CW00671402

PAUL & JUDAISM REVISITED

A STUDY OF DIVINE AND HUMAN AGENCY IN SALVATION

PRESTON M. SPRINKLE

FOREWORD BY STEPHEN WESTERHOLM

IVP Academic

An imprint of InterVarsity Press
Downers Grove, Illinois

InterVarsity Press
P.O. Box 1400, Downers Grove, IL 60515-1426
World Wide Web: www.ivpress.com
Email: email@ivpress.com

*InterVarsity Press® is the book-publishing division of InterVarsity Christian Fellowship/USA®, a movement of
students and faculty active on campus at hundreds of universities, colleges and schools of nursing in the United
States of America, and a member movement of the International Fellowship of Evangelical Students. For information
about local and regional activities, write Public Relations Dept., InterVarsity Christian Fellowship/USA, 6400
Schroeder Rd., P.O. Box 7895, Madison, WI 53707-7895, or visit the IVCF website at www.intervarsity.org.*

*Scripture quotations, unless otherwise noted, are from The Holy Bible, English Standard Version, copyright © 2001
by Crossway Bibles, a division of Good News Publishers. Used by permission. All rights reserved.*

Cover design: Cindy Kiple
Interior design: Beth Hagenberg
*Images: The Temple of Solomon, Jewish School /Dura-Europos Synagogue, National Museum of Damascus, Syria /
Photo © Zev Radovan / The Bridgeman Art Library*

ISBN 978-0-8308-2709-1 (print)
ISBN 978-0-8308-9563-2 (digital)

Printed in the United States of America ∞

Library of Congress Cataloging-in-Publication Data
A catalog record for this book is available from the Library of Congress.

P	21	20	19	18	17	16	15	14	13	12	11	10	9	8	7	6	5	4	3	2	1
Y	31	30	29	28	27	26	25	24	23	22	21	20	19	18	17	16	15	14	13		

For Joey Dodson

Who embodies the truism of Ben Sirach:
"A faithful friend is the medicine of life" (Sir 6:16)

Contents

Foreword by Stephen Westerholm. 9

Preface. 11

Abbreviations 17

  1 Paul and Judaism Revisited. 21

  2 Deuteronomic and Prophetic Restoration 38

  3 Restoration from the Curse of the Law 68

  4 The Eschatological Spirit 95

     EXCURSUS
     Moses, Paul and the Glory of the Old
     and New Covenants. 122

  5 Anthropological Pessimism in Paul and Qumran 125

  6 Justification in Paul and Qumran 145

  7 Judgment According to Works 172

     EXCURSUS
     Justification by Grace and Future Judgment
     Not by Grace? 204

  8 Divine and Human Agency in Early Judaism 208
    A Survey

  9 Paul and Judaism 239
    Soteriology Revisited

Author Index 250

Subject Index 251

Scripture Index 252

Foreword

Every New Testament scholar has been asked the question: Is there anything still to be said about the New Testament that has not been said already—and said again, and again, and yet again? There is, alas, a point to the question. Certainly no body of literature has been read more widely, studied more intensely or commented on more frequently than the books of Christian Scripture.

As if the assignment of contributing to a well-populated discipline were not challenging enough, Preston Sprinkle has opted for the task at its most formidable: no topic within New Testament scholarship has been more extensively discussed over the last thirty-five years than the New Perspective on Paul. To be sure, the issues raised by the discussion are crucial for an understanding of the apostle; but one could be forgiven for thinking that a debate now well into its fourth decade must have long since exhausted itself. If issues remain unresolved, must it not be the case that they permit no resolution? Is it not time to move on?

Sprinkle's study on Paul and Judaism serves to remind us not only that there are contributions still to be made, but also of factors that make new contributions possible. The Pauline texts have been much studied; but bring them into juxtaposition with other texts raising similar issues, and put new questions to them, and the distinctiveness of Paul's argument emerges with new clarity. In this study, Sprinkle proposes that Paul shared with his Jewish contemporaries a sense that Israel was experiencing the curse that followed unfaithfulness in their covenantal relationship with God. How was deliverance from that curse to be brought about? Would it be initiated, as Deuteronomy suggests, through the repentance of God's people and a return to Torah obedience? Or must God act unilaterally to end the curse, as a number of prophetic texts anticipate? Framing the question in these terms, Sprinkle looks not only for Paul's answers but for those outlined in a number of Jewish texts, primarily the Dead Sea Scrolls. The result is fresh insight into the apostle's thought and a more balanced perspective on its relation to contemporary Jewish thinking.

And so the debate moves forward. Anyone interested in its current state must carefully consider Preston Sprinkle's contribution.

Stephen Westerholm

PREFACE

Sometime during my second year at seminary, a friend recommended that I read a book by N. T. Wright about Paul's theology. My immediate reaction was that this would be a waste of time. I didn't know who N. T. Wright was, but I had already taken two courses on systematic theology and was therefore convinced that there was little more to be learned. But my friend insisted, so I stole away a few hours at a nearby coffee shop and dove into a borrowed copy of Wright's *What Saint Paul Really Said*.[1] Within minutes, I was hooked, and my view of Paul would never be the same.

The year was 2002 and little did I know that the next ten years would be occupied with my own quest to figure out what Paul really said. As I flipped page after page, Wright waved his rhetorical wand over me as I sat there dazzled by his eloquent prose and engaging argument. Wright actually made scholarship exciting—not an easy task—and enticed me to study the New Testament with eagerness and conviction. Most of all, Wright opened up a whole new world to me—the world of Second Temple Judaism. His portrait of Paul seemed so real and fresh, grounded in history and culture, and there was nothing more I wanted to do than to bury myself in books about Judaism.

And bury myself I did. As I looked to pursue doctoral studies, I didn't really care what I was going to research as long as I would learn more about Judaism. So I emailed Tom Schreiner of Southern Seminary, whom I had

---

[1]N. T. Wright, *What Saint Paul Really Said: Was Paul of Tarsus the Real Founder of Christianity?* (Grand Rapids: Eerdmans, 1997).

never met at the time, and he suggested that I study the use of Leviticus 18:5 in Paul and Second Temple Judaism. Apparently there was a longstanding debate over how Paul interpreted this verse in Romans 10:5 and Galatians 3:12, and looking at its Jewish usage would force me to dig into Jewish literature firsthand. I fired off an email to Simon Gathercole, my future doctoral supervisor at the time, and after some reflection he thought that this would be a fine topic to study.

The first year of my doctoral studies largely consisted of reading piles of Jewish literature, and I might as well have been in paradise. I also slugged my way through E. P. Sanders's *Paul and Palestinian Judaism* and various other books by James Dunn, Krister Stendahl, Richard Hays and others who questioned the traditional paradigm of both Paul and Judaism.[2] After my first year of research, I was fairly convinced—against the conviction of my supervisor—that the so-called New Perspective on Paul was correct. I found it hard to disagree with the arguments of Sanders and others; my own reading of the literature only seemed to confirm this. The only problem was that as I looked more closely at how Paul and his Jewish contemporaries interpreted Leviticus 18:5—a soteriologically loaded verse—I was becoming more convinced by those of a more "Old Perspective" mold. While I could no longer say that Judaism was legalistic in the Bultmannian sense, neither could I say that Paul and Judaism embraced the same way of thinking about salvation.

And then I read Francis Watson's *Paul and the Hermeneutics of Faith*.[3] More than any single book, Watson's tome crystallized my views on Paul, Judaism and salvation, which would end up shaping the conclusion of my own dissertation. Watson argued that Paul emphasized divine agency in salvation more than what we find in Jewish literature. This challenged the views of Sanders, Dunn and Wright in significant ways that I had not encountered. Watson was very careful and fair, and exhibited a wealth of knowledge of both Judaism and Paul—a blend that I wasn't finding in most

---

[2] E. P. Sanders, *Paul and Palestinian Judaism: A Comparison of Patterns of Religion* (Philadelphia: Fortress, 1977); James D. G. Dunn, *Jesus, Paul and the Law: Studies in Mark and Galatians* (Louisville, KY: Westminster John Knox, 1990); Krister Stendahl, *Paul Among Jews and Gentiles and Other Essays* (Philadelphia: Fortress, 1977); Richard Hays, *Echoes of Scripture in the Letters of Paul* (New Haven, CT: Yale University Press, 1989).

[3] Francis Watson, *Paul and the Hermeneutics of Faith* (New York: T & T Clark, 2004).

Old Perspective advocates. So at the end of my Ph.D., I concluded that Paul disagreed with his Jewish contemporaries on the meaning of Leviticus 18:5 and *therefore* on the very Jewish structure of salvation celebrated in the verse. Judaism used it to affirm that eschatological salvation is conditioned on law-obedience, while Paul believed that God accomplished salvation through the Christ event apart from any prior law-obedience. The difference between Paul and Judaism was seen in how they understood divine and human agency in salvation—at least, according to their interpretations of Leviticus 18:5. My dissertation was published the next year (2008),[4] and I thought that I was done figuring out Paul and Judaism. Such lofty ambitions are typical when you pass your *viva*,[5] but after coming back down to earth, I realized that my findings were quite limited. I figured out how Paul and Judaism understood one verse! However, as with any newly graduated Ph.D. student, I had a lot of findings that didn't make it into my dissertation, and a few other intuitions that I didn't have time to explore.

So that's where this book comes in. While researching the use of Leviticus 18:5 in Paul and Judaism, I noted various other passages and motifs that beg for comparison in order to shed further light on the discussion. And while I was quite confident in how Paul understood this one verse from Leviticus, there were many other facets of Paul's theology that were untouched during my Ph.D. Moreover, throughout my studies, I grew inclined to see more discontinuity between Paul and Judaism in terms of their soteriological structure. At the same time, scholars of all stripes are quick to affirm that more than any other Jewish sect, the authors of the Dead Sea Scrolls exhibit more continuity with the theology of Paul. Yet throughout my studies, I often noticed aspects of discontinuity that were either not detected or not emphasized among scholars, and thus the foundation for this book was laid: I wanted to explore more in depth what had been simply an educated hunch throughout my studies. This book is the fruition of that exploration—and my findings are both confirming and critical of my previous assumptions.

---

[4]Preston M. Sprinkle, *Law and Life: The Interpretation of Leviticus 18:5 in Early Judaism and in Paul*, WUNT 2.241 (Tübingen: Mohr Siebeck, 2008).
[5]*Viva* is short for *Viva Voce* ("living voice"), which refers to the much-dreaded oral examination of one's doctoral thesis, on which the entire degree hangs.

If I have learned anything during my few years as a scholar, it's that all good research is done in community, and this book is no different. I have several people to thank who devoted countless hours to helping me along the way. First, I thank Dan Reid and the folks at IVP for accepting my proposal for publication. Next, Jason Maston and Tom Schreiner read an early draft and offered many perceptive suggestions and critiques, some of which saved me from making embarrassing mistakes. Ben Reynolds, Andy Hassler, Kevin McFadden and my brother-in-law Benjamin Foreman all read portions of the book and offered many helpful corrections and improvements. Jonathan Moo and Daniel Gurtner read chapter eight (and other sections) and forced me to make some significant revisions for which I am very grateful. And my colleague and good friend Mark Beuving—editor *par excellence*—worked through the entire manuscript with the fine-toothed comb and offered a pile of improvements in my writing.

Portions of this book were presented at the Society for the Advancement of Ecclesial Theology (SAET) annual symposiums, and several members, including Scott Hafemann, Joel Willitts, John Yates, David Rudolph, David Morlan and Todd Wilson, have shaped (or critiqued!) my thinking on several issues in the book. John Barclay provided some much-needed encouragement in the initial conception of the book and helped crystallize my methodology. Kyle Wells contributed to some seminal ideas early on. And Simon Gathercole's push for clarity, precision and sound argumentation will always linger in the back of my head whenever I seek to interpret ancient texts. All remaining mistakes are, of course, my own.

I also want to thank my four children—Kaylea, Aubrey, Josie and Cody—for playing with me throughout the writing process. Our wrestling matches, long hikes, afternoons at the beach and many other fun-filled escapes were much-needed reminders that life is not all about research. And my wife Christine was incredibly encouraging through every stage of research. I thank you for holding down the fort while I had to spend some extra hours finishing up the book. But beyond that, nothing I do could be done without you in my life. Thanks for your joy and laughter, your wisdom and grace, your friendship and love.

It goes without saying, but it needs to be said, that the grace of Jesus Christ, which I have ventured to explain, sustained me through every tap of the keyboard. May Jesus be exalted all the more as a result of this study.

Last but not least, I thank my best friend Joey Dodson for reading portions of this book, but most of all, for your incessant encouragement, loyalty and wisdom. You are a model scholar and Christian leader, and I'm honored to call you my friend. I can't think of a more apt person to dedicate this book to—a small gesture to say that I love you like a brother.

ABBREVIATIONS

1 En.	*1 Enoch*
1 Macc	1 Maccabees
1QH^a	*1QHodayot^a*
1QM	*1QWar Scroll*
1QpHab	*1QPesher to Habakkuk*
1QS	*1QRule of the Community*
2 Bar.	*2 Baruch*
2 Macc	2 Maccabees
4QMMT	*4QHalakhic Letter*
4Q504	*4QWords of the Luminaries*
11QPs^a	*11QPsalms^a*
11QT^a	*11QTemple^a*
AB	Anchor Bible
ABG	Arbeiten zur Bibel und ihrer Geschichte
Abr.	Philo *De Abrahamo*
ABR	*Australian Biblical Review*
AGAJU	Arbeiten zur Geschichte des antiken Judentums und des Urchristentums
Alleg. Interp.	Philo, *Allegorical Interpretation*
AnBib	Analecta Biblica
ANE	Ancient Near Eastern
Ant.	Josephus *Jewish Antiquities*
Bar	Baruch
BETL	Bibliotheca Ephemeridum Theologicarum Lovaniensium
BBR	*Bulletin for Biblical Research*
BECNT	Baker Evangelical Commentary on the New Testament
Bib	*Biblica*
BJRL	*Bulletin of the John Rylands University Library of Manchester*

BST	Bible Speaks Today
BZAW	Beihefte zur Zeitschrift für die alttestamentliche Wissenschaft
BZNW	Beihefte zur Zeitschrift für die neutestamentliche Wissenschaft
CBQ	*Catholic Biblical Quarterly*
CBR	*Currents in Biblical Research*
CQS	Companion to the Qumran Scrolls
CD	*Damascus Document*
DJD	Discoveries in the Judean Desert
DSD	*Dead Sea Discoveries*
DSSSE	F. Garcia Martinez and E. J. C. Tigchelaar, eds. *Dead Sea Scroll Study Edition*. 2 vols. Grand Rapids: Eerdmans, 2000.
EC	*Early Christianity*
EKKNT	*Evangelisch-katholischer Kommentar zum Neuen Testament*
ESV	English Standard Version
HTR	*Harvard Theological Review*
ICC	International Critical Commentary
Int	*Interpretation*
JBL	*Journal of Biblical Literature*
JETS	*Journal for the Evangelical Theological Society*
JJS	*Journal of Jewish Studies*
Jos. As.	*Joseph and Aseneth*
JQR	*Jewish Quarterly Review*
JSHRZ	Jüdische Schriften aus hellenistisch-römischer Zeit
JSJ	*Journal for the Study of Judaism in the Persian, Hellenistic, and Roman Periods*
JSJSup	Supplements to the Journal for the Study of Judaism
JSNT	*Journal for the Study of the New Testament*
JSNTSup	Journal for the Studies of the New Testament Supplement
JSOT	*Journal for the Study of the Old Testament*
JSOTSup	Journal for the Study of the Old Testament: Supplement Series
JSP	Journal for the Study of the Pseudepigrapha
JSPSup	Journal for the Study of the Pseudepigrapha Supplements

JTI	*Journal for Theological Interpretation*
Jub.	*Jubilees*
KJV	King James Version
L.A.B.	*Liber antiquitatum biblicarum* (Pseudo-Philo)
Leg. All.	Philo *Legum Allegoriarum*
LNTS	Library of New Testament Studies
LSTS	Library of Second Temple Studies
LXX	Septuagint
m. Kidd.	*Mishnah Kiddushin*
m. Ned.	*Mishnah Nedarim*
MT	Masoretic Text
NIBC	New International Bible Commentary
NICNT	New International Commentary on the New Testament
NICOT	New International Commentary on the Old Testament
NIGTC	New International Greek Testament Commentary
NovT	*Novum Testamentum*
NovTSup	Novum Testamentum Supplement Series
NRSV	New Revised Standard Version
NTS	*New Testament Studies*
Pr Azar	Prayer of Azariah
Pss. Sol.	Psalms of Solomon
R & E	*Review & Expositor*
RB	*Revue biblique*
RevQ	*Revue de Qumran*
RSV	Revised Standard Version
SBEC	Studies in Bible and Early Christianity
SBLDS	Society of Biblical Literature Dissertation Series
SBLMS	Society of Biblical Literature Monograph Series
Sir	Sirach
SNTSMS	Society for New Testament Studies Monograph Series
Somn.	Philo *De Somniis*
STDJ	Studies on the Texts of the Desert of Judah
T. Abr.	*Testament of Abraham*
T. Jud.	*Testament of Judah*
T. Mos.	*Testament of Moses*

T. Reub.	*Testament of Reuben*
Them	*Themelios*
Tob	Tobit
TynBul	*Tyndale Bulletin*
VT	*Vetus Testamentum*
VTSup	Vetus Testamentum Supplement
WBC	Word Biblical Commentary
Wis	Wisdom of Solomon
WTJ	*Westminster Theological Journal*
WUNT	Wissenschaftliche Untersuchungen zum Neuen Testament
ZAW	*Zeitschrift für die Alttestamentliche Wissenschaft*
ZNW	*Zeitschrift für die Neutestamentliche Wissenschaft*
ZTK	*Zeitschrift für Theologie und Kirche*

1

PAUL AND JUDAISM
REVISITED

The phrase "Paul and Judaism" is an odd one, since Paul himself was a Jew. He was a "Hebrew of Hebrews," a descendant "from the tribe of Benjamin" and a member of the true "Israel of God."[1] But according to his own testimony, he was snatched from his aggressive pursuit of Judaism by the Messiah himself and was enlisted to proclaim a message quite different from anything in Judaism at the time.[2] Although Paul spoke as a Jew who belonged to the covenant people of God, he also believed that the Christian movement stood in opposition to at least some forms of Judaism.[3] Paul was a Jew, yet he was an "idiosyncratic Jew" who "engaged in critical dialogue with other Jews about a common heritage and identity."[4] As such, the phrase "Paul *and* Judaism" is fitting.

What this study will "revisit" is the soteriology of Paul and Judaism. Such a goal is, of course, unattainable—Judaism in the first century was much too diverse, and the idea of soteriology is far too anachronistic. So we will spend this chapter trimming our goal down to a manageable size, which will include a rather annotated definition of soteriology. But before we do that, we will summarize the last few decades of scholarship on this topic.

---

[1]Phil 3:5; Rom 11:1; Gal 6:16.
[2]Gal 1:14-16.
[3]Gal 2:11-16; 3:6-14; 4:21-31; 1 Thess 2:14-16.
[4]Francis Watson, *Paul and the Hermeneutics of Faith* (New York: T & T Clark, 2004), p. 1.

E. P. SANDERS AND THE NEW PERSPECTIVE ON PAUL

In 1977, E. P. Sanders published his groundbreaking book, *Paul and Palestinian Judaism*,[5] which has significantly altered the way scholars and students of the New Testament understand Paul and early Judaism. Previous to Sanders, most scholars understood first-century Judaism to be a legalistic religion governed by a system of merit and devoid of grace.[6] Sanders challenged this assumption by showing that the ancient Jewish documents themselves portray a religion that does not fit the dominant consensus. The Jewish writings leave little trace of a legalistic religion; rather, they hold grace and works in a healthy—one may say *biblical*—relationship. To describe this relationship, Sanders coined the phrase "covenantal nomism," which he defines as "the view that one's place in God's plan is established on the basis of the covenant and that the covenant requires as the proper response of man his obedience to its commandments, while providing means of atonement for transgression."[7] In other words, obedience to the law was not a means of *earning* God's grace but was the necessary covenant response to God's prior grace. So if Judaism was a religion based on grace, what did Paul find wrong with it? Sanders concluded in a now-famous dictum that Paul's problem with Judaism was simply that it was not Christianity.[8]

Paul and Palestinian Judaism created a wake of variegated responses. Some were critical of his method yet agreed with his overall correction of previous caricatures of early Judaism. Others believed that his understanding of Judaism was spot-on, while his view of Paul was less convincing. Still others reacted against his view of both Paul and Judaism, maintaining a more or less "Old Perspective" on the two.[9] The one who picked up the

---

[5]E. P. Sanders, *Paul and Palestinian Judaism: A Comparison of Patterns of Religion* (Philadelphia: Fortress, 1977).

[6]Among many others, see Rudolph Bultmann, *Primitive Christianity in Its Contemporary Setting*, trans. R. H. Fuller (London: Thames & Hudson, 1956 [1949]), pp. 59-71; Herman Ridderbos, *When the Time Had Fully Come: Studies in New Testament Theology* (Grand Rapids: Eerdmans, 1957), p. 63: "The Jew lived by a quantitative interpretation of the law. His fulfillment of each individual requirement of the law indicated merit, no matter how small."

[7]Sanders, *Paul and Palestinian Judaism*, p. 75, cf. 422.

[8]Ibid., p. 552.

[9]For a thorough overview of such responses, see Stephen Westerholm, *Perspectives Old and New on Paul: The "Lutheran" Paul and His Critics* (Grand Rapids: Eerdmans, 2004); for a shorter review, see Stephen Westerholm, "The New Perspective at Twenty-Five," in *Justification and Variegated Nomism*, Vol. 2: *The Paradoxes of Paul*, ed. D. A. Carson, P. T. O'Brien and M. A. Seifrid, WUNT 2.181 (Tübingen: Mohr Siebeck; Grand Rapids: Baker, 2004), pp. 1-38.

mantle with the most vigor is James D. G. Dunn, who in a flurry of publications moved the discussion to a whole new level.[10] It all started with his 1982 Manson lecture, "The New Perspective on Paul," which was published a year later.[11] The title of this essay gave his new view on Paul and Judaism its well-known moniker—so well-known that the abbreviation NPP (New Perspective on Paul) is now intelligible to many pastors, students of the New Testament and quite a number of biblio-bloggers, regardless of whether they have actually read anything by James Dunn. In agreement with Sanders, Dunn argues that Paul's problem with Judaism was its ethnocentrism, not its supposed legalism. According to Dunn, Paul (especially in Romans, Galatians and Philippians) was not arguing for salvation by grace alone *against* works-righteousness; rather, he was arguing for Gentile inclusion *against* Jewish ethnocentrism. Jews of Paul's day believed that a Gentile must first become a proselyte in order to become a member of the covenant. Paul argued against this, promoting the dangerous notion that the Gentiles need not take on the Jewish identity markers, such as circumcision, Sabbath keeping and food laws, in order to be genuine Christ-followers and covenant members. This is why Paul counters "works of the law" with "faith in Christ" (e.g., Rom 3:28; Gal 2:16). For Dunn, the phrase "works of the law" is shorthand not for legalism but for the "characteristically and distinctively Jewish practices ('identity marker[s]')"[12] that exclude Gentiles *as Gentiles* from becoming covenant members, while "faith in Christ" is "the only means for anyone, everyone, to receive God's righteousness."[13]

James Dunn is not the only one who has reread Paul in light of Sanders's portrayal of early Judaism. In fact, though Dunn coined the term New Per-

---

[10]Dunn's pre-1990 articles are collected in James D. G. Dunn, *Jesus, Paul and the Law: Studies in Mark and Galatians* (Louisville, KY: Westminster John Knox, 1990). Articles from 1990–2004, along with some older ones, are collected in James D. G. Dunn, *The New Perspective on Paul: Collected Essays*, WUNT 185 (Tübingen: Mohr Siebeck, 2005; Grand Rapids: Eerdmans, 2007). See also Dunn's *The Theology of Paul the Apostle* (Grand Rapids: Eerdmans, 1997), and his commentaries on *Romans 1–8, 9–16*, WBC 38a–b (Dallas: Word, 1988); and *Epistle to the Galatians* (Peabody, MA: Hendrickson, 1993).

[11]James D. G. Dunn, "The New Perspective on Paul," *BJRL* 65 (1983): 95-122; republished in Dunn, *Jesus, Paul and the Law*, pp. 183-214.

[12]Dunn, *Romans*, 1:188.

[13]Ibid., p. 167. Dunn's view of the phrase "works of the law" has shifted over the years, however. Whereas he used to limit "works of the law" to specific boundary markers, he now seems to allow for a more general meaning of requirements of the law with some emphasis on boundary markers depending on the context.

spective, it could be argued that N. T. Wright birthed it in his 1977 Tyndale lecture, published the following year, when he sought to "contribute" to the debate between Krister Stendahl and Ernst Käsemann "by offering a new way of looking at Paul which provides . . . *a new perspective* on other related Pauline problems."[14] Wright proceeded to unpack this new perspective by showing that Judaism was not a religion of works-righteousness,[15] and that the doctrine of justification was not the core of Paul's thought but was a polemical doctrine aimed at Jewish national pride.[16] Wright's lecture was a brilliant contribution to the discussion, especially since he had not yet completed his doctoral thesis.[17] Since then, he has gone on to write several influential books and articles that have proven to be foundational for the New Perspective, even though years later Wright would label his approach a "fresh," rather than "new," perspective on Paul.[18] Wright differs from Sanders and Dunn on several important facets of Paul's theology,[19] but all three believe that Judaism was not legalistic. God's grace was fundamental for salvation, and obedience to the law was a response to prior grace—a soteriological structure not wholly different from Paul's. All three, therefore, agree on one important feature that underlines the discussion: continuity.

CONTINUITY AND DISCONTINUITY
BETWEEN PAUL AND EARLY JUDAISM

Continuity can be an ambiguous term. Most theological students are familiar

---

[14]N. T. Wright, "The Paul of History and the Apostle of Faith," *TynBul* 29 (1978): 62-63.

[15]Ibid., p. 79.

[16]Ibid., p. 72.

[17]In 1981, Wright completed his doctoral thesis, which was examined by James Dunn.

[18]See N. T. Wright, *Paul: In Fresh Perspective* (Minneapolis: Fortress, 2005). Wright's narrative approach to Paul along with his counterimperial readings, both of which are neglected by Sanders and Dunn, constitute the freshness of his perspective (see, e.g., pp. 21-39, 59-79). Wright's other works that have contributed to the broad contours of the New Perspective include his *What Saint Paul Really Said: Was Paul of Tarsus the Real Founder of Christianity?* (Grand Rapids: Eerdmans, 1997), and "The Letter to the Romans," in *New Interpreter's Bible Commentary*, vol. 10, ed. Leander Keck (Nashville: Abingdon Press, 2002).

[19]For example, both Dunn and Sanders interpret the infamous *pistis Christou* phrase (e.g., Rom 3:22, 26; Gal 2:16) as an objective genitive, while Wright not only views it as a subjective genitive but believes that such interpretation is fundamental for Paul's theology. All three differ on their views of justification, and Wright's narrative and counterimperial readings of Paul are unparalleled in Dunn and Sanders. Many other differences can be seen in how they approach specific passages in Paul, such as Romans 2, which Wright believes is part and parcel of Paul's thought, while Sanders thinks the chapter as a whole was hijacked by Paul from a synagogue sermon.

with its use in discussions related to the Old and New Testaments. For instance, scholars often talk about continuity in terms of Israel and the church, or the old covenant and the new. But the term has been applied to the Paul and Judaism debate, and to my mind, this is really the crux of the issue. How much continuity is there between the nature of salvation in Paul and in Judaism? This is a much more concrete way of framing the discussion, rather than getting caught up on Old and New Perspectives on Paul.[20] Since there is so much diversity among scholars who would generally adhere to what we call an Old or New Perspective on Paul, we should be very cautious in using these general labels. Instead of using the terms "Old" and "New" to refer to one's perspective on Paul, I will use the terms "continuity" and "discontinuity" as a heuristic means of capturing the way scholars understand Paul's soteriology in relation to Judaism's. (We will get to the equally problematic term "soteriology" below.) Those who see more continuity argue that the relationship between divine and human agency in salvation is functionally the same in both Judaism and Paul, despite some obvious differences (the centrality of Jesus Christ, a law-free gospel, etc.). In both cases, God establishes the covenant relationship by grace, and the human agent responds in faith to this gracious offer. Obedience then flows from this covenant relationship; obedience is not a means of earning God's grace, but is a response to God's prior grace. For those who see more discontinuity, the reverse is true: in salvation, God responds to prior human action, a formulation seen in Judaism but not in Paul. Therefore, despite some conceptual similarities, Paul and Judaism promote two different structures of salvation.

Apart from the writings of Dunn and Wright, another thorough and rather convincing study that defends continuity is the published doctoral dissertation of Kent Yinger, entitled *Paul, Judaism, and Judgment According to Deeds*.[21] Yinger agrees with Sanders that early Judaism was not a religion of works-righteousness and that entrance into the covenant was by grace alone. One's obedience to the covenant stipulations was a response to God's prior grace, and it maintained one's status as a covenant member. Yinger

---

[20]I never really know how to respond to someone who asks me if I am "New Perspective," especially since the person is usually on a witch-hunt. And asking them to define their terms only fuels the flame.

[21]Kent Yinger, *Paul, Judaism, and Judgment According to Deeds*, SNTSMS 105 (New York: Cambridge University Press, 1999).

traces the motif of "judgment according to deeds" through a broad sampling of Second Temple texts and argues that the deeds of the righteous
"confirm or reveal one's fundamental loyalty to God,"[22] but they do not make
one righteous before God. In turning to Paul, Yinger finds the relationship
between grace and obedience largely the same as what we find in Judaism:
obedience is not a condition for entry into the covenant, but a condition for
maintaining one's status.[23] Yinger, therefore, sees much continuity between
the soteriological frameworks of Paul and Second Temple Judaism.[24] Bruce
Longenecker emphasizes this same point in an article that criticizes those
who stress discontinuity, arguing that these scholars have only "highlighted
the 'worst' features (from a Pauline perspective) of Jewish texts and . . . have
marginalised those that, even from a Pauline perspective, are admirable."[25]
Like Yinger, Longenecker believes that a more sensitive reading of Jewish
texts would show that Paul's soteriology was just as gracious as Judaism's.
"[B]oth Pauline and Jewish texts envisage God as empowering his people to
live acceptably before him."[26]

Against this view, there are those who see more discontinuity between
Paul and early Judaism. Not only are there differences with regard to the
content of faith (the centrality of Jesus, a law-free gospel, etc.), but also with
regard to the actual shape of the soteriological structure. Simon Gathercole,
for instance, engages the same general topic as Yinger does but concludes
that while there may be "continuity as to obedience being a criterion for final
judgment," there is "discontinuity as to the character of the obedience."[27] For
Paul, divine empowerment through the spirit generates the obedience necessary for the final day, and this is not paralleled in early Judaism. Likewise,
Francis Watson, John Barclay, Stephen Westerholm and others have argued

---

[22]Ibid., p. 285.

[23]Yinger notes the following differences between Paul and Judaism: 1) the Christ-event replaces
the law in defining one's membership in the people of God; 2) the role of the spirit in enabling
obedience among Christians, "while not absent, is certainly heightened significantly in Paul"
(Yinger, *Paul, Judaism, and Judgment*, p. 289).

[24]See also Kent Yinger, "The Continuing Quest for Jewish Legalism," *BBR* 19 (2009): 375-91;
idem, "Reformation *Redivivus*: Synergism and the New Perspective," *JTI* 3 (2009): 89-106.

[25]Bruce W. Longenecker, "On Critiquing the 'New Perspective' on Paul: A Case Study," *ZNW* 96
(2005): 270. Longenecker focuses on the work of Simon Gathercole (see below).

[26]Ibid.

[27]Simon Gathercole, *Where Is Boasting? Early Jewish Soteriology and Paul's Response in Romans 1–5*
(Grand Rapids: Eerdmans, 2002), p. 133.

for discontinuity between Pauline and Jewish soteriology, due to differences in their anthropology, their hermeneutics or their understanding of grace.[28] Most scholars who stress discontinuity see more of an emphasis in Judaism on the human agent in salvation, with Paul highlighting divine agency.[29]

This whole discussion may sound dangerously anachronistic. Are we not simply reading our modern theological debates between Calvinism and Arminianism (or Protestantism and Catholicism) back into these ancient texts? Certainly there can be an element of this,[30] but we need to keep in mind that similar debates were alive and well in the first century. In fact, when Josephus describes the various "philosophies," or sects, of Judaism, he defines them in terms of what they believed about predestination and free will.[31] And long before Arminius reacted against Calvin's doctrine, an ancient Jew named Jesus Ben Sirach argued passionately for a free-will theology that would delight a modern Arminian.[32] The opposite is true for the author of *4 Ezra,* who at around A.D. 100 espoused what in many ways sounds like a proto-Augustinian view of salvation. Paul seems to engage the same questions in the ninth chapter of his letter to the Romans. All that to say, by framing the discussion in terms of divine and human agency, we are not squeezing modern views into texts that were not asking these questions; rather, we are recognizing and analyzing the concerns that were in the air of the first-century Jewish world and have remained significant ever since.

Such questions concerning divine and human agency are at the forefront of recent discussions of Paul and Judaism. Significant works include Francis

---

[28]For anthropology, see Stephen Westerholm, "Paul's Anthropological 'Pessimism' in Its Jewish Context," in *Divine and Human Agency in Paul and His Cultural Environment,* ed. John M. G. Barclay and Simon J. Gathercole, LNTS 335 (New York: T & T Clark, 2006), pp. 71-98; for hermeneutics, see Watson, *Paul and the Hermeneutics of Faith*; for grace, see John M. G. Barclay, "'By the Grace of God I Am What I Am': Grace and Agency in Philo and Paul," in Barclay and Gathercole, *Divine and Human Agency,* pp. 140-57; John M. G. Barclay, "Unnerving Grace: Approaching Romans 9–11 from The Wisdom of Solomon," in *Between Gospel and Election,* ed. Florian Wilk and J. Ross Wagner, WUNT 257 (Tübingen: Mohr Siebeck, 2011), pp. 91-109.

[29]Sometimes Judaism is labeled synergistic and Paul monergistic; see Timo Eskola, *Theodicy and Predestination in Pauline Soteriology,* WUNT 2.100 (Tübingen: Mohr Siebeck, 1998); Timo Laato, *Paul and Judaism: An Anthropological Approach,* trans. T. McElwain (Atlanta: Scholars Press, 1995). But these modern theological terms are problematic unless clearly defined, and even then they tend to read back into the sources contours of modern theological debates. We will therefore avoid using them.

[30]See the fine critique by Yinger, "Reformation *Redivivus.*"

[31]Josephus *War* 2.119-66; *Ant.* 13.171-73; 18.11-25.

[32]Sir 15:14-17; 17:1-14.

Watson's *Paul and the Hermeneutics of Faith* (2004), Gathercole and Barclay's edited *Divine and Human Agency in Paul and His Cultural Environment* (2006), the unpublished doctoral dissertation by Kyle Wells, "Grace, Obedience, and the Hermeneutics of Agency" (2009),[33] and Jason Maston's recent *Divine and Human Agency in Second Temple Judaism and in Paul* (2010)[34]—all of which will be dialogue partners throughout this book. These works are only a sampling, however, of the recent publications that explore the relationship between divine and human agency in terms of continuity and discontinuity. Despite these fine studies, the discussion is in no way closed. More work is needed, different methods are required, and new light ought to be shed on these old issues. This book is an attempt to contribute to the discussion regarding continuity and discontinuity in the soteriological structures of Paul and Judaism; or more precisely, Paul and the Dead Sea Scrolls (see below).[35] And the word "contribute" is important. The issues are too complicated, and this book is far too limited in scope, to assume that it could resolve the debate, nor is it intended to do so. But if it raises some unfamiliar questions, answers a few old ones, and challenges a couple well-established assumptions, then the book will have hit its mark.

METHOD: SOTERIOLOGICAL MOTIFS IN PAUL AND THE DEAD SEA SCROLLS

Comparing Paul with Judaism has, of course, been done before—many times over. And yet scholars have made this comparison in a variety of ways. For instance, Sanders compared Paul with a wide range of Jewish literature spanning a large period of time (four hundred years), different genres and very diverse social settings. Casting such a wide net has its advantages, but it also has one major drawback: the array of literature surveyed by Sanders is much too disparate to be forced into one soteriological framework. This is seen, for instance, when one looks at a book that is more nationalistic (God is committed to the entire nation of Israel) alongside a book that is more sectarian (God is committed to a particular Jewish sect that repre-

---

[33]Kyle Wells, "Grace, Obedience, and the Hermeneutics of Agency: Paul and his Jewish Contemporaries on the Transformation of the Heart" (Ph.D. diss., Durham University, 2009).

[34]Jason Maston, *Divine and Human Agency in Second Temple Judaism and in Paul,* WUNT 2.297 (Tübingen: Mohr Siebeck, 2010).

[35]I will be using the terms *Qumran* and *Dead Sea Scrolls* somewhat interchangeably.

sents the true Israel).[36] In Sanders's study, the *Psalms of Solomon* are probably sectarian,[37] as are the Dead Sea Scrolls, while the apocalyptic book of *4 Ezra* is more nationalistic. These differences will inevitably shape the soteriology of the book, making the already troublesome task of determining its theology all the more difficult. Other studies have cast their net even wider than Sanders. The published dissertations by Gathercole and Yinger both look at a massive array of literature, leaving few stones unturned. To their credit, both Gathercole and Yinger were cautious about reductionism in their conclusions. But such an approach risks ignoring the particularities of the individual documents themselves. Bruce Longenecker's fine work went in the other direction.[38] Instead of surveying a large body of texts, he focused on comparing one document, *4 Ezra,* with (part of) Paul's letter to the Romans (chapters 1–11). This approach has the advantage of paying close attention to the particularities of each text; however, the implications of his conclusions are of limited value for understanding early Judaism as a whole. Others have entered the discussion through the side door by comparing how Paul and Judaism have interpreted a particular Old Testament passage that is packed with soteriological significance. Studies on Habakkuk 2:4, Genesis 15:6 and my own study on Leviticus 18:5 have made contributions but are admittedly limited in their conclusions.[39]

All of these approaches are helpful; diverse methods enlighten the discussion. But there is still room for imaginative comparisons that find yet new doors to enter through. Sound, consistent and historically viable approaches that break the mold of what has been done should be welcomed, and this has led me to contribute to the ongoing discussion about Paul and Judaism. In the following pages, I will compare Paul's soteriology with the Dead Sea Scrolls.[40] A common critique of comparative studies is that the

---

[36]See the fine work by Mark Elliot, *The Survivors of Israel: A Reconsideration of the Theology of Pre-Christian Judaism* (Grand Rapids: Eerdmans, 2000), which points this out.

[37]For a brief defense, see Preston Sprinkle, *Law and Life: The Interpretation of Leviticus 18:5 in Early Judaism and in Paul,* WUNT 2.241 (Tübingen: Mohr Siebeck, 2008), pp. 92-93.

[38]Bruce W. Longenecker, *Eschatology and the Covenant: A Comparison of 4 Ezra and Romans 1-11* (Sheffield: JSOT Press, 1991).

[39]See Benjamin Schliesser, *Abraham's Faith in Romans 4: Paul's Concept of Faith in Light of the History of Reception of Genesis 15:6,* WUNT 2.224 (Tübingen: Mohr Siebeck, 2007); A. Strobel, *Untersuchungen zum eschatologischen Verzögerungproblem auf Grund der spätjüdisch-urchristlichen Geschichte von Habakuk 2,2ff,* NovTSup 2 (Leiden: Brill, 1961); Sprinkle, *Law and Life.*

[40]There are many highly debated issues surrounding the Dead Sea Scrolls, which we do not have

diversity among the literature is often ignored in an attempt to (overly) systematize a theology without giving due attention to the historical and rhetorical context of the document(s).[41] By focusing on the Dead Sea Scrolls, however, this study will yield a more nuanced conclusion for the following reasons.

First, the Scrolls represent a voluminous collection of literature produced, or endorsed, by one Jewish sect.[42] Most other Second Temple documents stand alone and do not have sufficient complimentary literature to help round out our knowledge of what the author and his community believed. For instance, the *Psalms of Solomon* represent a collection of hymns written by a sectarian group of Jews, and yet our knowledge of what this group believed is limited to the psalms themselves. Likewise, the author of *4 Ezra*, as far as we know, did not write any other document that is still preserved today. Our knowledge of what its author believed is limited to one document. The composite work known as *1 Enoch* is quite a bit larger, and studying this literature would give us a relatively full-bodied understanding of what a particular Jewish community believed. With that established, we could helpfully compare these beliefs with Paul's. However, our knowledge of the practice and beliefs of the so-called Enochic community[43] is much

---

the time to discuss. Fortunately, none of these is crucial to the conclusions that will be drawn in this book. I will assume with F. M. Cross and others that most of the Scrolls were written between 150 B.C. and A.D. 68. The Scrolls were collected or written by a group of Jews who settled at Qumran, who were probably members of a larger Essene movement. For an overview of these issues, see, among others, James VanderKam and Peter Flint, *The Meaning of the Dead Sea Scrolls: Their Significance for Understanding the Bible, Judaism, Jesus, and Christianity* (New York: T & T Clark, 2002), esp. pp. 20-33, 239-54.

[41]Gone are the days when scholars can talk about early Judaism as a unified entity. There is too much diversity in the writings, staving off any attempt at making conclusions about *"the* Jewish view" of such and such.

[42]I originally set out by looking only at the scrolls that can be confidently labeled sectarian. However, several scholars pointed out to me that books that are endorsed by the Qumran community are just as influential for their theology as those books that they penned themselves. Moreover, it is quite difficult to determine whether some books are sectarian or not. And even among those that are clearly sectarian, there is diversity in theological expression. For all of these reasons, I will look at both sectarian and nonsectarian documents in this study.

[43]I am using the term *community* loosely. There is much discussion about the origins and socioreligious history of the authors who wrote, and the Jews who read and endorsed, the writings collected in what is now known as *1 Enoch*. And yet as Richard Bauckham notes, "The various Enoch writings form a distinctive tradition of thought and writing" (Apocalypses," in *Justification and Variegated Nomism*, Vol. 1: *The Complexities of Second Temple Judaism*, ed. D. A. Carson, P. T. O'Brien and M. A. Seifrid, WUNT 2.140 [Tübingen: Mohr Siebeck; Grand Rapids: Baker, 2001], p. 138).

more limited than what we know about the Qumran community.[44] In light of this, the Dead Sea Scrolls provide us with a unique window into the range of beliefs of one group of Jews roughly contemporary to Paul. With the Scrolls, as with Paul, we have many different texts, written under different circumstances and for different purposes, that yield a more comprehensive portrait of their theological beliefs—and for our purposes, their soteriological beliefs. For Paul, we have at least seven different letters, which provide a window into his thought.[45] It would make sense, then, to locate an equally diverse (roughly speaking) body of literature within Judaism for a more robust comparison.

Second, both Qumran and Paul exhibit similar eschatological frameworks.[46] That is, they both have an inaugurated eschatology and believe that God has established the new covenant with their community; as such, this will allow for a more accurate comparison. For instance, the Apocryphal book of Baruch anticipates God's future intervention (Bar 4:5–5:9). Its author is on a different side of the eschatological divide than Paul. Paul believed that God had already intervened and established the new covenant with his people. Comparing one who is looking forward to God's future intervention (Baruch) with one who is looking back and reflecting on it (Paul) will inevitably reveal differing conclusions—due to different perspectives about the eschatological time (or when God has acted), not neces-

---

[44]The term *Qumran community* is well known, but it is problematic. It implies that the sect who wrote and endorsed the Scrolls was limited to the few men who lived at Khirbet Qumran. However, it is clear from the Scrolls themselves that there were many "camps" or "communities" that were responsible for writing and collecting the Scrolls (see, e.g., CD 7:6; 14:3, 8-9; 1QS 6:1-8). I will therefore continue to use the terms *community* and *Qumran community* to refer to the wider "union of local communities" whose beliefs and practices are contained in the Scrolls found at Khirbet Qumran, following John J. Collins, "The Yaḥad and 'the Qumran Community,'" in *Biblical Traditions in Transmission: Essays in Honour of Michael A. Knibb*, ed. Charlotte Hempel and Judith M. Lieu, JSJSup 111 (Leiden: Brill, 2006), pp. 81-96 (esp. 88); and John J. Collins, "Forms of Community in the Dead Sea Scrolls," in *Emmanuel: Studies in the Hebrew Bible, Septuagint and Dead Sea Scrolls in Honor of Emmanuel Tov*, ed. S. M. Paul et al. (Leiden: Brill, 2003), pp. 97-111.

[45]I hold to Pauline authorship of all thirteen letters attributed to him, but some scholars hold to only seven. Recently, however, Colossians and 2 Timothy are gaining traction as genuine, as are Ephesians and 2 Thessalonians (to some extent). In any case, much of the debate about Paul's soteriology hinges on the undisputed letters of Romans, Galatians, Philippians and 1–2 Corinthians.

[46]See Heikki Räisänen, "Paul's and Qumran's Judaism," in *Judaism in Late Antiquity*, Part Five, *The Judaism of Qumran: A Systemic Reading of the Dead Sea Scrolls*, vol. 2, ed. A. J. Avery-Peck, J. Neusner and B. D. Chilton (Leiden: Brill, 2001), pp. 173-200 (esp. 177-79).

sarily because their theological frameworks are inherently different. Baruch and Paul viewed themselves as living in different scenes of the biblical drama, and we should not critique one for being in a different scene than the other. However, both the Scrolls and Paul situate themselves in the same scene, in the "already/not yet" epoch created by God's eschatological intervention. And this makes for a more fair and accurate comparison.

Third, and similarly, both Paul and Qumran independently show concerns for the same theological motifs. More than their "already/not yet" framework, they both have a pessimistic anthropology and a notable emphasis on God's grace in justification, and both give prominent attention to the role of the eschatological spirit in salvation—all of which will be studied further below. The similar interest in the same soteriological motifs lends itself to a more viable comparison than does, say, a comparison between Paul and the Wisdom of Solomon, since the spirit did not play a significant role in the latter though was fundamental for the former.[47]

Fourth, both Paul and Qumran were sectarian; both believed that their new covenant community was the true "Israel of God" (Gal 6:16; CD 3:12-16).[48] The soteriological framework of Jewish sects (including Paul) differs from the soteriological framework held by those who are more nationalistic. A nationalistic worldview understands one's covenant relationship with God to begin at birth, and one's covenant standing is maintained through persevering obedience.[49] But for sectarian groups, God's (new) covenant relationship is established through some eschatological act in calling out the sect *from* the nation. And entry into the sect, the true Israel, is usually gained through adherence to sectarian beliefs and codes of conduct. For Qumran, this means adhering to the community's interpretation of torah; for Paul, membership is determined by faith in Jesus and embracing one's role in the life of the church.

In light of these parallels,[50] it is safe to conclude, with Timothy Lim, that

---

[47]Joey Dodson in personal conversation reminded me, however, that the personification of Lady Wisdom in the Wisdom of Solomon stands in for the work of the spirit.

[48]See Timothy H. Lim, "Studying the Qumran Scrolls and Paul in their Historical Context," in *The Dead Sea Scrolls as Background to Postbiblical Judaism and Early Christianity*, ed. J. R. Davila (Leiden: Brill, 2002), p. 140.

[49]This is of course a broad generalization.

[50]Other reasons: (1) even though this body of literature may capture the thought of only a small group of Jews, their beliefs were known enough to capture the attention of Josephus, Philo and

"the Qumran scrolls and Pauline letters belong to the same religious milieu of sectarian Judaism,"[51] and therefore lend themselves to a fitting comparison.

Since I am focusing on the Dead Sea Scrolls and not the wider world of Second Temple Judaism, my conclusions will admittedly be limited to the views of the Qumran sect and not early Judaism as a whole. I am not confident that the latter can even be done with precision, any more than a comparison of the soteriology of the Ante-Nicene fathers with the Tanaaim. Such comparisons would unavoidably lead to dubious conclusions. However, in order to situate our comparison between Paul and Qumran in the wider context of early Judaism, I will include a more broad-brush survey of other Second Temple documents in chapter eight. This chapter will not pay as close attention to the particulars but will see if the general tenor of *Deuteronomic* and *Prophetic* patterns of restoration (see chapter two) can be evinced from other Jewish documents.

SOTERIOLOGY, GENRE AND THE POSSIBILITY OF AN UNBIASED READING

Throughout this book, I will be using the term *soteriology*, which opens up the danger of reading back into ancient texts a modern—and quite foreign—concept.[52] The term was derived from later attempts to systematize an aspect of Christian theology that centers on the death and resurrection of Christ, and it is nearly impossible to shake the term from all its Christian nuances.[53] But shake we must, if we are going to use it to describe the theology of the Scrolls and Paul. We will therefore use the term *soteriology* with

---

Pliny the elder. (2) The presence of nonsectarian writings among the Scrolls indicates *ipso facto* that at least some of their beliefs were shared by other Jews who may not have been part of the monastic community. (3) The letter 4QMMT, written to a person of authority in Jerusalem, reveals some measure of influence the Qumran community may have had on the temple cult in Jerusalem. For further reflection on the relationship between the Scrolls and Judaism at large, see VanderKam and Flint, *Meaning of the Dead Sea Scrolls,* pp. 275-92.

[51]Lim, "Studying the Qumran Scrolls," pp. 145-46; see also Räisänen, "Paul's and Qumran's Judaism."

[52]"Treatments of soteriology in the Dead Sea Scrolls must admit at the outset that the very search for a doctrine of salvation imposes on the material a foreign concept." Alex P. Jassen, "Survival at the End of Days," in *This World and the World to Come: Soteriology in Early Judaism,* ed. Daniel M. Gurtner, LSTS 74 (New York: T & T Clark, 2011), p. 196. For a meticulous discussion of the use of "soteriology" for understanding the theology of early Judaism, see Daniel M. Gurtner, "Introduction," in Gurtner, *This World,* pp. 1-4; see also Gathercole, *Where Is Boasting?* p. 22.

[53]See George W. E. Nickelsburg's brief discussion of soteriology in his "Salvation Among the Jews: Some Comments and Observations," in Gurtner, *This World,* pp. 299-300.

the basic sense of *the restoration God brings to those who belong to his covenant community.* This definition squares with the theological contours of Qumran and Paul, who both believed that their communities were experiencing the restoration promised in the Scriptures. We can expand the meaning of salvation to include the previously mentioned "already" aspect, when God established his new covenant with the community, and a "not yet" future, when God would complete their salvation. We can continue to fill out this definition by identifying several theological motifs that give shape to this restoration, all of which can be identified as important for Qumran and Paul independently. These motifs are: (1) the curse of the old covenant and how God will rescue his people from it; (2) the nature of the eschatological spirit's work among the community; (3) the view of the human condition, which among both Paul and Qumran amounts to a degree of anthropological pessimism; (4) justification—how the community members attain the status of righteous before a righteous God; and (5) the relationship between future judgment and works for those who are part of the covenant community. All five of these motifs are important aspects of the beliefs of both the Qumran community and Paul. We are not, therefore, projecting Pauline categories onto Qumran, or Qumran categories onto Paul. As we will see, all five concepts were to some measure important—and in some cases fundamental—for both. These five theological motifs, therefore, constitute various colors we have used to paint the portrait of restoration, which we will describe as Paul's and Qumran's *soteriology.* Scholars will continue to quibble over the meaning of this term, but what is beyond dispute is that Paul and the authors at Qumran wrote about similar theological concepts. For the sake of precision, therefore, we will compare Paul with the Scrolls in their understanding of the aforementioned theological motifs that are prominent in their writings.

Genre is another issue worth mentioning in laying a foundation for a more accurate comparison. Any student of hermeneutics knows how important genre is for understanding meaning, and yet some comparative studies seem to gloss over this when comparing Paul with Judaism. This is true especially of those more heavy-handed approaches that embark on a whistle-stop tour of large tracks of diverse literature, picking out phrases and terms to build a belief system of a particular group. The Qumran Scrolls are frequent victims of such rapacious assault. I believe there may be a place for a more global summary, a survey of the forest before examining the trees. But such an approach is ripe for caricature and misrepresentation. Now, when comparing Paul with Qumran, we are hard pressed to find perfect parallels in genre—Paul wrote letters to house churches composed of Jews and Gentiles, while the Qumranites, for the most part, wrote legal tracts, hymns, wisdom texts and didactic treatises instructing their own Jewish community. We are off to a certain disadvantage from the start. However, when given a closer look, there are actually a few rhetorical situations[54] within Qumran literature that correlate well with certain portions of Pauline literature, and these will be pointed out along the way. The one clear example, and one that we will revisit in chapter three, is the comparison between 4QMMT—one of Qumran's only letters—and Paul's letter to the Galatians. Both letters urge an aberrant group within the covenant to consider its destructive ways in order to avoid the curses of the covenant. Similar phrases and concepts are employed along the way, such as "works of the law"[55] and the righteousness of Abraham.[56] Given these similarities, 4QMMT and Galatians beg for comparison, which is why many scholars have done so.[57] But other Pauline documents and Qumran scrolls that exhibit related rhetorical situations have not been noticed. For instance, there are portions of the *Damascus Document* of Qumran that exhibit striking resemblances to Paul's letter to the Romans. Similar themes and analogous movements in thought make the arguments in these documents more worthy for comparison than, say, Romans with the *Thanksgiving Hymns*. Cross-genre comparisons can and will be done but must be tempered with caution. Therefore, for the sake of precision, we will put more emphasis on comparing soteriological motifs that are contained in documents written in

---

[54]I am drawing the phrase "rhetorical situation" from Lloyd Bitzer, "The Rhetorical Situation," *Philosophy & Rhetoric* 1 (1968): 1-14, who defines it as "a complex of person, events, objects, and relations presenting an actual or potential exigence which can be completely or partially removed if discourse, introduced into the situation, can so constrain human decision or action as to bring about the significant modification of the exigence" (p. 6).

[55]Gal 2:16; 3:2, 5, 10; 4QMMT C 27.

[56]Gal 3:6; 4QMMT C 27.

[57]See, among others, James D. G. Dunn, "4QMMT and Galatians," in Dunn, *The New Perspective*, pp. 333-40; Martin Abegg, "4QMMT, Paul and 'Works of the Law,'" in *The Bible at Qumran: Text, Shape, and Interpretation*, ed. Peter W. Flint (Grand Rapids: Eerdmans, 2001), pp. 203-16.

the same genres and comparable rhetorical situations.

Thus far, I have emphasized taking every step to make a more accurate comparison between Paul and the Dead Sea Scrolls. Does this mean that I am engaging these ancient texts without precommitments? Postmodernism has shown us that this is impossible; to suggest otherwise is naïve at best and dishonest at worst. I am a committed Christian and therefore believe in the inspiration and authority of Paul's letters as written Scripture. I do not hold the same view of Qumran texts. But this does not destroy our enterprise from the beginning; every scholar has precommitments, as Timothy Lim rightly states: "No one is entirely unbiased, but we can, and must, exercise a degree of objectivity by keeping biases in check and by continually questioning our own assumptions."[58] And this is the aim of our study: to compare soteriological motifs in Paul and Qumran in order to better understand how these two Second Temple Jewish communities understood divine and human agency in salvation. With regard to divine and human agency, I have no precommitments that require Paul to emphasize divine agency more than Qumran. Qumran can emphasize divine agency in salvation more than Paul and this would leave my faith unaffected. In fact, as we will see, I believe that there are variations in how agency is understood in restoration motifs in the Old Testament, which I also hold to be inspired and authoritative. Still, my faith is not altered by this tension.

PLAN OF THE BOOK

In comparing Paul with the Dead Sea Scrolls, I will compare the previously mentioned soteriological motifs that are important for both Paul and Qumran, in order to understand how both sets of writings articulated the relationship between divine and human agency. These motifs include: the curse of the covenant (chapter three), the role of the spirit (chapter four), anthropological pessimism (chapter five), justification (chapter six) and judgment according to works (chapter seven). This is not an exhaustive list. One could examine other motifs evident in both Paul and Qumran, such as predestination, messianism and the afterlife. But these have either already been the subject of thorough study, or do not reveal how the authors articu-

---

[58]Lim, "Studying the Qumran Scrolls," p. 136.

lated the relationship between divine and human agency as clearly as the motifs we will study in this book.[59]

But before we compare these motifs, we will look at the common foundation for both Paul and Qumran—the Old Testament. Both Paul and Qumran wrestled with how God was fulfilling his promises to Israel, and it is evident that their soteriological concepts are situated in the context of restoration motifs from the Old Testament. As we will show in the next chapter, the Old Testament offers multiple programs for restoration, and we will use these different programs as lenses through which to understand the individual soteriological motifs in Paul and Qumran. In short, the Old Testament says that Israel will be restored when it repents (which we will call a *Deuteronomic* restoration motif), but also that God will initiate restoration prior to repentance (which we will call a *Prophetic* restoration motif). Chapter two will explore in detail these different programs of restoration in order to prepare us to understand the Old Testament conceptual world of Paul and Qumran.

---

[59]The role of predestination is obviously relevant for our topic, and I originally planned to include it in the book. However, the topic has been discussed quite thoroughly by others, and I do not think I could contribute something that has not already been said. See, e.g., Timo Eskola, *Theodicy and Predestination;* Sigurd Grindheim, *The Crux of Election: Paul's Critique of the Jewish Confidence in the Election of Israel,* WUNT 2.202 (Tübingen: Mohr Siebeck, 2005); Armin Lange, *Weisheit und Prädestination: Weisheitliche Urordnung und Prädestination in den Textfunden von Qurman,* STDJ 18 (Leiden: Brill, 1995); Eugene H. Merrill, *Qumran and Predestination: A Theological Study of the Thanksgiving Hymns,* STDJ 8 (Leiden: Brill, 1975). As for messianism, such a topic is obviously significant for Paul, but Qumran's messianic concepts are quite diverse and unclear. (But if I were to add another chapter to this study, it would probably be on messianism, or supra-human saving agents.) Eternal life and other topics are only distantly related to our main focus on divine and human agency.

2

Deuteronomic and
Prophetic Restoration

The Old Testament[1] exhibits two different paradigms of restoration, which can be mapped on what Walter Brueggemann calls the "trajectory of pardon."[2] On one end of this trajectory, we find an eschatological pardon that is conditioned on Israel's repentance (1 Kings 8 *passim*; 2 Chron 7:13-14); on the other end we find "a full, unilateral pardon without reference to repentance" (Jer 31:31-34; 32:37-41; Ezek 36:22–37:14).[3] In this chapter, we will look at these two patterns of eschatological restoration set forth in the Old Testament: (1) a *Deuteronomic* model, where Israel's repentance precedes God's restorative action (forgiveness, blessings, renewed relationship), and (2) a *Prophetic* scheme, where God's restorative action is unilateral;[4] it is preceded by nothing on Israel's part.[5] The terms

---

[1] I will maintain the traditional label "Old Testament" against "Hebrew Bible," since I will be dealing with both the Hebrew and Greek Scriptures.

[2] Walter Brueggemann, "The Travail of Pardon: Reflections on *slḥ*," in *A God So Near: Essays on Old Testament Theology in Honor of Patrick D. Miller*, ed. N. R. Bowen et al. (Winona Lake, IN: Eisenbrauns, 2003), pp. 283-97 (esp. 293).

[3] Ibid. Brueggemann's trajectory actually extends past the conditional pardon to an absolute rejection of pardon (Deut 29:20; 2 Kings 24:4; Lam 3:42). However, for our purposes, we will only consider the conditional and unconditional pardon.

[4] I am using the term *unilateral* to refer to God's self-initiated action, which has no human preconditions.

[5] I will be using the italicized terms *Deuteronomic* and *Prophetic* to refer specifically to the respective types of restoration defined above. If I refer to general features of Deuteronomy (e.g., vocabulary, themes), I will use the unitalicized "Deuteronomic." I will use the term "Deuteronomistic" to refer to the literature of Deuteronomy through 2 Kings, abbreviated with DtrH. The unitalicized "Prophetic" will be used to refer to the books of Isaiah through Malachi.

Deuteronomic and *Prophetic* arise from the types of literature that emphasize each program of restoration. Deuteronomy and the so-called books of Deuteronomistic History (Joshua–2 Kings; hereafter DtrH) emphasize a more conditional restoration, where Israel must repent in order to be restored (brought back from exile) and forgiven. The Prophetic books, however, emphasize an unconditional restoration. To be sure, the different programs of restoration are not uniformly described in the different types of literature—Deuteronomistic literature contains some *Prophetic* restoration theology, and Prophetic literature often urges Israel to repent, as we will see below. But the emphasis is pronounced enough to warrant the respective labels given above.[6]

DEUTERONOMIC THEOLOGY OF RESTORATION

Deuteronomy is the wellspring of retributive eschatology and is saturated with conditional statements regarding law-obedience. Israel's obedience is the condition for possessing the land (Deut 4:1; 6:17-19; 8:1), attaining righteousness (Deut 6:24-25), receiving long life (Deut 6:1-2), maintaining a covenant relationship with God (Deut 7:12-13) and being rewarded with the covenant blessing of "the good" (Deut 12:25, 28; 19:13; 22:7). The most sustained treatment of these themes is found in Deuteronomy 28, where the conditional "if . . . then" gives structure to both the blessings (Deut 28:1-14) and the curses (Deut 28:15-44). In short, if Israel obeys torah, they will be blessed; if they disobey, they will be cursed.

And curses are expected to rain down on Israel in the future. Their rebellion and punishment are written into the script of Israel's history—curses will come. But restoration still awaits Israel, on the condition that they return to God. For instance, Moses says:

> I call heaven and earth to witness against you today, that you will soon utterly perish from the land that you are going over the Jordan to possess. You will not live long in it, but will be utterly destroyed. And the LORD will scatter you among

---

For a discussion on the use of the terms *Deuteronomistic* and *Deuteronomic*, see Richard Coggins, "What Does 'Deuteronomistic' Mean?" in *Those Elusive Deuteronomists: The Phenomenon of Pan-Deuteronomism*, ed. Linda S. Shearing and Steven L. McKenzie, JSOTSup 268 (Sheffield: Sheffield Academic Press, 1999), pp. 22-35.

[6]See H. W. Wolff, "The Kerygma of the Yahwist," *Int* 20 (1966): 132-58; Brueggemann, "Travail of Pardon." For an overview of Deuteronomic theology more generally, see among others John D. W. Watts, "The Deuteronomic Theology," *R & E* 74 (1977): 321-36.

the peoples, and you will be left few in number among the nations where the
LORD will drive you. And there you will serve gods of wood and stone, the work
of human hands, that neither see, nor hear, nor eat, nor smell. (Deut 4:26-28)[7]

The potential curse of exile is here viewed as inevitable: Israel *will* disobey
and *will* be cursed and exiled. Nevertheless, they will be restored in the end,
though this restoration is initiated by Israel: "But from there you will seek the
LORD your God and you will find him, if you search after him with all your
heart and with all your soul. When you are in tribulation, and all these things
come upon you in the latter days, you will return to the LORD your God and
obey his voice" (Deut 4:29-30). Israel takes the first step in seeking the LORD
wholeheartedly, thus responding to the demand for wholehearted obedience
(e.g., Deut 6:5).[8] In short, whether by condition or promise, Israel *will* disobey
and reap retributive punishment from Yahweh through curse and exile. As
for its restoration, Deuteronomy 4 sets out a hope, albeit in conditional terms.

The book of Kings is also governed by a theology of retribution.[9] This is
captured most clearly in Solomon's prayer of dedication in 1 Kings 8, where
repentance is set forth as a necessary prerequisite for restoration. Like Deuteronomy, the prayer assumes that Israel will apostatize and elicit God's
judgment (i.e., exile). If Israel will experience God's restoration, repentance
is the necessary condition:

> When your people Israel are defeated before the enemy because they have
> sinned against you, and *if they turn* (wĕšābû) again to you and acknowledge
> your name and pray and plead with you in this house, then hear in heaven
> *and forgive* (wĕsālaḥĕtā) the sin of your people Israel and bring them again to
> the land that you gave to their fathers. (1 Kings 8:33-34)

> When heaven is shut up and there is no rain because they have sinned against
> you, if they pray toward this place and acknowledge your name *and turn*
> (yĕšûbûn) from their sin, when you afflict them, then hear in heaven and

---

[7]Unless otherwise noted, all translations of the Old Testament are from the English Standard
Version (ESV).

[8]It is important to note, however, that human agency does not conflict with God's mercy,
according to the author. The next verse says: "For the LORD your God is a merciful God. He will
not leave you or destroy you or forget the covenant with your fathers that he swore to them"
(Deut 4:31). The demand for obedience is met with forgiveness and mercy, for *when* they
disobey, God is always willing to accept a penitent people.

[9]See, e.g., 1 Kings 2:1-4; 8:25; 9:4-5; 11:9-13, 38; 14:1-18.

forgive (wĕsālaḥĕtā) the sin of your servants, your people Israel, when you
teach them the good way in which they should walk, and grant rain upon your
land, which you have given to your people as an inheritance. (1 Kings 8:35-36).

If they turn their heart (wĕhēšîbû ʾel-libām) in the land to which they have
been carried captive, *and repent (wĕšābû)* and plead with you in the land of
their captors . . . *if they repent (wĕšābû)* with all their mind and with all their
heart in the land of their enemies . . . then hear in heaven your dwelling place
their prayer and their plea, and maintain their cause *and forgive (wĕsālaḥĕtā)*
your people who have sinned against you. (1 Kings 8:47-50)

The term *šûb* ("repent, turn") is central to Solomon's prayer (1 Kings 8:33, 35, 47,
48) and assures Israel that if they turn from their sin, then God will reverse the
covenant curses and restore them.[10] In each case, the nation's repentance elicits
God's forgiveness (1 Kings 8:34, 36, 50).[11] Solomon's prayer is not an isolated instance of conditionality but is programmatic for the book as a whole[12]—a book
written to justify God's punitive act of exile and set forth hope for future restoration. That hope will come to fruition if Israel first turns to God in repentance.[13]

Later in Kings, Josiah is singled out as the model king, not on account of
his enduring faithfulness, but precisely because he repented:

Because your heart was penitent, and you humbled yourself before the LORD,
when you heard how I spoke against this place and against its inhabitants, that
they should become a desolation and a curse, and you have torn your clothes
and wept before me, I also have heard you, declares the LORD. (2 Kings 22:19)

---

[10]See Wolff, "Kerygma of the Yahwist," pp. 92-93; Brueggemann, "Travail of Pardon," pp. 286-87.
The prayer assumes that Israel is under the covenant curses spelled out in Deut 28 and Lev 26.
For instance, they have been "defeated before the enemy" (1 Kings 8:33; Deut 28:25, 48; Lev
26:17, 25), "heaven is shut up and there is no rain because they have sinned" (1 Kings 8:35; Lev
26:19), and there are "famine . . . pestilence . . . locust . . . in the land" (1 Kings 8:37; Deut 28:21-
23, 38-42; Lev 26:16, 25-26).

[11]Brueggemann states: "The prayer in the mouth of Solomon is a bold and confident one,
counting on YHWH's readiness to accept repentance and to grant pardon to those who turn"
(Brueggemann, "Travail of Pardon," p. 287).

[12]See Iain Provan, *1 and 2 Kings,* NIBC (Peabody, MA: Hendrickson, 1995), p. 78; J. G. McConville,
"1 Kings VIII 46-53 and the Deuteronomic Hope," *VT* 42 (1992): 67-79.

[13]Benjamin Foreman questions my reading of 1 Kings 8, since the prayer "is more of a *petition* than
an actual restoration program" (personal conversation). This is certainly true—Solomon does
not describe the actual restoration. However, since there is no alternative vision of how God will
actually restore his people, we should take the pleas for repentance, which are prevalent
throughout the book, as capturing the author's anticipated means of restoration. This is different
from Jeremiah, for instance, who proclaims messages of repentance and yet promises that
restoration will be accomplished by God's initiative and *not* by Israel's repentance (see below).

> Before him [Josiah] there was no king like him, who turned to the LORD with
> all his heart and with all his soul and with all his might, according to all the
> Law of Moses, nor did any like him arise after him. (2 Kings 23:25)

Josiah is the "'turner' par excellence,"[14] who in the hour of judgment
sought the Lord, found forgiveness and staved off the covenant curses ready
to devour the nation. The reference to the heart, soul and mind of Josiah
alludes to the formula in Deuteronomy (Deut 6:5; 30:2, 10) and recalls the
Deuteronomic "if . . . then" of covenant obedience and restoration. The author
showcases Josiah, therefore, as a model for his exilic audience to follow.
They are experiencing the curses that Josiah's repentance evaded; but they
too, like Josiah, can still repent and find restoration from exile.

EZRA, NEHEMIAH AND CHRONICLES

Whereas the exilic generation stood in the midst of judgment, the postexilic
Judeans envisioned a hope through the dim mist of an ambiguous restoration. Although they are back in the land with a new temple and a Davidic
line, the full bounty of God's promise still hangs in the balance. They too
needed a message of hope and restoration, and the content of that message
was similar to the Deuteronomist's: repent and turn back to the law of
Moses. Indeed, the author(s) of Ezra–Nehemiah does not seem aware that
the sinaitic covenant had ended, and the Chronicler reinforces the theology
of retribution with even greater passion and consistency than Moses. Israel's history ends with an unmistakable call to return to the law.

This call is evinced clearly in Ezra and Nehemiah. Both books close on a
sour note, as the Israelites are once again mimicking their dark history by
marrying the people of the land (Ezra 9:1-4; 10:18-44; Neh 13:23-31). Ezra
bemoans the sin and cries out in a communal confession to God: "Our iniquities have risen above our heads, and our guilt has grown even to the
heavens" (Ezra 9:6 NASB). Once again, Israel faces impending judgment
(Ezra 9:15), and the hope of restoration hinges on Israel's repentance:

> We have broken faith with our God and have married foreign women from
> the peoples of the land, but even now there is hope for Israel in spite of this.
> Therefore *let us make a covenant* (nikrāt-běrît) with our God to put away all

---

[14]Brueggemann, "Travail of Pardon," p. 289.

these wives and their children, according to the counsel of my lord and of those who tremble at the commandment of our God, and let it be done according to the Law. (Ezra 10:2-3)

There is hope in spite of their sin; God will accept their renewal of the covenant[15] as long as they repent "according to the Law" and return to God "trembl[ing] at the commandment." If Ezra's generation will return to the Lord and seek him, they will obtain the covenantal blessings their fathers forfeited.[16]

The end of Nehemiah follows the same logic. Israel, though back in the land, is still in spiritual exile, since they have committed the sins of their fathers by failing to "separate" from the people of the land. Nevertheless, the penitent returnees engage in a covenant renewal ceremony, where they again seek the law of Moses (Neh 8), confess their sin (Neh 9) and make an agreement in writing (Neh 9:38–10:32 [10:1-33 Heb])[17] to "enter into a curse and an oath to walk in God's Law that was given by Moses the servant of God, and to observe and do all the commandments of the LORD our Lord and his rules and his statutes" (Neh 10:29). As long as the remnant of Israel continues in sin, they will remain in (spiritual) exile and thus under the covenant curse. But if they return to the law, God will restore them. However, the book of Nehemiah ends not with a return to the law (Neh 8–10) but a return to the Solomonic sin of intermarriage (Neh 13:23-29). Restoration, therefore, hangs in the balance, with a

---

[15]The phrase *nikrāt-bĕrît* ("let us make a covenant") is the usual form used in the Hebrew Bible to refer to divine-human covenants. Here, it is probably referring to a renewal of the sinaitic covenant and not to a general "solemn commitment." See F. Charles Fensham, *The Books of Ezra and Nehemiah* (Grand Rapids: Eerdmans, 1982), p. 134; Jacob Martin Myers, *Ezra, Nehemiah* (Garden City, NY: Doubleday, 1965), p. 83.

[16]Ezra previously modeled the posture of repentance when he evoked the favor of God for protection on his journey back to the land: "Then I proclaimed a fast there, at the river Ahava, that we might humble ourselves before our God, to seek from him a safe journey for ourselves, our children, and all our goods. For I was ashamed to ask the king for a band of soldiers and horsemen to protect us against the enemy on our way, since we had told the king, 'The hand of our God is for good on all who seek him, and the power of his wrath is against all who forsake him.' So we fasted and implored our God for this, and he listened to our entreaty" (Ezra 8:21-23). The emphasis on fasting (Ezra 8:21, 23), humbling oneself (Ezra 8:21), and seeking the Lord (Ezra 8:22) is typical of corporate repentance intended to elicit the favor of God in the postexilic period. Especially telling is the Deuteronomic formula spoken to the king: "The hand of our God is for good on all who seek him, and the power of his wrath is against all who forsake him" (Ezra 8:22).

[17]The phrase *'ănaḥnû kôrĕtîm 'ămānâ* (lit. "we have cut a faithful") in Neh 9:38 (10:1 MT) is unusual and is probably used here as a near-synonym for the more typical *kārat bĕrît* and is perhaps an allusion to Abraham in Neh 9:8 who was found "faithful" before the Lord. See Mark A. Throntveit, *Ezra-Nehemiah*, Interpretation (Louisville, KY: Westminster John Knox, 1992), p. 108.

question mark lingering over their profession of repentance.

Ezra and Nehemiah set forth repentance and a return to the law as the prerequisite for God's restorative action. But no book emphasizes covenant retribution as persistently as the book of Chronicles. Not even Deuteronomy or Kings can compare to the consistency with which the Chronicler promotes repentance as a prerequisite for eschatological restoration. No tensions; no ambiguity. Law-abiders will be blessed, lawbreakers will be cursed, and Israel's history is littered with examples of each.

We previously noted the centrality of Solomon's prayer for the book of Kings. Here in Chronicles, it is God's response to Solomon's prayer that is programmatic for restoration:

> When I shut up the heavens so that there is no rain, or command the locust to devour the land, or send pestilence among my people, if my people who are called by my name humble themselves, and pray and seek my face and turn from their wicked ways, then I will hear from heaven and will forgive their sin and heal their land. Now my eyes will be open and my ears attentive to the prayer that is made in this place. (2 Chron 7:13-15)

Verse 13 draws once again on the language of the covenant curses, stating that drought, locust and pestilence will cling to Israel when they disobey. The curses will be relieved, however, if the people turn to God in confession and repentance. Solomon's prayer here establishes several key words that form the theological backbone of the ensuing narrative about the divided kingdom (2 Chron 10–36), and in turn, inform the postexilic generation about what needs to happen if they are going to experience the covenant blessings.[18] The key words *humble (oneself)*,[19] *pray*,[20] *seek*[21] and *turn*[22] all

---

[18]On the theology of retribution in 2 Chronicles, see especially Raymond B. Dillard, "The Reign of Asa (2 Chron 14–16): An Example of the Chronicler's Theological Method," *JETS* 23 (1980): 207-18; Raymond B. Dillard, "Reward and Punishment in Chronicles: The Theology of Immediate Retribution," *WTJ* 46 (1984): 164-72; Raymond B. Dillard, *2 Chronicles* (Waco, TX: Word, 1987), pp. 58, 76-81.

[19]"Humbling oneself" (*nikna'* from *kāna'*), or the failure to do so, determines the divine response (2 Chron 12:6, 7, 12; 28:19; 30:11; 33:12, 19, 23; 34:27; 36:12).

[20]An obedient response to God is often correlated with prayer (1 Chron 4:10; 5:20; 21:26; 2 Chron 13:12-15; 14:11; 18:31; 20:9; 30:18, 27; 32:20, 24; 33:13, 18-19).

[21]Seeking God (*dāraš* or *biqēš*) reaps great reward; failing to do so is rewarded with punishment (1 Chron 10:13-14; 22:19; 28:9; 2 Chron 11:16; 12:14; 14:4, 7; 15:2, 4, 12, 13, 15; 16:12; 17:4; 18:4; 19:3; 20:4; 22:9; 25:20; 26:5; 30:19; 31:21; 33:12; 34:3).

[22]For *šûb* ("turn, repent"), see 2 Chron 15:4; 30:6, 9; 36:13.

echo the *Deuteronomic* pattern of restoration, and the Chronicler goes out of his way to reveal historical glimpses of this restoration. God's response to such repentance is seen in the words *hear*,[23] *forgive*[24] and *heal*,[25] which highlight God's restorative action. The final words of Yahweh are telling: "Now my eyes will be open and my ears attentive to the prayer that is made in this place" (2 Chron 7:15). God is waiting for his people to repent and seek his face, and *then* he will restore them.

The Chronicler's retelling (and reworking) of Rehoboam's reign is typical (2 Chron 10–12; cf. 1 Kings 12:1-24; 14:21-31).[26] The author of Kings makes note of Rehoboam's ascension (1 Kings 14:21), his wicked syncretism (1 Kings 14:22-24) and his encounter with Shishak, which ends in defeat (1 Kings 14:25-28). Theological judgments are made (e.g., 1 Kings 14:22-24), but no explicit theological explanation is given for the events included in his reign. Contrast this with the Chronicler, who is quick to show the theological reason behind virtually everything that happened in Rehoboam's reign. And the reason is simple: retribution. The Chronicler points out, for instance, that Rehoboam is awarded covenant blessings for his obedience: prosperity and power (2 Chron 11:5-12), support from the populace (2 Chron 11:13-17), and progeny (2 Chron 11:18-22), all of which are left out by Kings. More explicitly, the invasion of Shishak is identified explicitly as covenant retribution. Shishak was the victor "because they had been unfaithful to the Lord" and "abandoned the law of the Lord" (2 Chron 12:1-2). However, in keeping with the promise of 2 Chronicles 7:13-15, "the princes of Israel and the king humbled themselves" (i.e., they repented) and therefore God turned away his wrath, saying: "They have humbled themselves. I will not destroy them, but I will grant them some deliverance, and my wrath shall not be poured out on Jerusalem by the hand of Shishak" (2 Chron 12:7).[27] Nearly all of the changes the Chronicler makes to Kings highlight the fact

---

[23]*Šāmaᶜ* ("hear") is often used in the context of God's response to prayer (see note 19 above).

[24]For *Sālaḥ* ("forgive," "pardon"), see 2 Chron 6:21, 25, 27, 30, 39; 30:18. The concept of forgiveness is articulated in terms of God being "moved by" Manasseh's entreaty and hearing "his plea" in 2 Chron 33:13, 19.

[25]*Rāpāʾ* ("heal"). For healing as recompense for repentance, see 2 Chron 30:20; for withholding healing for disobedience, see 2 Chron 36:16.

[26]See especially Dillard, *2 Chronicles*, pp. 78-80, 102.

[27]Cf. 2 Chron 12:12: "And when he humbled himself the wrath of the Lord turned from him, so as not to make a complete destruction."

that God blesses obedience and punishes transgression.[28] And the Chronicler handles the rest of the Judean kings during the divided monarchy in like manner.

Retribution theology in Kings is often expressed negatively: God punishes sinners with covenant curses. Here in Chronicles, however, the author sends a positive message, seeking to convince his discouraged and doubting audience that God's forgiveness is ready to be poured out on the penitent hearts of the postexilic generation. Chronicles, therefore, though not formally part of Deuteronomistic literature, exemplifies an unprecedented *Deuteronomic* theology of restoration. Israel must repent and return to the law in order to lay hold of its covenant blessings.

Is the Deuteronomistic Literature Wholly Deuteronomic?

While Deuteronomy and DtrH are governed by a theology of retribution, this literature is not univocal. Several passages exhibit a more *Prophetic* eschatology of restoration, where God takes the initiative to restore Israel. The clearest example is seen when one compares the two "circumcision of the heart" passages in Deuteronomy.

Circumcise therefore the foreskin of your heart, and be no longer stubborn. (Deut 10:16)

And *the* LORD *your God will circumcise your heart* and the heart of your offspring, so that you will love the LORD your God with all your heart and with all your soul, that you may live. (Deut 30:6)

The first statement in Deuteronomy 10:16 is a command; Israel is to circumcise their hearts (i.e., render wholehearted obedience), while the latter statement is a promise. Inherent in the shift from command to promise is a change in agency. In Deuteronomy 10:16, Israel is the agent responsible to render obedience to God, while in Deuteronomy 30:6—which takes place in the postexilic future—God is the one who does what was once demanded. "Commanded *human* action has now become a promised *divine* gift."[29]

---

[28]As Dillard notes, the reign of Rehoboam "provides a virtual paradigm for the program announced in the divine response to Solomon's prayer at the dedication of the temple (7:14)" (Dillard, *2 Chronicles*, p. 101).

[29]Dennis T. Olson, *Deuteronomy and the Death of Moses: A Theological Reading* (Eugene, OR: Wipf & Stock, 2005), p. 127.

This is not the only time such a shift is made in Deuteronomy. In fact, this emphasis on divine agency and the surety of future grace is evident most clearly throughout Deuteronomy 29–32, the so-called covenant at Moab (Deut 29:1),[30] a passage characterized by this tension between command and promise.[31] While Moses continues to exhort Israel (Deut 29:9; 30:11-20; 31:12-13), he also knows that until God gives them an obedient heart (Deut 29:4), apostasy and failure to fulfill the covenant are inevitable (Deut 31:16-29). But grace will reign in the end, a reality seen most clearly in the song of Moses in Deuteronomy 32. "The Moses who speaks in the Song," says Francis Watson, "speaks not as lawgiver but as prophet." The "theme of his prophetic testimony is the unconditional divine saving act, in spite of the apostasy of God's people and of the world."[32] The entire song predicts Israel's covenant failure, God's righteous judgment and then God's unconditional salvation. "For the LORD will vindicate his people and have compassion on his servants, when he sees that their power is gone and there is none remaining, bond or free" (Deut 32:36); "I kill and I make alive; I wound and I heal; and there is none that can deliver out of my hand" (Deut 32:39). The song is all about God: *his* work of judgment and salvation. Nothing in the song even hints that Israel will marshal the strength to follow the *Deuteronomic* code of repentance in order to receive its covenant blessings.[33]

Deuteronomy itself is not entirely *Deuteronomic* in terms of God's restoration of Israel. Retribution theology is *dominant*, but other voices break through. The same is true for the rest of DtrH. The book of Judges,

---

[30]Some have argued that the covenant at Moab is captured in Deuteronomy 29–30, leaving out 31–32, but as Olsen has pointed out, after the superscription in Deut 29:1 ("these are the words of the covenant") the next superscription does not appear until Deut 33:1 ("this is the blessing"); Olsen, *Deuteronomy and the Death of Moses*, p. 129n1. It is important to note that this "new covenant" made at Moab is made in addition to the covenant made at Horeb (Deut 29:1). Therefore, Moab supplements Horeb, affirming the value and necessity of torah (Deut 12–26), but provides a solution to the inevitable failure of Israel to perform it. The solution is found in God's unilateral pardon and empowering agency in the age of restoration.

[31]Olsen designates Deut 29–32 as the "new covenant section," since these chapters articulate "a new relationship based not as much on *human* abilities and faithfulness as on the promise of *God's* faithfulness and *God's* active transformation of people and communities" (Olsen, *Deuteronomy and the Death of Moses*, p. 127).

[32]Francis Watson, *Paul and the Hermeneutics of Faith* (New York: T & T Clark, 2004), p. 453.

[33]Olsen writes: "The song of the new covenant of Moab in chapter 32 does not end with judgment or curse. God's last word in the new covenant poem is a word of compassion and of a hopeful future. It is God alone who ensures that hope" (Olsen, *Deuteronomy and the Death of Moses*, p. 138).

for example, while rich in retribution theology also contains a measure of unilateral grace. God certainly responds whenever Israel "cries out," but it is not clear that this cry includes repentance. God may be acting solely out of his own freedom and compassion whenever he responds to Israel's grief.[34] Likewise, the book of Kings contains large tracks of retribution theology (as we have seen), but traces of unmerited favor persist throughout. For instance, the author reminds his audience of God's unconditional commitment to David despite the continual disobedience of his sons (1 Kings 11:34; 15:4; 2 Kings 8:19). At other times, he declares that the obedience of the kings ensures the Davidic promise (1 Kings 2:4; 8:25; 9:4-5), a concept that is more in line with his *Deuteronomic* worldview. The latter emphasis on conditionality takes center stage toward the end of the book, where exile is the focus (2 Kings 16:1-4; 21:1-15; 23:31–25:26). However, almost out of nowhere, the Davidic promise is evoked in the last scene, where Jehoiachin is exalted to a high status well into the exilic period (2 Kings 25:27-30).[35] Retribution is the loudest voice heard in Kings, but it is not the only one.

In summary, for Deuteronomy and DtrH, retribution eschatology is a key motif that shapes the authors' understanding of how God has operated in the history of Israel and how God is expected to work in bringing it home from exile. However, the books are not stubbornly univocal. Portions of Deuteronomy and DtrH show signs of a more prophetic hope of restoration, where forgiveness and restoration will come through God's unilateral pardon.

THE PROPHETIC THEOLOGY OF RESTORATION

We have looked at the so-called *Deuteronomic* program of restoration, where God promises to respond to Israel's repentance. Another program of restoration envisions a more unilateral restoration, where God takes the initiative to restore Israel, enabling it to repent and fulfill the covenant demands. Since the prophets are the primary heralds of this scheme, we have

---

[34]See, e.g., Fredrick E. Greenspahn, "The Theology of the Framework of Judges," *VT* 36 (1986): 385-92; see also Preston M. Sprinkle, "The Hermeneutic of Grace: The Soteriology of Pseudo-Philo's *Biblical Antiquities*," in *This World and the World to Come: Soteriology in Early Judaism*, ed. Daniel M. Gurtner, LSTS 74 (New York: T & T Clark, 2011), pp. 50-67 (61-62).

[35]For this tension in Kings, see Provan, *1 and 2 Kings*, p. 13.

called this a *Prophetic* program of restoration. Three books exhibit this
pattern most clearly: Isaiah, Jeremiah and Ezekiel.[36]

Isaiah. With incessant beauty and vibrant imagination, the poet-
prophet depicts a future salvific act created by the sovereign hand of
Yahweh. Few portions of Scripture exhibit a more sustained and variegated
reflection on God's agency in the world. However, when we ask the more
specific question of whether this act of salvation is prefaced in any way by
Israel's repentance, the answer is not so clear. While scholars widely recognize that different portions of Isaiah have different theological emphases,
most would affirm without hesitation that Isaiah 40–55 accentuates God's
unilateral pardon.[37]

> Listen to me, you stubborn of heart,
>> you who are far from righteousness:
> I bring near my righteousness; it is not far off,
>> and my salvation will not delay;
> I will put salvation in Zion,
>> for Israel my glory. (Is 46:12-13)

Isaiah assumes that Israel is "far from righteousness," yet assures it that
God's salvation will find it nonetheless. There is no exhortation to repent or
return to the law. Nothing on Israel's part stands between its sinful state and
God's salvation. Salvation is simply identified as a gift and promise. Previously Isaiah says:

> Yet you did not call upon me, O Jacob;
>> but you have been weary of me, O Israel!
> You have not brought me your sheep for burnt offerings,
>> or honored me with your sacrifices.
> I have not burdened you with offerings. . . .
> But you have burdened me with your sins;
>> you have wearied me with your iniquities. (Is 43:22-24)

---

[36]The authorship of Isaiah is largely irrelevant for our discussion. I affirm single authorship of the
entire book and yet recognize that Is 1–39, 40–55 and 56–66 all contain different theological
emphases and rhetorical concerns. I will therefore treat these three sections as separate units of
thought written by the same author.

[37]See especially Mark J. Boda, *A Severe Mercy: Sin and Its Remedy in the Old Testament* (Winona
Lake, IN: Eisenbrauns, 2009), pp. 203-12. Unilateral pardon is not limited to Isaiah 40–55,
however. See, e.g., Is 6:7; 30:18-21; 57:14-21; 59:15-21; 60:1–62:12.

While the Chronicler would follow this indictment with a scathing word of judgment, Isaiah has God responding in grace:

> I, I am he
>> who blots out your transgressions for my own sake
>> and I will not remember your sins. (Is 43:25)

Though Israel's sins were a "burden" on God, its depravity is met with a divine pardon. Unlike the Deuteronomists, there is no mention of Israel repenting from its sins as a precondition for God's restorative action. And such is the theological tenor of restoration throughout Isaiah 40–55. God's eschatological redemption is the *ground for*, and not the *response to*, Israel's repentance. "I have swept away your transgressions like a cloud, and your sins like mist; return to me, *for I have redeemed you (kî gĕʾaltîkā*; Is 44:22 NRSV).[38] One could also trace the logic of other larger passages to see that God has reversed the spiritual condition of Israel unilaterally, without any prior repentance from Israel, as in, for instance, Isaiah 42:14–43:7, where Israel's blindness and deafness (Is 42:14-25) encounters God's redeeming grace (Is 43:1-7). God's motivation for redemption is not prior repentance but a concern for his own glory (Is 43:7). Several other recurring motifs in Isaiah 40–55 buttress God's unilateral pardon of Israel, motifs such as the second exodus (Is 42:13–44:23, esp. Is 43:16-19; 48:20-21; 51:9-11; 52:11-12), God's power in creation (Is 40:12-17, 21-31; 41:17-20; 44:24-28; 45:18) and the theocentric motivation for God's eschatological activity (Is 42:8-12; 43:7, 20-21; 45:6; 48:11). Intriguing also is the way in which Isaiah correlates God's future transformation of creation with his transformation of the human condition (Is 42:15-16; 43:19-21; 44:3), which in Isaiah 44:3 is achieved through the work of the spirit.[39] In short, for Isaiah 40–55, "Righteousness is

---

[38]For this understanding of the verse, see Klaus Baltzer and Peter Machinist, *Deutero-Isaiah: A Commentary on Isaiah 40–55* (Minneapolis: Fortress, 2001), p. 205; Antti Laato, *The Servant of YHWH and Cyrus: A Reinterpretation of the Exilic Messianic Programme in Isaiah 40–55* (Stockholm: Almqvist & Wiksell International, 1992), p. 104; and the discussion in B. Scheuer, *The Return of YHWH: The Tension Between Deliverance and Repentance in Isaiah 40–55* (Berlin: Walter de Gruyter, 2008), pp. 60-65. Scheuer argues for a slightly different understanding of this text, where the "relationship between salvation and the call for repentance is not that of cause and effect, but rather that of co-operation between two interdependent actors." However, she goes on to say that the "greatness of YHWH's redemption of the exiles lies . . . in the fact that he has taken the initiative to the renewal of relationship, and he has not waited for the people to change" (p. 65).
[39]On which see Thomas M. Raitt, *A Theology of Exile: Judgment/Deliverance in Jeremiah and*

still a requirement, but it is through divine grace that it is to be produced."[40]

Isaiah 56–66 is less consistent than Isaiah 40–55 in its conception of divine and human agency. This section stresses the ethical demands that Yahweh has placed before Israel much more than Isaiah 40–55 (especially Is 56:1–59:15; 63:7–66:17).[41] For instance, the opening statement is startling in light of all that has preceded it: "Thus says the LORD: 'Keep justice, and do righteousness, for soon my salvation will come, and my deliverance be revealed'" (Is 56:1).[42] But to say that God demands obedience is not the same as saying that God will require obedience as a prerequisite for eschatological restoration, as we will see below in Jeremiah and Ezekiel. In spite of the emphasis on obedience to the law in Isaiah 56–66, few passages depict Israel's repentance as a condition for eschatological salvation.[43] The themes of unilateral forgiveness, so pervasive in Isaiah 40–55, are still prominent in Isaiah 56–66.

> Because of the iniquity of his unjust gain I was angry,
>> I struck him; I hid my face and was angry,
>> but he went on backsliding in the way of his own heart.
> I have seen his ways, but I will heal him;
>> I will lead him and restore comfort to him and his mourners,
>> creating the fruit of the lips.
> "Peace, peace, to the far and to the near," says the LORD,
>> "and I will heal him." (Is 57:17-19)

Ezekiel (Philadelphia: Fortress, 1977), p. 140: "God's act of Transformation *[sic]* is amplified so that God as Creator stands forth in bold outlines, perfecting and refashioning all of nature as well as Israel's inner condition."

[40]John Oswalt, *The Book of Isaiah, Chapters 40–66,* NICOT (Grand Rapids: Eerdmans, 1998), p. 464.

[41]For a good discussion on the interplay of divine and human agency in Is 56–66, see Oswalt, *Isaiah 40–66,* pp. 7-11, 451-55, 461-65.

[42]Oswalt attempts to correlate this passage with the general tenor of Is 40–55 by pointing to the causal *because (kî)*: "Justice and righteousness are to be done *because my salvation* is at hand . . . obedience is to be lived out as a response to salvation" (*Isaiah 40–66,* p. 455). But the exhortation is immediate, while the salvation of God is in the near future ("at hand") so that latter cannot be the ground of the former.

[43]One of the clearer statements comes in Is 59:20: "And a Redeemer will come to Zion, and *to those who turn from transgression* in Jacob, declares the LORD" (NASB). This statement comes at the end of a lengthy section setting out God's ethical demands (Is 58:1-14) and Israel's failure to meet up to them (Is 59:1-15). Is 59:14-21 seems to assume both divine (Is 59:16-17) and human (Is 59:18-20) agencies in eschatological salvation. But if Mark Boda is correct, then perhaps Is 56–66 is more aligned with Is 40–55. Boda suggests that the "penitential agenda" of Is 56–64 was a failure, and that Is 65–66 (like Is 40–55) celebrates "the announcement and acts of divine grace" (*Severe Mercy,* pp. 212-22).

In this passage, "forgiveness is entirely the result of the divine initiative, without an insistence on prior repentance."[44] More clearly, Isaiah 60–62, which is often considered homogeneous to Isaiah 40–55, emphasizes again God's unconditional grace and sovereign ability to produce the obedience that the law demands. We can probably conclude that while Isaiah 56–66 emphasizes God's agency in salvation, the prophet wants to make clear that this does not erase God's call for law observance.

One passage seems to contradict Isaiah's emphasis on unilateral pardon.

> *Seek* the LORD while he may be found;
>   call upon him while he is near;
> let the wicked *forsake* his way,
>   and the unrighteous man his thoughts;
> let him *return* to the LORD, that he may have compassion on him,
>   and to our God, for he will abundantly pardon. (Is 55:6-7)

The passage is an anomaly for two reasons. First, it occurs at the climax of Isaiah 40–55. It is rather odd that this robustly theocentric oracle ends with an emphasis on Israel's repentance. Second, the passage stands out in light of its use of Deuteronomic terminology. Words such as *seek, forsake* and *return*,[45] along with the concept of conditional pardon, are not typical of this section of Isaiah but are all characteristic of Deuteronomistic literature. We could attempt to diminish the conditionality here by recognizing that God's initiative in Isaiah 55:1-5 grounds the call to repentance in Isaiah 55:6-7,[46] or by reading Isaiah 55 with Isaiah 56 and thus Isaiah 56–66 rather than with Isaiah 40–54, but both solutions betray an interpreter's craving for uniformity over the meaning of the text.[47] For now, we will content our-

---

[44]Donald E. Gowan, *Theology of the Prophetic Books: The Death and Resurrection of Israel* (Louisville, KY: Westminster John Knox, 1998), p. 172.

[45]Šûb ("turn, repent") occurs 16 times in Is 40–55 (Is 41:28; 42:22; 43:13; 44:19, 22, 25; 45:23; 46:8; 47:10; 49:5, 6; 51:11; 52:8; 55:7, 10, 11); see Scheuer, *Return of YHWH*, p. 33. Only two times is the root used to exhort Israel to turn to God in repentance, Isa 44:22 and 55:7; and the former exhortation is grounded in God's previous saving act: "Return to me, *because* I have redeemed you." This makes Is 55:7 the only use of the term with its characteristically *Deuteronomic* motif of repentance.

[46]Oswalt, *Isaiah 40–66*, p. 434.

[47]Another, slightly more nuanced, understanding of this passage is offered by Scheuer, who argues that the relationship between the repentance of the people and the forgiveness of Yahweh is not strictly causal: "Mercy is by no means to be understood as conditioned by returning, but

selves by concluding that Isaiah 55:6-9 is an exception to the norm for Isaiah 40–55: unilateral salvation is *nearly* uniformly proclaimed. As for Isaiah 56–66, while the dominant emphasis is, like Isaiah 40–55, on unconditional pardon, we do see some, albeit few, instances where God's ethical demands are woven into God's restorative act.[48]

In short, Isaiah 40–66 on the whole reveals a *Prophetic* theology of restoration. God's initiative is emphasized over against the conditional theology of restoration seen mostly in DtrH and postexilic literature.[49] Isaiah does not push the "trajectory of pardon" as far as he could. But Jeremiah and Ezekiel do.[50]

Jeremiah. Standing on the eve of exile, the prophet Jeremiah urged Israel to repent and obey God in order to avert God's impending judgment (e.g., Jer 26:3; 36:3). However, there is a difference between what is *hoped for* in restoration (i.e., repentance) and what is envisioned in the *actual* restoration in Jeremiah. "Though there may be many *calls* for Israel to return to her God," writes Benjamin Foreman, "the relationship is never *restored* through a human act of repentance."[51] The reason a *Deuteronomic* restoration will not work is because of Jeremiah's pessimistic view of Israel's condition. The prophet is not convinced that Israel has the ability to turn from its ways: "Can the Cushite change his skin or the leopard his spots? Then also you can do good who are accustomed to do evil" (Jer 13:23 my trans-

---

returning is encouraged because there is mercy to be obtained" (*The Return of YHWH*, p. 73). And again, "YHWH does not forgive because a person returns, but a person is urged to come back to YHWH because YHWH forgives" (p. 74). I think this makes good sense in light of the logic of Is 55:1-9 and the thrust of Is 40–55 as a whole. In any case, the passage is an exhortation, not a prophecy—there is no indication that Israel has or will actually return to God.

[48]My wording here is intentionally ambiguous in an effort to not go beyond what Isaiah says. I do not think that Isaiah 56–66 has sorted out with theological precision the relationship between divine and human agency.

[49]Even prophetic books written during the postexilic period exhibit a stronger *Deuteronomic* concept of restoration. See, e.g., Zech 1:3 ("Return to me . . . that I may return to you" NASB); Mal 3:7 ("Return to me, and I will return to you").

[50]Donald Gowan also recognizes this and explains the difference in terms of the focus of each book. While Jeremiah and Ezekiel envision a divinely initiated change in human nature, "Second Isaiah" speaks in more "broad, sweeping terms, with little specificity" of the people of God. "The author," continues Gowan, "feels the need to be very specific on one subject . . . and that is the nature of God" (Gowan, *Theology of the Prophetic Books*, p. 151).

[51]Benjamin A. Foreman, *Animal Metaphors and the People of Israel in the Book of Jeremiah* (Göttingen: Vandenhoeck & Ruprecht, 2011), p. 179. For an insightful treatment of how this line of thought unfolds in Jeremiah, see Boda, *Severe Mercy*, pp. 223-52.

lation). The two metaphors of the Cushite and leopard here are well known, and both require very little ingenuity to understand the point.[52] Israel is so bent towards evil that its ability to do good has been extinguished. "The point of comparison is not that sin is built in like skin, but that once acquired it is impossible to escape."[53] Humanly initiated change is impossible.[54] In a parallel passage, Jeremiah says:

> For my people are foolish;
>> they know me not;
> they are stupid children;
>> they have no understanding.
> They are "wise"—in doing evil!
> But how to do good they know not. (Jer 4:22)

The correlation between not knowing God and not knowing how to do good suggests that "doing good" means more than just good works, but "having a proper relationship with Yahweh."[55] The point is that Israel has severed its relationship with God and is unable to mend it.

That Israel is unable to repent from its evil ways is also made clear in Jeremiah 17:1-13. The whole section is pertinent, but the main point can be seen clearly in verses 1 and 9. "The sin of Judah is written with a pen of iron; with a point of diamond it is engraved on the tablet of their heart, and on the horns of their altars" (Jer 17:1). Three observations are important. First, the metaphor of a "pen of iron" with a "point of diamond" portrays an engraving that is irreversible. Sin is etched into the humanity of the Judeans. Second, the reference to their sin being engraved on the "horns of their altars" nullifies any hope of atonement through sacrifice. Their means of

---

[52]Most translations have "Ethiopian" instead of "Cushite" (e.g., KJV, RSV, NRSV, ESV) based on the LXX rendering, but the Hebrew word *kûšî* refers to the ancient land of Cush, which occupied modern-day Sudan, extending further south. Both the leopard and the Cushite are chosen here as metaphors because of their appearance. Leopards were well known in ancient Israel (Song 4:8; Is 11:6; Jer 5:6; Hos 13:7), as were the Cushites (Num 12:1; 2 Sam 18:21-32; Job 28:19; Jer 38:7; 39:16), who generally had a darker complexion than, say, an Ethiopian; see Foreman, *Animal Metaphors*, p. 175-76.

[53]Harry D. Potter, "The New Covenant of Jeremiah XXXI 31-34," *VT* 3 (1983): 351.

[54]Some scholars shy away from such a conclusion, asserting instead that the prophet is speaking hyperbolically. See, e.g., Jack R. Lundbom, *Jeremiah: A New Translation with Introduction and Commentary* (New York: Doubleday, 1999), p. 687. Although theologically troubling, there is nothing in the passage that points to hyperbole.

[55]Foreman, *Animal Metaphors*, p. 177.

forgiveness—the altar—is invalidated.[56] And third, the word "tablet" (*lûaḥ*) may allude to the Mosaic law along with the heart of the Judahites. In itself, "tablet of their heart" is quite odd, and twenty-nine of the forty-three occurrences of *lûaḥ* refer to the tablets of the Mosaic law. In any case, the reference to the law "written on their heart" in Jeremiah 31:31 is probably intended to contrast with Jeremiah 17:1, solving the problem of the sin-etched-into-the-heart condition of Judah.[57] "The notion of God writing on the heart," says Harry D. Potter, "was in response to what the prophet saw written there already; only so radical an intervention as one by God himself would suffice."[58]

A few verses later, Jeremiah again emphasizes the irreversible nature of Judah's innate sinful condition: "The heart is deceitful above all things and *incurable* (*wĕʾānūš*), who can know it?" (Jer 17:9, my translation). The word *ʾānūš* ("incurable") is often used by Jeremiah to refer to a fatal medical condition, usually depicting Israel's hopeless spiritual state.[59] The translations "desperately sick" (ESV) and "perverse" (RSV) do not capture the strength of the word, and the KJV's "desperately wicked" is generally true but misses the point. The term *ʾānūš* refers to a fatal condition where there is no cure in sight. It is defined as "refusing to be healed" in Jeremiah 15:18, and in Jeremiah 30:12-13 the "incurable" (*ʾānūš*) wound has "no medicine" and "no healing." The point is that the core of Israel's condition (viz. her heart) is utterly sinful and beyond repair.[60]

In light of Israel's condition, returning to the law is not possible. Israel is terminally ill and has been crushed by God's judgment, leaving it without hope: "The king of Assyria *devoured him,* and now at last Nebuchadnezzar king of Babylon *has gnawed his bones*" (Jer 50:17). Israel is a completely devoured sheep, whose carcass has attracted another predator

---

[56]"So deep-seated was the nation's sin that it had become engraved on the very horns of the altar where the blood of the sin offering which was supposed to wipe away sin was smeared" (Potter, "New Covenant," p. 352).

[57]Ibid.

[58]Ibid.

[59]See Jer 15:18; 17:16; 30:12, 15; cf. Job 34:6; Is 17:11; Mic 1:9; Foreman, *Animal Metaphors*, p. 171.

[60]In Jer 2:23-24, the prophet uses the common prophetic metaphor of whoredom to describe Israel's apostasy. But unlike a typical ANE prostitute, who has chosen such vocation as a means of survival—or perhaps as a means of worship—Israel is, like a wild donkey in heat, driven by its insatiable lust for sex.

(i.e., Babylon) now hungrily gnawing on its bones.[61] The odds of living again are about as good as a leopard mustering the strength to change his spots (Jer 13:23). The point is clear: Israel is spiritually dead with no hope of restoration.

But restoration it will find, solely through the free pardon and initiative of God. Carrying on from the previous passage, Jeremiah 50:19 depicts Israel now as a satiated sheep, grazing the luscious fields of Carmel and Bashan.

> I will restore Israel to his pasture, and he shall feed on Carmel and in Bashan, and his desire shall be satisfied on the hills of Ephraim and in Gilead. In those days and in that time, declares the LORD, iniquity shall be sought in Israel, and there shall be none, and sin in Judah, and none shall be found, for I will pardon those whom I leave as a remnant. (Jer 50:19-20)

The miraculous metamorphosis from a mangled corpse to a plump animal is wrought through the unilateral action of God: "I will restore Israel to his pasture. . . . I will pardon those whom I leave as a remnant" (Jer 50:19-20). The logic of unilateral restoration flows out of Jeremiah's pessimistic anthropology. And this is the point of the new covenant passage in Jeremiah 31:

> Behold, the days are coming, declares the LORD, when I will make a new covenant with the house of Israel and the house of Judah, not like the covenant that I made with their fathers on the day when I took them by the hand to bring them out of the land of Egypt, my covenant that they broke, though I was their husband, declares the LORD. But this is the covenant that I will make with the house of Israel after those days, declares the LORD: *I will put my law within them, and I will write it on their hearts.* And I will be their God, and they shall be my people. And no longer shall each one teach his neighbor and each his brother, saying, "Know the LORD," for they shall all know me, from the least of them to the greatest, declares the LORD. For I will forgive their iniquity, and I will remember their sin no more. (Jer 31:31-34)

Jeremiah describes a unilateral act of God whereby he reconstitutes Israel's

---

[61] Foreman notes that the words *'ākal* ("eat") and *'āṣam* ("gnaw") together depict a "totally devoured animal" that "cannot be restored" (Foreman, *Animal Metaphors*, p. 91).

"heart," pardoning it freely and enabling it to obey.[62] In stark contrast to the *Deuteronomic* program, which prefaces such pardon with a return to the law, Jeremiah speaks confidently of unilateral forgiveness, as Walter Brueggemann says: "The assurance of pardon and the forgetting of sin are voiced as a unilateral act by YHWH, without any seeking, calling, or turning—that is, without any repentance on the part of Israel. Pardon is a genuine *novum* on the part of YHWH, the breaking of all vicious cycles of alienation that permits a new start with YHWH."[63] The contrast with Deuteronomy is striking. Whereas Moses *exhorts* Israel to place the commandments "upon their heart," "teach them diligently to their children" and "write them upon the doorpost" (Deut 6:6-7, 9), Jeremiah *announces* that God will perform these tasks. Jeremiah uses Deuteronomic language, but the relationship between the prophet and Moses is one of "critical dialogue."[64] In the old covenant (i.e., "the covenant I made with their fathers"; Jer 31:32), the laws were written down on tablets of stone and were taught to the congregation. In the new covenant, God will write the law on their heart, erasing the need for such external teaching since every person will know God at the core of their being.

The same emphasis is seen in Jeremiah 32, where the prophet intentionally turns the *Deuteronomic* "if . . . then" on its head, creating an unconditional "I will."

> Behold, I will gather them from all the countries to which I drove them in my anger and my wrath and in great indignation. I will bring them back to this place, and I will make them dwell in safety. And they shall be my people, and

---

[62]The focus on the renewed heart here and elsewhere (Jer 24:7; 32:39-41) is intended to solve the problem of the wicked and stubborn heart of sin-plagued Judah (Jer 3:17; 7:24; 9:14; 13:10; 16:12; 17:1, 9; 18:12; 23:17).

[63]Brueggemann, "Travail of Pardon," p. 292; for a similar reading, see Robert P. Carroll, *Jeremiah: A Commentary* (Philadelphia: Westminster John Knox, 1986), pp. 613-14; Thomas M. Raitt, "The Prophetic Summons to Repentance," *ZAW* 83 (1971): 30-49 (47-48); Potter, "New Covenant," p. 351: "This is either a direct attack on the limitations of the Deuteronomic procedure or a considerable development from it." See also Terence E. Fretheim, *Jeremiah* (Macon, GA: Smith & Helwys, 2002), p. 449: "God's unilateral act of the forgiveness of Israel ('for my own sake,' Isa 43:25) is the basis upon which this new covenant is established."

[64]"I would regard the relation between 31.31-34 and the Deuteronomistic strand in the tradition to be one of critical dialogue. . . . The author of 31.31-34 transcends that limitation by asserting the divine initiative beyond human turning and making of a new *berit*. It is a post-Deuteronomistic hope but one which has learned its theology from Deuteronomism and made the leap of hope into the utopian future" (Carroll, *Jeremiah*, pp. 613-14).

I will be their God. I will give them one heart and one way, that they may fear me forever, for their own good and the good of their children after them. I will make with them an everlasting covenant, that *I will not turn away* (*lōʾ-ʾāšûb*) from doing good to them. And I will put the fear of me in their hearts, that *they may not turn from me* (*sûr mēʿālāy*). I will rejoice in doing them good, and I will plant them in this land in faithfulness, with all my heart and all my soul. (Jer 32:37-41)

By creatively using certain stock phrases from Deutoronomy, this passage picks up many *Deuteronomic* restoration themes and inverts them. First, the trio "in anger and fury and great wrath" occurs in Jeremiah 21:5 and elsewhere only in Deuteronomy 29:28 [29:27 Heb], suggesting that there is a deliberate allusion to Deuteronomy 29:28.[65] Second, the Hebrew word *šûb* ("repent, turn"), which is popular in Deuteronomy and DtrH and normally used as an *exhortation*, is used here as a *promise* that God will bring Israel back to the land.[66] This places God's initiative and action in critical dialogue with the exhortations of the Deuteronomists; God will *šûb* to Israel before Israel can *šûb* to God. Third, to "fear me/Yahweh forever" (lit. "all the days") is a standard phrase in Deuteronomy (Deut 4:10; 6:2; 31:13),[67] and the phrase "a heart to fear me" is held out as a hope laid on the people in Deuteronomy 5:29 (HCSB). "The dream of the Deuteronomists that the people should fear Yahweh all the days of their life will also be realized in the future because Yahweh will put that fear within them . . . so that they do not turn away from him."[68] Fourth, the phrase "I will rejoice in doing them good" is seen elsewhere only in Deuteronomy 28:63; 30:9,[69] suggesting that the restoration from exile envisioned in Deuteronomy will happen, though it will not be initiated by human agency. Fifth, and most significantly, with the phrase "with all *my* heart and with all *my* soul," the prophet uses language "normally reserved for the people and their commitment to Yahweh" as seen

---

[65]William Lee Holladay and Paul D. Hanson, *Jeremiah 2: A Commentary on the Book of the Prophet Jeremiah, Chapters 26–52* (Minneapolis: Fortress, 1989), p. 207. Jeremiah's more common phrase is simply "(my) anger and (my) wrath" (e.g., Jer 8:20; 32:31, 37; 33:5; 36:7; 42:18; see Lumdbom, *Jeremiah*, pp. 102-3).

[66]There seems to be a play on the meaning of *šûb*, which occurs here in the *hipʿil*—the only use of *šûb* in the *hipʿil* in Jeremiah (Holladay, *Jeremiah*, 2:208).

[67]See Lumbom, *Jeremiah*, p. 519.

[68]Carroll, *Jeremiah*, p. 630.

[69]Holladay, *Jeremiah*, 2:208.

throughout Deuteronomy and DtrH (Deut 4:29; 6:5; 10:12; 1 Kings 2:4; 2 Kings 23:3).[70] This can only be a deliberate challenge to Deuteronomy's stress on human agency, which is here transferred to divine agency.[71] As is often recognized, Jeremiah uses the language and motifs of Deuteronomy more than any other writer and therefore is considered the Deuteronomic prophet. But the appearance of such language does not mean Jeremiah embraced a *Deuteronomic* theology of restoration. It appears from Jeremiah 31 and 32 that Jeremiah uses Deuteronomic language as "a deliberate contrast to Deuteronomy, not a complement to it, or a restatement of it."[72]

---

[70]Lundbom, *Jeremiah*, p. 521.

[71]A few passages in Jeremiah seem to anticipate a more *Deuteronomic* restoration. Jer 26:3 and Jer 36:3 say that *if* Israel repents, *then* God will relent from exiling them. But this possibility is only hypothetical, since judgment and exile have already been decreed (Jer 29:10-11), which is reiterated in 36:31 (see Lundbom, *Jeremiah*, p. 589; Carroll, *Jeremiah*, p. 515, 658-59. Holladay (*Jeremiah*, 1:104) takes the exhortations in Jer 26:3; 36:3 as more real than hypothetical. As stated earlier, there is a difference between the demand for repentance and the actual way in which restoration is envisioned in Jeremiah. In Jer 29:14, Israel's restoration seems to be initiated by their repentance: "I will be found by you, declares the LORD, and I will restore your fortunes and gather you from all the nations and all the places where I have driven you, declares the LORD, and I will bring you back to the place from which I sent you into exile." And both Brueggemann and Carroll, who understand Israel's inability to repent to be a dominant theme in Jeremiah, believe this passage promotes a different program of restoration, where repentance will precede restoration. See Walter Brueggemann, *A Commentary on Jeremiah: Exile and Homecoming* (Grand Rapids: Eerdmans, 1998), p. 259, and Carroll, *Jeremiah*, pp. 558-59. However, Jer 29:10-11 grounds Israel's restoration in God's initiative, who "will visit you" and "fulfill to you my promise" and "bring you back to this place." God's future act is written into the script of the foreordained punishment that will last seventy years. Only then—that is, only after God has first intervened—will Israel call on the LORD and turn to him in obedience (Jer 29:13-14) (Foreman, *Animal Metaphors*, pp. 180-81; similarly Fretheim, *Jeremiah*, p. 404). Some have viewed Jer 24:4-7 as proof that Israel's repentance in exile will be the formal cause of her restoration. And grammatically, the final clause could hint in this direction: "*For (kî)* they shall return to me with their whole heart" (Jer 24:7b). See, e.g., Jeremiah Unterman, *From Repentance to Redemption: Jeremiah's Thought in Transition*, JSOTSup (Sheffield: JSOT Press, 1987), p. 82. However, as most commentators recognize, the only reason why Israel will be able to return to God with "their whole heart" is that God will have given them a heart to know him (Jer 24:7a). See Lundbom, *Jeremiah*, p. 232; Raitt, *Theology of Exile*, p. 178. For a mediating position, see Scheuer, *Return of YHWH*, p. 113. Moreover, preceding the return of Israel to God in Jer 24:7b is the return of God to Israel in Jer 24:4-7a. So like Jer 31:31-34 and Jer 32:37-41, God will take the initiative in restoring Israel and thus enabling it to return to him. The only passage in Jeremiah that seems to go against the dominant theme of unilateral redemption is Jer 50:4-5: "In those days and in that time, declares the LORD, the people of Israel and the people of Judah shall come together, weeping as they come, and they shall seek the LORD their God. They shall ask the way to Zion, with faces turned toward it, saying, 'Come, let us join ourselves to the LORD in an everlasting covenant that will never be forgotten.'" Though there are ways of smoothing out the theological inconsistency (see, e.g., Foreman, *Animal Metaphors*, pp. 72-73, 89-90), the solutions are not very convincing.

[72]Potter, "New Covenant," p. 350. Potter is thinking in terms of Jer 31:31-34 in particular, but, as

In summary, Jeremiah is indeed a prophet of repentance. Israel is wicked, and unless they repent they will face the fiery judgment of God through Babylon. But the prophet also knows that sin is too deeply ingrained in the heart of Israel, and therefore repentance is impossible apart from divine initiative. God will restore Israel through an unconditional pardon, when he writes his law on their hearts with all *his* heart, soul and mind.

Ezekiel. In many ways, the message of restoration proclaimed by Ezekiel is of the same cloth as Jeremiah. What is evident in Isaiah and prevalent in Jeremiah becomes unmistakable in Ezekiel: God will restore Israel through a unilateral act prefaced by nothing other than God's unconditional commitment to his own name. Breuggemann's "trajectory of pardon" is pushed to the limits in Ezekiel; nowhere does the prophet forecast that Israel's repentance will precede God's forgiveness.[73] And this is seen in more than a few passages here and there—it is integral to the book as a whole.

Like Jeremiah, Ezekiel's program of restoration arises out of his pessimistic anthropology. Israel is unable to turn from her wicked ways, a point made clear at the time of his call: "Surely, if I sent you to such, they would listen to you. *But the house of Israel will not be willing to listen to you, for they are not willing to listen to me*: because all the house of Israel have a hard forehead and a stubborn heart" (Ezek 3:6-7). Israel is a "rebellious people" (Ezek 2:3, 4, 5, 6, 7, 8; 3:7), and though they are able to understand the message, Israel will not be willing or able to respond to it. This is why God feeds the prophet a scroll filled front and back with messages of judgment; namely, "words of lamentation and mourning and woe" (Ezek 2:10). The fact that judgment is inscribed on this scroll points to its predetermination. Ezekiel

---

we have seen, his understanding applies to various passages in Jeremiah, not least Jer 32:37-41. Likewise, Duhm understands Jer 31:31-34 "as setting forth the contrast between the prophetic and the Deuteronomic conception of religion" (Bernhard Duhm, *Das Buch Jeremia* [Tübingen: Mohr Siebeck, 1903], p. 254, cited in Potter, "New Covenant," p. 350). J. Gordon McConville compares two so-called Deuteronomic texts (1 Kings 8:46-53 with Deut 29:17-27; 30:1-10) and astutely writes: "Too often, similar vocabulary or phraseology is taken, without further ado, to imply similar origin and meaning. The case I have examined shows that the writer's use of vocabulary may be self-conscious, and intended both to express a measure of identity with a tradition *and to criticize it* ("1 Kings VIII 46-53," p. 78, emphasis mine).

[73]"The causes of the restoration are nearly all expressed in priestly vocabulary and link to the unilateral work of Yahweh himself" (Boda, *Severe Mercy*, p. 287). While the verb *šûb* ("return, repent") is used in Ezekiel eight times in the imperative, calling Israel to repentance, none of these are in the context of eschatological restoration (see Scheuer, *Return of YHWH*, pp. 117, 120-21).

is not commissioned to turn Israel back from its sin but to announce God's unavoidable judgment.[74]

Israel's condition is beyond hope. They cannot turn from their wicked ways. The judgment of exile is inevitable. There is hope of restoration, however, on the other side of exile, but given the depth of their sin, the *Deuteronomic* paradigm will not work. God, therefore, will operate outside the confines of the Sinaitic covenant to deliver his blessing to the nation. As we will see, this new act of God takes center stage in Ezekiel 36–37, but it is also seen in two highly charged retellings of Israel's history that push the envelope of morality. Ezekiel 16 is a pornographic allegory that makes the most daring translators blush;[75] Ezekiel 20 is an imaginative story of Israel, where Ezekiel bends history to serve his own rhetorical purpose.[76] When the dust is settled, both are unparalleled in their depictions of unilateral grace.

The crude allegory in Ezekiel 16 depicts Israel as a helpless child (Ezek 16:3-6) who was cared for by Yahweh and later taken in marriage (Ezek 16:8). But Israel relentlessly pursued a life of whoredom (Ezek 16:15-52), idolatry (Ezek 16:15-19, 23-43), child sacrifice (Ezek 16:20-22) and neglect of the poor (Ezek 16:44-50). The most shocking feature of this scathing review of Israel's

---

[74]See Ezek 20:4; 22:2. The point is creatively driven home by the muteness of Ezekiel (Ezek 3:26). The significance of Ezekiel's muteness relates to the anthropology of the book in two important ways. First, it ensures that Ezekiel would not try to "reprove" the disobedient exiles (Ezek 3:26). The idea of "reprove" refers to speaking to elicit change, but this was not the function of Ezekiel's ministry. He was to announce judgment, not elicit change. Second, Ezekiel's muteness is intended to symbolically represent the spiritual condition of the nation. Just as his house confinement represents the nation's exilic state (Ezek 3:24-25), so also his muteness portrays the spiritual condition of the nation. Ezekiel is unable to speak; the nation is unable to repent. This is made clear as the book unfolds. Israel's future salvation is described in terms of the opening of the mouth (Ezek 16:63; 29:21), just as Ezekiel's mouth is opened preceding the oracles of salvation (Ezek 33:21-22). If the opening of the mouth correlates to the oracle of salvation (announced by Ezekiel and received by Israel), so the closing of the mouth correlates to the oracle of judgment. Part of God's judgment is to ensure that Israel cannot avoid it.

[75]See Daniel Block: "Through the priestly prophet Yahweh throws caution to the wind, speaking of a woman opening her legs wide to passersby (v. 25), the Egyptians with their enlarged penis (v. 26), the female genital fluid produced at sexual arousal (v. 36), and baring of the pudenda (vv. 36, 37). Such expressions are obviously of a piece with the references to lewdness (vv. 27, 43, 58), whoredom, and nudity (vv. 7, 22, 39), but they present serious problems for the commentator, who must clarify the author's intention, and even more so for the modern translator, who feels constrained to tone down the language in respect for sensitivities of the target readership" (Daniel I. Block, *The Book of Ezekiel: Chapters 1-24*, NICOT [Grand Rapids: Eerdmans, 1997], p. 467).

[76]See Katheryn P. Darr, "Ezekiel's Justifications of God: Teaching Troubling Texts," *JSOT* 55 (1992): 97-117.

moral atrocities, however, is that it ends *not* with God's judgment *nor* with Israel's repentance, but with God's unilateral forgiveness:

> Yet I will remember my covenant with you in the days of your youth, and I will establish for you an everlasting covenant. Then you will remember your ways and be ashamed when you take your sisters, both your elder and your younger, and I give them to you as daughters, but not on account of the covenant with you. I will establish my covenant with you, and you shall know that I am the LORD, that you may remember and be confounded, and never open your mouth again because of your shame, when I atone for you for all that you have done, declares the Lord GOD. (Ezek 16:60-63)

Israel responds with shame and remorse, but these emotions do not solicit God's saving act. God intervenes unilaterally with an "everlasting covenant" (*běrît ʿôlām*),[77] permeated by atonement and forgiveness. This covenant seems to usurp the previous "covenant with you" (Ezek 16:61), which, though debated, probably refers to the conditional Sinaitic covenant, which was never fulfilled.[78] In any case, God's unilateral grace takes center stage at the end of this historical allegory, anticipating God's saving intervention in Ezekiel 36–37.

Ezekiel 20 is equally *Prophetic*. From Egyptian bondage to Babylonian exile, Israel's history is sketched in terms of absolute failure (Ezek 20:5-26). There never has been a time, according to Ezekiel, when Israel has not run after idols—even while it was in slavery in Egypt (Ezek 20:7-8). Throughout this dark history, God had provided them with the law of Moses ("my statutes and . . . rules") in order to give them the covenant blessing of "life"—

---

[77]See too Ezek 37:26; cf. Jer 32:40; 50:5; Is 55:3; 61:8. Thomas Raitt understands the term *everlasting covenant* to convey the unconditional nature of the new covenant and thus captures the point of the Jer 31:31-34 and Jer 32:37-41. "Since an everlasting covenant founded on unconditional forgiveness, structure around law, and made possible by the transformation of human nature is wholly without precedent, every important implication of the 'new covenant' contained in Jeremiah 31:31-34 is subsumed under the promise of an 'everlasting covenant'" (Raitt, *Theology of Exile*, pp. 203-4).

[78]The Targum understands the phrase this way when it adds: "even though you did not observe the Torah" (cited in Block, *Ezekiel 1-24*, p. 518n309, though Block himself understands the phrase differently). Allen takes the view proposed here: "The context suggests that it is another manifestation of divine grace, here transcending the previous relationship" (Leslie C. Allen, *Ezekiel 1-19* [Waco, TX: Word, 1994], p. 246); see too Moshe Greenberg, *Ezekiel 1-20: A New Translation with Introduction and Commentary* (Garden City, NY: Doubleday, 1983), p. 292; John B. Taylor and Donald G. Wiseman, *Ezekiel: An Introduction and Commentary*, Tyndale Old Testament Commentaries (Downers Grove, IL: InterVarsity Press, 1983), p. 142.

if they would obey it (Ezek 20:11, 13, 21). The formula that Ezekiel uses to convey this offer of life comes right out of Leviticus 18:5 and has a distinct *Deuteronomic* ring to it: "I gave them my statutes and made known to them my rules, *by which, if a person does them, he shall live.*"[79] This formula, capturing as it does the conditional offer of "life," is repeated three times in this chapter and each time highlights Israel's *failure* to obey the law and lay hold of this offer of life. Yet God does more than just judge them for this failure; rather, he gives them over to death by giving them "statues that were not good and rules by which they could not have life" (Ezek 20:25). This is one of the most difficult verses in a very difficult book. What does it mean that God gave Israel no-good laws? Interpreters modern and ancient have tried to solve this dilemma, and there is no consensus as to what the prophet means here.[80] Regardless of the meaning of the no-good statutes and rules, it is clear that Ezekiel 20:25 was written in response to the threefold repetition of the Leviticus 18:5 quotation. The structure of the no-good laws statement (Ezek 20:25) and the Leviticus 18:5 citations (Ezek 20:11, 13, 21) is nearly identical, showing that the prophet is correlating the former to the latter.[81] In other words, the giving of no-good laws declares that the laws of Moses cannot give life to the nation. Wickedness is etched into Israel's bones, and this prevents torah from giving the life it offers for obedience.

But Israel's sin is not the final word. The narrative of Israel's apostasy (Ezek 20:5-32) is met with a promise of restoration (Ezek 20:33-38), which, as in Ezekiel 16, is not a response to Israel's confession, repentance or anything the nation has done. God acts unilaterally to redeem and forgive his people:

> As I live, declares the Lord GOD, surely with a mighty hand and an outstretched arm and with wrath poured out I will be king over you. I will bring you out from the peoples and gather you out of the countries where you are scattered, with a mighty hand and an outstretched arm, and with wrath poured out. . . . I will make you pass under the rod, and I will bring you into

---

[79]See Preston Sprinkle, *Law and Life: The Interpretation of Leviticus 18:5 in Early Judaism and in Paul*, WUNT 2.241 (Tübingen: Mohr Siebeck, 2008), pp. 34-40; and Preston Sprinkle, "Law and Life: The Use of Leviticus 18.5 in the Literary Framework of Ezekiel," *JSOT* 31 (2007): 55-73.

[80]For a discussion, see Sprinkle, *Law and Life*, p. 287.

[81]Ezek 20:25 *wĕgam-ʾănî nātatî lāhem ḥuqîm lōʾ tôbîm ûmišpāṭîm ḥuqîm lōʾ yiḥyû bāhem*; cf. Ezek 20:21b *ʾăšer yaʿăseh ʾōtām hāʾādām wāḥê bāhem*.

the bond of the covenant. I will purge out the rebels from among you, and those who transgress against me. I will bring them out of the land where they sojourn, but they shall not enter the land of Israel. Then you will know that I am the LORD. (Ezek 20:33-38)

The twofold reference to "a mighty hand and an outstretched arm" (Ezek 20:33, 34) evokes the exodus, and exhibits the common prophetic motif of a "second exodus" when God will intervene in similar ways.[82] In the exodus, of course, God was not responding to anything that Israel did; rather, he was moved out of pity for the nation and, even more so, motivated by a concern for his holy name. The same is true of the second exodus of Ezekiel 20: rebellion and salvation hinge not on repentance, but on unconditioned divine intervention.

Israel's *Prophetic* restoration is most clearly articulated in Ezekiel 36–37. "And I will give you a new heart, and a new spirit I will put within you. And I will remove the heart of stone from your flesh and give you a heart of flesh. And I will put my Spirit within you, *and cause you* (wĕʿāśîtî) to walk in my statutes and be careful to obey my rules" (Ezek 36:26-27). As with Jeremiah, Ezekiel believes Israel's spiritual condition is fatal. The only remedy for Israel's "heart of stone" is the divine gift of "a new heart." The most striking feature in this passage is the promise of the "new spirit" later identified as simply "my spirit," who is placed "within" the nation in order to "cause" them to obey.[83] The gift of the spirit enables Israel's eschatological obedience, which springs from restoration. And there is no prior act of repentance on Israel's part. Israel has a heart of stone and is therefore dead.

Israel's fatal condition and God's unilateral response is creatively portrayed in the dry bones vision in Ezekiel 37:1-14, which is linguistically and conceptually linked to Ezekiel 36:26-27.[84] In Ezekiel 37, the prophet is

---

[82]E.g., Is 12:1-6; 43:16-21; 52:10-12.

[83]This is captured by the *qal* wĕʿāśîtî ("and I will cause you"), which denotes causation. On this construction, see G. A. Cooke, *A Critical and Exegetical Commentary on the Book of Ezekiel* (Edinburgh: T & T Clark, 1936), p. 395; W. E. Gesenius, W. E. Kautzsch and A. E. Cowley, *Gesenius' Hebrew Grammar*, 28th ed. (Oxford: Oxford University Press, 1909 [1963]), §157.

[84]"The editorial function of 37.1-13 in its present position is to throw light on the gift of the spirit in 36.27a. . . . In turn 37.14a represents an editorial rounding off of the unit of vv. 1-13, which uses the vision with its ninefold occurrence of *rûaḥ* ('breath/spirit') as an illustration of the restoring power of God in 36.27a." Leslie Allen, "Structure, Tradition and Redaction in Ezekiel's Death Valley Vision," in *Among the Prophets: Language, Image and Structure in the Prophetic Writings*, ed. Philip R. Davies and David J. A. Clines, JSOTSup 144 (Sheffield: JSOT Press,

brought to a valley full of "very dry" skeletons (Ezek 37:2), which vividly portrays Israel's spiritual condition (very dry bones have been dead for quite some time). As Ezekiel prophesies over the skeletons, they stand on their feet, regaining sinews and flesh. But the bodies are still dead, so Ezekiel prophesies again, and "the *breath/spirit* (*rûaḥ*) came into them, and they lived" (37:10). In a summary-like statement, God ends the vision by declaring: "I will put my Spirit within you, and you shall live, and I will place you in your own land. Then you shall know that I am the LORD; I have spoken, and I will do it, declares the LORD" (Ezek 37:14).[85] The nation attains the covenant blessing of life, not through returning to the law, but through the spirit's unilateral agency. This "life-through-divine-agency" motif in Ezekiel 36–37 sums up a main theme of the book as a whole. The blessing of life held out as a *conditional* offer in Ezekiel 20:11, 13, 21, 25 is here granted to Israel *unconditionally* through the agency of the spirit. Israel, in fact, has been marching toward the grave throughout the book. They have received many calls to repentance, which, in theory, would reverse their deathly trajectory (e.g., Ezek 18:23, 32: "turn and live"), but no repentance has been found. At their wit's end, they cry out: "Surely our transgressions and our sins are upon us, and we are rotting away in them. *How then can we live?*" (Ezek 33:10), to which Ezekiel responds by showcasing the penitent law-abider as the one who will find life (Ezek 33:11-16). But no such persons can be found. So finally, the people of Israel find themselves in the grave in need of resuscitation (Ezek 37). Because of this, the only way in which God will grant his covenant blessings of life and forgiveness to the dead nation is through the agency of the divine spirit, who performs heart surgery on the nation and creates the obedience that torah commands.

In summary, the book of Ezekiel corresponds to Jeremiah in emphasizing the depth of depravity engrained on the heart of Israel, necessitating unilateral redemption. This redemption is underscored by the promise of the eschatological spirit of God, which will breathe life into the dead nation.

1993), pp. 140-41; followed by Thomas Renz, *The Rhetorical Function of the Book of Ezekiel* (Leiden: Brill, 1999), pp. 200-201.

[85] The summary statement in Ezek 37:14 corresponds to the gift of the spirit in Ezek 36:27: "And *I will put my spirit within you* (*wĕ'et-rûḥî 'etēn bĕqirbĕkem*), and cause you to walk in my statutes and be careful to obey my rules" (Ezek 36:27); "*and I will put my spirit within you* (*wĕnātatî rûḥî bākem*), and you shall live" (Ezek 37:14).

Dry, dusty skeletons do not repent, and neither will Israel, until they are first revitalized by a gracious act of divine intervention.[86]

SUMMARY

In this chapter, we have examined two programs of restoration, which we have labeled *Deuteronomic* and *Prophetic*. The former emphasizes a theology of restoration that is based more on retribution: if Israel repents and returns to the law, then God will restore it. The latter emphasizes God's unilateral act of restoration: God will redeem Israel and enable it to return to God. We have found that Deuteronomy and DtrH emphasize a *Deuteronomic* theology of restoration, while they maintain threads of *Prophetic* restoration. Ezra, Nehemiah and especially Chronicles portray a *Deuteronomic* restoration much more consistently. For the prophetic books, we have surveyed Isaiah, Jeremiah and Ezekiel and found that Isaiah emphasizes a *Prophetic* restoration (esp. Is 40–55), though not as pervasively as Jeremiah and Ezekiel, where the *Prophetic* scheme is ironed out with remarkable consistency and clarity.[87]

---

[86]Ezekiel 18 does not run against the grain of Ezekiel's otherwise pessimistic view of Israel. While it is true that the chapter urges Israel to repent in order to find life (explicitly in Ezek 18:23, 32, and implied throughout), the function of this chapter is to prove that God's judgment on the exilic generation is just (see Ezek 18:2). Ezekiel, in other words, does not set forth the manner in which God will restore them. Paul Joyce rightly states that "the primary purpose" of Ezekiel 18 is "to highlight responsibility for the crisis which has engulfed the nation rather than to issue a realistic call to repentance which might avert disaster and thereby secure the future" (Paul Joyce, *Divine Initiative and Human Response in Ezekiel* [Sheffield: JSOT Press, 1989], p. 128). This is made clear towards the end of the chapter, when the prophet states clearly that Israel is wicked and they will die (see Ezek 18:25, 29). The rhetoric about the hypothetical wicked person in Ezek 18:5-23 slides from a hypothesis to an indictment on the nation of Israel toward the end of the chapter. Moreover, the final command in Ezekiel 18:31 to "make yourselves a new heart and a new spirit" is clearly left unfulfilled as the book unfolds. The correlation between the new heart and new spirit that is here stated as a command, and the new heart and new spirit that is created through divine agency in Ezekiel 36, is intentional. Like the circumcision of the heart motif in Deuteronomy, God will create what he commands in the age of restoration. See further Joyce, *Divine Initiative*, pp. 33-60; Michael Fishbane, "Sin and Judgment in the Prophecies of Ezekiel," *Int* 38 (1984): 131-50 (esp. pp. 147-48); Greenburg, *Ezekiel 1-20*, p. 341: "It is true that the principles of retribution and repentance that Ezekiel enunciated are highly theoretical and hardly take realities into account."

[87]Examining the Twelve is beyond the scope of this chapter. However, Mark Boda, with whom I am in essential agreement on Isaiah, Jeremiah and Ezekiel, finds a similar relationship between divine and human agencies in the Twelve. He says that much of the Twelve highlights Israel's inability to respond in repentance, while emphasizing God's future unilateral intervention (esp. Hosea, Amos and Micah). The books of Joel and Jonah, however, are different in that they hold out hope for a positive response of repentance. Mark Boda, "Repentance," in *Dictionary of the*

The point of this chapter is not to determine which books the Qumranites and Paul will use to depict their understanding of restoration; rather, it is to show that the Scriptures hold out diverse paradigms of restoration, which no doubt shape the way early Jewish interpreters—including Paul—will understand God's saving act. In some cases, we will find explicit endorsement of a particular paradigm; in other cases, we will find that Paul or Qumran will follow the inner logic of one of the motifs. We will therefore use the categories of *Deuteronomic* and *Prophetic* as heuristic lenses to understand and compare the soteriological structures of Paul and Qumran.

Old Testament Prophets (Downers Grove, IL: IVP Academic), pp. 668-69; see also Boda, *Severe Mercy*, pp. 294-350.

3

RESTORATION FROM
THE CURSE OF THE LAW

As the Old Testament draws to a close, Israel stands under the covenant curse looking forward to restoration. For the Deuteronomists and postexilic historians, this restoration will come when Israel returns to the law in repentance and obedience. For the Prophets, however, the human condition is too dire, and therefore God will intervene to implant his spirit or law in their hearts, thereby enabling their obedience.[1] The Old Testament ends, therefore, with two different trajectories of how God will restore the nation. And Second Temple writers pick up on these motifs and integrate them into their own reflection on how God will—or has—restore(d) his people.

In this chapter, we will look at the "curse motif" through the lens of the two patterns of restoration surveyed in the previous chapter. It is evident that both Paul and Qumran believed that national Israel still lived under the curse of the covenant, yet both writers believed that their respective communities had escaped this curse. The question is whether or not we can see evidence of either a *Deuteronomic* or *Prophetic* pattern of restoration in Paul and Qumran—a task to which we now turn.

RESTORATION FROM THE CURSE IN THE DEAD SEA SCROLLS

Curse and blessing language abounds in the Scrolls, often in contexts where

---

[1]Once more, my terms *Deuteronomists* and *Prophets* point to theological emphases and not uniformity.

covenant restoration is the focal point.[2] The community[3] at Qumran believed that their sect had escaped the covenant curse and received (at least
in part) the blessings, while the rest of the nation of Israel remained under
the curse of the Sinaitic covenant. This theme, in fact, is quite pervasive in
the literature, leading to the question: Did they believe that God's people
needed to repent and return to the law in order for God to remove the covenant curse (*Deuteronomic*), or did they believe that God had acted unconditionally to remove the curse prior to repentance (*Prophetic*)? To answer
this, we will look at five documents that address the theme directly.

The Temple Scroll (11QTᵃ). The *Temple Scroll* (11QTᵃ) is the largest and
one of the most well preserved nonbiblical scrolls found at Qumran. For
the most part, the scroll is a law-code resembling much legal material in the
Pentateuch (Ex 25–31; Deut 12–23).[4] But one passage in particular, the so-
called law of the king (11QTᵃ 59:4-13), breaks from this legal genre and
delves into an eschatological discourse:

> And during all this, *their cities shall become a waste* [Lev 26:31-32], and a
> mockery and a ruin. And their *enemies will be appalled at them* [Lev 26:32].
> And they themselves, in the lands of their enemies, will sigh and cry out
> under a heavy yoke. And they will call but I will not listen; they will shout but
> I will not reply to them, because of the evil of their deeds. *And I will hide my
> face from them* [Deut 31:17-18], and they will be fodder and prey and spoil,
> and no one will save them because of their wickedness, for they broke my
> covenant and their soul loathed my law, so that they became guilty of all
> wrongdoing. (11QTᵃ 59:4-9)[5]

This passage describes the plight of Israel in terms of the covenant curses of
Deuteronomy 28–31 and Leviticus 26.[6] While Israel is in their wicked state,
no one will save them, not even God, for he has "hidden his face from them"
and "will not listen" or "reply" to their cry of misery. But, as the following

---

[2]See Bilhah Nitzan, *Qumran Prayer and Religious Poetry*, STDJ 12 (Leiden: Brill, 1994), pp. 123-43.

[3]See chap. 1, n. 43 for how I am using the term "community."

[4]See James C. VanderKam and Peter W. Flint, *The Meaning of the Dead Sea Scrolls: Their Significance for Understanding the Bible, Judaism, Jesus, and Christianity* (New York: T & T Clark, 2005), p. 211.

[5]Unless otherwise noted, all translations of the Dead Sea Scrolls are my own. Translations from F. Garcia Martinez and E. J. C. Tigchelaar, eds., *Dead Sea Scroll Study Edition*, 2 vols. (Grand Rapids: Eerdmans, 2000), will be noted as *DSSSE*.

[6]Other passages alluded to include Deut 28:36-37, 48, 64; 31:17-18; and Lev 26:15, 31-32.

section indicates, if they repent, turn from their wicked ways and revert back to the law with all their hearts, then God will save them from the covenant curse:

> Afterwards they will come back to me *with all their heart and with all their soul* [Deut 30:3] in agreement with all the words of this law, and I will save them (*whûšt'tîm*) from the hand of their enemies and redeem them (*wpdîtîm*) from the hand of those who hate them and bring them into the land of their fathers, and I will redeem them (*wpdîtîm*), and multiply them, and rejoice in them. And I will be their God and they will be my people. (11QT[a] 59:9-13)

Israel takes the initiative to return to God, and therefore this passage resonates with a *Deuteronomic* view of restoration. Israel will be redeemed from the curses of the covenant when they first return to God "with all [their] heart and with all [their] soul" (Deut 30:3) and revert back to the law.[7] Israel's obedience is a precondition to God's restorative act.

The Damascus Document (CD). The *Damascus Document* (hereafter CD) contains several historical narratives about the establishment of the sectarian community.[8] Like many scrolls from Qumran, CD frequently draws on the book of Deuteronomy, specifically on the theme of covenant curses and blessings. The first occurrence of curse language comes in the first of three speeches, where the author describes the waywardness of Israel:

> "Like a stray heifer so has Israel strayed" [Hos 4:16], when the scoffer arose, who poured out over Israel waters of lies and made them stray into a wilderness without path, causing the everlasting heights to sink down, diverging from tracks of righteousness and removing the boundary with which the forefathers had marked their inheritance, so that the *curses of his covenant* (*'lôt brîtû*) [see Deut 29:19-21] would cling to them. (CD 1:13-17 DSSSE)

The "scoffer" was probably a former member of the sect who was influential in Israel around the time that the Qumran community was established, and

---

[7]Yigael Yadin, *The Temple Scroll* (Jerusalem: Israel Exploration Society, 1977), 2:65-70.

[8]The *Damascus Document* has been known to modern scholarship for almost one hundred years since it was first discovered in Cairo (hence the abbreviation CD, or Cairo Damascus) and subsequently published by Solomon Schechter in 1910. Its significance was augmented with the Qumran excavations in the 1940s and 1950s when ten fragmentary manuscripts of the *Damascus Document* were found among the Dead Sea Scrolls. These manuscripts are referred to as 4Q266-73, or the 4QD manuscripts, 5Q12 and 6Q15. For a detailed discussion, see Charlotte Hempel, *The Damascus Texts* (Sheffield: Sheffield Academic Press, 2000), pp. 26-43.

the "boundary . . . which the forefathers had marked" is a reference to the law of Moses.[9] The specific historical details of the situation are difficult to reconstruct, but the theological framework is clear: by straying from the law, national Israel has incurred the covenant curses. The Qumran community, however, has escaped these curses, since they are the righteous remnant. Philip Davies notes that this remnant theme is "one of the central themes of CD as a whole." This remnant group is "the Israel with whom God is presently dealing. The rest of 'Israel,'" writes Davies, "has been and is rejected, subject to the covenant vengeance of God."[10]

While CD 1:13-17 describes Israel as a nation under the covenant curse, it does not specify the means through which the community has escaped this curse. But several other passages do. First, in CD 1:8-11, the author describes the early stage of the community's existence, prior to the rise of the Teacher of Righteousness.

> They recognized their sin and knew that they were guilty. But they were like blind people and like those who grope for a path over twenty years. But God approved their deeds, because they sought him with an undivided heart. And he raised up for them a Teacher of Righteousness in order to steer them in the path of his heart. (CD 1:8b-11a *DSSSE*)

Noteworthy is the statement that God "raised up for them a Teacher of Righteousness" and "appraised their deeds *because* (*kî*) they sought him with an undivided heart."[11] God's gift of this leader and his approval of their deeds was a response to their prior upright behavior. This pattern of restoration is therefore *Deuteronomic*.

Second, CD 2:14–3:20 narrates the waywardness of historic Israel, which climaxes in the establishment of a (new) covenant with the members of the community. As in CD 1, God restores them, since they are the only ones who have obeyed the law:

> Through it, the very first to enter the covenant made themselves guilty and

---

[9]See 4Q266 *frag.* 11 12-13.

[10]Philip R. Davies, *The Damascus Covenant: An Interpretation of the "Damascus Document"* (Sheffield: Sheffield Academic Press, 1983), p. 71.

[11]There is much debate over the identity and function of the Teacher of Righteousness, which is not relevant for our study. At the very least, he was a main catalyst for the early establishment of the community.

were delivered up to the sword, for *having deserted God's covenant* [Deut 29:25] and having chosen their whims, and *having followed the stubbornness of their heart* [Deut 29:19],[12] each one doing his desire. But with those who remained steadfast in God's precepts, with those who were left from among them, God established his covenant with Israel forever, to reveal *to them hidden things* [Deut 29:28] in which all Israel had gone astray: his holy Sabbaths and his glorious feasts, his just stipulations and the paths of his truth, and the wishes of his will, *which if the man does he will live by them* [Lev 18:5]. (CD 3:10-16)

While the terms *curse* and *blessing* are not used, similar concepts from Deuteronomy 28–29 abound. The "first to enter the covenant" refers to historic Israel, and being "delivered up to the sword," "deserting God's covenant," and "followed the stubbornness of their heart" are all phrases that describe an Israelite who has committed apostasy and has incurred the curses of the covenant. The phrase "his covenant" that God makes with the sectarian community is most likely a reference to the "new covenant." This covenant consists of new laws that were hidden from the wayward nation of Israel but now revealed to the Qumranites.[13] The passage shows that the sect had already demonstrated a certain level of obedience to the (revealed) law of Moses, and *this is why* God chose to reveal to them the "hidden matters in which all Israel went astray." For it is "with those who remained steadfast in God's precepts" that "God established his (new) covenant."

Both CD 1:8a-11b and 3:11b-16a portray a *Deuteronomic* paradigm of restoration: the community's obedience to the revealed law is the precondition for God's restorative act in removing them from the curse that resides over the nation. CD 1:13b-17a, while not identifying the explicit means of restoration, also refers to wayward Israelites (i.e., those outside the sectarian community) as being under the "curses of the covenant." Read together, these opening sections of CD show that the community has escaped the covenant curses by means of their return to the law. And other passages in CD concur. In CD 15, the author describes a member's ongoing adherence to sectarian law as a "return to the law of Moses with the whole heart and

---

[12]The allusion to Deut 29:19 (29:18 MT) is typical in Qumran literature; see CD 8:8, 19; 19:20, 33; 20:9-10; 1QS 1:6; 2:13-14, 26; 3:3; 5:4.

[13]See A. Shemesh and C. Werman, "Hidden Things and Their Revelation," *RevQ* 18 (1998): 410-14.

with the whole soul" (CD 15:9, 12). The language of the eschatological return to the law in Deuteronomy 30 is reapplied to the ongoing adherence to sectarian law. Again, apostasy from the community would result in coming back under the "curses of the covenant" that reside over the nation (CD 15:3). CD, therefore, emphasizes that the community has escaped the curses of the covenant through a *Deuteronomic* program of salvation.

The Community Rule (1QS). Every year the Qumran community would go through a covenant renewal ceremony, where they would admit newly qualified members into the sect while excommunicating those who had fallen away.[14] A detailed description of this event is recorded at the beginning of the *Community Rule* (1QS), where the priests pronounce blessings on all those who are part of the community (1QS 2:1-4) and the Levites pronounce curses on all those who are not (1QS 2:4-9). Subsequently, the priests and Levites come together to pronounce curses on the one who has committed apostasy:

> And the priests and the Levites will continue, saying: "Cursed by the idols which his heart reveres whoever enters this covenant [1QS 1:18, 20; Deut 29:12], and places the obstacle of his iniquity in front of himself to fall over it. *When he hears the words of this covenant, he will congratulate himself in his heart, saying 'I will have peace, in spite of my walking in the stubbornness of my heart'* [Deut 29:19/29:18 MT]. However, his spirit will be obliterated without mercy, the dry with the moist. May God's anger and the wrath of his judgments consume him for everlasting destruction. May all the *curses of this covenant* (*ʾlôt hbrît hzôt*) stick fast to him [Deut 29:20/29:19 MT]. May God separate him for evil, and may he be cut off from the midst of all the sons of light because of his straying from following God on account of his idols and obstacle of his iniquity. May he assign his lot with the cursed ones forever (*ʾrûrî ʿôlmîm*)." And all those who enter the covenant will respond and will say after them: "Amen, Amen." (1QS 2:11-18)

This passage describes the apostate, who once joined the community but later fell away, thus moving back into the realm of covenant curse. The

---

[14]The Scriptural basis for this comes from Moses' prescriptions in Deuteronomy 27, where he instructs Israel to recount the blessings and curses of the covenant once they have entered the land. This was carried out by Joshua after the conquest of Ai (Josh 8), and it is picked up by the Qumran community, who transformed it into an annual ceremony.

author draws on Deuteronomy 27–29 extensively throughout this passage, even quoting at length Deuteronomy 29:19 (29:18 MT) and applying it to the apostate. The underlying assumption is that deliverance from the covenant curses is achieved by entering into the Qumran sect and returning to the law. To move outside the realm of the covenant community—whether by choice or by excommunication for not following the law—is to move into the realm of the covenant curse that resides over national Israel.

As far as agency is concerned, the covenant member takes the initiative to escape the curse, as seen in 1QS 3:1-12, the final section of this ceremony. Here, the author reflects on the reason why the apostate has not remained with the community:

> For it is *by the spirit* (*brûḥ*) of the true counsel of God that are atoned the paths of man, all his iniquities, so that he can look at the light of life. And it is *by the holy spirit of the community* (*wbrûḥ qdôš lîḥd*), in its truth, that he is cleansed of all his iniquities. And *by the spirit* (*wbrûḥ*) of uprightness and of humility his sin is atoned. *And by the compliance* (*wbʿnôt*) of his soul with all the laws of God his flesh is cleansed by being sprinkled with cleansing waters and being made holy with the waters of repentance. (1QS 3:6b-9a *DSSSE*)

We will look at this passage in more detail in the next chapter where we discuss the eschatological spirit. For now, we can simply point out that despite the *rûaḥ* language, divine agency is not in view. The "holy spirit of the community"[15] refers to the quality of the Qumran sect—they are a holy community—and the final reference to the "spirit of uprightness and humility" parallels "the compliance of his soul with all the laws of God" and together refer to human agency in "being made holy." In short, 1QS 3:1-12 draws out what is only implicit in 1QS 1–2: the human is the primary agent as he moves from the realm of covenant curse (national Israel) to covenant blessing (the Qumran community).

This *Deuteronomic* pattern of restoration is supported by 1QS 5, where

---

[15]R. W. Kvalvaag understands "the holy spirit of the community" as a clear reference to divine agency. See "The Spirit in Human Beings in Some Qumran Non-Biblical Texts," in *Qumran Between the Old and New Testaments*, ed. F. H. Cryer and T. L. Thomson (Sheffield: Sheffield Academic Press, 1998), pp. 159-80 (171); contra B. D. Smith, who sees it as a human quality: "'Spirit Holiness' As Eschatological Principle of Obedience," in *Christian Beginnings and the Dead Sea Scrolls*, ed. J. J. Collins and C. A. Evans (Grand Rapids: Baker, 2006), pp. 87-89.

the author refers to the moral transformation of the community in terms of a circumcision of the heart:

> No-one should walk in the stubbornness of his heart in order to go astray following his heart and his eyes and musings of his inclination. Instead, he should circumcise in the Community the foreskin of his tendency and of his stiff neck in order to lay a foundation of truth for Israel, for the Community of the eternal covenant (1QS 5:4b-6a *DSSSE*).

The metaphor of "heart circumcision" is drawn from Deuteronomy and refers to an internal moral transformation. It was first used in Deuteronomy 10:16, where the *human* is the agent of change—"[You] circumcise therefore the foreskin of your heart, and be no longer stubborn." In Deuteronomy 30:6 the metaphor is used again, but this time God is the agent of transformation: "And the LORD your God will circumcise your heart and the heart of your offspring, so that you will love the LORD your God with all your heart and with all your soul, that you may live." The Qumran author understands the metaphor in light of the paraenetic section of Deuteronomy 10, thus prioritizing human agency in moral transformation.[16]

This priority of human action is seen throughout 1QS 5. The author frequently identifies the member as one who "freely volunteers" (1QS 5:1, 6, 8, 10, 22), and his entry into the community is described as a return "to the law of Moses with all that it decrees, with whole heart and whole soul" (5:8-9). Those who fail to separate from the "men of sin" and have failed to "learn the hidden matters" will incur the "curses of the covenant" (5:10-12).

In short, the covenant renewal ceremony of 1QS 1–3, along with 1QS 5, emphasizes human agency in the context of escaping the covenant curse and receiving the covenant blessings. The structure of restoration is *Deuteronomic:* the curse will be lifted from the one(s) who first repents from his wicked ways and reverts to the law of Moses as interpreted by the community. God's eschatological restorative action is conditioned on prior human action.

Miqṣat Ma'aśeh ha-Tôrāh (4QMMT). The document known as *Miqṣat Ma'aśeh ha-Tôrāh* ("some of the works of the law" or MMT) is a letter written by a member of the Qumran community to a certain person of authority in

---

[16]See Kyle Wells, "Grace, Obedience, and the Hermeneutics of Agency: Paul and His Jewish Contemporaries on the Transformation of the Heart" (Ph.D. diss., Durham University, 2009), pp. 50-54.

Jerusalem.[17] The addressee apparently has great influence over matters related to the temple service (or at least he thinks he does), since the letter is written with the intent to reform what the author believes to be aberrant behavior among the priests in Jerusalem.[18] The letter lists certain "works of the law," which the author believes have been ignored by the Jerusalem priests or have been performed incorrectly. The expressed intent of the letter is to elicit change in these priestly practices so that the covenant curses may be lifted from the nation of Israel. It is here where the letter bears witness to our theme. The author of MMT believes that the covenant curses reside over the nation of Israel because of its disobedience, and that a return to a more accurate understanding and practice of the law will thus remove this curse. The author believes that since he and his community have already removed themselves from these sinful practices, they have escaped the covenant curse and are participating in the blessings. This letter is a plea that the addressee and those under his influence would do the same.[19]

To support his argument, the author cites two important texts from Deuteronomy that point to the future reality of the covenant curse and the means of escape: Deuteronomy 31:29 and Deuteronomy 30:1-2.

> And it is written that [you will stray] from the path and that calamity will meet [you]. And it is written "and it shall come to pass, when all these things [be]fall you" [Deut 31:29], at the end of days, the blessing and the curse, "[then you will take] it to hea[rt] and you will return unto him with all your heart and with all your soul" [Deut 30:1-2]. (MMT C 12-16)[20]

---

[17]For various essays written in the wake of the publication of 4QMMT, see J. Kampen and M. J. Bernstein, *Reading 4QMMT: New Perspectives on Qumran Law and History* (Atlanta: Scholars Press, 1996). The original composition of the document probably dates to the time when Jonathan (the Wicked Priest?) most likely was occupying the high priesthood (i.e., 159–152 B.C.). The manuscripts known as 4QMMT (4Q394–399) have been dated from around 75 B.C. to A.D. 50. See Elisha Qimron and John Strugnell, *Qumran Cave 4, V: Miqsat Ma'aśé ha-Torah*, DJD 10 (Oxford: Clarendon, 1994), pp. 109, 121. Typically, the document is considered to be one of the earliest explanations for the Essene separation from Judean society.

[18]N. T. Wright, "4QMMT and Paul: Justification, 'Works,' and Eschatology," in *History and Exegesis: New Testament Essays in Honor of Dr. E. Earle Ellis for His 80th Birthday*, ed. Aang-Won [Aaron] Son (New York: T & T Clark, 2006), p. 108.

[19]A common assumption is that the author(s) of MMT (identified with the "we" group throughout) is the Teacher of Righteousness representing his community, and the recipient is the so-called Wicked Priest, whom Hanan Eshel identifies as Jonathan the Hasmonean in *The Dead Sea Scrolls and the Hasmonean State* (Grand Rapids: Eerdmans, 2008), pp. 46-51.

[20]For MMT, I will be using the translation from Qimron and Stugnell, *Qumran Cave 4.5*.

Moses predicted that Israel would turn from God, break his covenant, and yet repent and return to the law in the end. The Qumran author believes that Moses is describing the current situation. Israel has rebelled and is under the curse as foretold by Moses. All they need to do, according to the rhetorical and exegetical persuasion of our author, is to "return to him with all your heart and with all your soul" (MMT C 16; Deut 30:2). The author goes on to support his point by appealing to Israel's history.

> Remember the kings of Israe[l] and reflect upon their works (*m'śêhmh*), how whoever of them feared [the la]w was delivered from troubles; and these were people who stu[d]ied the law (*mb[q]śê tôrh*) and whose transgressions were forgiven. Remember David, how he was a man of the pious and was [de]livered from many troubles and received forgiveness. (MMT C 23-26)

The Qumran author desires that his addressee would follow in the footsteps of the kings of old by returning to the law. Such repentance would result in forgiveness, just as it did for king David, and it would thus end the curse of the covenant.

In the final section of this letter, the author ends with a plea for his audience to obey these "works the law" so that God would pour out his eschatological "good" on the nation of Israel.

> We have written to you *a selection of the works of the law* (*mqṣt m'śê htôrh*) which we consider to be for your good and that of your people Isr[a]el. For we have noted in you an understanding and a knowledge of the law. Consider all these things, and seek from before him that he will make straight your counsel and keep far from you evil thoughts and the counsel of Belial. Thus you shall rejoice in the last time in finding that this selection of our words is true. *And it shall be reckoned to you for righteousness* (*wnḥšbh lk lṣdqh*)[21] when you do what is right and good before him, for your good and that of Israel. (MMT C 26-32)

N. T. Wright correctly summarizes the eschatological rhetoric of the passage as "aimed at persuading the readers to join those who are, in the present time, turning to God with all their heart, and so experiencing the eschatological covenant blessing, the real return from exile promised in

---

[21]I have emended the translation to correspond to the allusion to Gen 15:6 and Ps 106:31.

Deuteronomy."[22] The author of MMT certainly believes that he and his community have escaped the covenant curse and are enjoying, in part, the covenant blessings by means of their adherences to the "works of the law," some of which have been described earlier in the document. In doing so, the author's community is living out the script of Deuteronomy 30:1-4.

But Wright shies away from seeing these "works" as the means of eschatological blessing. Instead, the works "mark them [Qumran community] out in the present time as the true, returned-from-exile, covenant people of Israel."[23] Apparently Wright is concerned that some might use this passage to support the traditional caricature of Judaism as promoting works-righteousness. Therefore, he insists that "these 'works' will not *earn* them membership in God's eschatological people; they will *demonstrate* that they are God's people."[24] Wright seems to erect a false dichotomy, believing that either one must view the passage in a covenantal context or retreat to an older legalistic (mis)reading. A true covenantal reading, however, goes beyond what Wright argues for. In both Deuteronomy and in MMT, not least in many other scrolls at Qumran (e.g., 11QT³, CD, 1QS), a return to the law in the eschatological age is a means of eliciting the covenant blessing, not merely a way to identify who the righteous really are. Conversely, the disobedience of wayward Israelites is the means of inviting the covenant curse; it is not merely the identity marker of the apostates. This interpretation is supported by the author's use of Genesis 15:6 (cf. Ps 106:31) in C 31: "And it shall be reckoned to you for righteousness (*wnḥšbh lk lṣdqh*) when you do what is right and good before him, for your good and that of Israel." Righteousness here is used more or less synonymously with the eschatological "good" (C 31) and covenant "blessing(s)" (C 14, 20) that God will give to Israel if they return to the law. Inasmuch as Deuteronomy itself refuses to

---

[22]Wright, "4QMMT and Paul," p. 115.

[23]Ibid., p. 166, emphasis original.

[24]"It is because *these works of Torah will mark them out in the present time as the true, returned-from-exile, covenant people of Israel.* These 'works' will not *earn* them membership in God's eschatological people; they will *demonstrate* that they are God's people" (Wright, "4QMMT and Paul," p. 166). Wright goes on to agree with Sanders that the works of the law here are about "staying in" and not "getting in" the covenant and should be understood "*within* the broader covenantal and eschatological scheme" of Deuteronomy, rather than being "abstracted . . . into a wider 'legalism' to which Paul's doctrine of justification, in its traditional Reformation sense, could then be opposed" (p. 117).

be read legalistically, so also this reading of MMT should not be considered a retreat to a Protestant misreading of Judaism. It is simply good *Deuteronomic* eschatology, an eschatology that depicts God's restorative action as a response to Israel's prior repentance and return to the ("works of the") law.

For MMT, then, the works of law here are the halachic deeds of the community by which they have escaped the covenant curse and obtained covenant blessing. In failing to do these works, the Jerusalem priests mirror the same disobedience of Israel's past that elicited the covenant curses. The scheme of restoration is essentially *Deuteronomic*.

The Words of the Luminaries (4Q504). Another document that contains a restoration from the curse theme is the fragmentary collection of prayers known as the *Words of the Luminaries.*[25] These prayers were recited each day of the week and consist of pleas for deliverance from the covenant curses. Like the documents examined thus far, these prayers reveal hope that God will restore his covenant fortunes to the nation of Israel, and they contain many themes typical in Deuteronomy along with sustained reflection on Leviticus 26. However, unlike 4QMMT and others, these prayers exhibit a more *Prophetic* outlook on how God will rescue the nation from the covenant curses. Restoration necessitates law-obedience, but such obedience can only happen through a prior act of God.

After acknowledging that Israel has broken the covenant, the author prays that God would "Circumcise the foreskin of [our heart]" and "Strengthen our heart to do [. . .]" (4Q504 *frag.* 4 iii 10-12). Again, drawing on Deuteronomy though emphasizing divine agency, the author pleads for

---

[25]The fragmentary manuscripts 4Q504 and 4Q506 (4QDibHam), or *Words of the Luminaries* (*dbry hm'rôt*), are a collection of liturgical prayers believed to have been recited each day of the week, either at sunset or sundown. The manuscript 4Q504 is the oldest of this collection, dated to the mid-second century B.C., while 4Q506, which overlaps 4Q504 considerably, is dated to the mid-first century A.D. Therefore, *Words of the Luminaries* was being copied at least two hundred years after its original composition, giving evidence that it had a longstanding function and popularity in the Qumran community. The collection of prayers were probably written prior to the Essene settlement in Qumran and are *nonsectarian*. That is, they envision the restoration of the nation as a whole and not merely a sect within the nation (see Esther Chazon, "Is *Divrei Ha-Me'orot* A Sectarian Prayer?" in *The Dead Sea Scrolls: Forty Years of Research*, ed. Devorah Dimant and Uriel Rappaport, STDJ 10 [Leiden: Brill, 1992], pp. 3-17). An excellent summary of all the introductory issues in these prayers can be found in D. Falk, *Daily, Sabbath, and Festival Prayers in the Dead Sea Scrolls*, STDJ 27 (Leiden: Brill, 1998); see also Preston M. Sprinkle, *Law and Life: The Interpretation of Leviticus 18:5 in Early Judaism and in Paul*, WUNT 2.241 (Tübingen: Mohr Siebeck, 2008), pp. 77-78.

God to "implant your law in our heart, [so that we do not stray from it,] either to the right or to the left" and to "heal us of madness/ blindness/ and confusion" (*frags.* 1-2 ii 13-14).[26] The most explicit prioritization of God's initiative comes in the Friday prayer:

> You did favors to your people Israel among all [the] lands where you had exiled them, in order that they might be made to return to their heart and to turn to you and to listen to your voice, [according to] all that you commanded through the hand of Moses your servant. [Fo]r you have poured your holy spirit upon us, [to be]stow your blessings to us. (*frag.* v 11-15)

The author remains firmly committed to the exile-restoration theme of Deuteronomy, and yet acknowledges that God must take the initiative in restoring Israel from the curses. This *Prophetic* scheme of restoration is seen in the phrase "to place upon their heart to turn to you and to listen to your voice" and in the acknowledgment that God has "poured your holy spirit upon us."[27] God's initiative in restoration from covenant curses, therefore, is emphasized.

Summary of Qumran Literature. In the five texts examined in this section (11QT^a, CD, 1QS, 4QMMT, 4Q504), we observed that through repentance and return to the law the community believed that they had escaped the covenant curse that resides over the nation of Israel. Despite some differences in context, wording and argumentation, the structure of restoration is more *Deuteronomic.* The Qumran community believed that since it had returned to the law—or, for MMT, the "works of the law"—it had therefore escaped the covenant curse and was enjoying the covenant blessings. The one exception is 4Q504, where the author pleads for divine enablement in order to return to the law, which anticipates a more *Prophetic* restoration without leaving the thought world of Deuteronomy. The difference between divine priority (4Q504) and human priority (11QT^a, et al.) may be due to diverse perspectives—the library at Qumran is not uniform— or it may be due to genre. In other words, the hymnic nature of the prayers

---

[26]These curses are drawn from Deut 28:28. Other covenant curses are mentioned in 4Q504 *frags.* 1-2 iii 7-9: "You have raised us over the years of our generations . . . /evil/illnesses, famine, thirst, plague, the sword . . . requital of your covenant." These five curses are drawn from Deut 28:21, 48, 59. See further Sprinkle, *Law and Life,* pp. 79-81.

[27]See Rodrigo J. Morales, *The Spirit and the Restoration of Israel,* WUNT 2.282 (Tübingen: Mohr Siebeck, 2010), pp. 52-55.

of 4Q504 may explain the emphasis on divine agency—it would be more natural when praying to ask God for assistance in obeying the law. We will discuss the importance of genre in later chapters, especially when we interact with the *Hodayot* (1QH[a]). For now, we can conclude cautiously by observing that according to didactic and legal texts, redemption from the curse of the covenant is more *Deuteronomic*, while in hymnic literature, it is more *Prophetic*.

As we move from Qumran to Paul, it may be helpful to recognize the striking similarities between MMT and Galatians 3. Many have observed the obvious parallels between Paul's *ergōn nomou* and MMT's *m'śê htôrh*,[28] along with the citations of Genesis 15:6 (cf. Ps 106:31) in Galatians 3:6 and 4QMMT C 31,[29] and similar terminology of separation (*sprsnû* 4QMMT C7; *aphōrizen hauton* Gal 2:12). James Dunn and others have also noted that both texts operate within the framework of the covenant blessings and curses of Deuteronomy 27–30 (4QMMT C 13–32 and Gal 3:8-14).[30] These parallels are well known, but what is rarely observed is that both Paul and the author of MMT discuss *the efficacy of "works of the law" in escaping the covenant curse,* and that both Paul and MMT consider their own communities to be the true "Israel of God" (cf. Gal 6:16) who have escaped the curse. The conceptual resemblance between this letter and Paul's argument in Galatians 3:10 is striking. For MMT, the way of escape is through adherence to the correct "works of the law." Paul will have a rather different view on the matter.

PAUL AND THE CURSE OF THE LAW IN GALATIANS 3:10-14

In agreement with the Qumran community, the apostle Paul believed that

---

[28]Wright is correct to note that the "works of the law" in MMT refer to extrabiblical applications of the law, while Paul's use of the phrase points to actual biblical commands (e.g., circumcision, dietary laws, etc.). However, as Abegg points out, the parallel in usage still stands, since "'works of the law' is quite agile and allows for any number of strictures, the only condition being that they find their source in torah and are concerned with practice which defines relationship to God in a particular sort of Judaism" (M. Abegg, "4QMMT C 27, 31 and 'Works Righteousness,'" *DSD* 6 [1990] 141). I wonder, therefore, whether the author of MMT would have considered the laws promoted in the document as extrabiblical.

[29]See Wright, "4QMMT and Paul"; M. Abegg, "4QMMT C 27, 31"; and James D. G. Dunn, *The New Perspective on Paul: Collected Essays*, WUNT 185 (Tübingen: Mohr Siebeck, 2005; Grand Rapids: Eerdmans, 2007), pp. 333-39.

[30]Dunn, *New Perspective*, pp. 333-39.

Israel was still under the curse of the law. An even though he discussed this motif in only one section of his letters, Galatians 3:10-14 has been hailed one of the most important passages in all of Paul, even if it is the most difficult to interpret.[31] Theological concepts are abbreviated and then jammed into one tight and terse argument. But one thing is clear: Paul's concepts about restoration from the covenant curse are of the same pool of thought as what we saw at Qumran. His conclusion, however, is quite different. In order to hack our way through Paul's thick train of thought, we will need to identify and discuss three separate, though related, issues. (1) Why does Paul cite Deuteronomy 27:26 in Galatians 3:10 as an indictment against his opponents—the agitators? (2) Why is it that the "works of the law" are an inadequate means of escaping the curse? And (3) what is the function of his citations of Habakkuk 2:4 and Leviticus 18:5 in Galatians 3:11-12?

Paul's Citation of Deuteronomy 27:26 in Galatians 3:10. One glance at Galatians 3:10 reveals a problem. To prove that those who are "of works of the law" are cursed, Paul cites a passage that states the opposite—Deuteronomy 27:26 says that everyone who *does not* do the law is cursed: "For all who are of works of the law are under a curse; for it is written, 'Cursed be everyone who does not abide by all things written in the Book of the Law, and do them'" (Gal 3:10; Deut 27:26).[32] Unfortunately, the apostle does little in the ensuing verses to resolve his apparent hermeneutical lapse, and scholars therefore have offered reasons for the incongruity. Some try to relieve the tension by supplying a missing premise; namely, that the law requires perfect (sinless) obedience, a standard of which those who are "of works of the law" have fallen short.[33] Others say that those who are "of works of the law are under a curse" because—to put it bluntly—Deuteronomy 27:26 says so. That is, Paul's attraction to Deuteronomy 27:26 is due merely to the presence of the terms "law" and "curse" in the citation—the original

---

[31]"[Gal 3:10-14] is one of the most difficult passages anywhere in his letters" (Richard Hays, "The Letter to the Galatians," in *The New Interpreter's Bible*, ed. Leander Keck [Nashville: Abingdon Press, 2000], 10:257); "The meaning of almost every phrase in Gal 3:10-14 is disputed" (N. H. Young, "Who's Cursed—And Why? (Galatians 3:10-14)," *JBL* 117 [1998]: 79-92 [79]; "This is one of the most complicated and controverted passages in Paul" (N. T. Wright, *The Climax of the Covenant : Christ and the Law in Pauline Theology* [Minneapolis: Fortress, 1991], p. 137).

[32]Unless otherwise noted, all translations of the New Testament are my own.

[33]T. R. Schreiner, "Is Perfect Obedience to the Law Possible? A Re-examination of Galatians 3:10," *JETS* (1984): 151-60.

context of Deuteronomy 27:26 bears no significance for Paul's argument. Paul believes that Christ is the means of blessing, and therefore all other attempts—including those of the law—will only end in curse.[34] Still others argue that those who are "of works of the law are under a curse" because in maintaining such boundary markers they are essentially excluding Gentiles *as Gentiles* from the covenant blessings. James Dunn says that "works of the law" (Gal 3:10; cf. Gal 2:16; 3:2, 5) are the demands of the law that separate the Jew from the Gentile. Living by works of law is "a mode of living wholly Jewish in character."[35] The promise made to Abraham that God would bless the *nations,* however, has been realized outside the boundaries of Jewish existence. Thus, any attempt to restrict the blessing to those who are "wholly Jewish in character" have actually *failed to keep the law.*[36]

While all of these approaches have merit, none of them fully captures the redemptive-historical tenor of Paul's argument. The belief that national Israel was still under the covenant curse was widely held in the Judaism of Paul's day.[37] One would expect, therefore, that Paul, in mentioning the curse of the law, is tapping into this same motif, even if he argues for a different solution. As such, Paul argues in Galatians 3:10 that those who are "of works of the law are under a curse" because in their attempt to uphold such law-works, they have identified themselves with a cursed covenant. When Paul cites Deuteronomy 27:26, he assumes the wider context of Deuteronomy

---

[34]E. P. Sanders, *Paul and Palestinian Judaism: A Comparison of Patterns of Religion* (Philadelphia: Fortress, 1977), pp. 483-84; E. P. Sanders, *Paul, the Law, and the Jewish People* (Philadelphia: Fortress Press, 1983), pp. 26-27.

[35]Dunn, *New Perspective,* p. 219.

[36]This reading has some merit, but it does not do justice to the correlation between "works of the law" and "flesh" (Gal 3:2-5), which we will discuss below. Moreover, this reading interprets Paul's use of Lev 18:5 *nonsoteriologically;* in other words, "'the one who does these things *will live by them'* refers to *the maintenance of life by the law*" (Dunn, *Theology,* p. 153) or "of doing the law and of living within its terms" (Dunn, *Galatians,* p. 175). It is noneschatological life, says Dunn, that is in view. But a nonsoteriological understanding of the "life" held out in Lev 18:5 is nearly impossible. For one, Paul correlates the terms blessing, justification and *life* in Gal 3:8-14, and since the first two are soteriological, so the third must be. Moreover, early Jewish interpreters understood Lev 18:5 as a soteriological promise: obedience to the law would bring eternal life. It seems best, therefore, to understand Paul's problem with Lev 18:5 to be the insufficiency of the law to give life (Gal 3:21), rather than a critique against the Gentile-excluding manner of life in which one lives. For a thorough defense of this reading, with bibliography, see Sprinkle, *Law and Life,* pp. 138-42.

[37]Along with the passages examined in the Qumran literature, see also 2 Macc 7; *1 En.* 85–90; *T. Levi* 16:1-2, 5; *T. Jud.* 24:1-3; Tob 13:5-18; 14:4-7; Bar 1:15–3:8; Pr Azar; Sir 36:1-17.

27–32, a passage that anticipates the curse as the inevitable outcome of God's Sinaitic covenant with Israel.

This approach was first articulated by Martin Noth over forty years ago and has been developed independently by N. T. Wright and James M. Scott, who have termed it the "exile-restoration" view.[38] While the exile-restoration framework to my mind over-reads Paul's argument,[39] I do think that situating Paul's argument in the context of Israel's covenant history does justice to the actual language and scriptural texts that Paul uses, as we will see. In any case, scholars often critique the exile-restoration view,[40] since Deuteronomy 27:26 refers to individuals and not the nation of Israel.[41] However, the wider context of Deuteronomy 28–32 describes the nation as a whole, and in light of Paul's addition of the phrase "all things written in the book of the law" to the citation of Deuteronomy 27:26 in Galatians 3:10, he most likely has this wider context in view. This phrase occurs throughout Deuteronomy 28–30 (LXX 28:58, 61; 29:19, 20, 26; 30:10), suggesting that Paul is reading Deuteronomy 27:26 in light of the larger context.[42] Furthermore,

---

[38]See Martin Noth, "For All Who Rely on Works of the Law Are Under a Curse," in *The Laws in the Pentateuch and Other Studies,* ed. M. Noth (Edinburgh: Oliver & Boyd, 1966), pp. 118-31; Wright, *Climax of the Covenant,* pp. 141-47; and James M. Scott, "'For as Many as Are of Works of the Law Are Under a Curse' (Galatians 3.10)," in *Paul and the Scriptures of Israel,* ed. Craig A. Evans and James A. Sanders (Sheffield: JSOT Press, 1993), pp. 187-221. See also Hays, "Letter to the Galatians," pp. 257-62; and Joel Willitts, "Context Matters: Paul's Use of Leviticus 18:5 in Galatians 3:12," *TynBul* 54 (2003): 105-22.

[39]Rather than using the label "exile-restoration" to describe the passage, I think it is better to use "curse-restoration," since this is the language Paul actually uses. Perhaps Paul thinks that the nation of Israel is in spiritual exile, and certainly the ultimate curse of the Sinaitic covenant is exile, but building a case for this is unnecessary and distracting. The surface of Paul's argument identifies the "works of the law" people as under the curse of the Sinaitic (Gal 3:16-19) covenant. It is best to leave it at that and not parse out the details beyond what Paul says.

[40]Critics include N. Bonneau, "The Logic of Paul's Argument on the Curse of the Law in Galatians 3:10-14," *NovT* 39 (1997): 61-62; Seyoon Kim, *Paul and the New Perspective: Second Thoughts on the Origin of Paul's Gospel* (Grand Rapids: Eerdmans, 2002), pp. 136-41; and Norman H. Young, "Who's Cursed?" pp. 79-92 (esp. 83-84).

[41]See C. D. Stanley, "'Under a Curse': A Fresh Reading of Galatians 3.10-14," *NTS* 36 (1990): 484; Bonneau, "Logic of Paul's Argument," pp. 61-62; Kim, *Paul and the New Perspective,* p. 139; and Timothy G. Gombis, "The 'Transgressor' and the 'Curse of the Law': The Logic of Paul's Argument in Galatians 2–3," *NTS* 53 (2007): 81-93 (esp. 84n10).

[42]See Francis Watson, *Paul and the Hermeneutics of Faith* (New York: T & T Clark, 2004), pp. 427-34. Wisdom rightly notes that Paul's incorporation of "things written in the book of the law" highlights the aspect of apostasy in Jeffrey R. Wisdom, *Blessing for the Nations and the Curse of the Law: Paul's Citation of Genesis and Deuteronomy in Gal 3.8-10* (Tübingen: Mohr Siebeck, 2001), p. 173. And in light of the context of Deut 27–32, it can be assumed that Paul is implying that the nation as a whole has committed such apostasy.

this addition intensifies the aspect of judgment that inevitably fell on the nation of Israel. "In each case," notes Francis Watson, "'the book of this law' is associated with the threat—and indeed the certainty—that the law's curse represents the destiny of the entire people, and not just of individual law-breakers."[43] As the narrative unfolds, the threat of curse becomes a promised reality: the nation (not just certain individuals) will commit apostasy and fall under the curse (see, e.g., Deut 29:22-29; 30:1; 31:14-22, 27-29; 32:1-43).[44] Moreover, when Deuteronomy envisions restoration, it comes to the nation, not an individual.[45] Sensitivity to the theological movement of Deuteronomy 27–32, then, sheds light on the way in which Paul might be reading Deuteronomy 27:26.

Equally suggestive is Jeremiah's application of Deuteronomy 27:26[46] to accuse Israel—as a nation—of breaking the covenant and eliciting the curse.

> Cursed is the person who does not hear the words of this covenant (*'rûr h'îš 'šr l' yšm' 't-dbrê hbrît hz't ('rûr h'îš 'šr l' yšm' 't-dbrê hbrît hz't*). (Jer 11:3 my translation)

> Cursed is every person who does not remain in all the words of this law to do them (*'rûr 'šr l' yqîm 't-dbrê htôrh-hz't l'śût 'ôtm*). (Deut 27:26 my translation)

Jeremiah 11:3 is almost certainly drawing on Deuteronomy 27:26; no other passage in the Hebrew Bible (or LXX)[47] resembles the language as

---

[43]Watson, *Paul and the Hermeneutics of Faith*, p. 432.

[44]Dennis Olson rightly observes that a "focus on human freedom and ability to choose wisely to obey and act righteously ('if . . . then') is here juxtaposed with a focus on a determined future which no human choice can avert: 'all these curses shall come upon you'"; D. T. Olson, "How Does Deuteronomy Do Theology? Literary Juxtaposition and Paradox in the New Moab Covenant in Deuteronomy 29–32," in *A God So Near: Essays on Old Testament Theology in Honor of Patrick D. Miller*, ed. Brent A. Strawn and Nancy R. Bowen (Winona Lake, IN: Eisenbrauns, 2003), p. 206; D. T. Olson, *Deuteronomy and the Death of Moses* (Minneapolis: Fortress, 1994), pp. 122, 152; see also D. J. McCarthy, *Treaty and Covenant: A Study in Form in the Ancient Oriental Documents and in the Old Testament* (Rome: Pontifical Biblical Institute, 1963), p. 178; and P. A. Barker, "The Theology of Deuteronomy 27," *TynBul* 49 (1998): 277-303 (esp. 292).

[45]The prediction of restoration in Deut 30:1-10 happens only after the blessing and curse have come on the nation as a whole (Deut 30:1; 31:29).

[46]This of course assumes that Jeremiah is writing after Deuteronomy. From the canonical perspective (or from a Pauline perspective), though, the historical-critical questions of date and authorship are largely irrelevant.

[47]Deut 27:26 LXX: *epikataratos pas anthropos hos ouk emmenei en pasin tois logois tou nomou toutou tou poisai autous*; Jer 11:3 LXX: *epikataratos ho anthropos hos ouk akousetai tōn logōn tēs diathēkēs tautēs.*

closely.[48] Furthermore, Jeremiah goes on to say: "And then I answered and said, 'amen'" (Jer 11:5 my translation), which seems to echo the corporate affirmation of Deuteronomy 27:15-26, "and all the people shall say, 'Amen.'" Jeremiah, then, has patterned his indictment of the nation of Israel on the curse ceremony of Deuteronomy 27 and has specifically alluded to Deuteronomy 27:26 in his pronouncement.[49] While Deuteronomy 27:26 threatens a curse to individuals who break the laws of Deuteronomy 27:15-25, it is clear that Jeremiah uses this text to pronounce a curse on Israel as a whole.[50]

In short, the potential rebellion and ensuing curse on the individual in Deuteronomy 27:15-26 fades quickly into a prophetic forecast of national rebellion—the individual in Deuteronomy 27 simply embodies the nation of Deuteronomy 28–32. This movement from individual to nation is picked up by Jeremiah, who uses Deuteronomy 27:26 to accuse Israel of national rebellion. Paul cites Deuteronomy 27:26 in a similar manner in order to accuse national Israel, and all law-workers who identify with it, of covenant rebellion. According to Galatians 3:10, those who are "of works of the law" are identifying with historic Israel and are therefore under the same cursed covenant. And seeking to alleviate this curse through law-works only exacerbates the problem—a concept to which we now turn.

Works of the Law. We have argued that Paul assumes the widespread idea that Israel as a nation is under the curse of the covenant and that he cites Deuteronomy 27:26 in support of this assumption. If this argument is correct, it still needs to be shown why "works of the law" are an inadequate means of escaping this curse. To be sure, Paul does not say that his opponents are relying on, or seeking to do, "works of law" in Galatians 3:10. He simply identifies his opponents as those who are "of works of law."[51] However, it is clear from his previous references to "works of law" (Gal 2:16; 3:2, 5) that these

---

[48]Other terms in Jer 11:3-5 are drawn from Deuteronomy (e.g., Deut 4:20; 7:8; 8:18; 26:8-9; 31:20). See further William Lee Holladay and Paul D. Hanson, *Jeremiah 1: A Commentary on the Book of the Prophet Jeremiah, Chapters 1-25* (Philadelphia: Fortress, 1986), p. 350.

[49]See Holladay and Hansen, *Jeremiah*, p. 350: "Jer 11.3-5 are a deliberate variation on the pattern of Deut 27:15-26." See also J. A. Thompson, *The Book of Jeremiah* (Grand Rapids: Eerdmans, 1980), pp. 341-42; and Peter C. Craigie, Page H. Kelley and Joel F. Drinkard, *Jeremiah 1-25*, WBC 26 (Dallas: Word, 1991), p. 170.

[50]See Jer 11:10: "The house of Israel and the house of Judah have broken my covenant which I made with their fathers." They have all "walked, each one, in the stubbornness of his evil heart" and thus God has brought on them "all the words [= curses] of this covenant" (Jer 11:8).

[51]Hays, "Letter to the Galatians," pp. 257-58.

people were identified as such because they believed that adherence to these works is necessary for justification (Gal 2:16), the reception of the spirit (Gal 3:1-5) and the attainment of covenant blessings (Gal 3:8-9, 14). Therefore, underlying Paul's identification of his opponents as those who are of "works of the law" is the assumption that the same group is seeking to attain eschatological blessing by means of these works. This pattern of restoration, akin to what we have seen in Qumran, is viewed as a dead end by Paul. But why?

Galatians 3:1-5 may shed light on this question. Here, Paul highlights the powerlessness of "works of the law" for attainting eschatological blessing (i.e., the spirit) by correlating "works of the law" with "being perfected *by the flesh*" (*sarki*):[52]

> I only wish to learn this from you; did you receive the spirit by works of the law (*ex ergōn nomou*) or by a report of faith (*ex akoēs pisteōs*)? Thus are you so foolish, having begun by the spirit are you now being perfected by the flesh (*sarki epiteleisthe*)? Have you suffered such things in vain—if indeed it was in vain? Therefore, the one who supplies you with the spirit and works miracles among you, (does he do it) by works of the law or by a report of faith (*ex ergōn nomou ē ex akoēs pisteōs*)? (Gal 3:2-5)

Though there are interpretive difficulties here,[53] Paul implies that the Galatians are trying to maintain the spirit's work among them by doing "works of the law," a feat Paul describes as "being perfected *by the flesh*" (*sarki*).[54] With *sarx*, Paul could be referring to the act of circumcision or to the

---

[52]See J. B. Tyson, "'Work of Law' in Galatians," *JBL* 92 (1973): 423-31 (esp. 427); Richard Longenecker, *Galatians*, WBC 41 (Dallas: Word, 1990), p. 103; and A. Oepke, *Der Brief des Paulus an die Galater* (Berlin: Evangelische Verlagsanstalt, 1973), p. 69.

[53]Along with interpretive issues surrounding *ergōn nomou*, the phrase *akoēs pisteōs* is also troublesome, since it can have at least four different meanings: 1) hearing with faith, 2) hearing "the faith" (i.e., the gospel), 3) the message that enables, or elicits, faith, or 4) the message of "the faith" (i.e., the gospel-message). See Richard B. Hays, *The Faith of Jesus Christ: The Narrative Substructure of Galatians 3:1-4:11* (Grand Rapids: Eerdmans, 2002), pp. 124-32; and J. Louis Martyn, *Galatians: A New Translation with Introduction and Commentary* (New York: Doubleday, 1997), pp. 286-89. Though not crucial to my argument, I have followed the fourth view here, that *akoē* refers to a message rather than the act of hearing. This is the most probable reading in light of Romans 10:16-17 and 1 Thessalonians 2:13, following Hans Joachim Eckstein, *Verheißung und Gesetz: Eine exegetische Untersuchung zu Galater 2,15-4,7*, WUNT 2.86 (Tübingen: Mohr Siebeck, 1996), pp. 86-88; Heinrich Schlier, *Der Brief an die Galater* (Göttingen: Vandenhoeck & Ruprecht, 1971), p. 122.

[54]John M. G. Barclay, *Obeying the Truth: Paul's Ethics in Galatians* (Minneapolis: Fortress, 1988), p. 203.

weakness of human nature.[55] J. Louis Martyn argues for the former interpretation based on Galatians 6:12-13, where this meaning is almost certain,
and on the association of "flesh" and "circumcision" in Genesis 17.[56] John
Barclay, however, while agreeing that *sarx* refers to circumcision in Galatians 6:12-13, sees a more general sense of "that which is merely human"
when *sarx* is opposed to *pneuma* as it is here in Galatians 3:3.[57] For Paul, the
spirit-flesh dualism designates activity that is merely human as opposed to
divine activity through the spirit.[58] This latter interpretation finds support
in Galatians 2:16, where *pasa sarx* designates humanity in general terms,
probably highlighting its weakness. Significant also, as Barclay points out, is
the contrast between Ishmael who was born "according to the flesh" and
Isaac who was born "according to the spirit (or promise)" (Gal 4:23, 29).
Ishmael was born through *merely human* means, while Isaac's birth was the
result of divine initiative; he was born "by means of promise" (*di epangelias*,
Gal 4:23).[59] The contrast between God and human is amplified in Galatians
3:5, where God is the one who "supplies the spirit and works powers among
them."[60] God freely gives the divine spirit, the effective agent (*pneumati*)
through whom the community is enlivened, and God does this through the
faith-message of the crucified Christ and not through the merely human
endeavor of law-obedience.[61] The point here is that since the Galatians
began their Christian lives by receiving the spirit through the faith-message,
they cannot maintain that same divine power through human means. God
alone is the source of their miraculous experiences (Gal 3:5).

When Paul mentions again (for the last time) "works of the law" as an
identity marker of the agitators in Galatians 3:10, he assumes his previous
critical evaluation of these works—they are a merely human way to escape
the curse and attain the covenantal blessing of the spirit, justification and

---

[55]Paul also uses *sarx* to refer to an evil inclination or desire (Gal 5:17, 24) but this nuance cannot
be intended here; see F. Mußner, *Der Galaterbrief* (Freiburg: Herder, 1974), p. 209.

[56]"Covenant . . . in your flesh" and "the flesh of your foreskins" (Gen 17:11, 13, 14, 23-25); see
Martyn, *Galatians*, pp. 289-94.

[57]Barclay, *Obeying the Truth*, pp. 202-9.

[58]Ibid., p. 206; see also Franz Mußner, *Der Galaterbrief* (Freiburg: Herder, 1974), p. 209.

[59]On this point, see Watson, *Paul and the Hermeneutics*, pp. 202-8. The divine and human
antithesis also seems evident in 1 Cor 3:1-3 and Phil 3:3 (cf. Heb 7:16-19).

[60]Hays, *Faith of Jesus Christ*, p. 170.

[61]See Eckstein, *Verheißung und Gesetz*, p. 86.

life.[62] Paul, therefore, argues against the sort of *Deuteronomic* scheme of restoration evinced in the Qumran literature, and probably promoted by the agitators, where returning to the law (e.g., 11QT^a 59; CD 1–3; 1QS 1–3, 5) or to "works of the law" (e.g., 4QMMT C) was the only way to escape the curse. In short, "works of the law" are more than just identity markers; they are the prescribed means of escaping the covenant curse—according to the *Deuteronomic* scheme.

But interpreters are quick to overlook this. For instance, Wright's robust covenantal reading of Galatians 3 seems to fizzle out once he compares the role of "works of the law" in Paul with Qumran. He says: "The 'works' which MMT commends were designed to mark out one group of Jews from the rest, whereas the agitators' 'works' were designed to mark out Jews from pagans."[63] But Wright's view does not do justice to his own reading of Deuteronomy 27–30 as the scriptural context of Galatians 3. According to Deuteronomy, Israel is punished by the curse for their disobedience, and they will be rewarded with blessing *for their return to the law*—something that the Qumran writers found to be quite unambiguous. According to the *Deuteronomic* scheme, "works of the law" do more than just mark out the obedient ones; rather, they are the necessary means of attaining the covenant blessings held out in Deuteronomy 27–30. But Paul argues that given God's intervention in Christ, this *Deuteronomic* scheme does not work. And Paul's citations of Habakkuk 2:4 and Leviticus 18:5 tell us why.

Habakkuk 2:4 and Leviticus 18:5 in Galatians 3:11-12. One of the greatest challenges to any reading of Galatians 3:10 is making sense of Galatians 3:11-12, where Paul cites Habakkuk 2:4 and Leviticus 18:5 respectively: "Now it is clear that no one is justified before God by the law, for 'The righteous shall live by faith' [Hab 2:4]. But the law is not of faith, but 'The

---

[62]Paul has already forged a chasm between justification (= righteousness) and the law in Gal 2:20-21, and will do the same for the attainment of "life" in Gal 3:21. All three eschatological concepts—the spirit, justification and life—are correlated in Gal 3:8-14 and refer to the variegated blessings that lie on the other side of covenant curse. See Hans Dieter Betz, *Galatians: A Commentary on Paul's Letter to the Churches in Galatia* (Philadelphia: Fortress, 1979), p. 142; Hays, *The Faith of Jesus Christ*, pp. 173-77; and Schlier, *Der Brief an die Galater*, pp. 130-31. The correlation between justification and life is explicit in Gal 3:21: "For if a law was given *which was able to make alive* (*hodynamenos zōopoiēsai*), then *righteousness* (*hē dikaiosynē*) would have really been through the law" (see Sprinkle, *Law and Life*, pp. 139-40).

[63]Wright, "4QMMT and Paul," p. 130.

one who does them shall live by them' [Lev 18:5]." I have put my own hand to the herculean task of making sense of Paul's citations in my dissertation on Leviticus 18:5 and will therefore sum up my previous argument here. As with any interpretive dilemma, scholars have proposed several different avenues to solve the problem. To my mind, the best way to unlock Paul's understanding of these texts is to look to their original scriptural contexts.

Habakkuk as a whole instills hope in future divine action while questioning the effectiveness of the law. The only reference to torah in the entire book is Habakkuk 1:4, where the prophet questions its effectiveness: "The law (*tôrâ*) is paralyzed (*tāpûg*),[64] and justice never goes forth. For the wicked [Judeans] surround the righteous; so justice goes forth perverted." The vision oracle itself (Hab 2:2-5), from which Paul cites the prophet (Hab 2:4 in Gal 3:11), focuses on the certainty of God's future act of salvation, an act that is *not a response to prior law-obedience*. Like Isaiah before him, the "if . . . then" construct of Deuteronomic eschatology is banished. The assurances of God's future saving act rests on the reliability of a vision, which, although it may delay, is sure to come (Hab 2:2–3).[65] This vision is the referent of the much-discussed pronoun of Habakkuk 2:4: "But the righteous will live by *its* reliability (*wĕṣadîq beʾĕmûnātô yiḥyeh*)."[66] The content of the

---

[64]Although the meaning of *tāpûg* is debated, the sense of "ineffective" is clear from the context and its use elsewhere. In Gen 45:26, it refers to Jacob becoming "numb" or "fainthearted." In Ps 77:2 (77:3 MT) it refers to "a wearing paralysis." In Ps 38:8 (38:9 MT) it means "broken" or "numbed;" see further Marshall Johnson, "The Paralysis of the Torah in Habakkuk 1:4," *VT* 35 (1985): 257-66 (esp. 259-60). But is Habakkuk's complaint directed to the torah itself or the failure among the Judeans to obey it? Johnson argues that Habakkuk's complaint is directed at a failure inherent in the torah. Habakkuk, according to Johnson, was a "disillusioned deuteronomist" who could not understand why the "righteous" were not being blessed as the torah promised (Johnson, "Paralysis," p. 264). While Johnson's understanding would fit Paul's thought well, his argument that the prophet was concerned with the failure of torah to mediate the blessings of Deuteronomy goes beyond the evidence in Habakkuk. It seems best to side with the majority of interpreters that Habakkuk's complaint is directed toward the ethical breakdown in society; see R. D. Haak, *Habakkuk* (Leiden: Brill, 1992), p. 34; J. G. Janzen, "Eschatological Symbol and Existence in Habakkuk," *CBQ* 44 (1982): 394-414 (esp. 397-99); Ralph Smith, *Micah-Malachi*, WBC 32 (Waco, TX: Word, 1984), p. 99. In any case, Habakkuk critiques the efficacy of the torah, whether by its own inherent ineffectiveness or because of its inability to keep the wicked from persecuting the righteous.

[65]The delay can refer to either the coming of God or the coming of the vision, although the two cannot be separated completely. For a discussion of this difficult passage, see Francis Anderson, *Habakkuk: A New Translation and Commentary*, AB 25 (New York: Doubleday, 2001), pp. 205-8.

[66]So J. G. Janzen, "Habakkuk 2:2-4 in the Light of Recent Philological Advances," *HTR* 73 (1980): 53-78 (esp. 54-61); J. G. Janzen, "Eschatological Symbol," pp. 395, 406; Haak, *Habakkuk*, p. 59; Anderson, *Habakkuk*, p. 214.

vision most likely refers to the theophany of Habakkuk 3,[67] which promises salvation to Judah and judgment on its enemies. In short, the *'ĕmûnâ* that mediates "life" to the righteous one is the reliability that God will intervene to perform a future act of salvation. The reliability of the vision (and thus of God) is meant to evoke a response of "faith" from the prophet and all who are "righteous," but in the vision oracle of Habakkuk 2:2-5 and the theophany of Habbakuk 3, the emphasis lies in divine action as the solution to the problem of wickedness. In short, Habakkuk sidelines a *Deuteronomic* restoration (Hab 1:4) for a more *Prophetic* one, casting all confidence on God's unilateral power to save. In Galatians 3:11, Paul leaves out the original pronoun in his citation of Habakkuk 2:4, so it is not clear whose "faith" he has in mind. The righteous will simply live "by faith," though in the context of Galatians 3, it is more likely that human faith is in view.[68] In any case, it makes more sense of Paul's argument if we understand his citation of Habakkuk 2:4 in light of Habakkuk's own context. The faith that justifies, which is contrasted with the law that does not (Gal 3:12), is faith in God's eschatological saving action accomplished on Calvary.

This reading of Habakkuk is strengthened when contrasted with Leviticus 18:5, a passage that exhibits a conceptual world similar to that of the Deuteronomists: blessing will come to those who obey the law. In its widespread usage, both in the Old Testament and in early Judaism, Leviticus 18:5 was often correlated with the blessings and curses of Israel's covenant, capturing as it does so the conditional structure of the Sinaitic law.[69] In the original context of Leviticus 18, the "life" held out refers to the covenant blessing given to the "one who does these things"; that is, the obedient Isra-

---

[67]Johnson, "Paralysis," p. 263; similarly Anderson, *Habakkuk*, pp. 205, 207, but see p. 202. The content of the vision is a matter of dispute. It may refer to (1) the coming of the Chaldeans in Hab 1:5-11; (2) the set of woe oracles in Hab 2:6-20; (3) the theophany of Hab 3; (4) the oracle in Hab 2:4-5a (William H. Brownlee, "The Placarded Revelation of Habakkuk," *JBL* 82 [1963]: 324; similarly Janzen, "Habakkuk 2:2-4," p. 76); or (5) the content of the book as a whole (Watson, *Paul*, p. 143). All of these views except (1), however, are either related to or include the theophany of chapter 3.

[68]The reference to human faith does not mean that Paul emphasizes human *agency* in salvation, since "the efficacy of the path of faith lies in what Christ has done *for* those cursed by the law" (Stephen Westerholm, *Perspectives Old and New on Paul: The "Lutheran" Paul and His Critics* [Grand Rapids: Eerdmans, 2004], p. 304). Faith, then, is a human response to God's prior saving act in Christ. And for Paul, even the human response is created by divine action (esp. 2 Cor 4:6; see also Rom 4:18-22; 1 Cor 2:4-5, 10; 1 Thess 2:13).

[69]See Sprinkle, *Law and Life.*

elite (see the blessings of Lev 26). Ezekiel alludes to Leviticus 18:5 to sum up the stipulations and potential reward (viz. "life") of the Sinaitic covenant, a covenant that Israel failed to keep (Ezek 20:11, 13, 21). But Ezekiel anticipates that the blessing of life (held out in Lev 18:5) will be granted unconditionally in the end. Israel's failure to "do these things" led to death (Ezek 33:10), and their future life will be given through a unilateral act of God (Ezek 36:26-27; 37:1-14).[70]

In early Judaism, Leviticus 18:5 was quoted quite frequently, but it was not understood in the same sense in which Ezekiel used it. The Leviticus formula is inherently *Deuteronomic,* and early Jewish interpreters understood it as such. This is seen especially in the Dead Sea Scrolls.[71] The citation of Leviticus 18:5 in CD 3, a passage cited earlier, is typical:

> But with those who remained steadfast in God's precepts, with those who were left from among them, God established his covenant with Israel forever, revealing to them hidden matters [Deut 29:28] in which all Israel had gone astray: his holy Sabbaths and his glorious feasts, his just stipulations and his truthful paths, and the wishes of his will *which man must do in order to live by them* (*'šr y'śh h'dm whyh bhm*) [Lev 18:5]. (CD 3:12b–16a)

The Qumran community believes that it has obeyed the law, thus escaping the covenant curse and gaining the blessing of life. Their obedience and subsequent blessing is captured in Leviticus 18:5, a passage they believe is an accurate description of their eschatological situation. They have "done these things" so as to gain "life by them."

The blessings and curses are reiterated at the end of the document in 4Q266.[72] The context here is an annual expulsion ceremony, where a member has committed apostasy and is therefore cut off from the community. The following allusion to Leviticus 18:5 is embedded in a prayer prayed over the one being expelled:

> You chose our fathers and gave their descendants your truthful ordinances and your holy judgments, *which the man will do and live* (*'šr h'dm y'śh whyh*).

---

[70]Preston M. Sprinkle, "Law and Life: The Use of Leviticus 18.5 in the Literary Framework of Ezekiel," *JSOT* 31 (2007): 55-73.

[71]4Q504 *frag.* 6 ii, 17; CD 3:16; 4Q266 11 i-ii, 12.

[72]4Q266 contains material that would have been contained in the text that we know as the *Damascus Document* (CD).

> And you established boundaries for us and you curse those who cross them.
> And we are your people of your ransom and the flock of your pasture. You
> curse those who cross them and we have established [this curse]. (4Q266 11
> i-ii, 9–14a *DSSSE*)

The Qumran community has established the "boundaries" (i.e., the law)
and has attained the life held out in Leviticus 18:5. Those who cross the
boundaries, however, are cursed. Again, the life held out in Leviticus 18:5 is
contrasted with the curse of the covenant and is attained by obedience to
the law.

Other passages could be examined, but these three cited above (Ezekiel,
CD, 4Q266) demonstrate that the life offered in Leviticus 18:5 was understood more specifically as the *covenant blessing of life* awarded to the community that returns to the law. The Qumran community believes that they
have done so, and thus have inherited the blessing of life, while Ezekiel
speaks of Israel's *failure* to "do these things" and envisions a unilateral gift of
life through the spirit in the eschatological age.

The correlation between Leviticus 18:5 and the blessings and curses of
the law, evinced among the Qumran texts, Ezekiel and in Leviticus itself,
dovetails nicely with Paul's argument. While Qumran cited Leviticus 18:5
positively to underscore their return to the law and attainment of covenant
blessing, Paul cites it negatively—as does Ezekiel—to highlight Israel's
failure to achieve blessing through law-works. Paul argues, therefore, that it
is the human response to what God has done in Christ, and not the divine
response to what Israel (or the agitators) has done in the law, that delivers
"us" from the curse of the law. And this contrast is emphasized in Galatians
3:13, where Paul abruptly and emphatically underscores divine agency in
rescuing Christians from the curse of the law: "*Christ* redeemed us from the
curse of the law."[73] Paul's assertion implies a contrast with other potential
avenues of redemption, including the path of law-works promoted by Leviticus 18:5. Regarding Paul's language in Galatians 3:13, Richard Longenecker rightly notes that "the asyndeton (absence of a connective where one
would normally be expected), particularly after the consistent use of con-
necting particles in vv 10-12, lends rhetorical force to the change of subject."[74]

---

[73]Greek *Christos hēmas exēgorasen ek tēs kataras tou nomou.*
[74]Longenecker, *Galatians*, p. 121.

The rhetorical force of Galatians 3:13, therefore, not only indicates the means through which the curse has been relieved, but it challenges and critiques all other means; namely, the avenue of "works of the law" (Gal 3:10) sanctioned by Leviticus 18:5 (Gal 3:12). This confirms the emphasis between divine (*Prophetic*) and human (*Deuteronomic*) agency in relieving the covenant curse that Paul is pushing for in his redemptive-historical argument.

CONCLUSION

I have suggested that in Galatians 3:10-13, Paul argues along similar redemptive-historical lines as Qumran. He believes that God has restored his remnant people—the true "Israel of God"—from this curse, though not through the *Deuteronomic* scheme of returning to the law, but rather through the *Prophetic* scheme of unilateral divine intervention. Paul's citation of Deuteronomy 27:26 in Galatians 3:10 situates Paul's argument in this context, and his citations of Habakkuk 2:4 and Leviticus 18:5 in Galatians 3:11-12 carry the argument forward. Thus, the forecast of the Hebrew prophets (Habakkuk, Ezekiel, et al.) of a unilateral act of God, which circumvents the *Deuteronomic* paradigm, finds its realization in God's redeeming activity in Christ.

The curse of the law motif, fundamental for Paul's argument in Galatians 3, was widespread at Qumran as well. In didactic and legal texts, Qumran underscores the *Deuteronomic* motif of returning to the law in order to escape the curse and find the covenant blessing of life. The discontinuity between these passages and Galatians 3 could not be sharper. In fact, it seems that the tradition that fueled the agitators' view of the curse of the law is the same tradition witnessed among the Scrolls. However, we saw some disparity within the scrolls in 4Q504, where the author believed that divine action will precede and create a human return to the law. Though this is similar to Paul, the two do not completely see eye to eye, since 4Q504 still envisions a return to the law, albeit divinely empowered. Paul actually radicalizes the *Prophetic* vision of covenant restoration by evading "works of the law"—divinely empowered or not—altogether. With this particular soteriological motif, therefore, there is a measure of continuity between Paul and 4Q504, but the overarching assessment between Pauline literature and the Scrolls is one of discontinuity.

4

THE ESCHATOLOGICAL SPIRIT

Paul's understanding of the spirit is essential to his soteriology—although, as we will see, it carries with it multiple interpretive issues.[1] Qumran's view of the spirit[2] is even more complicated and has attracted quite a number of scholarly tomes. In order to stay on track, we will focus our comparative study on how each interpreted the prophetic promise of the spirit in Ezekiel 36–37. This is a fair avenue of comparison, since Ezekiel's promise was a source of reflection for both Qumran and Paul on more than one occasion.

As we saw in chapter two, Ezekiel 36–37 envisions a future unilateral work of the spirit, who will quicken the dead and enable Israel to obey. More than any other Old Testament book, Ezekiel is clearly *Prophetic* in its view of how God will restore the nation. The leading question for this chapter, then, is: Did Paul and the covenanters at Qumran envision the same *Prophetic* paradigm of restoration when they read Ezekiel 36–37? After addressing this question head-on, we will widen our lens to capture a more comprehensive understanding of their respective views of the spirit as it pertains to divine and human agency in salvation.

PAUL AND EZEKIEL'S LIFE-GIVING SPIRIT

Paul discusses the role of the spirit throughout most of his letters; however,

---

[1]For an overview, see Gordon D. Fee, *God's Empowering Presence: The Holy Spirit in the Letters of Paul* (Peabody, MA: Hendrickson, 1994).

[2]I use the lowercase "spirit" for both Paul and Qumran's use of *pneuma* and *rûaḥ* respectively. I found this to be the least cumbersome way to discuss how each viewed the work of the spirit, especially when studying the intersection of their views.

two sections draw on Ezekiel 36–37 most clearly: 2 Corinthians 3:1-7 and Romans 7:6–8:13. Although other passages could be examined,[3] for the sake of concision we will concentrate our study on these two passages.

2 Corinthians 3:1-7. Second Corinthians comprises a defense of Paul's apostolic ministry against the attacks of certain opponents.[4] Apparently, Paul's sufferings gave these contenders much fodder for their degrading assertions about his apostolic authority. In 2 Corinthians 2:14–4:6, Paul defends his ministry by correlating it with the power of the new covenant and setting it in opposition to the old covenant ministry of Moses (esp. 2 Cor 3:7-18). Paul's external weakness (in speech and possibly in stature) and ongoing suffering led the opponents to question the legitimacy of his apostolic office. In this passage, Paul defends his apostleship by arguing that his weakness and suffering provide a better conduit for God's power and grace.

As we approach 2 Corinthians 3, we must acknowledge that Paul's argument here is an exegetical minefield. The interpretation of nearly every verse is widely disputed, and Paul's quirky interpretation of Exodus 34:29-35 only adds to the ambiguity. With this in mind, it will be crucial to stay focused on the question at hand: *Did Paul understand the role of the spirit along the same lines as we saw in Ezekiel 36–37?*[5]

Paul refers to the spirit in 2 Corinthians 3:3, 6, and he seems to ground his argument in the eschatological promises of Ezekiel: "being manifested that you are an epistle of Christ ministered by us, being written not with ink but with the spirit of the living God, not on tablets of stone but on tablets of

---

[3] Paul alludes to the promise of Ezek 36–37 in 1 Cor 15:42-49; 1 Thess 4:8; and perhaps throughout Gal 5:16-25.

[4] While the identity and doctrine of these opponents is impossible to determine with certainty, they likely bore a message similar to Paul's opponents who troubled the churches of Galatia and were probably of some sort of Jewish background (2 Cor 11:22-23; cf. 2 Cor 11:4). Scott Hafemann sums up the situation well: "Instead of calling the Corinthians to a life of faithful endurance and love in the midst of adversity, Paul's opponents promised them deliverance from suffering and a steady diet of spiritual experiences. Instead of demonstrating the fruit of the spirit in their own lives, they supported their claims to be true apostles with letters of recommendation from other churches (cf. 2 Cor 3:1), by trumpeting their ethnic heritage as Jews (2 Cor 3:4-18; 11:21-22), by displaying professional rhetorical flash (2 Cor 10:10; 11:6), and by boasting in their spiritual experiences and supernatural signs (2 Cor 10:12; 11:12, 18; 12:12)." Scott J. Hafemann, *2 Corinthians* (Grand Rapids: Zondervan, 2000), pp. 29-30.

[5] Paul refers to the spirit six times in 2 Cor 3:1-18 (2 Cor 3:3, 6 twice, 8, 17 twice), and according to Fee, "This is one of the most significant spirit passages in the Pauline corpus" (Fee, *God's Empowering Presence,* pp. 296-97). Since we are not concerned as much with the *identity* of the spirit, the issues related to the "Lord" and the "spirit" in 2 Cor 3:17-18 will not be discussed.

fleshly hearts" (2 Cor 3:3).[6] In itself, the phrase "spirit of the living God" is not directly correlated to any specific Old Testament passage, but the reference to the "tablets of fleshly hearts" (*plaxin kardiais sarkinais*) alludes to Ezekiel 36:26, where God will "remove the *heart of stone* [LXX *tēn kardian tēn lithinēn*] from your flesh" and give Israel "a *heart of flesh*" (LXX *kardian sarkinēn*). In Ezekiel, this gift of a new heart is linked to the endowment of Yahweh's spirit, in Ezekiel 36:27, who causes Israel to render the obedience that was not forthcoming under the old covenant (cf. Ezekiel 20). While the spirit in 2 Corinthians 3:3 is the agent of writing and not the content of the gift as in Ezekiel, the occurrence of both "spirit" and "fleshly hearts" confirms the allusion to Ezekiel.

But Ezekiel is not the only passage in view here. The reference to the "epistle of Christ" being "written" by the spirit "on the hearts of flesh" almost certainly alludes to Jeremiah 31:33 (38:33 LXX), where God will "write it [the law] on their hearts."[7] Although the Jeremiah allusion is difficult to prove with certainty, it is most probable since Paul clearly cites Jeremiah 31:31 (38:31 LXX) in 2 Corinthians 3:6 with his reference to the "new covenant."[8] Paul, therefore, in referring to the "writing by the spirit of the living God" and "tablets of fleshly hearts," conflates the promises of Jeremiah 31 and Ezekiel 36, both of which highlight the unilateral transformative work of God.

Moreover, this divine work is explicitly and surprisingly contrasted with the law, here referred to as "tablets of stone" (*plaxin lithinais*, 2 Cor 3:3), a phrase that alludes to the stone tablets of the law that Moses received on Sinai.[9] But any reader with an ear to the ground will hear another echo. The reference to tablets of *stone* reminds the reader of Ezekiel's "hearts of *stone*" (Ezek 36:26) to which the "hearts of flesh" stand in contrast.[10] The corre-

---

[6]Greek *Phaneroumenoi hoti este epistolē Christou diakonētheisa hyph hēmōn, engegrammenē ou melani alla pneumati theou zōntos, ouk en plaxin lithinais all' en plaxin kardiais sarkinais.*

[7]John Yates, *The Spirit and Creation in Paul*, WUNT 2.251 (Tübingen: Mohr Siebeck, 2008), pp. 108-9; contra Scott J. Hafemann, *Suffering and the Spirit: An Exegetical Study of II Cor. 2:14–3:3 Within the Context of the Corinthian Correspondence* (Tübingen: J. C. B. Mohr, 1986), pp. 204-7, who says that Jer 31 doesn't come into play until 2 Cor 3:6.

[8]Richard Hays, *Echoes of Scripture in the Letters of Paul* (New Haven: Yale University Press, 1989), p. 128.

[9]Exodus 31:18 (2x); cf. Exod 24:12; 32:15; 34:1 (3x), 4 (2x); Deut 4:13; 5:22; 9:9-10; see Yates, *Spirit and Creation*, p. 108; Paul Barnett, *The Message of 2 Corinthians*, BST (Downers Grove, IL: InterVarsity Press, 1988), p. 169.

[10]See Hays: "Paul's . . . pejorative reference to stone hearts becomes the ground of intertextual

lation between the "stone tablets" of the law and the "stone hearts" of the
rebellious Israelites is both striking and daring: Paul asserts that the law has
contributed to the death of Israel.

This critical evaluation of the law is seen again in 2 Corinthians 3:1-3,
when Paul tethers the ineffectual nature of the law ("tablets of stone," 2 Cor
3:3) to the ineffectual nature of the "letters of commendation" (2 Cor 3:1). He
begins by pointing out that the legitimacy of his apostolic ministry is witnessed in the transformed nature of the Corinthians, whom he describes as
a "letter of Christ" (2 Cor 3:3). This "letter of Christ" that Paul carried is
contrasted with the "letters of commendation" that his opponents so
proudly displayed. The substance of the contrast is the agency of writing:
the letters of the opponents were written with the human agency of "ink,"
while the "letter of Christ" was written with the agency of "the spirit of the
living God" (2 Cor 3:3). This contrast between human and divine agency—
the proof of the latter evidenced in the transformation of the Corinthians—
is taken a step further when Paul correlates the letters written with ink to
the "stone tablets" of the law (2 Cor 3:3):[11]

| not (*ou*) with ink | but (*alla*) with the spirit of the living God |
| not (*ouk*) on tablets of stone | but (*all'*) on tablets of fleshly hearts |

---

plausibility for Paul's daring interpretive act of imputing negative connotations to the stone
tablets on which God once wrote at Sinai. It is hardly mere coincidence that Paul, rather than
referring to Ezekiel's stone hearts, uses the very phrase (*plakas lithinas*) that describes the tablets
of the law in Exodus and Deuteronomy, and sets these 'stone tablets' in antithesis to Christ's
letter written on fleshy hearts" (*Echoes*, p. 129).

[11]Hafemann, however, does not see a correlation of "ink" with "tablets of stone" and "spirit" with
"tablets of fleshly hearts." The first contrast, according to Hafemann, is between the power of
the spirit in the new covenant and the lack of this power (i.e., mere ink) in the old. But the
second contrast between tablets of stone and tablets of fleshly hearts is a neutral one: "In 3:3b,
Paul had established a contrast between God's work in the past under the old covenant, in
which he engraved his covenant document on stone tablets, and his present work under the
new covenant, in which he engraves his 'letter of Christ' on the 'tablets of human hearts.' . . .
Against this backdrop, Paul's concern is not with two distinct messages, but with the two
materials on which God wrote, corresponding to the two basic ages within the history of
salvation. If anything is to be assumed as implicit in Paul's contrast in regard to the law, it is that
those who have received the Spirit are now keeping the law, just as Ezekiel prophesied"
(Hafemann, *2 Corinthians*, p. 131). So the contrast between tablets of stone and tablets of fleshly
hearts is simply between "two basic ages within the history of salvation." Paul is not describing
the former age ("tablets of stone") critically. God is at work in the past through the law and he
is also at work in the present through the spirit. While there is some truth to this theologically,
it seems much more likely here that Paul intends a contrast, as we will see below.

The parallel between *ou . . . alla* and *ouk . . . all'* suggests a parallel between "ink" and "tablets of stone," which is contrasted with "spirit" and "tablets of fleshly hearts," respectively.[12] In other words, his move from "epistles of commendation" to "written with ink" to "tablets of stone" is intended to correlate the ministry of the opponents and their ineffectual letters with the ministry of the old covenant and its ineffectual law. In the same way that the letters of the opponents were unable to substantiate ministerial authority—written, as they were, with the human agency of ink—so also the law is unable to effect moral transformation among the Corinthians. Like the "letters of commendation," the "stone tablets" of the law lack the power to transform and engender the power to kill.

Some will find this interpretation too abrasive, perhaps anachronistic, but it seems to be exactly what Paul says in 2 Corinthians 3:6: "Who made us sufficient to be ministers of a new covenant, not of the letter but of the spirit; for the letter kills, but the spirit gives life."[13]

The death-bringing outcome of the law-letter and the life-giving power of the spirit draw us back into Ezekiel's world. Though the law intended to bring life (Ezek 20:11, 13, 21), it produced death (Ezek 20:25-26; 33:10), carving out room for the spirit's transformative work in the eschaton, which Paul saw taking place during his ministry in Corinth. The reference to "a new covenant" (*keinēs diathēkēs*) refers to the promise of Jeremiah 31:31 (38:31 LXX),[14] and the description of the "spirit" who "gives life" picks up on the dry bones vision of Ezekiel 37:1-14.[15] By correlating the promises of Jeremiah 31 and Ezekiel 37, Paul asserts that his sufficiency as a minister of the new covenant comes from the life-giving power of the spirit, which shapes the new covenant itself.

The "letter" that "kills" (2 Cor 3:6) is the law, which overlaps with the

---

[12]But Hafemann does not agree. He says that "Paul here establishes *two* contrasts, not one: a contrast between the two *means* of writing (human agency of ink versus the spirit) and a contrast between two *spheres* of the writing (the old covenant tablets of the law versus the new covenant 'tablets' of the human heart)" (Hafemann, *2 Corinthians*, p. 117).

[13]Greek *hos kai hikanōsen hēmas diakonous kainēs diathēkēs, ou grammatos alla pneumatos; to gar gramma apoktennei, to de pneuma zōopoiei*.

[14]Contra Heikki Räisänen, *Paul and the Law* (Philadelphia: Fortress, 1986), pp. 240-45, who does not see an allusion to Jeremiah here.

[15]In Ezek 37:14, for instance, the vision is summarized by God, who says, "And I will give *my* spirit (*to pneuma mou*) in you and *you will live* (*zēsesthe*)" (cf. Ezek 37:6).

"ministry of death which was *engraved with letters on stones*" (2 Cor 3:7).[16] This connection between 2 Corinthians 3:6 and 7 offers the clearest proof for Paul's letter/law correlation. The "ministry of death" connotes the old covenant as a whole, while the phrase "engraved with letters on stones" picks up on the "stone tablets" of 2 Corinthians 3:3 and thus refers to the Mosaic law. There is no indication here—and it would destroy the logic if it were so— that the new covenant somehow incorporates these letter-engraved stones ("tablets of stone," 2 Cor 3:3).[17] The letter-engraved stones are the catalyst for the ministry of death and are therefore set in contrast to the "new covenant" that is "of the spirit which gives life" (2 Cor 3:6)—a clear allusion to the unilateral work of the spirit in Ezekiel 37:1-14. Once again, the continuity between Ezekiel and Paul here is striking. Paul does not simply adapt life-giving language from the prophet but sums up the entire motif of the law-covenant leading to death and the spirit-covenant generating life that is so fundamental to Ezekiel's own book.

Grounding Paul's argument in Ezekiel's prophecy clarifies the somewhat ambiguous and much-debated contrast between letter and spirit in Paul, which has spawned many different interpretations.[18] According to Origen, the "letter" represents the literal meaning of Scripture, while the "spirit" represents the allegorical sense. Most modern scholars, however, do not consider this to be a legitimate interpretive option. Another view that is fading away is the one advocated by Rudolf Bultmann and others, who say that the "letter" equates with human striving after righteousness, or legalism, while the "spirit" represents a proper dependence on God. In addition to these older views, recent interpreters find more continuity between the letter and the spirit in this passage. Scott Hafemann, for instance, takes the "letter" to

---

[16]See Francis Watson, *Paul and the Hermeneutics of Faith* (New York: T & T Clark, 2004), pp. 288-89. Watson points out that the giving of the law immediately resulted in death (Ex 32–34), and that "the post-Sinai history of Israel in the wilderness is a history of catastrophe" (p. 277). Paul's assertion that the "letter kills," therefore, is not simply a dogmatic assertion but a responsible hermeneutical conclusion.

[17]Sigurd Grindheim, "The Law Kills but the Gospel Gives Life," *JSNT* 84 (2001): 97-115 (esp. 101). Grindheim goes on to point out that 2 Cor 3:10 says that the old covenant had glory, but with the coming of the new, it no longer has any glory. If Paul meant to portray the old and new covenants as a continuum rather than contrast, he would have said that the old covenant has reached its full glory in the new, rather than being terminated (pp. 102-3).

[18]Cf. Rom 2:28-29; 7:5-6. For a survey of views with extensive bibliography, see Grindheim, "The Law Kills."

represent the law without the spirit and the "spirit" to represent the law with the spirit. The latter, then, is not so much a critique of the former as it is an improvement on it: what was good simply got better.[19]

Despite strengths in each of these approaches, I find it more plausible to interpret the letter/spirit contrast in line with the messages of Jeremiah and Ezekiel as a whole.[20] According to these prophets, Israel is horribly wicked, and the old covenant has failed to alleviate the problem. The spirit is the divine agent who effects Israel's moral transformation in response to Israel's failure to gain life through the law. Paul takes this a step further and argues that the law, being bound to the old covenant, only kills, while the new covenant spirit gives life. Paul maintains Jeremiah's and Ezekiel's emphasis on divine agency in the new covenant and uses this motif to confront the ineffectual nature of his opponents' ministry—empowered, as they themselves have argued, through letters of commendation. Paul's reference to the "letter," therefore, refers to the law *in its old covenant function of offering life conditioned on obedience,* whereas the spirit is the divine agent who grants the covenant blessing of life unilaterally.

Paul contrasts the letter with the spirit again in Romans 2:28-29: "For the Jew is not one who is simply a visible one, neither is circumcision merely the external circumcision in the flesh, but the true Jew is internal and circumcision is of the heart by the spirit and not by the letter, whose praise is not on a human basis but on the basis of God." Paul says that the Gentile, who does not have the law, actually keeps the law if his heart has been circumcised by the spirit (Rom 2:29). This common Old Testament metaphor

---

[19]Scott J. Hafemann, *Paul, Moses, and the History of Israel,* WUNT 2.81 (Tübingen: Mohr Siebeck, 1995), pp. 284, 361; see also pp. 177-80; Carol K. Stockhausen, *Moses' Veil and the Glory of the New Covenant,* AnBib 116 (Rome: Editrice Pontificio Istituto Biblico, 1989), pp. 73-86.

[20]One of the strengths of Hafemann's argument is that neither Jeremiah nor Ezekiel envisions a doing away with of the Mosaic law with the coming of the new covenant. While it is true that Jeremiah and Ezekiel envision a renewed obedience to the law, it is not clear that Paul maintains this same emphasis on *law* obedience. In 2 Cor 3:3, for instance, it is the *epistle of Christ,* and not the law, that is written on the fleshly hearts of the Corinthian believers. Moreover, this divine act, being set in opposition to the law ("tablets of stone"), suggests that Paul maintains Jeremiah's emphasis on divine agency in transformation but has detached this act from the law. Paul does the same thing with Ezekiel in 2 Cor 3:6, where the agency of the spirit does not just improve on, but is contrasted with, the agency of the "letter." In short, while Jer 31 and Ezek 36–37 envision a renewed obedience to the Mosaic law, Paul does not maintain this aspect of the Prophetic promises. Ezekiel also sees a return to the land as integral to the promise of the spirit (Ezek 37:12-14), yet this is another aspect that Paul does not emphasize.

of heart circumcision (Deut 10:16; 30:6; Lev 26:41; Jer 4:4; 9:25; Ezek 44:6-9) differs from passage to passage in terms of its emphasis on human or divine agency. Deuteronomy reveals both emphases, as we saw in Romans 2. In Deuteronomy 10:16, Israel is exhorted, "Circumcise therefore the foreskin of your heart," thus emphasizing human agency, while in Deuteronomy 30:6 heart transformation is accomplished through divine agency: "*God will circumcise your heart*" (Deut 30:6). In Romans 2:29 Paul erases all ambiguity concerning which agency he has in mind, for it is the spirit who circumcises the heart of the Gentile. Paul has probably integrated the promise of the spirit in Ezekiel 36–37 with the eschatological promise of heart circumcision from Deuteronomy 30:6.[21] This understanding of Romans 2:28-29 correlates to what we have argued for in the letter/spirit contrast in 2 Corinthians 3:6. In both passages, Paul highlights the efficacy of the spirit's agency in transforming the person. The law in its old covenant function kills, while the spirit in his new covenant ministry gives life. The gift of the spirit is not simply an improvement on the old paradigm; rather, it is the divine response to the failure of the old.[22] And this is why Paul and his apostolic band can be so confident (Rom 2:16; 3:4-5, 12; 4:1-6), because it is God who is at work in them as bearers of the new covenant ministry.

In sum, 2 Corinthians 3:1-7 reveals a great deal of continuity between Paul and Ezekiel's promise of the spirit, who gives life and enacts the new covenant.

Romans 7:6–8:13. While interacting with 2 Corinthians 3, Gordon Fee notes in passing that "in many ways Romans 8:2 serves as Paul's own commentary on this passage."[23] Indeed, as Fee points out, the references to the "spirit of life" in Romans 8:1-4 and the spirit's work in raising the dead in Romans 8:9-11 alludes to Ezekiel 37, which we will discuss in more detail below. Moreover, Paul's whole argument about the spirit in Romans 8 begins not in 8:1 but in 7:5-6, where he contrasts (for the second time in Romans; cf. Rom 2:29) the letter with the spirit. Therefore, we have grounds to expand

---

[21]The combination of the circumcision of the heart metaphor with Ezekiel's spirit is not new to Paul; cf. *Jubilees* 1:23: "And I shall cut off the foreskin of their heart and the foreskin of the heart of their descendants. And I shall create for them a holy spirit, and I shall purify them so that they will not turn away from following me from that day and forever." See too Ps 51; Col 2:11; *Odes of Solomon* 11:1-3, on which see E. Käsemann, *Commentary on Romans*, trans. and ed. G. W. Bromiley (Grand Rapids: Eerdmans, 1980), p. 75.

[22]A similar contrast between old and new covenants can be seen in Gal 4:21-31.

[23]Fee, *God's Empowering Presence*, p. 306.

on Fee's observation about the connection between 2 Corinthians 3 and Romans 8:2; it seems that Romans 7:6–8:13[24] as a whole is a commentary on Paul's letter/spirit contrast. In fact, we could say that Romans 7:7-25 is an explanation of how "the letter kills," while 8:1-13 articulates how the spirit "gives life." The letter/spirit contrast in Romans 7:5-6 states *in nuce* what Paul will argue in greater detail in Romans 7:7–8:13.[25]

To state my conclusion up front, I will argue that Paul again believes that the eschatological work of the spirit in Ezekiel 36–37 has been accomplished through the Christ event to solve the problem of sin—a problem that was only strengthened by the law. Paul maintains in Romans 8 the same emphasis on divine agency through the work of the spirit that he does in 2 Corinthians 3.

Paul summarizes his marriage illustration (Rom 7:1-4) by stating that "the passions of sins are energized (*enērgeito*) through the law" and the result is that they "bear fruit unto death" (Rom 7:5). Paul then counters the potential objection that the law is itself identified with sin (Rom 7:7) by explaining that it is sin (or, Sin) itself that uses the law to produce death (Rom 7:8-9).[26] Paul then calls the *egō* to the stand to testify.[27] The *egō* affirms that

---

[24]Maston, Moo and others argue that Paul's train of thought runs through Rom 8:13 instead of ending at Rom 8:11. Jason Maston, *Divine and Human Agency in Second Temple Judaism and in Paul*, WUNT 2.297 (Tübingen: Mohr Siebeck, 2010), p. 127n14; Douglas J. Moo, *The Epistle to the Romans*, NICNT (Grand Rapids: Eerdmans, 1996), p. 473.

[25]In a phone conversation, I asked Tom Schreiner what he thought about the letter/spirit contrast in Rom 7:5-6 setting up Paul's argument in Rom 7:7-25 (letter) and Rom 8:1-11 (spirit). He said that he thought it was "too neat" and therefore unlikely. While I admire the exegetical caution, I still think that this "neatness" is intentional. In Rom 7:5-6, Paul deliberately states his larger argument of Rom 7:7–8:11 *in nuce*. Brenden Byrne, in *Romans* (Collegeville, MN: Liturgical Press, 1996), rightly considers Rom 7:14-25 and Rom 8:1-13 as "panels of a diptych" (p. 213), which he labels "Life Under the Law—Ethical 'Impossibility'" (224) and "Life in the Spirit— Ethical 'Possibility'" (p. 234) for Rom 7:14-25 and Rom 8:1-13 respectively (see also Maston, *Divine and Human Agency*, p. 130).

[26]The "law" (*nomos*) is used interchangeably with "the commandment" (*hē entolē*) here.

[27]The identification of *egō* in Romans 7 is notoriously difficult. The various views can be grouped into four general categories, or "directions" of interpretation, as Moo rightly calls it (*Romans*, p. 424): The *egō* is (1) Adam, (2) Israel, (3) Paul (autobiographical view), or (4) a rhetorical figure. While all of these views have staunch defenders, the strongest view, in my opinion, is that the *egō* is referring predominantly to Adam. An early defense of this view was given by S. Lyonnet, "L'histoire du salut selon le chapitre VII de l'épître aux Romains," *Bib* 43 (1962): 117-51; S. Lyonnet, "'Tu ne convoiteras pas' (Rom. vii 7)," in *Neotestamentica et Patristica: Eine Freundesgabe, Herrn Professor Dr. Oscar Cullman zu seinem 60. Geburtstag überreicht*, ed. W. C. van Unnik, NovTSup 6 (Leiden: Brill, 1962), pp. 157-65. See now H. Lichtenberger, *Das Ich Adams und das Ich der Menschheit: Studien zum Menschenbild in Römer 7*, WUNT 164 (Tübingen: Mohr Siebeck, 2004).

he was alive before the commandment, but when the commandment came "sin sprang to life" (*hē hamartia anezēsen*)[28] and the *egō* died. The commandment, though it was "unto life,"[29] only brought death (Rom 7:10). Romans 7:7-12 teaches, therefore, that the law has become a victim to the power of sin and has been used as sin's agent to effect death in humanity. It is not only the lack of obedience on the part of humanity that is the barrier to life, but also the powerlessness of the law itself to conquer sin, release the death sentence and grant life to sinful people. The law has been transformed through sin from a "commandment unto life" (Rom 7:10) into a "law of sin and death" (Rom 8:2; cf. 2 Cor 3:6).

Although the following passage is one of the most disputed (Rom 7:13-25), it almost certainly depicts a non- or pre-Christian failing to find deliverance from sin through the law.[30] The law is not itself sin but has been hijacked and forced into the service of sin. The exact type of person Paul seeks to identify with the *egō* is not essential for our purpose. What is pertinent is Paul's solution in Romans 8:1-4 to the plight depicted in Romans 7:7-25:

> There is therefore now no condemnation to the ones in Christ Jesus. For the law of the spirit of life has set you free from the law of sin and death. For what the law was unable to do, being weak through the flesh, God did by sending

---

[28]Although *anazaō* retains its full force as "to live again" in Luke 15:24, most commentators rightly interpret it as "to become enlivened" here in 7:10. See, e.g., C. E. B. Cranfield, *On Romans: And other New Testament Essays* (Edinburgh: T & T Clark, 1998), p. 352; Moo, *Romans*, p. 438n53. L. Ann Jervis, however, retains the full force of the verb here: "'The Commandment Which Is for Life' [Romans 7.10]: Sin's Use of the Obedience of Faith," *JSNT* 27 (2004): 193-216 (esp. 200).

[29]*Hē entolē hē eis zōēn* ("the commandment which [was] unto life"). The sense of *eis* is unclear. It could refer to God's original intention of giving life through the law or the *egō's* own (wrong) belief that the law could give life.

[30]Moo lists the best arguments for this view (*Romans*, p. 445), the strongest of which are: (1) The connection between *egō* and "the flesh" (Rom 7:14, 18, 25) suggests that the *egō* is unregenerate, since Rom 7:5 refers to those "in the flesh" as unregenerate; (2) the *egō* is said to be "under the power of sin," and yet Paul already said that believers are free of sin's power (Rom 6:2, 6, 11, 18-22); (3) Rom 7:23 says that the *egō* is a "prisoner of the law of sin," yet Rom 8:2 says that believers have been set free from the same "law of sin (and death)"; (4) while Paul says that believers will struggle with sin (Rom 6:12-13; Gal 5:17), the portrait of Rom 7:14-25 is more of a defeat by sin than it is a struggle. See further Käsemann, *Romans*, p. 192; Joseph A. Fitzmyer, *Romans: A New Translation with Introduction and Commentary*, AB (New York: Doubleday, 1993), p. 465; and the extensive bibliography in Don B. Garlington, *Faith, Obedience, and Perseverance: Aspects of Paul's Letter to the Romans*, WUNT 2.79 (Tübingen: Mohr Siebeck, 1994), p. 198n5. Both Cranfield, *Romans* 1:241-47, and James D. G. Dunn, Romans (Dallas: Word, 1988), 1:407, see Rom 7:14-25 as the struggle of a Christian.

his own son in the likeness of sinful flesh and as an offering for sin, by which he condemned sin in the flesh, in order that the righteous requirement of the law would be fulfilled in us, who do not walk according to the flesh but according to the spirit. (Rom 8:1-4)

Paul connects his argument to Romans 7 by referring to the law (*nomos*) three times in this passage. While disputed by some, the first reference to the law ("the law of the spirit of life") does not refer to the Mosaic law but more generally to a principle, norm or authority.[31] This seems clear from Paul's use of the term in Romans 8:2, where the "law of the spirit and life" performs an act of liberation *from* "the law of sin and death," and in Romans 8:3, where the law is *unable* to do what God has done through the "law of the spirit of life" in Christ. If *nomos* refers to the Mosaic law in all three instances, then how can the law be the effective liberator (Rom 8:2a), the thing from which we have been liberated (Rom 8:2b), and at the same time unable to liberate (Rom 8:3a)? It seems best to take, with most interpreters, the "law of the spirit of life" as the *principle* (or authority) of the spirit who gives life, while understanding the next two references to *nomos*—"the law of sin and death" (Rom 8:2) and the "law" that was unable to redeem (Rom 8:3)—as the Mosaic law.

Romans 8:1-4 solves the dilemma of Romans 7:7-25. God has liberated humanity from sin and death through his decisive act in Christ and through the power of the spirit who gives life, a life that the law failed to give in Romans 7:10. There is an underlying antithesis between God, who through Christ and the spirit redeems and gives life, and the law, which lacked the ability to do so.[32] This contrast is especially emphatic in the Greek, which literally reads: "For the inability of the law, in which it was weak through the flesh, *God* . . . by sending his own Son in the likeness of sinful flesh and as a sin-offering, condemned sin in the flesh."[33] The elliptical expression to-

---

[31] Fitzmyer, *Romans*, pp. 482-83; Leander Keck, *Romans* (Nashville: Abingdon, 2005), pp. 196-97; Fee, *God's Empowering Presence*, pp. 523-24; contra Dunn, *Romans*, 1:416-18. Moo (*Romans*, pp. 476-77) takes both occurrences of *nomos* in Rom 8:2 to refer to a binding principle or authority.

[32] See Fitzmyer: "It is God himself who brings about the fulfillment of the law through Christ and the Spirit" (*Romans*, p. 488).

[33] Greek *to gar adynaton tou nomou, en hō esthenei dia tēs sarkos, ho theos ton heautou huion pempsas en homoiōmati sarkos hamartias kai peri hamartias katekrinen tēn hamartian en tē sarki.* The ellipsis in my English translation depicts a missing verb in the Greek. Paul probably borrowed the verbal notion from the word "inability," which is assumed in the first translation given above: "For what the law was *unable to do* . . . God *did.*"

gether with the emphatic placement of *ho theos* ("God") jars the reader and forces them to see the contrast between the ineffectual nature of the law and the effectual work of God through Christ.

The result of God's decisive action is that the "righteous requirement of the law would be fulfilled in us" (*to dikaiōma tou nomou plērōthē en hēmin,* Rom 8:4).[34] It is possible that the phrase "fulfilled in us" (*plērōthē en hēmin*) refers to the active fulfilment of the law by believers. Paul will say something similar in Romans 13:10, where he argues that "love is the fulfilling of the law" (cf. Gal 5:14). If this reading is correct, then Paul grounds human action in prior divine action: "The outcome of God's act is that believers, in contrast to the *egō,* will be obedient."[35] More likely, however, is the reading that Paul is not referring to the active fulfillment of the law by believers, but to the act of God in satisfying the sum total of the requirements of the law through Christ and the spirit.[36] This interpretation understands Romans 8:4

---

[34]The meaning of the phrase "righteous requirement" (*to dikaiōma*) is disputed. The word is used in Romans 5:16, 18, although the meaning there is equally debated (the plural is used in Rom 1:32). In all three instances (Rom 5:16, 18; 8:4), it could mean "justification," "judgment," "righteous act" or "righteous requirement." The context is paramount in determining its meaning in all three passages, and here in Romans 8:3 it should be rendered "righteous requirement" since the active sense of "justifications" would be awkward. This is further supported by the frequent use of the plural *dikaiōmata* in the LXX and NT to refer to the ordinances or commandments of the law (Moo, *Romans,* p. 481n55). Therefore, *to dikaiōma tou nomou* that is "fulfilled in us" is probably the sum total of what the law requires (see note 36 below).

[35]Maston, *Divine and Human Agency,* p. 166.

[36]This is the best understanding of the phrase for two reasons. First, the passive voice of *plērōthē* "points not to something that we are to do but to something that is done in and for us" (Moo, *Romans,* p. 483). Schreiner is correct to point out that the use of the passive does not in itself exclude human action, since Paul elsewhere uses the passive of *plēroō* to include human action (2 Cor 10:6; Phil 1:11; Col 1:9; Eph 5:18). See Schreiner, *Romans,* BECNT (Grand Rapids: Baker Books, 1998), p. 405. However, in the context of Rom 8:1-4, where divine action in Christ is pitted against human inability to fulfill the law, it is more likely that the passive highlights what God has done in and for believers. Second, the singular *to dikaiōma* instead of the plural *dikaiōmata* signifies something different than carrying out the individual commandments of the law (see note 34 above). Some have suggested that the singular refers to the love command of Rom 13:8-10; thus, believers who love their neighbor as themselves have "fulfilled the law" (so Maston, *Divine and Human Agency,* pp. 164-67). While this is certainly true, it is questionable whether this is what Paul has in mind in Rom 8:3, where the love command is absent from the near context. It seems that Paul's argument is more salvation-historical than it is ethical in Rom 8:4, though the ethical implications will be the focus in Rom 8:5-8. To be sure, on first hearing the letter, the Roman believers would not have understood Rom 8:4 to refer to *their* fulfilment of the law through the love command, an understanding that could only be reached after hearing Rom 13.

as the climactic statement about God's legal satisfaction of the law's condemning power over humanity. Or in the words of Brendan Byrne, "The fulfilment spoken of here is in no sense something achieved by Christians themselves; it is something which God, the author of all, works in us through the Spirit as a consequence of the Christ-event. There is a fulfilment of the moral demand . . . [but this] righteousness is entirely the creation of God operating through the Spirit."[37] This reading is not entirely at odds with the former "ethical" reading; it simply views Romans 8:5-13 (instead of Rom 8:4-13) as the ethical "outcome of God's act" described in Romans 8:1-4.

The emphasis on divine agency in giving life to believers is reiterated again in Romans 8:9-11, where the spirit, who raised Christ from the dead, will also "give [resurrection] life to your mortal bodies through his spirit who dwells in you."[38] Spirit-generated resurrection life—this is almost certainly read off the pages of Ezekiel 37. In fact, there are many parallels between Romans 8 (esp. Rom 8:2-4, 9-11, 13) and Ezekiel 36–37. First, there is the common theme of redemption through the spirit who indwells believers (Rom 8:9-11), which is very similar to Ezekiel 36:26-27, where God will put his spirit "within" Israel. Second, the reference to "the righteous requirement" (*to dikaiōma*) is the same word used in Ezekiel 36:27 (*tois dikaiōmasin*) to refer to the requirements of the law.[39] Third, the reference to

---

[37]Brenden Byrne, "Living Out the Righteousness of God," *CBQ* 43 (1981): 557-81 (esp. 569); see also Keck: "God is the doer who actualizes the right requirement of the law *in us*" (*Romans*, p. 200); Fitzmyer, *Romans*, p. 488, and J. C. Beker, *Paul the Apostle: The Triumph of God in Life and Thought* (Philadelphia: Fortress, 1980), pp. 105-7, 186; contra Cranfield, *Romans*, 1:384-85; Fee, *God's Empowering Presence*, pp. 534-37; and others in Moo, *Romans*, p. 482n61. However, my interpretation does not necessarily mean that Christ fulfilled the law's demand for perfect obedience, which is mediated to us through our incorporation in him (contra Moo, *Romans*, pp. 483-84). Rather, Paul has in mind God's act in the death of Christ, not the active obedience of Christ's life (cf. Rom 5:18-19).

[38]With most interpreters, I am taking the genitive *tou enoikountos autou pneumatos* (א A C 81 Cyril-Jerusalem, Hippolytus) over the accusative *to enoikoun autou pneuma* (B D F G Y). See Cranfield, *Romans*, 1:391-92; Dunn, *Romans*, 1:414; Moo, *Romans*, p. 471n12; and Bruce M. Metzger, *A Textual Commentary on the Greek New Testament*, 2nd ed. (Stuttgart: Deutsche Bibelgesellschaft, 1994), p. 456, which gives it a "B" rating. Fee (*God's Empowering Presence*, pp. 552-53), followed by Keck (*Romans*, p. 205), goes with the accusative and understands the spirit's role to be a *guarantee* rather than an active *agent* of future resurrection. However, Käsemann (*Romans*, p. 225) and Fitzmyer (*Romans*, pp. 491-92) are probably correct that the spirit's activity in generating resurrection life can be conveyed by either reading.

[39]The change from the plural in Ezekiel to the singular in Paul is due to a shift in theological perspective—Paul does not think that believers need to do the "righteous requirements" of the

"walking" is evident in both Ezekiel 36:27 (*poreuēsthe*) and Roman 8:4 (*peripatousin*), referring to the spirit-created obedience of the redeemed.[40] Finally, the phrase "spirit of life" (*pneuma zōēs*) is probably a direct allusion to LXX Ezekiel 37:5 (cf. variant Ezek 37:10).[41] Given these connections to Ezekiel 36–37, it seems clear that Paul in Romans 8 is interpreting Ezekiel's promise of the eschatological spirit.

The resemblance between the above analysis and our previous examination of law and life in Ezekiel is striking. Ezekiel refers to Leviticus 18:5 (Ezek 20:11, 13, 21) to show that Israel has failed to meet the demands of the law and thus forfeited the life therein. By obeying "no-good laws by which they could not live" (Ezek 20:25-26), Israel died (Ezek 33:10-11; 37:11). In order to receive the life offered by Leviticus 18:5, God acts unilaterally to create life through his spirit (Ezek 36:26-27; 37:1-14). Eschatological salvation will be achieved, not by performing the conditional demands of the law (Lev 18:5), but through divine agency. Here in Romans, the pattern is remarkably similar. The law, though it was "unto life" (Lev 18:5), became entangled with sin and therefore leads to death. The solution to the plight comes not through the law, but through the atonement of Christ and life-giving power of the spirit (Rom 8:1-4). In short, Romans 7:7-25 explains why the "oldness of the letter" brought death and became a "law of sin and death" (Rom 8:2), while Romans 8:1-11 explains how Ezekiel's "spirit of life" intervened through Christ to grant life unilaterally. Paul, therefore, reads Ezekiel in line with the prophet's own theological concerns.

Summary. In chapter two, we saw that the prophetic promises of Ezekiel and Jeremiah envision a future unilateral work of God in response to the Sinaitic covenant, a covenant which Israel failed to keep. In our study of 2 Corinthians 3 and Romans 7–8, we have seen that Paul interprets this prophetic promise in terms of God's saving act in Christ and the spirit. Christ and the spirit are not just new identity markers for the new covenant believer, nor are they merely the marks of the eschatological age. Christ and

---

Mosaic law—while maintaining a connection to Ezek 36.

[40]These three connections are noted by Seyoon Kim, *Paul and the New Perspective: Second Thoughts on the Origin of Paul's Gospel* (Grand Rapids: Eerdmans, 2002), p. 159.

[41]For the phrase "spirit of life," see LXX Ezek 1:20, 21; 10:17; cf. Gen 6:17; 7:15; and Judith 10:13. For early Jewish literature, see *T. Abr* 18:11; *T. Reub.* 2:4; *Jos. As.* 16:14; 19:11; *4 Ezra* 3:5; throughout Philo; cf. Rev 11:11. I thank John Yates for alerting me to these references.

the spirit are the effective agents through whom God unilaterally redeems and transforms his people.

THE DEAD SEA SCROLLS AND EZEKIEL'S LIFE-GIVING SPIRIT

In a recent study on the role of the spirit in Paul and Judaism, John Yates says that "members of the *yaḥad* [i.e., Qumran] understood themselves to possess the promised eschatological spirit of Ezekiel 37."[42] If this is true—and to some extent I think it is—the question still follows whether or not they maintained the same theological emphasis inherent in Ezekiel 37. Put simply: Did the Qumranites believe that they had been spiritually transformed through the unilateral act of God's spirit as Ezekiel promised? Thus far, we have seen that Paul maintains the same Ezekielian emphasis on divine agency in reflecting on the eschatological work of the spirit. In turning to Qumran, our task of answering this same question is much easier, since we have among the Scrolls a commentary on Ezekiel 37.

4QPseudo-Ezekiel. The scroll known as 4Q*Pseudo-Ezekiel* rewrites Ezekiel's dry bones vision (Ezek 37) and applies the resurrecting work of God to the new covenant community at Qumran.[43] The relevant portion of the text reads:

> "Yahweh, I have seen many men from Israel who have loved Thy Name and have walked in the ways of righteousness; and these (things) when will they be, and how will they be recompensed for their loyalty?" And Yahweh said to me: "I will make the children of Israel see, and they will know that I am Yahweh." [And he said:] "Son of man, prophesy over the bones and say: be ye joined bone to its bone and joint [to its joint." And it wa]s so. And he said a second time: "Prophesy, and sinews come upon them and let them be covered with skin [above." And it wa]s s[o]. And he said again: "Prophesy

---

[42]Yates, *Spirit and Creation*, p. 65. In an interesting contrast, Alex Deasley, "The Holy Spirit in the Dead Sea Scrolls," *WTJ* 21 (1986): 45-73, says that "nowhere is it stated that the presence of the Spirit in the Community is the eschatological fulfillment of prophetic promises" (p. 57). Again: "Indeed, it is as noteworthy regarding the future work of the spirit as its present work that no appeal is make [sic] by the Qumran writers to the forecasts by the great prophets of a singular coming of the spirit in the end-time" (p. 60).

[43]4Q*Pseudo-Ezekiel* is preserved in five or possibly six manuscripts (4Q385, 386, 387, 388, 389, 390). According to J. Strugnell and D. Dimant, the number of manuscripts indicates that it was probably a very popular document among the Qumran community. Whether or not it is a sectarian composition is disputed; see further J. Strugnell and D. Dimant, "4Q Second Ezekiel (4Q 385)," *RevQ* 13 (1988): 45-58 (esp. 45-46).

concerning the four winds of heaven and let the win[ds of heaven] blow
[upon them and they shall revive] and a great crowd of people shall stand up,
and they shall bless Yahweh Sabaoth wh[o] has given them life again."
(4Q385 *frag.* 2 2-9a)[44]

The preserved section picks up in mid-thought with the query: "When
will these things happen?" In light of what follows, it is probable that
some sort of statement about the restoration of Israel prompted the
question. In any case, the next concern—"how will they be recompensed
for their loyalty?"—refers back to the "many in Israel . . . who love your
name and walk in the paths of righteousness." What is striking is that
lines 4-9 clearly rewrite the dry bones prophecy of Ezekiel 37 and imply
that the resurrection referred to therein is the reward for those who have
kept the covenant.[45] The difference between the Qumran commentary
and Ezekiel could hardly be more striking. In Ezekiel, the dry bones represent the hopeless spiritual state of the entire nation—they are wicked to
the core and unable to live. But in 4QPseudo-Ezekiel, the resurrection of
the dry bones is a reward for those who have demonstrated love, righteousness and covenant faithfulness toward Israel's God.[46] But this is not
the most striking feature in the text. What stands out above anything else,
what distances 4QPseudo-Ezekiel from its biblical counterpart and from
Paul in even more surprising ways, is one significant missing element:
there is no work of the spirit.[47]

If we considered this text alone, we would have to conclude that Qumran
did not view the prophecy of God's intervention through his spirit in Ezekiel
37 as coming true in their community in any significant way. 4QPseudo-

---

[44]The translation is by J. Strugnell and D. Dimant, "4Q Second Ezekiel," p. 49.

[45]It is debated whether or not this text reveals a belief among the Qumran community in a literal
bodily resurrection. For an argument that they did, see N. T. Wright, *The Resurrection of the Son
of God* (Minneapolis: Fortress, 2003), p. 188.

[46]The word for "reward" is *shlm* and is used throughout the Hebrew Bible in the *pi'el* or *pu'al* to
speak of a positive or negative retribution for human behavior (see Ruth 2:12; 1 Sam 24:19; 2
Kings 9:26; Is 65:6; Prov 20:22). The same word is used in Palestinian Aramaic in the *hitpa'el* as
it is here, with the same connotation; see also 11QPsª 22:10 (Strugnell and Dimant, "4Q Second
Ezekiel," p. 53). The word translated "loyalty" is *ḥsd*.

[47]That is, the surviving fragments make no mention of the spirit and give no obvious indication
that the spirit was mentioned in the now-missing parts (thanks to Jason Maston for pointing
this out). While *rûaḥ* occurs twice, it is in the plural and clearly refers to the "four *winds* of
heaven" and not the work of the eschatological spirit as in Ezekiel.

Ezekiel stands in marked contrast with both Ezekiel and Paul's interpretation of the prophet.[48]

But the discussion is not that simple. We have many more texts from Qumran that speak of the spirit, some of which draw on Ezekiel, so we have much more work ahead of us.

Ezekiel's Eschatological Spirit at Qumran.

In seeking to understand the work of the spirit at Qumran, we run into immediate problems in figuring out what the authors mean by *rûaḥ* ("spirit"). The word can refer to various things, as it does in the Bible, and we have examples of the full spectrum of meanings throughout the Scrolls. *Rûaḥ* is used to refer to the *wind* or *breath* (1QHª 15:23), the *inner nature* of a person (1QHª 9:15; 12:31; 1QS 7:18, 22-23; CD 3:2, 8), the *quality* of a person (1QS 8:3; 11:1; 1QM 7:5; 8:3; 14:7), *supernatural beings* (1QS 3:24; CD 12:2; 1QM 13:1-2; 1QHª 9:10-11; 18:8; 19:13) or to the *holy spirit* from God (1QS 3:7-8; 1QHª 12:31; CD 5:11; 7:4, among others).[49] Even this last idea, which sounds in itself quite Pauline, could either refer to a divine person or power (the holy spirit that comes from God) or to a human moral quality or principle (the spirit or principle of holiness evident in a person) that is a gift of God. And even in those places where we can conclude with some degree of confidence that it is a divine person or power, we still must be careful not to read into this some sort of proto-Trinitarian idea of a personal member of the Godhead. With these issues in view, we will proceed with great caution to evaluate those passages that offer the clearest evidence for Ezekiel's promise of the spirit.

The clearest allusion to the spirit in Ezekiel among the Scrolls is seen in the phrase "the spirit given to/in me," which occurs four times in the *Ho-*

---

[48]The same point is made by Kyle Wells, "Grace, Obedience, and the Hermeneutics of Agency: Paul and His Jewish Contemporaries on the Transformation of the Heart" (Ph.D. diss., Durham University, 2009), pp. 36-40.

[49]According to Karl G. Kuhn, *Konkordanz zu den Qumrantexten* (Gottingen: Vanderhoeck & Ruprecht, 1960), the term *rûaḥ* is concentrated in four documents among the Scrolls: 1QHª (60x), 1QS (38x), 1QM (13x) and CD (9x); see Deasley, "Holy Spirit," p. 48. A. E. Sekki has found 217 occurrences of the term *rûaḥ* in the nonbiblical Scrolls as a whole. A. E. Sekki, *The Meaning of Ruach at Qumran*, SBLDS 110 (Atlanta: Scholars Press, 1989), *passim*. Sekki breaks down the meaning of the term as follows: the spirit of man (97x), an angel or demon (58x), the spirit of God (35x) and wind (27x); see too R. W. Kvalvaag, "The Spirit in Human Beings in Some Qumran Non-Biblical Texts," *Qumran Between the Old and New Testaments*, ed. F. H. Cryer and T. L. Thompson, JSOTSup 290 (Sheffield: Sheffield Academic Press, 1998), p. 159.

dayot[50] (1QH^a 5:24-25; 8:19; 10:11-12; 21:14 *bottom*).[51] Three of these references exhibit similar themes and so will be quoted together:

> Only by your goodness is man acquitted, [purified] by the abundance of [your] compa[ssion.] You embellish him with your splendor, you install [him over an abun]dance of pleasures, with everlasting peace and length of days. For [you are the truth, and] your word does not depart. *Blank* And I, your servant, have known thanks to *the spirit you have placed in me* [. . .] and all your deeds are just, and your word does not depart. (1QH^a 5:22b-25 *DSSSE*)

> And I, the Instructor, have known you, my God, through *the spirit which you gave in me,* and I have listened loyally to your wonderful secret through your holy spirit. You have [op]ened within me knowledge of the mystery of your wisdom, and the source of [your] power. (1QH^a 20:11b-13 *DSSSE*)

> [And I, cr]eature from dust, I have known by *the spirit which you have given in me* (1QH^a 21:14 *bottom DSSSE*)

This phrase is most likely an allusion to the same phrase in Ezekiel 37:6, 14, where God says: "And I will give my spirit in/to them and they will live and they will know that I am Yahweh."[52] Other than the commonalities in language, we also see in the three Qumran passage above the common theme of knowledge, which parallels Ezekiel 37:6, 14, where the result of the spirit's saving work is that Israel "*will know* that I am Yahweh." In the *Hodayot* pas-

---

[50]There are eight copies of the *Hodayot* discovered at Khirbet Qumran, with 1QH^a being the fullest copy by far. The other seven copies (1QH^b, 4QH^{a-f}) do not contain any additions or variations significant for our study. See Eileen Schuller, "The Cave 4 Hadayot Manuscripts: A Preliminary Description," *JQR* 85 (1994): 137-50; Eileen Schuller, "Some Contributions of the Cave Four Manuscripts [4Q427-432] to the Study of the Hadayot," *DSD* 8 (2001): 278-87. When the *Hodayot* were first discovered, scholars quickly asserted that they were written by the "Teacher of Righteousness," the supposed founder and key figure for the sect. However, this was challenged early on by research on the Scrolls, and authorship continues to be open to discussion. There do seem to be some hymns that were written by an individual and some that were written by a community, hence the common designations of "teacher hymns" and "community hymns." These two categories, however, continue to be refined and challenged in recent years. For a recent discussion with extensive bibliography on these background issues, see Maston, *Divine and Human Agency*, pp. 75-80. For our study, debates about authorship and background do not need to be resolved. Therefore, I will use the general designation of author, authors or the like to designate the writer(s) of these hymns. For a discussion of the phrase "the spirit given to/in me," see Yates, *Spirit and Creation*, p. 78; Maston, *Divine and Human Agency*, pp. 106-7.

[51]I will be following the column and line numeration from F. Garcia Martinez and E. J. C. Tigchelaar. eds., *Dead Sea Scroll Study Edition*, 2 vols. (Grand Rapids: Eerdmans, 2000).

[52]My translation. Similar phrases are only seen in Is 42:1 and Eccles 12:7, but even here the language is not exactly the same (see Yates, *Spirit and Creation*, pp. 78-79).

sages, the gift of the spirit is the means by which the community member is able to come to a special knowledge of God.[53] The spirit effects, therefore, cognitive renewal.[54]

While there is some continuity between these *Hodayot* passages and Ezekiel 37, there is also some discontinuity in terms of the nature of moral transformation. The passages in Qumran depict the spirit's work solely in terms of cognitive transformation. For the hymnist, of course, obedience is only possible through cognitive transformation, so we should not downplay the importance of the latter. However, despite some overlap, these three passages in the *Hodayot* do not depict the total reconstitution of the human person portrayed in Ezekiel 36–37, where God unilaterally rips out the heart of stone and gives the deceased a new heart and eschatological life. For the hymnists, the cognitive transformation may lead to a total reconstitution (cf. 1QS 4:18-23), but the divinely caused break between the wicked past and obedient present is not as sharp.

In short, while these three passages borrow language from Ezekiel 36–37, they do not capture the contours of the spirit's unilateral transformative work from Ezekiel.

The fourth passage in the *Hodayot* that speaks of the spirit being "given to" the author is 1QH[a] 8:19-20. Here, the spirit is a conduit of divine kindness and purification.

> And since I know that you have recorded *the spirit of the just man*, I have chosen to purify my hands in accordance with [your] will and your servant's soul detests every work of iniquity. I know that no-one besides you is just. I have appeased your face by *the spirit which you have placed [in me,]* to lavish

---

[53]This parallels many other passages in the Scrolls where God enables the covenant member to receive a special knowledge of divine mysteries:1QH[a] 10:14; 12:5; 14:11-12; 15:20-22, 25-27; 19:9-10, 15-17; 1QS 11:15-16; CD 2:14-16; 6:2. See Wells, "Grace," pp. 87-89.

[54]Though not specified in this hymn, the revelation of knowledge was probably derived from the correct interpretation of scripture practiced by the community, which was first revealed to their leader, the Teacher of Righteousness; see 1QpHab 2:1-10; 7:1-5; CD 1:10-12. For the saving significance of the Teacher's hermeneutic, see 1QH[a] 10:18 and 16:35-36: "You have made the tongue in [my] mouth strong . . . to give life to the spirit of those who stagger, and to support the fatigued with a word." See Wells: "It is the revelation of an accurate Torah-hermeneutic that can be marked as *the inceptive salvific act* in the community's history which separates it from the rest of 'apostate' Israel and enables a person 'to do' Torah" ("Grace," p. 60). While divine agency is highlighted in the revelation of knowledge, this esoteric hermeneutic is quite different from what Ezekiel has in mind.

your [kind]nesses on [your] serv[ant] for[ever,] to purify me with *your holy spirit*, to bring me near by your will according to the extent of your kindnesses. (1QH[a] 8:19-20)

The first occurrence of *rûaḥ* ("the *spirit* of the just man") probably refers to a human quality, while the latter two ("the *spirit* which you have placed [in me,] . . . with your *holy spirit* ") most likely refer to God's own spirit and allude to Ezekiel 37:6, 14. Here the spirit's transformation and empowerment are articulated by the three purpose clauses that follow the spirit's work: "to lavish your [kind]nesses . . . to purify me . . . to bring me near" (1QH[a] 8:20). The hymn as a whole highlights God's enabling power for obedience: "You have resolved . . . to take pity [on your servant,] to show me favour by the spirit of your compassion . . . to you belongs the justice because you have done al[l this]" (8:16-17).[55] Like Ezekiel before him, the Qumran hymnist believes that obedience flows from God's prior transformative work through his spirit.[56]

In short, of the four passages in the *Hodayot* that bear some linguistic resemblance to Ezekiel 37, one (8:19-20) captures Ezekiel's emphasis on the priority of divine agency through the spirit in restoration.

Another important passage that seems to bear multiple allusions to Ezekiel 36:25-27 occurs at the end of the so-called Treatise of the Spirits in the *Rule of the Community* (1QS):

Then God, with his truth, will refine all man's works and will purify for himself the composition of man, tearing out every *spirit of injustice* from the innermost part of his flesh, and cleansing him with the *spirit of holiness* from all deeds of wickedness. He will sprinkle over him the *spirit of truth* like radiant water (in order to cleanse him) from all the abhorrence of deceit and (from) the defilement of the unclean spirit. (1QS 4:20b-22a)

Several commonalities in language connect this passage to Ezekiel 36, including the words "cleanse" (*thr*, line 21a), "flesh" (*bśr*, line 21a) "sprinkle"

---

[55]See also 1QH[a] 8:15, though the text is fragmentary: "to be strengthened by [you] ho[ly] spirit, to adhere to the truth of your covenant." On the divine agency in this hymn, see Maston, *Divine and Human Agency*, pp. 116-19.

[56]Human action clearly flows from prior divine action. For instance, the hymnist says that "I have chosen to purify my hands" but this is in response to God's prior decree of "recording" the spirit of the just man and is "in accordance with [your] will."

(*zrq*, line 21b), "water" (*mym*, line 21b), and "spirit" (*rûḥ*, lines 20 and 21 [twice]). Additionally, the references to God purifying for himself an unclean people and ripping from the innermost part the spirit of injustice are both conceptually parallel to the action of God in Ezekiel 36:25-26. The emphasis on divine action drawn from Ezekiel clarifies the potential ambiguity surrounding the meaning of *rûaḥ* in this passage. No doubt the first reference to the spirit points to a human quality, and the third one probably does as well, although it is not as clear. With the middle phrase "spirit of holiness," however, God's spirit is most likely in view, since the whole passage is rooted in Ezekiel's promise, where God is the agent of purification.[57] It is worth pointing out, however, that unlike the passages in the *Hodayot*, 1QS 4:20-22 refers to the spirit's work that is still to come. Lines 18-19 say that God "has determined an end to the existence of injustice and on the appointed time of the visitation he will obliterate it forever."[58] So despite the inaugurated eschatology of the community, they still await the total reconstitution of their community through the divine work of the spirit.

In short, while the word *rûaḥ* occurs in the midst of clear allusions to Ezekiel 36, this passage in the *Community Rule* does not refer to a present transformative work of God's spirit as promised in Ezekiel.

The Qumran scrolls exhibit diversity in terms of direct interaction with Ezekiel 36–37. Of the six clear allusions to Ezekiel 36–37 we looked at, three focus on cognitive transformation (1QH^a 5:24-25; 10:11-12; 21:14 *bottom*), two capture Ezekiel's emphasis on total reconstitution (1QH^a 8:19-20, in the present; 1QS 4:10-22, in the future), while one exposes a stark contrast with the prophet's anticipation of God's unilateral work (*4QPseudo-Ezekiel*). Thus far, there is evidence of both *Deuteronomic* and *Prophetic* motifs of restoration.[59]

---

[57]Contra Deasley, "Holy Spirit," p. 53.

[58]The future orientation can also be observed by the two occurrences of the word "then" ('z) in lines 19-20.

[59]There are a few other scrolls that come close, though not close enough to warrant a thorough consideration. For instance, in the so-called *Messianic Apocalypse* (5Q521), we read that "the Lord will consider the pious, and call the righteous by name, and *his spirit will hover upon the poor*, and he will renew the faithful with his strength" (*frag.* 2 ii 6). This is a clear allusion to Gen 1:2, and yet in line 12 it says that "he will heal the badly wounded and will make the dead live." This could refer to the resurrection of the dead from Ezek 37, but the context is not that clear

MORAL TRANSFORMATION THROUGH THE SPIRIT IN QUMRAN

Apart from clear allusions to the work of the spirit from Ezekiel 36–37, do the Scrolls make reference to the work of the spirit in moral transformation without making any explicit connection to Ezekiel? We will address this question by first examining references to "the holy spirit" and then references to "the spirit" without any qualifier, which we have not looked at in relation to Ezekiel 36–37 above.

The Holy Spirit at Qumran. While the term "holy spirit" only occurs twice in the Old Testament (Ps 51:11; Is 63:10-12), it occurs at least fifteen times among the Scrolls.[60] Seven of these thirteen may refer to God's spirit, as the term does in its Old Testament usage.[61] For our purposes, we are concerned only with those references that depict some sort of moral trans-

---

and the previous reference to *rûaḥ* clearly alludes to Gen 1:2, not Ezekiel. Another passage that could have Ezek 36–37 in mind occurs in the Zadokite fragments on skin disease (4Q266, 269, 272), in which the phrase "the spirit of life" occurs (the only occurrence of this phrase among the Scrolls). This passage, though, refers to the manner in which the body is healed from a skin disease and is therefore not set in an eschatological context (cf. 4Q418 122 ii 11). It is very unlikely that this passage alludes to the life-giving work of the spirit in Ezek 36–37. On the role of the spirit in 4Q521 and the Zadokite fragments, see Yates, *Spirit and Creation*, pp. 43-45.

[60]1QS 3:7; 4:21; 8:16; 9:3; 1QH^a 5:18; 6:12-13; 8:15, 20; 15:6-7; 20:11-12; CD 2:12; 5:11; 7:4; 4Q504 *frag.* 4 iii 5; *frags.* 1-2 v 15.

[61]The identity of the spirit is debated in some of the passages that I will not consider. For instance, some see a reference to God's holy spirit in 1QS 9:3: "When these exist in Israel in accordance with these rules in order to establish the spirit of holiness in truth." But the fact that it is the community who "establishes" this "spirit of holiness" indicates that it is probably not God's spirit that is in view. Furthermore, throughout this section, there are parallel references to holiness as a human attribute rather than a description of a divine agent: "men of perfect holiness" (8:20), "men of holiness" (8:23), "most holy community" (9:6) and "men of holiness" (9:8). Moreover, the author frequently speaks of "men of perfect behavior" (or similar phrases) with no reference to the spirit's empowerment (see 8:18, 21; 9:2, 5, 6, 8, 9). Therefore, the "spirit of holiness" in this context seems to speak of the moral quality of the men of Qumran (contra Kvalvaag, "Spirit in Human Beings," p. 16n41). In 1QSb 1:1-2, there is a reference to "those who fear [God, do] his will, keep his commandments, remain constant in his holy co[ven]ant." The last phrase translated "holy covenant" is fragmentary and could be reconstructed as "holy spirit" (*brûḥ qôdšû*), though most prefer the reading "holy covenant" (*bbrît qôdšû*). See García-Martínez and Tigchelaar, *Study Edition*, p. 105; J. T. Milik, "Recueil des Bénédictions (1QSb)," in *Qumran Cave 1*, ed. D. Barthélemy and J. T. Milik, DJD 1 (Oxford: Clarendon, 1955), p. 120; contra Barry D. Smith, "The Spirit of Holiness as Eschatological Principle of Obedience in Second-Temple Judaism," in *Christian Beginnings and the Dead Sea Scrolls*, ed. J. J. Collins and C. A. Evans (Grand Rapids: Baker Academic, 2006), p. 9. Another possible reference to God's holy spirit comes in 1QH^a 8:15, "to be strengthened by [your/a] ho[ly] spirit." While the reconstruction "holy" is probably correct, there is no way of telling whether or not the spirit is "a" or "your" holy spirit. The fragmentary nature of the text makes a reference too ambiguous to consider.

formation or enablement for obedience.[62] This leaves us with three passages, one from the *Hodayot* (1QHᵃ),[63] one from *The Rule of the Community* (1QS) and one from the *Words of the Luminaries* (4Q504). First, the *Hodayot*:

> I give you thanks, Lord, because you have sustained me with your strength, you have spread *your holy spirit* over me so that I will not stumble, you have fortified me against the wars of wickedness. (1QHᵃ 15:6-7 *DSSSE*)

In this text, the author refers to the holy spirit as God's enabling power to prevent him from moral failure. God's power is mediated through the spirit empowering the human agent toward obedience and staving off "the wars of wickedness." The hymn as a whole highlights divine agency in obedience, where God has "establish[ed] my heart" (15:13), "established me for your covenant" (15:19-20), "established my foot on the le[vel ground]" (15:25), and "straighten[ed] my steps on the paths of justice, to walk in your presence on the frontier of [lif]e along tracks of glory" (15:14-15). This passage, therefore, highlights divine agency in obedience.

Another potential reference to God's holy spirit comes at the end of an important section of 1QS, where a former member is expelled and thus forfeits the atonement for sin experienced by the covenant community:

> For it is by the *spirit of the true counsel of God* that man's paths are atoned for—all his iniquities—so that he can look at the light of life. And it is by *the holy spirit of the community* in its truth that he is cleaned from all his iniquities, and by the *spirit of uprightness and of humility* that his sin is atoned. (1QS 3:6b-8a)

We addressed this passage briefly in chapter three, where we concluded that the "holy spirit of the community" is probably not a reference to a divine agent.[64] *Rûaḥ* occurs three times in this passage, and despite Robert Kval-

---

[62]This excludes 1 QS 8:16 and CD 2:12, which refer to the holy spirit as the source of prophetic revelation, and 1QHᵃ 17:32, which refers to the holy spirit as the source of joy (see further, Deasley, "Holy Spirit," p. 50). 1QHᵃ 20:11b-13 listed above also refers to the holy spirit, but as the source of God's secret knowledge. CD 5:11 and 7:4 both use the phrase "holy spirit," but the context shows clearly that a human quality is in view.

[63]Excluding 1QHᵃ 8:19-20, which we discussed above.

[64]Contra Robert Kvalvaag, who says that the second *rûaḥ* "refers to an act of God while 3.6 and 3.8 refers to acts of humans" (Kvalvaag, "Spirit in Human Beings," p. 16). Kvalvaag goes on to conclude: "The submission and humility of the human spirit makes atonement possible, but only God, by the spirit of holiness, can purify humans and purge them of all their iniquities" (p. 16).

vaag's optimism, the second one is not "easy to identify . . . as God's spirit."[65] The last one ("spirit of uprightness and of humility") no doubt refers to a human quality, while the first two are more difficult to identify. But it does seem best to take all three as referring to God-given human qualities for three reasons. First, all three seem to be synonymous, and while the first two are ambiguous, the last one clearly refers to a human quality, suggesting that the first two do as well. Second, the second *rûaḥ* is qualified by "of the community," which is better taken as the human quality of holiness that resides in the sect. This is confirmed by the variant reading in 4Q255 of the same passage, which says: "And it is by *his* holy spirit of the community."[66] This cannot refer to God, since in the previous line the two references to "his" (i.e., "*his* iniquities," "*he* can look at") refer to the one being expelled, and not God, as does the reference that follows: "*He* is cleansed of all his iniquities."[67] And third, the "spirit of the true counsel of God," which is an agent of atonement, parallels the third *rûaḥ*—a human quality, which is also an agent of atonement. The qualification "of the true counsel of God," like the "holy spirit *of the community*," refers to the Qumran community as the emanation of truth. For these reasons, it is better to understand the middle reference to "the holy spirit" as a reference to something other than a divine agent.

The final reference to God's holy spirit comes in the *Words of the Luminaries* (4Q504), which we discussed previously in connection with the curse of the law.[68] This passage is significant since the gift of the spirit is viewed through the lens of redemptive history, much like 2 Corinthians 3 and (I would argue) Romans 8:1-13:

> You did favors to your people Israel among all [the] lands where you had exiled them, in order that they might be made to return to their heart and to turn to you and to listen to your voice, [according to] all that you com-

---

[65]Ibid.

[66]Barry Smith rightly notes that the point of this phrase, "holy spirit of the community," means that "this principle of obedience is accessible only to those who enter the community" (Smith, "Spirit of Holiness," p. 88).

[67]Ibid.

[68]This text is most likely nonsectarian; see Esther G. Chazon, "Is Divrei Ha-me'orot a Sectarian Prayer?," in *The Dead Sea Scrolls: Forty Years of Research*, ed. D. Dimant and U. Rappaport (Leiden: Brill, 1992), pp. 3-17; see also Daniel K. Falk, *Daily, Sabbath, and Festival Prayers in the Dead Sea Scrolls* (Leiden: Brill, 1998), pp. 61, 85.

manded through the hand of Moses your servant. [Fo]r you have poured your holy spirit upon us, [to be]stow your blessings to us so that we would look for you in our anguish. (4Q504 *frags.* 1-2 v 11b-16)

The reference to the holy spirit comes in a prayer to God, thanking him for taking the initiative in restoring Israel. God places "upon their heart to turn to you and to listen to your voice," which points to God's returning Israel from exile and instilling in them the heart to obey (cf. Deut 30:1-10). Following from this, the statements about God "pour[ing] your holy spirit upon us" and bestowing "your blessing to us" shift from the third person to the first person, indicating that the author views this action to have recently taken place, perhaps in forming the Qumran community or an early form of it. In any case, it is clear that the author alludes to Isaiah 44:3 for his understanding of the redemptive-historical work of the spirit in the author's present situation.[69] Both passages, Isaiah 44:3 and 4Q504 *frags.* 1-2 v 15, speak of the "spirit" (*rûḥ*) and "blessing" (*brkh*) being "poured out" (*yṣq*) on God's people on their return from exile. Though not influenced by Ezekiel 36–37, this passage depicts the unilateral work of the spirit, drawn from prophetic literature and applied to the restoration of God's people in the eschatological age.[70]

Synthesis: Qumran's View of the Spirit

The very title of this subsection is bound to elicit a violent reaction from any scholar who has worked on this issue—or on any issue in the Scrolls—since we cannot expect to find a unified view on much of anything at Qumran, let alone their understanding of the spirit.[71] Keeping this in mind, it would be safe to conclude that there was no single view, but various *views* of the spirit among

---

[69]For a thorough discussion, see Rodrigo J. Morales, *The Spirit and the Restoration of Israel*, WUNT 2.282 (Tübingen: Mohr Siebeck, 2010), pp. 52-55.

[70]Other sections in these prayers highlight God's agency in enabling obedience. For instance, 4Q504 *frags.* 1-2 ii 13-16 says that God "implant(s)" his "law in our heart, so that we do not stray from it" and "in spite of our sins you did call us . . . and you freed us from sinning against you." This seems to allude to the promise of Jer 31:31-34 where God takes the initiative in restoring Israel. Again, in *frag.* 4 iii 11-12 the author calls on God to "Circumcise the foreskin of [our heart]" and to "Strengthen our heart to do [. . .]." While the text is fragmentary, there seems to be hope that God will enable obedience. However, unlike the previous passage, this statement asks God to do something, rather than reflecting on what God has already done.

[71]Sekki's otherwise fine study *(Meaning of Ruach)* has been severely criticized on these same grounds; see, e.g., M. Horgan's review of Sekki's work in *CBQ* 54 (1992): 544-46; see also Kvalvaag, "Spirit in Human Beings," pp. 19-20.

the Scrolls. Indeed, we have seen an exegesis of Ezekiel 37 that as far as we can tell leaves out the spirit's work entirely, and also statements that depict the Qumran sect as a "community of the spirit" (1QS 3:7), showing that the *rûaḥ* was part and parcel with their identity. Some passages in the *Hodayot* allude to Ezekiel 36–37 but seem to limit the spirit's work to an individual enlightenment of hidden knowledge, while others capture the full dynamics of Ezekiel's prophecy of God's *rûaḥ*. Other passages do not draw on Ezekiel at all, and yet bear similar connotations of divine agency in moral transformation. One text in particular (4Q504 *frags.* 1-2 v 15) draws on Isaiah 44:3 to underscore the spirit's work in bringing the eschatological blessings of the covenant to the nation of Israel. In light of such diversity, we can safely conclude this short analysis with the simple observation that the Qumran literature reveals diverse perspectives on the eschatological work of the spirit that cover the full spectrum of the *Deuteronomic* and *Prophetic* paradigms of restoration.[72]

QUMRAN, PAUL AND EZEKIEL'S LIFE-GIVING SPIRIT

In the previous chapter, we saw more discontinuity than continuity between Paul and Qumran on the restoration of the curse motif, though there is one passage in the scrolls (4Q504) that reveals the latter. With the eschatological work of the spirit, there is an even spread of discontinuity and continuity. Paul believes that Ezekiel's promise of a total reconstitution of the human has begun through the present indwelling of God's holy spirit. As in the prophet, Paul believes this gift of the spirit is unilateral: no individual, community or nation is inherently worthy of the gift prior to its endowment. This perspective exhibits a good deal of continuity with two texts from Qumran where Ezekiel's promise is in view, 1QHᵃ 8:19-20 and 1QS 4:20-22, although the latter, unlike Paul, depicts the work of the spirit in wholly future terms. The pouring out of the spirit in 4Q504 also aligns well with the *Prophetic* paradigm of restoration.

---

[72]W. D. Davies goes even further by concluding that only 1QS 4:18-23 speaks of an eschatological fulfillment of the spirit drawn from the Prophets, and yet he agrees that this passage is still future from Qumran's perspective. But even in this passage, Davies does not see the same connotation of the spirit's empowerment that we find in the Old or New Testaments. "Paul and the Dead Sea Scrolls: Flesh and Spirit," in *The Scrolls and the New Testament*, ed. K. Stendahl and J. H. Charlesworth (New York: Crossroad, 1992), pp. 157-82. In contrast to Davies, Sekki believes that Qumran saw themselves as the heirs of the eschatological spirit of Ezek 36:27 (Sekki, *Meaning of Ruach*, pp. 87-88).

The sharpest point of discontinuity between Paul (and Ezekiel) and the scrolls is seen in Qumran's own commentary on Ezekiel 37, where the new life is no longer a unilateral gift but a reward for obedience. One can only wonder how the author of this commentary would get along with the hymnists of the *Hodayot,* should the question of pneumatology ever come up. In any case, several other passages in the *Hodayot* highlight the spirit's agency in obedience (1QHᵃ 5:25; 20:11-12; 21:14 *bottom*), though the byproduct is limited to cognitive transformation and therefore is not an exact parallel with Paul. To my mind, the thickest wedge that separates the Qumran literature from Paul is the sheer disparity in clear references to the spirit of God. In Paul's thirteen letters, *pneuma* occurs 145 times, most of which unambiguously refer to the holy spirit of God (or Christ), along with the 24 uses of the adjective *pneumatikos*.[73] And for most of Paul's letters, obedience can hardly be mentioned apart from the spirit's empowerment.[74] We see some similarities in Qumran, but only a small handful of passages within a large body of literature depict the *rûaḥ* as a divine agent who effects obedience (1QHᵃ 8:19-20; 15:6-7; 4Q504 *frags.* 1-2 v 15-16). Most of the 217 occurrences of *rûaḥ* in the Scrolls do not unmistakably refer to a divine agent.[75] This, I suggest, is a major point of discontinuity between Qumran's and Paul's soteriology.

---

[73]For the breakdown of the statistics, see Fee, *God's Empowering Presence,* pp. 14-36.

[74]This is true especially in Romans, 1-2 Corinthians, Galatians and Ephesians, though less so in Philippians, Colossians and the Pastorals.

[75]A. E. Sekki says that thirty-five of the 217 occurrences of *rûaḥ* refer to God's spirit, but he includes references that are either ambiguous or very unlikely (*Meaning of Ruach,* pp. 71-93). For instance, he includes 1QS 3:7 ("the holy spirit of the community") as one of the references to the spirit of God, but this is unlikely as shown above.

Excursus

Moses, Paul and the Glory of the
Old and New Covenants

We have emphasized a good amount of *discontinuity* between the old and new covenants in 2 Corinthians 3:1-7, but Paul seems to see a measure of continuity in 2 Corinthians 3:8-18. While the new covenant has more glory than the old, Paul affirms that the old covenant did have some glory. So how do we understand the seemingly negative statements about the old covenant—"letter kills" (2 Cor 3:6), "ministry of death" (2 Cor 3:7), "ministry of condemnation" (2 Cor 3:9)—in light of the seemingly positive statements that affirm a certain measure of glory in the old covenant (2 Cor 3:7-11)? To state my conclusion up front, in 2 Corinthians 3:7-18 Paul argues that the old covenant only had a measure of glory before the coming of the new, but with the coming of the new, the old now has no glory at all. So the discontinuity between the letter and spirit, or old covenant and new, is maintained.

This understanding of 2 Corinthians 3:8-18 is supported by a few key exegetical observations. First, we see that any glory belonging to the old covenant and the law that was bound to it has been "nullified" *by* the coming of the new. The much-debated use of *katargein* (2 Cor 3:7, 11, 13, 14) most likely means "to nullify, to invalidate, to render ineffectual" and not "to fade away."[76] Moreover, as Richard Hays points out, the participle *katargoumenēn* in 3:7 implies not an innate property of the noun ("glory that fades") but "an action performed upon it": the "glory . . . *has been nullified*" by something else, namely the new covenant.[77] In doing so, Paul situates his understanding of the old and new covenants firmly within the framework of salvation history. As he does in Galatians 3:15-29, Paul sees a positive role that the old

---

[76]See the thorough study of this term in Garrett, "Veiled Hearts," pp. 729-72.
[77]Hays, *Echoes*, p. 134.

covenant played in God's redemptive plan; and as he does in Romans 7:12-14, Paul sees an inherent goodness in the law. However, when the law is tethered to a heart of stone, it only leads to sin, death and condemnation. What Paul says in Romans and Galatians, then, is very much of the same cloth as his argument here in 2 Corinthians 3:8-18: the old law-covenant exhibited a measure of glory, but only for a time. God's act in Christ has nullified the old covenant and stripped the law of its condemning power for Christians.

Second, discontinuity between the old and new covenants is maintained in 2 Corinthians 3:8-18 with regard to the transforming power of the presence of God. In fact, the main point that Paul makes by bringing up Moses in the first place is revealed in 2 Corinthians 3:18 and bleeds over into 2 Corinthians 4:1-6; namely, that the old covenant only allowed one person, Moses, to gain momentary glimpses of the presence of God, while those in the new covenant gaze continually on the presence, or glory, of God in Christ.[78] As a result, they are being "transformed into the same image" (2 Cor 3:18), a motif that picks up on the previous references to the transforming work of the "letter of Christ" (2 Cor 3:3) and the "life-giving spirit" (2 Cor 3:6). This is set in stark contrast to the Israelites of Moses' day, who were not even allowed—or able—to catch a mere glimpse of God's glory being reflected as it was off the face of Moses. The veil that prevented the Israelites from being transformed by the presence of God still remains over the hearts of those who seek to be transformed by the old law-covenant—or by letters of commendation written by Jesus-denying super-apostles (cf. 2 Cor 11:4-5)!

Third, this emphasis on the transforming power of the presence of God (which correlates well with the temple motif so prevalent in the Corinthian correspondence; e.g., 1 Cor 3:16; 6:19-20; 2 Cor 6:16-17) helps make sense of 2 Corinthians 3:13—perhaps the most disputed verse in the entire passage. Here, Paul says that the veil prevented the Israelites from "gaz[ing] *at the outcome* (*eis to telos*) of what was being brought to an end." Since *katargein* does not mean "fade away" but "nullify" (or "render ineffective"), the *telos*

---

[78]The figure of Moses is complex and variegated in this passage. It seems that Paul refers to Moses as the mediator of the old covenant (2 Cor 3:7, 13), a synonym for the old covenant itself (2 Cor 3:15), and at the same time has him "prefigure Christian experience" (implied in 2 Cor 3:16-18; see Hays, *Echoes*, p. 144).

cannot be the fading nature of the old covenant ministry—which would not make sense anyway of Exodus 34 or of Paul's argument here. (Why would the Israelites need to keep from seeing the transitory nature of the old covenant?) Rather, in keeping with the purpose of the transforming presence of God in 2 Corinthians 3:18, the *telos* of that which is being nullified most likely refers to the same: the presence of God which was fully revealed in Christ (2 Cor 3:18; 4:4, 6).[79] The presence of God was a reality in the old covenant, but it was hidden behind a veil in the temple and merely reflected off the face of Moses at Sinai. But under the new covenant, the life-giving spirit has unleashed on those who "turn to the Lord" (2 Cor 3:16) the full presence of God in Christ.

Paul admits that the old covenant had a measure of glory, but this glory was not able to transform the Israelites because it was veiled both then and now. The discontinuity between the old and new covenants articulated clearly in 2 Corinthians 3:1-7 is maintained in 2 Corinthians 3:8-18, albeit through an unexpected turn in the argument.

---

[79]"Behind the veil is nothing other than the glory of God, which is made visible in Jesus Christ" (Hays, *Echoes,* p. 146). The parallel between the "face of Moses" (2 Cor 3:7) and the "face of Christ" (2 Cor 4:6), both of which reflect the glory of God, strengthens this interpretation of *telos.*

5

ANTHROPOLOGICAL PESSIMISM
IN PAUL AND QUMRAN

In our study thus far we have seen that Paul and Qumran had somewhat diverse opinions about how God has rescued the "Israel of God" from the curse of the law (chapter three), and about the nature of the spirit's eschatological work among their communities (chapter four). We have seen points of continuity and discontinuity with both motifs, though with the curse of the law, the dominant picture was one of discontinuity. Regarding the spirit's work, on some occasions Qumran and Paul see eye to eye, while on others the unilateral work of the spirit is clearer in Paul than in Qumran (compare, e.g., 4QPseudo-Ezekiel with Rom 8:1-13).

In this chapter, I will return to a theme that arose in chapter two, when we looked at prophetic literature in the Old Testament: anthropological pessimism. As we saw through Jeremiah and Ezekiel, humanity's inability to repent and return to the law necessitates a unilateral act of God. Conversely, the *Deuteronomic* promise that God will forgive a penitent nation requires a degree of human ability in repenting and returning. Again, a spectrum of anthropological assumptions are evident in the Old Testament, but in terms of emphasis, the restoration motifs from the Prophets exhibit more pessimism than the Deuteronomists.

In the following, we will examine the anthropological assumptions of Paul and Qumran. But first, we will get our bearings by situating our approach in the broader discussion regarding anthropological pessimism in Paul and Judaism.

ANTHROPOLOGY IN PAUL AND JUDAISM: A BRIEF SKETCH

In *Paul and Palestinian Judaism*, E. P. Sanders argued for a good measure of continuity between Paul and Judaism in terms of their soteriological structures. But when responses to Sanders's work came out, several argued that the soteriological pattern in Judaism described by Sanders seems synergistic, while Paul's is clearly monergistic.[1] In other words, Judaism believed that people were capable of contributing something to their salvation, while Paul believed that people could contribute nothing to their salvation. Covenantal nomism itself, the critics say, assumes a rather positive view of the human condition, while Paul clearly had a pessimistic view. While some scholars pointed this out early on, a full-scale treatment of the anthropology was lacking until Timo Laato published his dissertation, *Paul and Judaism: An Anthropological Approach*.[2] Laato argued that Paul's pessimistic view of the human condition calls for a more radical emphasis on divine agency in salvation. But after surveying passages from Second Temple and Rabbinic writings, Laato concludes that Judaism believed that humankind has "free will," "has also the power always to *do* good," and even though they may have "an inborn propensity" to do evil, they do not have a "hereditary compulsion to disobedience." In short, "it is self-evident that the Jews generally hold fast to human power of decision in the area of soteriology."[3]

Many opponents of Sanders and the New Perspective have taken Laato's conclusion at face value. They have assumed that Laato's study ended the discussion, hammering the proverbial nail in the coffin. For instance, P. T. O'Brien, a defender of discontinuity in the second volume of *Justification and Variegated Nomism*, simply cites Laato's study and then concludes that "the anthropological presuppositions of Judaism clearly differed from those of the apostle."[4] Early Jewish anthropology was

---

[1]E.g., R. H. Gundry, "Grace, Works, and Staying Saved in Paul," *Bib* 66 (1985): 1-38, and Timo Eskola, *Theodicy and Predestination in Pauline Soteriology*, WUNT 2.100 (Tübingen: Mohr Siebeck, 1998).

[2]Timo Laato, *Paul and Judaism: An Anthropological Approach* (Atlanta: Scholars Press, 1995). Laato's original dissertation was published in 1991 as *Paulus und das Judentum: Anthropologische Erwagungen* (Turku, Finland: Åbo Akademis Förlag, 1991).

[3]Laato, *Paul and Judaism*, p. 73.

[4]Peter T. O'Brien, "Was Paul a Covenantal Nomist?" in *Justification and Variegated Nomism*, Vol. 2: *The Paradoxes of Paul*, ed. D. A. Carson, P. T. O'Brien and M. A. Seifrid (Grand Rapids: Baker Academic, 2004), p. 270.

"thoroughly optimistic"; free will and the ability to obey are considered inherent to humankind. O'Brien does not revisit the early Jewish texts themselves to see if these things are so; Laato's study is proof enough. O'Brien, though, admits in a footnote that "the single but significant exception" to Judaism's optimistic view of humanity "is the Qumran literature."[5] More on this anon.

Is Laato's work the final word on anthropology? Despite much scholarly faith in his study, I think there is much more to be said. Laato's claims would indeed have devastating effects on those who argue for soteriological continuity, but his study lacks in one major area—evidence. His conclusions are governed by a mere six pages of isolated quotations from Jewish writings, mostly Rabbinic material.[6] There is no exegesis, no interaction with opposing scholarly views, only a handful of quotations from Second Temple literature. Moreover, the passages cited give only a caricatured one-sided portrait of an early Jewish view of the human condition. One could easily turn around and cite six other passages that would sound quite predestinarian, even within the same document.[7]

While some scholars have simply adopted Laato's conclusion, others have re-examined the evidence. Stephen Westerholm, for instance, revisited the literature more thoroughly. Even though his twenty-five page essay is a broad survey, Westerholm's treatment is characteristically cautious. He carefully examined the literature—including Qumran—and made moderate conclusions, exhibiting a calm awareness of the limitations that such broad-brush surveys necessarily carry. Still, Westerholm arrives at a conclusion similar to Laato's: "Paul's anthropology, in corresponding to his 'soteriology,' is a good deal more 'negative' than the anthropology typical

---

[5] O'Brien, "Was Paul a Covenantal Nomist?" p. 271n80; see too Laato, *Paul and Judaism*, p. 72.

[6] Laato, *Paul and Judaism*, pp. 67-72. The only texts that he cites from the Second Temple period are: Sir 15:11-20; *Pss. Sol.* 9:4-5; *4 Ezra* 8:55-58; *2 Bar.* 54:15, 19; 85:7; Philo, *Quod Deus* 10, 45, 50. His Rabbinic references include: *Avot* 3:15; *Sifre* Deut 11:26; *Mekh. Ex* 15:26; *BT Berakhot* 33b; *BT Niddah* 16b.

[7] For instance, *Pss. Sol.* 9:5 is cited by Laato ("Our works are in the choosing and power of our souls, to do right and wrong in the works of our hands"), while 16:3-4 is ignored ("Thus my soul was drawn away from the Lord God of Israel, unless the Lord had come to my aid with his everlasting mercy. He jabbed me as a horse is goaded to keep it awake; my savior and protector at all times saved me").

among his contemporary Jews."[8] The situation is more complex when it comes to the Scrolls, however. Some passages clearly affirm that "human[s] are deemed able to do both good and evil"[9] yet others insist that "each individual deed done by the righteous and the wicked alike has been predetermined by God."[10] With regard to the Qumran literature, Westerholm concludes that anthropologically, "the Qumran literature occupies a halfway position between"[11] Paul and the rest of Judaism.

The question of continuity and discontinuity between Paul and Judaism regarding the human condition, therefore, has not been sufficiently answered. There is much work to be done. Such an important topic no doubt deserves a book-length treatment, and I acknowledge the limitations of treating it in a single chapter. But treat it we must, and this chapter serves as a modest contribution to the task. We will begin by looking at Paul, focusing our study, in the words of Westerholm, on "the question of the capacity of humankind."[12] In other words, *does humanity possess the unaided ability to initiate a return to God and obey his laws?* The Chronicler and (to some extent) the Deuteronomists say yes, but Jeremiah and Ezekiel say no. Where on the spectrum do we situate Paul and Qumran?

ANTHROPOLOGICAL PESSIMISM IN PAUL

Two sections in Paul's letter to the Romans are pertinent: Romans 1–3 and 5–8.[13] Paul begins by affirming that all people have rebelled against their creator and stand under divine wrath (Rom 1:18-23). In an act of judgment, God gives them over to their sinful desires, which has the effect of pushing humanity further down its chosen path of destruction (Rom 1:24-32). The Jew fares no better than the Gentile in this regard (Rom 2:1-29). All people

---

[8]Stephen Westerholm, "Paul's Anthropological 'Pessimism' in Its Jewish Context," in *Divine and Human Agency in Paul and His Cultural Environment*, ed. J. M. G. Barclay and S. Gathercole (New York: T & T Clark, 2006), p. 97.

[9]Ibid., p. 94.

[10]Ibid., p. 95.

[11]Ibid., p. 98.

[12]Westerholm, "Paul's Anthropological Pessimism," p. 71.

[13]Romans reveals Paul's most comprehensive understanding of humanity's condition. Paul uses the term *hamartia* ("sin") forty-eight times in Romans, which constitutes nearly three quarters of Paul's sixty-four uses. Moreover, forty-one of the forty-eight occurrences in Romans refer not to "sins" as specific misdeeds, but to "sin" as a singular enslaving power over humanity. See James D. G. Dunn, *The Theology of Paul the Apostle* (Grand Rapids: Eerdmans, 1998), p. 111.

regardless of their ethnicity are "under sin" (Rom 3:9). There is no one who is righteous, none who seek after God, and no one who does good (Rom 3:10-11). "All have turned aside; together they have become worthless" (Rom 3:12). As Paul says elsewhere, everyone is "imprisoned . . . under sin" (Gal 3:22). The only way humanity can turn to God is if God first turns to them through the intervention of Christ (Rom 3:21-26). Performing "works of the law" is a dead end and only makes matters worse (Rom 3:19-20; 4:15). In short, humanity does not possess the unaided capacity to turn to God.

Paul's argument in Romans 5–8 is even more explicit. Humanity's moral condition at the time of redemption is characterized by wickedness; they were "ungodly," "sinners" and "enemies" of God (Rom 5:6-11; 8:7-8). And such rebellion is rooted not just in their sins—particular transgressions—but in their condition, which dates back to Eden. As sons and daughters of Adam, humanity is born condemned (Rom 5:12-21); they do not merely commit acts of sin but possess an inherently sinful nature. Everyone is born "dead in [their] trespasses and sins" and are "by nature children of wrath" (Eph 2:1-3).

The inability to turn from sin is magnified by Paul's statements about sin as an enslaving power. For Paul, sin is not simply something humans choose, but sin chooses us. It controls us, enslaves us, deceives us, manufactures lust in our hearts and ultimately kills us (Rom 6:6, 17-23; 7:8, 11, 13, 17). Sin "reigns" over Adam's race (Rom 5:21), confining all its subjects to slavery and death (Rom 6:6; cf. 1 Cor 15:56). Unless God intervenes to reconstitute our nature, we will remain hostile to God and unable to please him (Rom 8:6-8).

The idea of sin as an enslaving power is taken further and may include suprahuman forces.[14] In Romans, sin as an outside force is left ambiguous; the connection between sin and demonic powers is not articulated. Elsewhere, however, Paul says that "the god of this world has blinded the minds of the unbelievers, to keep them from seeing the light of the gospel" (2 Cor 4:4), and that "the prince of the power of the air . . . is now at work in the sons of disobedience" (Eph 2:2).[15] This does not mean that humans are mere

---

[14]Among others, see J. Louis Martyn, *Galatians: A New Translation with Introduction and Commentary*, AB (New York: Doubleday, 1997), pp. 370-73, 393-406; M. C. de Boer, "Paul and Jewish Apocalyptic Eschatology," *Apocalyptic and the New Testament: Essays in Honor of J. Louis Martyn*, ed. J. Marcus and M. L. Soards (Sheffield: JSOT, 1989), pp. 169-90.

[15]Although debated, Paul's mention of unbelievers being "enslaved to the elementary principles [or spirits] of the world" (Gal 4:3) could also refer to human enslavement to demonic forces.

victims, enslaved to sin against their will. Demonic and other suprahuman forces only ensure that humans will not escape their predicament under their own power. Again, humankind does not possess the unaided ability to turn to God.

Central to Paul's pessimistic anthropology is the term "flesh" (sarx),[16] a word Paul uses with "bewildering variety."[17] Sometimes sarx simply denotes the human body or part of it; other times it emphasizes the mortality or frailty of humankind, which is its typical OT meaning. In some places, though, Paul uses sarx to refer to the moral depravity of humankind. Paul speaks of humankind's sinful nature as our flesh (Rom 7:18; 8:3; 13:14), as in "works of the flesh" or "desires of the flesh" (Gal 5:16-24), and sometimes sarx describes humanity's unregenerate state, when "we were living in the flesh" dominated by "our sinful passions" (Rom 7:5; cf. 2 Cor 10:3; Gal 2:20; Phil 1:22). But does the term sarx say anything about humankind's capacity to obey God? In at least one passage, it does:

> For those who are according to the flesh, set their minds on the things of the flesh, but those who are according to the spirit, the things of the spirit. For the mindset of the flesh is death, but the mindset of the spirit is life and peace. Because the mindset of the flesh is at enmity toward God, for it does not submit to the law of God, *for neither is it able to* (oude gar dynatai). And those who are in the flesh are not able to please God. (Rom 8:5-8)

Paul's pessimism about humanity's ability to turn to God could not be more clear. Paul here separates humanity into two camps: those in the flesh and those in the spirit. The assumption is that believers are in the spirit and unbelievers are in the flesh; there is no middle ground. Romans 8:7-8 paint a portrait of humanity similar to that of the Prophets. Unbelievers, being in the "flesh," not only fail to submit to the law, but are unable to do so (Rom

---

[16]Sarx ("flesh") is used ninety-one times in his thirteen letters, twenty-six times in Romans alone. For a survey of the complicated issues related to Paul's use of this term, see Dunn, *Theology of Paul*, pp. 62-73; Robert Jewett, *Paul's Anthropological Terms: A Study of Their Use in Conflict Settings* (Leiden: Brill, 1971), pp. 95-116.

[17]John M. G. Barclay, *Obeying the Truth: Paul's Ethics in Galatians* (Minneapolis: Fortress, 1991), p. 203. For an investigation into the background of Paul's flesh-spirit antithesis, see Jörg Frey, "Flesh and Spirit in the Palestinian Jewish Sapiential Tradition and in the Qumran Texts: An Inquiry into the Background of Pauline Usage," in *The Wisdom Texts from Qumran and the Development of Sapiential Thought*, ed. Charlotte Hempel, Armin Lange and Hermann Lichtenberger, BETL 159 (Leuven: University Press, 2002), pp. 367-404.

8:7). Paul then makes a more general statement that everyone outside of Christ lacks the ability to please God (Rom 8:8).[18] Paul does not believe that humans possess the capacity to turn to God apart from prior divine intervention (cf. Rom 8:1-4).

The depravity of the mind (*nous*) and heart (*kardia*) also capture Paul's pessimistic anthropology. *Nous* refers to the deliberative or intellectual aspect of humankind, which includes, in some cases, the will (as in, e.g., Rom 12:1-2; 14:5; Eph 4:23). A desperate picture of sin's effect on the mind is painted in Romans 1:28: "God gave them up to a *debased mind* (*adokimon noun*) to do what ought not to be done." The phrase "debased mind" does not just mean that intelligence is lacking or that humanity is "void of discernment."[19] Such a mind, rather, "perversely rejects that which it knows to be true."[20] Humanity's will is so bent toward evil (Rom 1:18-32) that it lacks the volitional capacity to turn to God under its own power. The same is true of the heart of man (*kardia*). *Kardia* is sometimes used interchangeably with "mind" (Rom 1:21; 2 Cor 3:14-15), but it appears to be more central to the human person, encompassing the mind and including emotions, desires and convictions, which inform beliefs and actions (Rom 9:2; 10:1; 2 Cor 2:4; Phil 1:6-7; cf. Rom 5:5; 6:17; 10:9-10; 1 Cor 4:5).[21] Romans 1:21 underscores the depth of sin's infection of the heart: "Although they knew God, they did not glorify God nor did they give thanks, but they became worthless in their reasonings and *their senseless hearts were darkened*" (*eskotisthē hē asynetos autōn kardia*). "The senseless" (*hē asynetos*) heart depicts one who not only fails to seek after God (Rom 10:19-20; cf. Sir 15:7), but one who has been stripped of all autonomous ability to obey.[22] Humanity goes from bad to worse.

Much more could be said about Paul's pessimistic anthropology, but the

---

[18]On the flip side, believers are frequently described as pleasing God (1 Cor 7:32-34; 1 Thess 4:1); see R. Jewett, *Romans: A Commentary*, Hermeneia (Minneapolis: Westminster John Knox, 2007), p. 488-89.

[19]F. Godet, *Commentary on St. Paul's Epistle to the Romans*, trans. Talbot W. Chambers (Grand Rapids: Kregel, 1998 [1883]), p. 109.

[20]Jewett, *Anthropological Terms*, p. 387; see also Jewett, *Romans*, p. 182.

[21]Kyle Wells, "Grace, Obedience, and the Hermeneutics of Agency: Paul and His Jewish Contemporaries on the Transformation of the Heart" (Ph.D. diss., Durham University, 2009), p. 191; Dunn, *Theology*, p. 75.

[22]See Wells, "Grace," pp. 191-92.

point is not a major contention among scholars.[23] Paul believes that humanity lacks the unaided capacity to turn to God.

Anthropological Pessimism in the Dead Sea Scrolls

Most studies on Jewish and Pauline anthropology recognize that the Scrolls present a pessimistic view of humankind that is unmatched by other Jewish texts. Even O'Brien, Westerholm and Laato, all of whom think that Judaism on the whole has an optimistic anthropology, believe that the Dead Sea Scrolls are an exception. However, few have taken a sufficient look at the anthropology of Paul and Qumran with soteriological questions in mind.[24] In the following, we will first compare Romans 1–3 with the *Damascus Document* 2–3, which employ analogous arguments. We will then situate our findings within the context of the Scrolls as a whole. Finally, we will look at the one document that feels notably Pauline in its anthropology: the *Hodayot*.

Anthropological Assumptions in Romans 1–3 and the **Damascus Document 2–3.** To my knowledge, no scholar has recognized the striking similarities between Romans 1:18–3:26 and CD 2:14–3:20, yet the resemblance begs for analysis. The authors follow the same pattern of thought to depict God's solution to the plight of humanity; their arguments, however, are fueled by different anthropological assumptions. As noted above, Romans 1:18–3:20 asserts that all humanity, Israel included, is under sin and incapable of turning to God. The solution to such a plight is God's intervention through the atoning sacrifice of Christ (Rom 3:21-26), which satisfies God's wrath and creates a new covenant community. This general line of thought is curiously close to CD 2–3, where all humanity, Israel included, falls headlong into sin and stands under the deathly consequences of their re-

---

[23]For Paul's pessimistic anthropology, see Dunn, *Theology of Paul,* pp. 51-127; Thomas R. Schreiner, *Paul, Apostle of God's Glory in Christ: A Pauline Theology* (Downers Grove, IL: IVP Academic, 2001), pp. 127-50; Wells, "Grace," pp. 187-210; Jason Maston, *Divine and Human Agency in Second Temple Judaism and Paul: A Comparative Study,* WUNT 2.297 (Tübingen: Mohr Siebeck, 2010), pp. 141-52; Simon Gathercole, "Sin in God's Economy," in Barclay and Gathercole, *Divine and Human Agency in Paul,* pp. 158-72, among many others. Debates about Paul's pessimistic anthropology surround his view of Adam, the origin of the fall and the entrance of evil, but none of these change the conclusion we have made about humanity's capacity to turn to God.

[24]Both Wells ("Grace") and Maston (*Divine and Human Agency*) are notable exceptions, though Maston's work is limited to the *Hodayot*.

bellion (CD 2:14–3:11). The only solution is God's intervention in forming a new covenant community with the Qumranites (CD 3:12-20).

There is a good deal of overlap between CD and Romans. First, the texts move from plight to solution in much the same way. CD describes the plight of all humanity—which includes Israel (CD 2:14–3:11)—and then points to God's eschatological intervention as the solution (CD 3:12-20). Paul's argument flows in the same direction: the plight of all humanity (Rom 1:18-32)—which includes Israel (Rom 2:1-29; 3:10-20)—is met with God's eschatological intervention (Rom 3:21-26). Second, both narratives emphasize humanity's rebellion against their creator (CD 2:21; 3:7; Rom 1:18-23) and highlight their disobedience against God's commandments (CD 2:18, 21; 3:5-6, 8; Rom 1:18-32; 2:1-5, 17-24). Third, both narratives say that God's wrath is poured out toward those who break his commandments. For Paul, the wrath of God is at work against wayward humanity now (Rom 1:18-32; 3:5) and will be poured out at the final judgment on the wicked (Rom 2:5-11; 3:19-20), while CD situates the outpouring of God's wrath in Israel's history (CD 2:21; 3:8). Fourth, CD and Romans consider death to be the consequence of rebellion (Rom 1:32; 3:12-18). For Paul, breaking God's commandments makes one worthy of death (Rom 1:32), and everyone is guilty (Rom 2:7-13). Sin has transformed humanity into a walking corpse (Rom 3:12-18). The author of CD views humanity's predicament along the same lines. CD narrates the effects of the "guilty inclination" (CD 2:20-21) that has burrowed its way into humanity's heart, effecting death through all generations (CD 3:7, 9-11).[25] Death and wrath reign as humankind falls away from its creator. Fifth, both texts highlight the sins of Israel. This is fundamental to Paul's argument, where both Jews and Gentiles are under God's wrath (Rom 2:17–3:9), and CD makes the same point. All humanity, including Israel, are guilty of sin and have fallen away, though for Qumran—and this is where Qumran and Paul part company—Abraham, the patriarchs and the founders of the Qumran community are notable exceptions (CD 3:2-5a, 12-14). Lastly, both Paul and CD describe the formation of a community. For Qumran, the community consists of those who "remained steadfast in God's precepts" (CD 3:12); for Paul, those who are "of the faith of Jesus"

---

[25]Terms connoting death or expulsion (e.g., "cut off," CD 3:1, 7, 9; "died," 3:9; "perished," 3:10) abound and signify the consequence of submitting to the "guilty inclination."

(Rom 3:26; cf. Rom 3:22; 4:1-25) are beneficiaries of God's intervention.

Such abundant resonances ensure that we are not forcing two disparate texts to dialogue with each other against their wills. The points of comparison, weighed cumulatively, suggest similar patterns of thought stemming from comparable beliefs about the human dilemma. Both narratives about God's eschatological intervention provide solutions to humanity's condition. But do Romans 1-3 and CD 2-3 portray humanity in equally pessimistic terms? A close look at their solutions in light of their plights suggests that they do not. There is considerable discontinuity between Paul and Qumran in terms of humanity's capacity to turn to God. Qumran's humanity contains the unaided ability to render unto God sufficient obedience to make them worthy of God's intervention.

> But with those who remained steadfast in God's precepts, with those who were left from among them, God established his covenant with Israel[26] forever, *to reveal (lglôt)* to them *hidden things (nstrôt)*[27] in which all Israel had gone astray: his holy Sabbaths and his glorious feasts, his just stipulations and his truthful paths, and the wishes of his will *which if a man does he will live by them* (Lev 18:5). (CD 3:12b-16a)

A select portion of obedient Israelites ("those who remained steadfast . . . who were left among them") elicit God's redeeming activity—they alone are worthy recipients of God's saving intervention. But the notion that some Israelites "remained steadfast" in God's commandments *prior to* God's saving act is foreign to Paul. Therefore, E. P. Sanders's claim that God's revelatory act in CD 3:13-14 "emphasize[s] the initiating grace of God" cannot be substantiated.[28] Divine action is a response to human initiative, and this

---

[26]The term *Israel* here is used to designate the community as elsewhere in CD (see 1:4-5; 4:4-5; 12:2; 15:5; cf. 1QS 2:22); see further P. R. Davies, "The Judaisms in the Dead Sea Scrolls: The Case of the Messiah," in *The Dead Sea Scrolls in Their Historical Context*, ed. Graeme A. Auld, et al. (Edinburgh: T & T Clark, 2000), pp. 219-32 (esp. 31-32); Joseph M. Baumgarten and Daniel R. Schwartz, "Damascus Document (CD)," in *The Dead Sea Scrolls: Hebrew, Aramaic, and Greek Texts with English Translations: Damascus Document, War Scroll, and Related Documents*, ed. James H. Charlesworth (Louisville, KY: Westminster John Knox, 1995), p. 17; contra Markus Bockmuehl, "1QS and Salvation at Qumran," in *Justification and Variegated Nomism*, Vol. 1: *The Complexities of Second Temple Judaism*, ed. D. A. Carson, P. T. O'Brien and M. A. Seifrid (Grand Rapids: Baker Academic, 2001), pp. 381-414 (esp. 393n44); E. P. Sanders, *Paul and Palestinian Judaism: A Comparison of Patterns of Religion* (Philadelphia: Fortress, 1977), p. 247.

[27]These two phrases probably allude to Deut 29:29 (29:28 MT); cf. 4Q508 2, 4.

[28]Sanders, *Paul and Palestinian Judaism*, p. 269.

is quite different from Paul in Romans 1–3. Paul in Romans also traces humanity's plight (Rom 1:18-32), including Israel (Rom 2:1-29), and his argument resonates with many underlying motifs in CD's narrative, as we have seen. But Paul moves beyond his Jewish counterpart by insisting that there were none who remained steadfast in God's commandments prior to God's saving action in Christ (Rom 3:21-26). The mere suggestion that God would justify his wicked enemies (Rom 4:4-5; 5:6-11) radicalizes Paul's anthropological assumptions. Humanity does not possess the unaided capacity to turn to God.

Again, assessing Romans 1–3 alongside CD 2–3 would be unfair if the two passages betrayed different preoccupations, but the passages are strikingly similar. Both documents are didactic treatises aimed at informing their respective communities about their redemptive historical situation and God's ethical demands that follow.[29] The overlap in rhetorical movement and theological assertions only serves to highlight the stark difference in their anthropological assumptions. Paul's view of humanity is decidedly more pessimistic than the author of CD's.

Qumran's more optimistic view of humanity is evident elsewhere. As we saw in chapter three, CD 1 depicts the original founders of the community as possessing the unaided ability to initiate a return to God: "God appraised their deeds, because they sought him with an undivided heart, and raised up for them a Teacher of Righteousness, in order to direct them in the path of his heart" (CD 1:10-11). God's gift of the Teacher, who would rightly interpret the law, came in response to their behavior. This passage assumes the unaided capacity to turn to God on the part of the covenanters, and there is no clear act of God that preceded or enabled this turn.[30] Other passages that

---

[29]P. R. Davies argues that CD 2:14–4:12 is "catechetical" and is directed to "initiates in the process of making their choice" whether to join the community or not. Philip R. Davies, *The Damascus Covenant* (Sheffield: JSOT Press, 1983), p. 77. M. Knibb is similar, and probably correct, when he says that this discourse is oriented toward those who are either on the verge of entering the community or those who have just recently entered. Michael A. Knibb, *The Qumran Community* (Cambridge: Cambridge University Press, 1987), pp. 27-28. J. Murphy-O'Connor takes a different view, believing that the audience is not part of the Essene movement; hence, his description of this section as a "missionary document"; see his "An Essene Missionary Document? CD II, 14–VI, 1," *RB* 78 (1971): 201-29.

[30]Through personal conversations, Joel Willitts pointed out that God's preservation of a remnant highlights the priority of divine agency. For instance, CD 1:4-5 says: "But when he remembered the covenant with the forefathers, he saved a remnant for Israel and did not deliver them up to

depict the community's deliverance from the curse of the law, which we looked at in chapter two, confirm the point. The *Temple Scroll, Manual of Discipline* and *Miqṣat Maʿaśeh ha-Tôrâ* all contain passages that assume that the community retained the unaided ability to turn to God *prior to* his eschatological saving act.[31] 4QPseudo-Ezekiel even goes against what his biblical counterpart says about the human condition. Ezekiel's anthropology, much like Paul's, is exceptionally pessimistic—there are none who do good. But the author of *Pseudo-Ezekiel* does not see his own situation in such dismal terms. Unlike Ezekiel's dry bones, the Qumran exegete sees "many in Israel who love your name and walk on the paths of [justice]" (4Q385 2:2-3). This text, therefore, "stands on completely different anthropological premises"[32] than both Ezekiel and Paul. Again, as we have seen in CD and other documents, Israel is able to turn to God unassisted. Though humans are weak, there are still some who seek after God. They have not all turned aside.

Everything changes, however, when we read the hymns of Qumran.

Anthropological Pessimism in the Hodayot. The *Hodayot* (hereafter 1QHª) paint a pessimistic portrait of the human condition that on the whole goes far beyond the passages above. 1QHª is the only Qumran document that extensively and consistently portrays humans as utterly sinful, even depicting *those who are part of the covenant* as wicked, frail and unable to please God apart from divine grace. For the authors of the *Hodayot*, they are filled with sin (5:21-22; 9:22; 17:13), composed of "dust" and are mere "vessels of clay" (5:21; 11:23-24), governed by a "perverse spirit" (5:21), belonging to "the assembly of worms" and "wicked humanity" (11:9-10), and have "forsaken your covenant" (12:36) even after they have entered it. While the hymnists believe that they may be more righteous than some of their wicked neighbors, compared to God they have no righteousness.[33] Therefore, when judgment day comes, their only hope is to throw themselves on the mercy of God (17:14-17; cf. 9:25).

---

destruction." But this statement does not specify the divine-human relationship in the preservation process. As Wells rightly notes, CD 1:3-4 "says nothing as to whether the remnant's seeking was within their power or somehow spurred by God; it only tells us that the previous covenant was a necessary condition for God's redeeming act" (Wells, "Grace," p. 71n94).

[31] See the discussion in chapter three.

[32] Wells, "Grace," p. 67.

[33] In the *Hodayot*, righteousness does not belong to humans (1QHª 12:31) but to God alone (1QHª 4:32; 6:26; 7:37; 8:27, 29; 9:28; 12:32, et al.) See Maston, *Divine and Human Agency*, p. 87.

If these authors were to enter the age-old debate about Romans 7, they would no doubt conclude that Paul describes his life as a believer. They would be eager to affirm, with Paul, that "nothing good dwells in ... my flesh" and that they have been "sold under sin" (Rom 7:14, 18). Or in their own words: "I am a creature of clay, fashioned with water, a foundation of shame and a source of impurity, an oven of iniquity and a building of sin, a spirit of error and depravity without knowledge, terrified by your just judgments. What can I say which is not known?" (1QH^a 9:21-23 *DSSSE*). Such anthropological pessimism, pervasive throughout 1QH^a, is evident in other hymns at Qumran. The *Manual of Discipline* concludes with a hymn that depicts mankind in most desperate terms: "I belong to evil humankind, to the assembly of unfaithful flesh; my failings, my iniquities, my sins, [...] with depravities of my heart, belong to the assembly of worms and of those who walk in darkness" (1QS 11:9-10 *DSSSE*).[34] The language here is very close to what we find throughout the *Hodayot*. The author affirms humanity's degenerate condition even after they have become community members. Another text known as the *Barki Nafshi* hymns (4Q434-38)[35] assumes a pessimistic anthropology similar to the *Hodayot*:

> In the abundance of his mercy he has favoured the needy and has opened their eyes so that they see his paths, and their ear[s] so that they hear his teaching. He has circumcised the foreskin of their hearts and has saved them because of his mercy and has set their feet firm on the path ... he turned darkness into light before them, and rough paths into a plain. (4Q434 *frag.* 1 i 3-4, 9 *DSSSE*)

Unlike CD 3, where divine agency is conditioned on human initiative, for this hymn the sole agent responsible for turning human darkness into light is God. And in contrast to 1QS 5:5, where heart circumcision is an act of man, here it is God who has "circumcised the foreskin of their hearts and

---

[34]Cf. 1QS 10:11; 11:20-22.

[35]The *Barki Nafshi* ("Bless, O My Soul") hymns refer to a series of five texts (4Q434-38), which are probably of sectarian origin. The title of the work derives from Ps 103 and Ps 104, which open with the same phrase: "Bless, O My Soul, the Lord." See further David Seely, "Implanting Pious Qualities as a Theme in the *Barki Nafshi* Hymns," in *The Dead Sea Scrolls Fifty Years After Their Discovery: Proceedings of the Jerusalem Congress, July 20-25, 1997*, ed. L. H. Schiffman, et al. (Jerusalem: Israel Exploration Society/Shrine of the Book, Israel Museum, 2000), pp. 322-23; David Seely, "The 'Circumcised Heart' in 4Q434 *Barki Nafshi*," *RevQ* 17 (1996): 527-35 (esp. 527-28).

saved them because of his mercy." Such need for divine agency in salvation reveals a pessimistic anthropology.[36]

Summary of the Qumran Literature. It would seem that Qumran has space for the same type of pessimism that Paul assumes throughout his letters, especially in Romans, and scholars have indeed taken this view based largely on the *Hodayot*.[37] But what do we do with the seemingly inconsistent portrait of the human condition among the Scrolls? How do we reconcile the anthropological pessimism in, say, 1QH[a] with the optimism in CD?

One answer is that we do not. Qumran exhibits diverse perspectives on the human condition: 1QH[a] is pessimistic while CD is more optimistic. If we take this approach, we could conclude that there is continuity between Paul and 1QH[a], *Barki Nafshi* and other hymns, while there is discontinuity between Paul and CD, 4QMMT and other didactic texts. But there are other factors to consider.

First, there is the question of genre. Anthropological pessimism in the Scrolls is largely confined to hymnic material (1QH[a], 1QS 10–11, 4Q434; 4Q504), while anthropological optimism dominates ethical or didactic material (CD, 1QS 1–9). This raises an important question: How much of Qumran's pessimistic anthropology is dictated by the genre rather than the actual beliefs of the community? On one extreme, Chris VanLandingham wants to discount the pessimism altogether, since hymnic material is not a suitable picture of what people actually believe.[38] But most scholars are not ready to dismiss the material so quickly.[39] Jason Maston more cautiously points out that not all hymns have a thoroughgoing pessimistic anthropology. In some

---

[36]As we have seen in chapters three and four, the *Words of the Luminaries* (4Q504) credits heart circumcision to the work of God (4Q504 *frag.* 4 iii 11), recognizes the priority of the spirit's work in communal repentance (4Q504 *frags.* 1-2 v 15-16) and highlights divine agency in restoration from exile (4Q504 *frags.* 1-2 v 13-14), all of which assume a measure of pessimism in the human condition.

[37]See, e.g., Udo Schnelle, *The Apostle Paul: His Life and Theology*, trans. M. Eugene Boring (Grand Rapids: Baker, 2003), pp. 504-5.

[38]"The Theology of the *Hodayot* ª, then, reflects more the language of its genre than the distinctive theology of the Qumran Community." Chris VanLandingham, *Judgment and Justification in Early Judaism and the Apostle Paul* (Peabody, MA: Hendrickson, 2006), p. 122.

[39]Speaking more broadly of divine and human agency, D. A. Carson writes: "Hymns must not be divorced from doctrine, because they are often the most innocent expression of it." *Divine Sovereignty and Human Responsibility: Biblical Perspectives in Tension* (Atlanta: John Knox, 1981), p. 82.

hymns, the pessimism is even ignored (citing 1QM 12–14 and 4Q403-7). According to Maston, "While hymns are more suited than legal texts for contrasting God's righteousness with human sinfulness the hymn or prayer genre is not bound to this contrast."[40] We cannot simply discount Qumran's pessimistic anthropological tendencies because they occur in hymns. E. P. Sanders falls somewhere between VanLandingham and Maston in the *Hodayot*'s portrayal of humanity. Sanders shows that in hymnic material, the author often contrasts God's righteous actions with humanity's sinful deeds. When the focus is on praising God, the necessary offset will be a pessimistic view of humanity. For Sanders, therefore, the hymnic genre naturally allows the author to magnify human inability in light of God; the genre does not dictate the author's theology, but it does shape it.

While I affirm Maston's point that genre does not determine one's theology, I do think that Sanders makes a valid observation. In other words, it is not simply that genre dictates the pessimism; rather, it is the divine and human contrast, *which often (though not always) occurs in hymns,* that draws out the pessimism. When the divine and human relation is brought to the fore, anthropological pessimism is aroused.

This can be seen, for instance, in 1QH[a] 9, where the author contrasts God with humankind and ends up with a dark portrait of the latter: "To you, you, God of knowledge, belong all the works of justice and the foundation of truth; but to the sons of Adam belongs the service of iniquity and the deeds of deception" (9:26-27 *DSSSE*). Compared to God, humanity is wicked. But a few lines down, the same author turns to his audience to exhort, and the pessimism fades away: "Listen, wise men, and you, meditating on knowledge, and (you) impetuous ones, be of staunch purpose! [. . .] increase in cleverness! O righteous men, put away iniquity! And all of you, of perfect way, strengthen [. . .] the poor!" (9:36-37 *DSSSE*). Sanders rightly observes that the author "changes from describing the inability and unrighteousness of man to speaking of the 'righteous' and the 'perfect of way.'"[41] It is not so much the hymn *qua* hymn that governs the pessimism, but the contrast between God and humanity that naturally arises from the hymn.[42]

---

[40]Maston, *Divine and Human Agency,* p. 80.

[41]Sanders, *Paul and Palestinian Judaism,* p. 292.

[42]For explicit divine and human contrasts that showcase humankind's condition, see 1QH[a] 20:27-38.

If pessimism is largely governed by the divine/human contrast, then we would expect there to be less pessimism when humans are compared to fellow humans. And this is exactly what we see. Compared to God, the entire Qumran community is an incubator for sin, but such rhetoric is not displayed when the covenanters compare themselves to the "wicked" Jews outside their community, let alone to their Gentile neighbors. This point can be clearly seen in 1QH[a] 17:

> I know th[at] there is hope, thanks to your [ki]ndness, and trust, thanks to the abundance of your strength, for no-one is pronounced just in your ju[dgme]nt, or inno[cent at] your trial; one man may be more just than another man, a guy wiser [than] his [neighbour], flesh may be respected more than something made from [clay,] one spirit more powerful than another spirit, but compared to your mig[ht], no-one is strong, and there is no [limit] to your glory. (1QH[a] 17:14-17 DSSSE)

This hymn provides a window into the inner logic of the righteousness of God and humanity. When one is compared to God, they cannot be considered righteous, since only God is righteous. But when a human is compared to a fellow human, then they can be considered righteous or unrighteous.[43] This is why the hymnist believes that he and the community are unrighteous—"Who is just before you when he goes to court?" (1QH[a] 15:28)—and yet also affirm that "at the judgment you pronounce guilty all those who harass me, separating the just from the wicked through me" (1QH[a] 15:12). While the author is plagued with sin, he is still much more righteous than those outside the community. So the authors of 1QH[a] and 1QS 10–11 can at the same time be righteous (compared to others) and unrighteous (compared to God)—the latter being naturally emphasized in hymnic material.[44]

Set against the backdrop of God's character, humanity is portrayed very pessimistically. However, in ethical or didactic material, such pessimism is not apparent. And this is important for the purpose of our study, since

---

[43]See too 1QH[a] 9:15-20; 12:5-25; 15:12.

[44]This explains why some passages in the *Hodayot* affirm that the author (and his community) is righteous (4:23-25; 7:9-14; 9:34-37; 10:13, 28; 12:22), while other passages say that no one is righteous (8:19; 17:14-15).

Paul's anthropological pessimism is evident in his didactic letters.[45] Again, this is where our comparison between Romans 1–3 and CD 2–3 is telling, since here we are comparing theological assumptions embedded in similar rhetorical situations. So even if we took the more cautious route and concluded that Romans and 1QH[a] exhibit the same pessimism, the comparison is not entirely accurate in light of the different genres. Romans and CD (or Galatians and 4QMMT) are much closer in genre, and when they stand toe to toe, Paul's letter exudes a much greater degree of anthropological pessimism than CD.

Second, there is the issue of transference. While the *Hodayot*'s anthropology is pessimistic, so is the solution. In other words, the transference from darkness to light is not that extreme, as Kyle Wells rightly observes: "Sons of Light" are never "to think of themselves as having been Sons of Darkness."[46] The radical reconstitution of the human person will take place at the eschaton (e.g., 1QS 4:18-22), but for the present, "transformation is primarily understood as a cognitive process of becoming more aware of who one is, of what God requires, and of God's control of history."[47] Though a beneficiary of God's saving acts, the hymnist at the end of 1QS writes: "I belong to evil humankind, to the assembly of unfaithful flesh; my sins, my iniquities, my sins, [. . .] with the depravities of my heart belong to the assembly of worms and of those who walk in darkness" (1QS 11:9-10).

For Paul, the upshot of his pessimistic anthropology is a dramatic transference from humanity's wicked condition. God reconstitutes evil humanity from a debased mind to a renewed mind (Rom 1:21; 12:1-2); from a depraved heart to a new heart (Rom 1:28; 2:29); from death to life (Rom 7:6–8:11); from nonglory to a divine-like glorified existence (Rom 1:21-23; 8:18-23).[48] The degree of transference could not be more pronounced. God's

---

[45]We focused on Romans in our treatment of Paul, but anthropological pessimism can be seen across most of his letters (1 Cor 1:18-31; 2:14-16; 6:9-11; 2 Cor 3:1–4:6; Gal 1:4; 3:15-25; 4:1-7; 5:16-26; Eph 2:1-10; 4:17-24; 5:6-14).

[46]Wells, "Grace," p. 87.

[47]Ibid., p. 87; see also C. A. Newsom, *The Self as Symbolic Self: Constructing Identity and Community at Qumran*, STDJ 52 (Leiden: Brill, 2004), p. 72.

[48]For the transference of glory in Romans, see Preston Sprinkle, "The Afterlife in Romans: Paul's Glory Motif in Light of the *Apocalypse of Moses* and *2 Baruch*," in *Lebendige Hoffnung – ewiger Tod?! Jenseits-vorstellungen im Hellenismus, Judentum und Christentum*, ed. Manfred Lang and

saving action through Christ and the spirit has "condemned sin in the flesh," stripping the flesh of its power over freshly redeemed humanity. Paul agrees with the *Hodayot* that "those who are in the flesh cannot please God" (Rom 8:8), but goes on to says that those who are in Christ are no longer in the flesh. Total transference from flesh to spirit—from darkness to light—has taken place, whereas in the *Hodayot*, such transference is limited to new knowledge through hermeneutics: redeemed humanity now has the ability to rightly interpret, understand and therefore follow God's law.[49] But the power of one's sinful nature is alive and well (1QHᵃ 5:19; 7:24). In short, for the *Hodayot*, where anthropology is most pessimistic, God's saving acts lack the transforming power that we see in Paul.[50]

Moreover, the *Hodayot*'s solution to humanity's condition is expressed primarily in cognitive terms. The psalmist, for instance, praises God "because you have taught me your truth, you have made me know your wonderful mysteries" (1QHᵃ 15:25-27) and "have enlightened my face for your covenant" (1QHᵃ 12:5). God's gift of special knowledge is considered to be a merciful act of salvation: "Your compassion [is] for all the sons of your approval, for you have taught them the secret of your truth and have instructed them in your wonderful mysteries" (1QHᵃ 19:9-10, 30-31; cf. 18:29). Or more thoroughly:

> These things I know through your knowledge, since you opened my ears to wonderful mysteries even though I am a creature of clay, fashioned with water, a foundation of shame and a source of impurity, an oven of iniquity and a building of sin, a spirit of error and depravity without knowledge, terrified by your righteous judgments. What can I say which is not known? (1QHᵃ 9:21-23)

Michael Labahn, ABG 24 (Leipzig: Evangelische Verlagsanstalt, 2007), pp. 161-93.

[49]Two hymns may suggest a more complete transference: 1QHᵃ 8:16-23 and 11:20-26. Regarding the former, Maston argues that "God acts in a certain manner to overcome the ill effects of the human's creaturely, sinful nature" (*Divine and Human Agency*, p. 97). A close look at this passage validates Maston's conclusion. This hymn refers to God transforming the hymnist through "the spirit which you have placed [in me]" (8:19). The threefold result of the spirit's work is "to lavish your [kind]nesses on [your] serv[ant] for[ever,] to purify me with your holy spirit, to bring me near by your will according to the extent of your kindnesses" (8:19-20). A good measure of transference seems to take place in this hymn. As for 11:20-26, however, a close look shows that it is a prayer of thanksgiving "not for being brought out of a state of wickedness and into a state of righteousness, but for God's preserving and protecting mercy during a time when the psalmist was surrounded by the wicked community" (Wells, "Grace," p. 83).

[50]This reading, of course, assumes that Paul is not speaking about his postconverted state in Rom 7:14-25, which we have briefly addressed in chapter four.

The author's pessimistic anthropology is largely due to lack of knowledge, and therefore salvation is conceived as God "open[ing] my ears to wondrous mysteries."[51] Such enlightenment is not an end in itself, however. Maston rightly observes that cognitive transformation leads to obedience: "With knowledge comes the power to avoid wickedness and to live righteously."[52] Or in the words of the hymnist, God is the one "who puts wisdom in the heart of [your] servant to kn[ow al]l these matters, to unders[tand . . .] to restrain oneself when faced with the deeds of wickedness" (1QHᵃ 6:8-9). Although it leads to obedience, this concept of a reconstituted mind softens the pessimism in the *Hodayot*'s anthropology in one important way: the divine gift of knowledge does not seem to be granted unilaterally. In some hymns, there are qualifications when God gives the gift of knowledge. For instance, in 1QHᵃ 6, one of the only hymns that discusses a person's entrance into the community, the recipient of salvific knowledge already possesses a degree of intellect prior to entering the community: "I have enjoined my soul with an oath not to sin against you [and n]ot to do anything which is evil in your eyes. In this way I was brought near in the community of all the men of my counsel. According to his [int]elligence I bring him near, I love him in proportion to the abundance of his inheritance" (1QHᵃ 6:17-19 *DSSSE*). The phrase "in this way I was brought near" points back to the hymnist's commitment to obey. He was considered worthy to enter the community and receive salvific knowledge because of his prior "[int]elligence." This "partial competence of moral agents"[53] qualifies the recipient of divine grace as worthy. Such prior demonstration of knowledge and desire to obey is frequently expressed in the *Manual of Discipline* (1QS 5:7-11, 20-22) and, as we have seen, in the *Damascus Document* (e.g., CD 3:12-16).

---

[51]See too 1QHᵃ 5:19-23; 7:24; 14:7; 20:11-24; 22:31. In four different places in these hymns, the agent of this cognitive transformation is the spirit of God (1QHᵃ 5:24-25; 8:19; 20:11-12; 21:14 *bottom*). "And I, your servant, have known thanks to the spirit you have placed in me" (1QHᵃ 5:24-25). Though the gift of the spirit is expressed in terms similar to Ezek 36:26-27, Ezekiel's vision of a total reconstitution of the person does not seem to be echoed by the *Hodayot*, as we saw in chapter 4. See John Yates, *The Spirit and Creation in Paul*, WUNT 2.251 (Tübingen: Mohr Siebeck, 2008), pp. 80-81.

[52]Maston, *Divine and Human Agency*, p. 116.

[53]Wells, "Grace," p. 70.

CONCLUSION

We conclude by returning to our opening question: *Does humanity possess the unaided ability to initiate a return to God and obey his laws?* Our answer is that according to didactic texts, yes, they do, and according to some hymnic texts, no, they do not. The portrait at Qumran is not uniform, and this should not surprise us, since ancient authors probably did not share our modern obsession with systematized thought. Moreover, we should not expect such unanimity across multiple authors writing documents over more than a century.[54] So, generalized statements about *the* anthropology of Qumran are naïve and unwarranted.

We can recognize, however, that while there is a good deal of continuity between Paul and some of the hymns at Qumran in terms of their pessimism (e.g., *Barki Nafshi, Words of the Luminaries*), there are also discernible points of discontinuity. Even in the *Hodayot*, which are thought to be just as pessimistic as Paul, we observed some points of discontinuity. On the whole, we can sum up our study as follows. (1) When Qumran's didactic treatises are compared to Paul's didactic treatises (e.g., CD with Romans), there is observable discontinuity. (2) Paul's pessimism is not limited to instances where he contrasts God with humanity; rather, it penetrates many levels of discourse. (3) Believers, for Paul, are said to have been transferred from wickedness to righteousness; everyone in Adam belongs to the "sons of darkness." Therefore, (4) the degree of transference is more radical in Paul than even in the hymns of Qumran. (5) In some Qumran hymns, only qualified people who demonstrate a measure of intelligence are given the gift of salvific knowledge, while Paul's pessimism casts its net equally over all humanity. There are no preconditions or qualifications for God's saving action. God justifies the ungodly, as the next chapter will show.

---

[54]When I asked Simon Gathercole what he thought about the diversity of thought among the Scrolls, he quickly pushed back with tongue in cheek: "Does *your* library contain a uniform theology?"

6

JUSTIFICATION IN
PAUL AND QUMRAN

Thus far, we have been comparing various soteriological motifs in Qumran and in Paul through the lenses of *Prophetic* and *Deuteronomic* restoration. As two ends of a spectrum, *Deuteronomic* and *Prophetic* paradigms of restoration carry differing emphases on divine and human agency. The former views repentance and obedience as a condition for God's restorative act, while the latter envisions a unilateral intervention from God in restoring his people. We have seen through the motifs of the curse of the law, the spirit and anthropological pessimism that Qumran exhibits elements of both paradigms, while Paul is thoroughly *Prophetic*. In this chapter, we will look at the Pauline doctrine that has been the bread and butter of recent discussions, if not of Protestantism as a whole: justification. This soteriological motif is not uniquely Pauline—it can be observed among the Dead Sea Scrolls, as many scholars have noted, so it provides a fitting point of comparison.[1]

In order to avoid getting bogged down in the layers of issues related to justification, we will stay focused on specific soteriological questions. Does Paul's understanding of justification exhibit a greater emphasis on divine agency than his Qumran contemporaries (discontinuity)? Or, do Paul and Qumran understand the dynamics of divine and human agency in jus-

---

[1]See, above all, Siegfried Schulz, "Zur Rechtfertigung aus Gnaden im Qumran und bei Paulus: Zugleich ein Beitrag zur Form- und Überlieferungsgeschichte der Qumrantexte," *ZTK* 56 (1959): 155-85.

tification in the same way (continuity)? And as in the previous chapters, we will focus more narrowly on those aspects of justification where Paul and Qumran intersect. That is, we will locate and compare specific themes within their respective statements about the nature of justification, leaving aside any aspect of the doctrine that is emphasized by only one of our dialogue partners. Such convergence can be seen in three areas: (1) the possibility of God justifying the ungodly; (2) the nature of God's justification of Abraham in general, and specifically the interpretation of Genesis 15:6 as it relates to Abraham; and (3) the interpretation of Habakkuk 2:4. All of these motifs can be observed in both Paul and Qumran within the general purview of justification. Lastly, (4) we will widen our parameters a bit to examine a hymn from Qumran (1QS 10–11) that speaks of justification in ways that seem downright Pauline. But to get us up to speed, we will first review how recent scholars have tackled justification in relation to Qumran and Paul.

JUSTIFICATION BY FAITH AND THE
NEW PERSPECTIVE ON PAUL: A BRIEF SKETCH

Prior to Sanders, most New Testament scholars assumed that Paul's soteriology was antithetical to Judaism's, and justification by faith was the primary reason why.[2] Paul formulated his doctrine of justification by faith in response to Judaism's belief that justification was by works. The relationship between divine and human agency in each of these views of justification was not at the forefront of the scholarly discussions; however, the implication is clear: Judaism placed much more emphasis on human agency for justification, and this is what Paul was reacting against. Sanders, of course, set out to dismantle the caricature of Judaism as a religion driven by meritorious works, though his articulation of justification was mediocre at best, as even his most sympathetic interlocutors agree.[3] Ac-

---

[2]For a survey of views, see E. P. Sanders, *Paul and Palestinian Judaism: A Comparison of Patterns of Religion* (Philadelphia: Fortress, 1977), pp. 1-12; Mark Seifrid, *Justification by Faith: The Origin and Development of a Central Pauline Theme*, NTS 68 (Leiden: Brill, 1992), pp. 1-77; see also Preston M. Sprinkle, "The Old Perspective on the New Perspective: A Review of Some 'Pre-Sanders' Thinkers," *Them* 30 (2005): 21-31.
[3]See the critical evaluation of Sanders's reading of Paul in James D. G. Dunn, "The New Perspective on Paul," in *The New Perspective on Paul: Collected Essays*, WUNT 185 (Tübingen: Mohr Siebeck, 2005), p. 93; N. T. Wright, *What Saint Paul Really Said: Was Paul of Tarsus the Real Founder of Christianity?* (Grand Rapids: Eerdmans, 1997), p. 19.

cording to Sanders, there is both continuity and discontinuity between Paul and Qumran when it comes to justification. Discontinuity is seen in Paul's distinctive use of justification language (*dikaioō*) as "transfer terminology," or how one "gets in" to the covenant community. "The verb [*tsadiqah*] in Qumran means 'be righteous,' that is, be upright or perfect of way, not 'be justified' in the sense of 'saved,' as in Paul."[4] For Qumran, then, righteousness describes one who is already a covenant member; maintaining one's righteousness ensures that one will "stay in" the covenant, but the verb "justify" is never used to describe conversion into the covenant. Strictly speaking, Paul's concept of justification by faith is not paralleled among the Scrolls. Surprisingly, then, Sanders actually argues for a certain measure of discontinuity when it comes to Paul and Qumran in their views of justification. However, such discontinuity does not curtail Sander's painstaking endeavor to find many other strands of soteriological continuity between Paul and Qumran. "The difference is not located in a supposed antithesis of grace and works," says Sanders, "on grace and works there is in fact agreement."[5] To my mind, Sanders did not sufficiently recognize the implications of the different ways that Paul and Qumran conceived of justification—differences which Sanders himself affirmed.

Since Sanders, the discussion about Paul and Judaism regarding justification has splintered in several different directions. With regard to divine and human agency James Dunn, N. T. Wright and others have argued for continuity; namely, that Paul and Qumran understand the dynamics between divine and human agency to be very similar, if not the same. For James Dunn, Paul's understanding of justification by faith is not entirely unique. Not only is it rooted in the Old Testament, it also finds much in common with his contemporary Jews. So for Dunn, "fundamental to Jewish self-understanding and covenant theology is this recognition and affirmation that Israel's standing before God was due entirely to the initiative of divine grace," and "this is where Paul derived his emphasis on the initiative of divine grace within his teaching on justification." Paul's seemingly radical departure from his former beliefs is a modern invention. Justification by

---

[4]Sanders, *Paul and Palestinian Judaism*, p. 545.
[5]Ibid., p. 548.

faith for Paul "was simply a restatement of the first principles of his own ancestral faith."[6] This naturally opens up the question: What was Paul reacting against when he pitted justification by faith against justification by works of law? For Dunn, Paul was arguing against "Jewish *restrictiveness*— the tendency in Judaism to restrict the covenant grace of God, covenant righteousness to Israel."[7] The discontinuity between Paul and Judaism has to do with the ethnic inclusiveness of justification; it is *by faith* and not by one's ethnic—namely *Jewish*—heritage that one is declared right with God.

This, of course, shapes Dunn's interpretation of Paul's phrase "works of the law" (*ergōn nomou*, e.g., Rom 3:20, 28; Gal 2:16; 3:2, 5, 10), which often occurs in contrast to justification by faith. The phrase in itself, according to Dunn, refers to all that the law requires, but "in a context where the relationship of Israel with other nations is at issue certain laws would naturally come more into focus than others," such as circumcision and food laws.[8] And Paul has such a context in view when he uses the phrase in Romans and Galatians. Therefore, when Paul contrasts justification by faith with justification by works of the law, he is not contrasting divine initiative (faith) with human initiative (works), but ethnic inclusivity (faith) with ethnic exclusivity (works). Ethnocentrism, not legalism, is what fuels Paul's polemic.[9]

There is, therefore, discontinuity between Paul and Judaism regarding justification, but it is limited to the ethnic inclusivity and not the means or the theological contours of justification. In other words, there is continuity between Paul and Qumran in the *content* of justification but discontinuity in how they understand its *scope*. For Paul, God justifies Jews along with Gentiles on the same basis—faith. Yet with regard to divine and human agency, both Paul and his Jewish contemporaries regarded God's work as central and prior to all human action.

Dunn and others have attracted many dissenters, however, who see more discontinuity between Paul and Qumran in their understanding of justification. Among the most prolific has been Mark Seifrid, who argues that

---

[6]James D. G. Dunn, "Paul and Justification by Faith," in *The New Perspective*, p. 364; see also James D. G. Dunn, *The Theology of Paul the Apostle* (Grand Rapids: Eerdmans, 1998), pp. 366-67.
[7]Dunn, "Paul and Justification by Faith," p. 366.
[8]Ibid., p. 372.
[9]See also Michael Cranford, "Abraham in Romans 4: The Father of All Who Believe," *NTS* 41 (1995): 71-88.

Paul's doctrine of justification is unparalleled in early Judaism. Although some resemblance in language can be found in the Scrolls, the structure of justification is fundamentally different. For Qumran, "The proper observance of *Torah* maintained by the community was thought to atone for sins."[10] Qumran conceived of righteousness in behavioral, not forensic, terms. This is why proper observance of torah constituted their righteousness.[11] But the main difference between Paul and Qumran lies in the timing of justification. For Qumran, righteousness (i.e., upright behavior) will be vindicated *in the eschaton* at the judgment of God, and therefore behavioral righteousness maintains one's covenant standing and ensures one's final vindication. Paul, however, uses justification language to refer to the initial entry into salvation. And since one's condition prior to initial salvation is one of wickedness, Paul asserts that God justifies the wicked. Sanders acknowledged the difference in the timing of justification between Paul and Qumran as we saw above, but he failed to recognize the implications—implications that Seifrid drives home. "A distance existed between Paul and Qumran," writes Seifrid, "since the gift of righteousness there [at Qumran] was conceived of in terms of the practices of the community,"[12] whereas for Paul, justification comes on behalf of the ungodly, who have no righteousness in themselves.

Both Paul and Qumran, as we will see, speak of justification on several occasions, making this motif a fitting point of comparison. We will hone our discussion by locating specific features that surround justification language in both Paul and Qumran: God's justification of the ungodly, Abraham and Genesis 15:6, and the use of Habakkuk 2:4. We will conclude by looking at the justification language in the hymn at the end of 1QS, which seems to correlate with Paul.

JUSTIFICATION IN PAUL

Paul's discussion of justification is largely confined to two of his letters:

---

[10]Seifrid, *Justification*, p. 94, citing 1QS 3:6, 8; 5:6, 7; 8:6, 10; 9:4. At the same time, in light of the predestinarian undertone among the Scrolls, "this atoning work of the community was considered to be a gracious gift of God" (p. 95). Atonement is through obedience; obedience is the outworking of grace.

[11]Ibid., 97-98.

[12]Ibid., p. 211.

Romans and Galatians. In Galatians, his statements about justification are more asserted than explained. But in Romans, the nature, basis and means of justification is the hub of Paul's argument in Romans 3–5, so for the sake of space, this section will occupy our focus.

Justification of the Ungodly. After declaring all humanity to be wicked and "under sin" (Rom 1:18–3:20), Paul says that the sole solution is found in the atoning sacrifice of Christ, which is received through the response of faith (Rom 3:21-26). God is still just, in that his wrath is satisfied through the death of Christ, and yet is able to justify—pronounce righteous—the one who is "of the faith of Jesus" (Rom 3:26). Regardless of the nature of faith in Romans 3:22-26, it is clear that both the moral person (Rom 2:1-16) and the law-possessing Jew (Rom 2:17-29) have not rendered the obedience that would be sufficient for justification. The verdict that "both Jews and Greeks are under sin" and that "none is righteous, no, not one" (Rom 3:9-10) serves as a fitting summary of Paul's argument leading up to Romans 3:21-26. And the whole scope of Paul's point is stated succinctly in Romans 3:23-24: "All have sinned . . . and are justified by his grace as a gift, through the redemption that is in Christ Jesus." Despite the various interpretive difficulties scattered throughout Romans 1–3—the meaning of "righteousness of God," "faith of Jesus" and "works of law"—and despite how much emphasis one finds on the Jew/Gentile issue, both New Perspective and Lutheran readings agree: humans are justified by the grace embodied in the death and resurrection of Christ, and this act is prefaced by nothing but sin. James Dunn could not have summed up Paul's argument any better:

> The gospel is that God sets to rights man's relationship with himself by an act of sheer generosity which depends on no payment man can make, which is without reference to whether any individual in particular is inside the law/covenant or outside, and which applies to all human beings without exception. It is this humbling recognition—that he has no grounds for appeal either in covenant status or in particular "works of the law," that he has to depend *entirely* from start to finish on God's gracious power, that he can receive acquittal only as a gift which lies at the heart of faith for Paul.[13]

Paul's thorough argument in Romans 1–3 is summed up in Romans 4 with

---

[13]Dunn, *Romans*, 1:179 (emphasis original).

the crisp and enticing assertion that God "justifies the ungodly," using none other than Abraham as an example:

> If Abraham was justified by works, he has something to boast about, but not before God. For what does the Scripture say? "Abraham believed God, and it was counted to him as righteousness" [Gen 15:6]. Now to the one who works, his wages are not counted as a gift but as his due. And to the one who does not work but believes in *him who justifies the ungodly* (*ton dikaiounta ton asebē*), his faith is counted as righteousness. (Rom 4:2-5)[14]

This description of God as the one "who justifies the ungodly" captures for Paul a central feature of justification and reveals a fundamental aspect of God's identity.[15] God pronounces righteous not the morally upright but the wicked. Paul argues for this in Romans 1-3, more or less assumes it in Romans 4, and rehearses it again in Romans 5:

> For while we were still weak, at the right time Christ died for *the ungodly* (*asebōn*). For one will scarcely die for a righteous person—though perhaps for a good person one would dare even to die—but God shows his love for us in that while we were still *sinners,* Christ died for us. Since, therefore, we have *now been justified by his blood* (*dikaiōthentes nyn en tō haimati*), much more shall we be saved by him from the wrath of God. (Rom 5:6-9)

Here, Paul highlights Christ's self-giving death for the ungodly and sinners in Romans 5:6-8 and then concludes, "therefore, we have now been *justified by his blood.*" That is, Christ's death for the ungodly sums up the meaning of justification (Rom 5:9) and therefore captures the same point Paul made in Romans 4:2-6 and Romans 3:21-26. The atoning work of Christ is understood as the ground of justification, which enables God to be righteous even as he justifies wicked people (Rom 3:26). Paul is eager to erase any notion that justification takes into account a certain measure of right-

---

[14]In this chapter all NT translations are ESV unless otherwise noted.

[15]God is defined by three assertions in Rom 4. He is the "one who justifies the ungodly" (Rom 4:5), the "one who gives life to the dead and calls into being that which does not exist" (Rom 4:17), and the "one who has raised Jesus our Lord from the dead" (Rom 4:24). Therefore, the justification of the ungodly must be considered a fundamental aspect of Paul's understanding of God and the nature of justification; see Francis Watson, "The Triune Divine Identity: Reflections on Pauline God-language, in Disagreement with J. D. G. Dunn," *JSNT* 80 (2000), pp. 99-124; see also Simon J. Gathercole, "Justified by Faith, Justified by his Blood: The Evidence of Romans 3:21-4:5," in *Justification and Variegated Nomism*, Vol. 2: *The Paradoxes of Paul*, ed. D. A. Carson, P. T. O'Brien and M. A. Seifrid (Grand Rapids: Baker, 2004), pp. 147-84 (esp. 165-68).

eousness or inherent worth in the one who receives the gift of justification. For the apostle, justification is preceded only by sin, as he took pains to demonstrate in Romans 1:18–3:26. Even Abraham, who "kept the commandments of God" (Gen 26:5), was *initially* accepted by God before he was obedient, as argued through the stark contrast between belief and works in Romans 4:4-5. Such contrast seems to be a slam-dunk in favor of a Lutheran reading of Paul.

But what does Paul mean by "works" in Romans 4:2-6? Is he speaking about human behavior, obedience to the law, or specific boundary markers that divide Jews from Gentiles? The first two options would affirm everything we have said regarding justification thus far, while the third option, made popular by James Dunn and championed in recent years by his former student Michael Cranford, would set Paul's argument in Romans 4 on a different path. For instance, Cranford argues that "works" in Romans 4 is a simple shorthand for "works of the law," which focuses on boundary markers and not obedience in general. This would mean that Paul does not contrast grace with human deeds but with acceptance of Gentiles into the covenant. "What is rejected as the basis for boasting," says Cranford, "is not obedience . . . but rather works which designate membership in Israel."[16]

Cranford's interpretation is not convincing for three reasons. First, Paul uses the term "works" in Romans 4:4-5 without qualification (e.g., "of law"), which elsewhere in Romans refers to human deeds in general or obedience to the law in particular. The former meaning is clear in Romans 9:10-11, where Isaac is elected before he had done anything "either good or bad—in order that God's purpose of election might continue, *not because of works* (*ouk ex ergōn*) but because of him who calls." The term "works" here is parallel to doing good or bad and therefore refers to human behavior in general, not boundary markers (nor lawkeeping). These "works" are correlated with

---

[16]Cranford, "Abraham in Romans 4," p. 78, also pp. 71, 88; see also John M. G. Barclay, *Obeying the Truth: Paul's Ethics in Galatians* (Minneapolis: Fortress, 1988), pp. 246-47; James D. G. Dunn, *Theology of Paul*, pp. 135-36; Dunn, *Jesus, Paul and the Law*, pp. 238-39. The emphasis on ethnocentrism does seem to be the main point of Rom 4:9-25, where Abraham is shown to be the father of Jews *and* Gentiles. Gentile inclusivity is the main point to which Paul will turn, but this emphasis cannot be read back into Romans 4:1-8. "The scope of God's promise," writes Gathercole, "does become prominent in 4:9-25, but here in 4:1-8, Paul is establishing first and foremost that the Jewish understanding of obedience and justification is seriously mistaken" (Gathercole, "Justified by Faith," p. 160).

Paul's statement that election is not based on "human will or exertion" (Rom 9:16), confirming therefore that "works" in Romans 9:11 refers to human behavior in general. This gives us traction for understanding Paul's next reference to works in Romans 9:32 in like manner: "Israel who pursued a law that would lead to righteousness did not succeed in reaching that law. Why? Because they did not pursue it by faith, but *as if it were based on works*" (*hōs ex ergōn*) (Rom 9:31-32). Cranford's view of "works of the law" makes more sense here, but ultimately it does not satisfy Paul's flow of thought. Paul moves from contrasting God's election with human behavior (Rom 9:10-16) to contrasting again divine and human agency in terms of the work of Christ (Rom 10:5-11). Situated in between is Paul's assertion about Israel missing Christ because of their zeal for strict observance of the law in Romans 9:31-32. The flow of the argument, therefore, suggests that "works" in Romans 9:32 does not *primarily* critique Israel's desire to separate from Gentiles by establishing boundary markers.[17] Again, in Romans 11 Paul says that election "is by grace" and "no longer on the basis of works; otherwise grace would no longer be grace" (Rom 11:6). Paul's contrast between "works" and "grace" is essentially between human and divine agency. The former assumes that God's election is maintained by obedience; the latter believes, with the Prophets, that such obedience did not exist in Israel and therefore God creates and maintains his election unconditionally.[18] Therefore, the unqualified references to "works" throughout Romans suggest that "works" in Romans 4:4 should not be limited to boundary markers. Depending on the context, it may refer either to law-obedience (Rom 9:30-32) or behavior in general (Rom 9:10-11).

Second, in the context of Romans 1–3, there is evidence that the term "works" correlates with other terms that refer to obedience in general, and not boundary markers. It is true that Paul's reference to "works of the law" in Romans 3:28 emphasizes a certain element of Jewishness in Paul's cri-

---

[17]See my more thorough defense of this reading with bibliography in Preston Sprinkle, *Law and Life: The Interpretation of Leviticus 18:5 in Early Judaism and in Paul*, WUNT 2.241 (Tübingen: Mohr Siebeck, 2008), pp. 173-75.

[18]The rather strange "*no longer* on the basis of works" may allude to the *Deuteronomic* structure of the old covenant, whereby blessing is contingent on works. See, e.g., Ulrich Wilckens, *Der Brief an die Römer*, EKKNT 6 (Zurich: Benziger; Neukirchen-Vluyn: Neukirchener Verlag, 1978-1982), 2:238. As much as this would support my overall reading of Paul, it seems best here to understanding this phrase logically and not temporally.

tique, as the follow-up question makes clear: "Or is God the God of Jews only? Is he not the God of Gentiles also?" (Rom 3:29). But according to Paul's argument in Romans 1–3, the main problem with celebrating one's Jewishness is not that it excludes Gentiles, but that it has not been accompanied by obedience. This point is clear in Romans 2:12-24 and particularly acute in Romans 2:25-29, where Paul contrasts circumcision with law-obedience. That is, the problem with circumcision, in Paul's most explicit discussion, is not that it puts up barriers between Jews and Gentiles, but that it has not been tethered to a holistic law-obedient life. Paul, in fact, condemns disobedience to the law throughout Romans 2. He articulates this with phrases that are in the same linguistic purview as "works of the law" (ergōn nomou): "those who *practice (prassontes)* such things" (i.e., "God's decree," *to dikaiōma tou theou*, Rom 1:32), "the doers of the law" (*hoi poiētai*, Rom 2:13), "obey the law" (*prassiēs*, Rom 2:25), "keeps the precepts of the law" (*ta dikaiōmata tou nomou phylassē*, Rom 2:26) and "keeps the law" (*ton nomon telousa*, Rom 2:27). Each of these phrases is, in the words of C. E. B. Cranfield, "naturally connected with the phrase *ergōn nomou*" and it is not "at all feasible to see a reference to circumcision" or other so-called ethnic boundary markers.[19] This is apparent in the phrase "the work of the law" (*to ergon tou nomou*), which is "written on their hearts" (Rom 2:15).[20] It seems more likely that "works of the law" (Rom 3:20) is similar to "work of the law" (Rom 2:15), both referring to law-obedience in general and not specific Gentile-excluding boundary markers. To be sure, the *scope* of justification (viz. its extension to the Gentiles on equal grounds) is important for Paul, but the driving force behind his argument is the gracious *content* of God's justifying act toward the wicked apart from anything they have done.

Third, the grace/works contrast is crystallized in Paul's use of the wage metaphor in Romans 4: "To the one who works, his wages are not counted as a gift but as his due" (Rom 4:4). The antithesis between gift and obligation "is a clear rejection of a work-for-reward view of salvation as one can imagine."[21] The antithesis between "gift" (*charis*) and "obligation" (*opheilēma*)

---

[19]C. E. B. Cranfield, "'The Works of the Law' in Romans," in *On Romans: And Other New Testament Essays* (Edinburgh: T & T Clark, 1998), p. 7.
[20]I discuss this verse in more detail in the next chapter.
[21]Michael F. Bird, *The Saving Righteousness of God: Studies on Paul, Justification, and the New Perspective* (Milton Keynes: Paternoster: 2007), p. 145.

was typical in the ancient world; no one would miss the commercial logic of Paul's statement.[22] Those who work are compensated with the appropriate "wages" (*misthos*),[23] but one who gives a "gift" (*charis*) does so not out of obligation or to compensate the receiver; otherwise, it would not be a gift. Since Paul refers to "works" without qualification, he probably has in mind human behavior. In the context of Romans 1–4, of course, the type of human behavior would be law-obedience, but any form of human behavior is logically excluded (as in Rom 9:10-12). Paul's point is unmistakable: if God justified Abraham as an obligatory response to his works, then it would no longer be a gift but divine compensation for human deeds.[24]

In short, the "works" in Romans 4:4 should not be limited to ethnic boundary markers. In the context of Romans 4, Paul has in mind obedience to the law, which he excludes as the basis for justification. This reading is supported by other passages where Paul speaks of works without qualification, similar phrases throughout Romans 1–2, and the wage metaphor in Romans 4:4. Put simply, though without much originality, God justifies the ungodly on the basis of grace and not anything humans have done—this is the heart of Paul's argument.

---

[22]See, e.g., Thucydides *Hist.* 2.20.4; Aristotle *Eth. Nic.* 1165a3; A. Andrew Das, "Paul and Works of Obedience in Second Temple Judaism: Romans 4:4-5 as a 'New Perspective' Case Study," *CBQ* 71 (2009): 795-812 (esp. 805); Robert Jewett, *Romans: A Commentary,* Hermeneia (Minneapolis: Fortress, 2006), p. 313.

[23]*Misthos* refers to "pay" or "wages." See Xenophon, *Anab.* 1.2.11; 7.7.14; Epictetus, *Diss.* 3.26.27; Jewett, *Romans,* p. 312.

[24]According to Kent Yinger, Abraham's ungodly state in Rom 4:4-5 highlights his uncircumcised status at the time of justification (cf. Rom 4:9-16) and *not* his moral condition. That God justifies the "ungodly" means that he justifies uncircumcised Gentiles, of which Abraham is a striking example. Yinger concludes that "verses 4-5 are not about grace versus works-righteousness, but are about the conditions required for membership in the new people of God—faith in Christ or law-works." Kent Yinger, *Paul, Judaism and Judgment According to Deeds,* SNTSMS 105 (Cambridge: Cambridge University Press, 1999), p. 186. But this interpretation is flawed on two accounts. First, it too quickly correlates the unqualified "works" with "works of the law," which as we have seen is unwarranted in light of other passages, such as Rom 9:10-16 and Rom 11:6 (see also the wage metaphor of Rom 4:4). Second, Yinger reaches to other passages in Paul where future judgment is according to works (e.g., Rom 2:6; 1 Cor 3:8, 14; 2 Cor 5:10) in order to show that works, and not faith alone, are rewarded by God. Thus Paul would be contradicting himself if he meant to separate faith from works in Rom 4:4-5 (pp. 184-87). But Yinger's argument neglects the crucial difference in Pauline thought between the criteria of initial justification and final justification. For Paul, works do not contribute towards our initial justification, which is Paul's point in Rom 4:2-6 (cf. Rom 3:19-26). But spirit-generated works do factor in our final judgment before God.

Justification and Abraham. Paul stands apart from his Jewish contemporaries not only in declaring that God justifies the ungodly, but also in his use of Abraham as paragon of such unconditional grace in Romans 4:1-5.[25] According to Paul, God did not justify Abraham in response to his obedience, since Abraham was in an ungodly state at the time of his justification, a point he cites Genesis 15:6 to support. Paul's use of Abraham here is polemical. That is, he argues against the common Jewish belief about their forefather; namely, that he was justified by works and not by faith alone.[26] In Jewish literature, Abraham was depicted as a model of faithful obedience and was rewarded accordingly, as in 1 Maccabees 2:51-52: "Remember the deeds of the ancestors, which they did in their generations; and you will receive great honor and an everlasting name. Was not Abraham found faithful when tested, and it was reckoned to him as righteousness?" The testing most probably refers to the binding of Isaac, where Abraham demonstrated obedience to God; Genesis 15:6 is conflated with the binding of Isaac in Genesis 22. Such is also the case in Sirach 44:20-21, where Abraham is said to have "kept the law of the Most High, and entered into a covenant with him; he certified the covenant in his flesh, and when he was tested he was found faithful" (Sir 44:20). In response to Abraham's "faithfulness," God promises "that the nations would be blessed through his offspring" (Sir 44:21). It is not mere trust that is credited to Abraham as righteousness (as in Gen 15:6) but his obedience displayed on the mountains of Moriah. And this obedience makes him worthy of the divine promise that the nations will be blessed through him. Again, the author of *Jubilees* asserts: "Abraham was perfect in all of his actions with the LORD and was pleasing through righteousness all of the days of his life" (*Jub.* 23:10).

Therefore, Paul in Romans 4 seems to intentionally turn this view of Abraham on its head by arguing that the patriarch was found wicked, not righteous, when God reckoned to him righteousness. We will explore below whether or not Qumran agrees with Paul on his view of Abraham and justification.

---

[25]Contra Joseph A. Fitzmyer, *Romans: A New Translation with Introduction and Commentary*, AB (New York: Doubleday, 1993), p. 375, who thinks that Paul does not imply here that Abraham was "ungodly."

[26]Which seems to be shared by James 2:14-26.

Justification and Habakkuk 2:4. The third lens through which both Paul and Qumran understand justification is Habakkuk 2:4: "The righteous shall live by his faith." The text seems to be more fundamental to Paul than Qumran, but the latter did leave behind a commentary on the prophet, which reveals with little ambiguity how they understood the verse. For Paul, Habakkuk 2:4 captures *in nuce* his understanding of justification by faith, and he cites the passage two times (Rom 1:17; Gal 3:11) in theologically packed arguments. As we saw above in chapter three, Paul turns to Habakkuk 2:4 to support the notion that righteousness comes through faith and not through works in Galatians 3:11-12: "Now it is evident that no one is justified before God by the law, for 'The righteous shall live by faith' [Hab 2:4]. But the law is not of faith, rather 'The one who does them shall live by them' [Lev 18:5]." Several interpretive issues surround this passage, some of which have been worked out above, but one thing is clear: Paul contrasts Habakkuk 2:4 with Leviticus 18:5—a verse that promotes law-obedience as a means to eschatological life. Habakkuk 2:4 captures a *Prophetic* means of restoration, while Leviticus 18:5, by contrast, summarizes the *Deuteronomic* principle of restoration.

Though less explicit, the same contrast is evident in Paul's other citation of Habakkuk in Romans 1:16-17: "For I am not ashamed of the gospel, for it is the power of God for salvation to everyone who believes: to the Jew first and also to the Greek. For in it the righteousness of God is revealed from faith for faith, as it is written, 'The righteous shall live by faith' [Hab 2:4]." The immediate significance of the Habakkuk text is unclear. But Paul will go on for three chapters to unpack the substance of righteousness by faith (Rom 1:18–4:25), which comes to full view in Romans 3:21-26.[27] This latter passage is Paul's own commentary on Habakkuk 2:4. God has disclosed his saving righteousness through the atonement of Christ, and the benefits are mediated through faith and not through law-works (Rom 3:19-20). Leaving aside the host of interpretive debates in Romans 1–4, it is clear that Paul believes Habakkuk 2:4 excludes law-works as a basis for justification.

Justification of the Ungodly: A Theme* in Prophetic *Restoration. While nothing I have argued for thus far is original, few scholars understand Paul's

---

[27]The correlation between Rom 1:16-17 and Rom 3:21-22 is unmistakable; the latter picks up on and explains the former.

"justification of the ungodly" theme in the context of the *Prophetic* restoration motifs in the Old Testament.[28] Interpreters have grown accustomed
to Paul's justification language, but anyone steeped in the Jewish Scriptures
will inevitably be taken aback by the apostle's claims. On the surface, Paul's
statement that God "justifies the ungodly" contradicts Moses, who said that
God "will not justify the ungodly" (Exod 23:7; LXX *kai ou dikaiōseis ton asebē*).
Moses' statement is echoed by several other Old Testament writers (Prov
17:15; 24:24; Is 5:23; cf. Sir 42:2) and therefore creates an interesting tension
with Paul's claim, especially since the apostle also grounds his doctrine in
the Jewish Scriptures. Exodus 23 fits well with Sinaitic retribution theology
where righteousness is rewarded and wickedness is punished.[29] If Israel is
to enact justice in the courts, they too must apply this principle. But as the
Scriptures unfold, we find friction between the sinfulness of the nation and
God's unconditional commitment to Abraham and his seed. On the eve of
exile, the Hebrew prophets pronounced both judgment on the rebellious
nation and assurance that God would intervene at a future time to unconditionally redeem them. Put differently, for God to fulfill his covenant and
keep his promise with the ungodly nation, he must justify the wicked.[30] And
this, I suggest, forms the basis for Paul's statement in Romans 4–5 that God
justifies the wicked.

Thus, Paul's doctrine of justification was not only a polemic against his
contemporaries but was also an expression of the *Prophetic* program of unilateral redemption trumpeted by Isaiah, Jeremiah, Ezekiel and others.[31] As
we saw in chapter two, the Prophets looked forward to the restoration of
Israel through an unconditional act of God. I suggest that the theological
contours of *Prophetic* restoration have contributed to Paul's formulation of
the justification of the ungodly by faith. Isaiah, in fact, provides Paul with

---

[28]The notable exception is Otfried Hofius, "Rechtfertigung des Gottlosen als Thema biblischer
Theologie," in *Paulusstudien*, WUNT 51 (Tübingen: Mohr Siebeck, 1989), pp. 121-47; see also
Gathercole, "Justification," pp. 166-67. In many ways, Francis Watson argues for a similar point
throughout his *Paul and the Hermeneutics of Faith* (New York: T & T Clark/Continuum, 2004).

[29]The original context of Ex 23:7 refers to a human law court, and therefore is not immediately
soteriological. However, God's affirmation of justice in the courts is reflective of a *Deuteronomic*
principle of righteous retribution.

[30]I hesitate saying that God *must* do anything. However, the Scriptures portray God as bound to
his own promises, which include the salvation of his people. It is in this sense that I use the term
"must": God is compelled by his own character to save wicked people.

[31]See Hofius, "Rechtfertigung des Gottlosen," pp. 91-100, who also discusses Hosea.

more than just the *concept* of justification, but even the *terminology*.[32] The verb *dikaioō* is particularly frequent in Isaiah 40–55 and often conveys forensic notions of declaring one to be in the right (Is 43:9, 26; 45:25; 50:8; 53:11). The noun *dikaiosynē* is also used throughout Isaiah in contexts where God rules or judges in an eschatological sense (Is 42:10-13; 49:13; 51:4-11). And this section in Isaiah is shaped by God's unilateral pardon of Israel. While Isaiah did not use the exact phrase "God justifies the ungodly," he very well could have without altering his message. A few passages are of particular importance.

In Isaiah 45, the prophet contrasts God with idols and concludes:

Only in the Lord, it shall be said of me,
    are righteousness (*dikaiosynē*) and strength;
to him shall come and be ashamed
    all who were incensed against him.
In the Lord all the offspring of Israel
    shall be justified (*dikaiōthēsontai*) and shall glory. (Is 45:24-25)

A courtroom scene surrounds this passage (see Is 45:20-23), and the parallel between "righteousness" and "justified" shows that the latter is a soteriological statement. Moreover, the entire nation of Israel is ungodly, and therefore we have a compelling prototype for Paul's concept of God justifying the ungodly that is situated in a section of Scripture that Paul quoted quite frequently.[33]

Isaiah will later say: "The one who justifies me is near, who will contend with me? . . . Who will declare me guilty?" (Is 50:8-9 my translation). The use of *dikaioō* within the context of judicial imagery suggests that the prophet understands justification to be forensic, and Paul alludes to this passage in Romans 8:33-34: "Who shall bring any charge against God's elect? It is God who justifies. Who is to condemn?" Here, as in Romans 3:21-26; 4:25, it is the death and resurrection of Christ that secures the justification of the ungodly, an idea that is not altogether foreign to Isaiah. Of particular significance is Isaiah 53:11 where the suffering servant will "justify the many, and

---

[32]Of course, Hab 2:4 and Gen 15:6 are the main sources for Paul's justification language.
[33]Compare Is 45:9-10 with Rom 9:20-21, and Is 45:22-23 with Rom 14:11-12 and Phil 2:10-11. Isaiah as a whole was fundamental for Paul's argument in Romans. See Ross Wagner, *Heralds of the Good News: Paul and Isaiah "in Concert,"* NovTSup (Leiden: Brill, 2002).

he shall bear their iniquities." Since Isaiah does not envision Israel's repentance in Isaiah 40–55, Israel's ("the many") justification and forgiveness
through the servant must be unconditional.[34] The servant, in other words,
through his atoning death justifies the ungodly.[35]

The striking conceptual and linguistic similarities between Paul's justification of the ungodly and Isaiah's unilateral pardon through the servant
suggest that the apostle had an eye on the prophet when he penned Romans
and infused *dikaioō* with its distinct Pauline sense. In short, Paul's doctrine
of the justification of the ungodly through faith should be understood
through the lens of *Prophetic* restoration. Conceptually, Paul finds roots for
his doctrine in many of the ancient heralds—Ezekiel, Jeremiah and Hosea—
but it is the great prophet Isaiah who has passed the mantle to Paul in an-
nouncing Yahweh's unilateral pardon of the ungodly seed of Abraham. All
the ingredients (linguistic and conceptual) for Paul's belief that God justifies the ungodly are prevalent in Isaiah 40–55, a passage that was formative
for much of the apostle's thought. It is on these grounds that we find Paul's
understanding of justification of the ungodly to exhibit the contours of *Prophetic* theology.

JUSTIFICATION AT QUMRAN

How did the Dead Sea Scrolls understand the idea of justification? Would
they agree with Paul (and Isaiah) that God justifies the wicked, or with
Moses that God would justify the righteous? In order to wrestle with these

---

[34]It is not clear that Paul had Is 53:11 in mind when he constructed his phrase "God justifies the
ungodly"; however, the Isaiah text probably does underlie Rom 4:25 and Rom 5:18-19.
According to Bird, "the Servant" of Isaiah 53 "suffers and is justified in the heavenly courtroom
upon seeing 'the light,'" which may suggest resurrection, since light is associated with
resurrection elsewhere (see Job 33:28, 30; Ps 49:19; 1 *En.* 58:3; 92:3-5; 108:12-13; *Pss. Sol.* 3:12;
Bird, *Saving Righteousness*, p. 55).

[35]"The result of the Servant's own resurrection-justification is that he will 'justify many'" (Bird,
Saving Righteousness, p. 77). In Rom 4:25, Jesus' death atones for the sins of the transgressors,
and his resurrection secures our justification, and similar contours are found in Is 53:10-11,
suggesting a deliberate allusion on Paul's part. Isaiah's influence on Paul is even clearer in Rom
5:19, where he not only uses the language of "justification" and "many," but also the concept of
corporate solidarity, both drawn from Is 53:11. Shiu-Lun Shum is correct to point out that "what
Paul draws on from the Suffering Servant song is not simply (Second) Isaiah's language, but the
prophet's concept of a *one-many-solidarity-relationship*" (*Paul's Use of Isaiah in Romans*, WUNT
2.156 [Tübingen: Mohr Siebeck, 2002], p. 199; italics and parentheses original; cited in Jewett,
Romans, p. 387).

questions, we will consider the three primary motifs that traverse Paul's letters and the Scrolls at Qumran: (1) God's justification of the ungodly, (2) the justification of Abraham and meaning of Genesis 15:6, and (3) the interpretation of Habakkuk 2:4. We will conclude by looking at justification language in hymnic material, which seems to have received an extra endowment of grace-language (esp. 1QS 10–11).

Justification of the Ungodly. According to Qumran, does God justify the ungodly? The Scrolls present a ready answer in statements that parallel Paul's own formulation. In at least two passages, the community either abhors the idea that God would justify the ungodly, or they celebrate God's justification of the righteous. Both statements are found in the *Damascus Document.*

> For they sought smooth things, chose delusions, scrutinized loopholes, chose the handsome neck, and they *justified the guilty, and pronounced guilty the just (wyṣdîqû ršᶜ wyršᶜû ṣdîq)*, violated the covenant, broke the precept, banded together against the life of the righteous man, their soul abominated everyone who walks in perfection, they hunted them down with the sword and provoked the dispute of the people. (CD 1:18-21)

The key phrase "justified the guilty, and pronounced guilty the just" stems from Exodus 23:7 and other such commandments in the Old Testament.[36] In the human courts, righteous people were to be declared innocent, while the wicked were condemned. Qumran's abhorrence of the wicked here critiques injustice in the courts. We should be careful, therefore, not to invest this statement with soteriological significance. The author is not saying that God pronounces people to be righteous based on their deeds. However, the Qumran courtroom is analogous to how God accepts people, and this is seen clearly later in CD, where the idea is shaped by soteriological concerns: "the holy men of old, for whom God atoned, and who *justified the righteous, and pronounced the wicked to be wicked (wyṣdîqû ṣdîq wyršᶜû ršᶜ)*" (CD 4:6-7). There is gap of undetermined length that precedes this statement, so the full context is difficult to reconstruct.[37] Philip Davies argues convincingly, however, that the gap in the text once contained a list of the names and

---

[36]Prov 17:15; 24:24; Is 5:23; cf. Sir 42:2.
[37]For a discussion, see P. R. Davies, *The Damascus Covenant: An Interpretation of the "Damascus Document,"* JSOTSup 25 (Sheffield: Sheffield Academic Press, 1983), pp. 96-100.

deeds of the author's community. If so, God's atonement and justification is prefaced by righteous action, which is not altogether foreign to CD's worldview (cf. 3:12-16). In any case, from the content we do have, God "justifies the righteous, and pronounced the wicked to be wicked," and this statement is soteriological (i.e., the author is not talking about earthly courts). God's justifying act is connected to his atoning work toward the members of the community.[38] The act of atonement is credited to God, but those who are atoned for are the righteous remnant of the author's community. God justifies those who have already demonstrated through obedience to the commandments that they are righteous. Contrary to Paul, God explicitly does not justify the ungodly, but the righteous.[39]

This reading of CD 4:6 squares with the underlying contours of divine and human agency in CD 1–4. Throughout the context, obedience to the Mosaic Torah is a precondition for entrance into the community covenant (CD 3:12-16). Once in, the members must demonstrate sufficient obedience to sectarian law (e.g., the "hidden matters" that were "disclosed" to the community), and as a response to such obedience, God atones for their sin. We see this in CD 2, which is one of the strongest predestinarian passages in CD, if not the Scrolls as a whole:

> God loves knowledge. He has established wisdom and counsel before him; prudence and knowledge are at his service; patience is his and abundant forgiveness, *to atone for those who repent from sin.* However, might and power and a great wrath with flames of fire by the hand of all the angels of destruction upon those who turn aside from the path and abhor the precept— there will be neither remnant nor survivor. (CD 2:3-7)

Atonement is God's response to those who repent from sin. Such formulation aligns well with old covenant law (e.g., Lev 5:1-6) but is fundamentally different from Paul, who says that justification and atonement come unilaterally to those who are ungodly (Rom 4:5; cf. Rom 3:21-26; 5:10). Paul's "justification of the ungodly" formula is not just different than the type of justification endorsed by Qumran—it seems to be in critical dialogue with it.

---

38. Cf. CD 3:18; 4:9-10.
39. For similar phrases, see 1QS 5:6-7; 1QH^a 14:32; 15:12.

Justification and Abraham. As we saw earlier, Paul stands apart from his Jewish contemporaries not only in declaring that God justifies the ungodly, but also in his use of Abraham as an archetype of such unconditional grace. Qumran's understanding of Abraham correlates with the common Jewish view—Abraham's obedience is credited to him as righteousness (cf. 1 Macc 2:51-52, cited above).[40] For the author of CD, Abraham is an *exception* to the ungodly condition of humanity; for Paul, he is the epitome of it. "Abraham did not walk in it, and was considered a friend for keeping God's commandments and not following the desire of his spirit" (CD 3:2-3). The "it" that Abraham did not walk in refers to the "guilty inclination" (CD 2:16) that has infected humanity and the fallen angels (CD 2:17–3:12). The author's chronological sweep of ungodly humanity excludes Abraham, who was "counted as a friend for keeping God's precepts." Abraham's obedience was fundamental for his acceptance with God—and no first-century reader would have batted an eye at this statement. Abraham is an example of God declaring the just man just.

Qumran's perspective on Abraham and justification is implicitly affirmed in 4QMMT. At the end of this letter sent to Jerusalem, the author cites Genesis 15:6 to support his argument that God will remove the covenant curse and justify the righteous if they are obedient to sectarian law.[41]

> We have written to you *a selection of the works of the law (mqšt m'śy htôrh)* which we consider to be for your good and that of your people Isr[a]el. For we have noted in you an understanding and a knowledge of the law. Consider all these things, and seek from before him that he will make straight your counsel and keep far from you evil thoughts and the counsel of Belial. Thus you shall rejoice in the last time in finding that this selection of our words is true. *And it shall be reckoned to you for righteousness (wnḥšbh lk lṣdqh)* when

---

[40]Sir 44:19-20; 1 Macc 2:52; *Jub.* 19:8-9; cf. 23:9-10; CD 3:2-3; Jos. *Ant.* 1.233-4; *m. Kidd.* 4:14; *m. Ned.* 3:11; G. Walter Hansen, *Abraham in Galatians: Epistolary and Rhetorical Contexts,* JSNTSup 29 (Sheffield: JSOT, 1989), pp. 175-79. See too Das, "Rom 4," p. 808.

[41]The author could also have Ps 106:31 in mind. In fact, the passive voice of *wnḥšbh* ("it will be reckoned") along with the priestly context of the letter suggest a closer connection to Ps 106 than to Gen 15. However, Benjamin Schliesser is probably correct in saying that "the immediate appeal probably is to Ps 106:31" but "Gen 15:6 still constitutes the wider background, which is evident in the unique authority the 'Book of Moses' possesses" (B. Schliesser, *Abraham's Faith in Romans 4: Paul's Concept of Faith in Light of the History of Reception of Genesis 15:6,* WUNT 2.224 [Tübingen: Mohr Siebeck, 2007], p. 199). For other allusions to Gen 15:6, see Ps 106:31; *Jub.* 14:6; 1 Macc 2:51-52; Philo *Alleg. Interp.* 3.228.

you do what is right and good before him, for your good and that of Israel.
(4QMMT C 26-32)

The Jerusalem priests will trigger God's covenant blessing if they obey the sectarian laws laid out in this halachic letter. The final statement is telling: their "righteousness" is constituted in doing "what is right and good"; namely, obedience to the sectarian laws articulated in the letter. In fact, the author drives home the notion of works by conflating Genesis 15:6 with Deuteronomy 6:25: "And it will be righteousness for us, if we are careful to do all this commandment before the LORD our God."[42] In using Deuteronomy 6:25 to interpret Genesis 15:6, the author has created a view of faith that is quite different from Paul. In Romans 4:2-5, Paul takes pains to show that initial acceptance with God comes through faith apart from works, and he uses Genesis 15:6 to prove his case. But the argument in 4QMMT runs in the opposite direction. Good deeds are smuggled into Genesis 15:6, rendering mere faith without deeds as insufficient grounds for justification.

Another citation of Genesis 15:6 is found in 4QPseudo-Jubilees (4Q225): "And [Abraham] be[lieved] Go[d], and righteousness was reckoned to him" (*frag.* 2 i 7-8).[43] While there is no interpretive gloss that reveals how the author understands the relationship between faith and deeds, the text immediately jumps from Genesis 15 to Genesis 22 and uses the latter to understand the former. The binding of Isaac (Gen 22) is a test to see "whether he would not be found faithful" (4Q225 *frag.* 2 ii 8). It seems that Abraham's faith in Genesis 15:6 is viewed through the lens of "faithfulness" as manifested in Genesis 22, similar to how James 2:21 understands it. This may suggest that the author was not comfortable with the distance between Abraham's trust (Gen 15) and his deeds (Gen 22) and therefore correlated the two, as did the author of 1 Maccabees (2:51-52). If this is the case, then it provides more evidence for discontinuity between Paul and Qumran in their views of Abraham's justification. However, this understanding is not altogether clear, and on the surface 4QPseudo-Jubilees says nothing more

---

[42]See Schliesser, *Abraham's Faith*, pp. 197-200; E. Qimron and J. Strugnell, *Qumran Cave 4*, DJD 10 (Oxford: Clarendon Press, 1994), p. 63.

[43]4QPseudo-Jubilees was most likely composed in the second century B.C. before the founding of Qumran and is therefore probably not sectarian; see G. Vermès, "New Light on the Sacrifice of Isaac from 4Q225," *JJS* 47 (1996): 140-46; Schliesser, *Abraham's Faith*, pp. 183-85.

than that genuine faith will lead to faithfulness, which in itself is quite Pauline. In short, 4Q*Pseudo-Jubilees* does not reveal significant evidence for either continuity or discontinuity between Paul and Qumran.

Both Paul and some scrolls from Qumran view Abraham as significant evidence for the way in which God justifies, but they come to different conclusions. For Paul, Abraham's encounter with the justifying God highlights human dependency on divine agency, while Qumran (for the most part) assumes that the Exodus 23 principle of God justifying the righteous applies to how God acts toward the sectarians. They are—at least in comparison with other Jews—righteous, and God therefore declares them to be so.

Justification and Habakkuk 2:4. We also find similar points of discontinuity between Paul and Qumran regarding justification from their respective interpretations of Habakkuk 2:4. In Qumran's commentary on Habakkuk (1QpHab), the author writes:

> "See, it is conceited and does not give way [his soul within him]" [Hab 2:3]. Its interpretation: they will double upon them [. . . and] find [no] mercy at being judged. [. . .] [. . .] "But the righteous man will live because of his faith in him" [Hab 2:4]. Its interpretation concerns all *doers of the law* (*'ûsy htôrh*) in the House of Judah, whom God will deliver from the house of judgment on account of their toil and of their faith in the Teacher of Righteousness. (1QpHab 7:15–8:3)

But before we highlight any discontinuity, it will be helpful to note several points of continuity. First, the commentator understands Habakkuk 2:4 to speak of an eschatological situation that is a present reality for the Qumran community. The writer has been interpreting Habakkuk as speaking about "what was going to happen to the last generation" and "the consummation of the era" (1QpHab 7:1-2) throughout his commentary (cf. 2:5-6, 7; 7:7, 12). Second, the *'mûnh*, or "faith," of Habakkuk 2:4 is probably understood by the Qumran commentator in the Pauline sense of "belief" or "trust," rather than the more typical Hebraic sense of "faithfulness."[44] This is supported by

---

[44]Following Watson, *Hermeneutics of Faith,* p. 120; William H. Brownlee, *The Midrash Pesher of Habakkuk,* SBLMS (Missoula: Scholars Press, 1979), p. 125; contra Heinz-Wolfgang Kuhn, "The Impact of Selected Qumran Texts on the Understanding of Pauline Theology," in *The Bible and the Dead Sea Scrolls,* Vol. 3: *The Scrolls and Christian Origins,* ed. James H. Charlesworth (Waco, TX: Baylor University Press, 2006), pp. 153-85 (esp. 171-72).

several other passages, where the writer uses the verb "believe" to speak of the posture of the righteous (or lack thereof among the wicked) toward God and the Teacher of Righteousness (see 1QpHab 2:3-4, 6-7).[45] Third, the Teacher of Righteousness is portrayed as the central human agent of God's redeeming activity; those who seek to be saved "on the day of judgment" (1QpHab 12:14) and delivered "from the house of judgment" (1QpHab 8:2) must put their faith in him. The conceptual paradigm, garnered from Habakkuk 2:4, is strikingly Pauline. Watson, therefore, is correct to argue that "the pesherist and the apostle are agreed that it [i.e., Hab 2:4] is of fundamental importance, speaking of the divinely ordained way to salvation with a clarity and brevity virtually unparalleled in the rest of Scripture."[46]

Along with such continuity, however, there is one crucial point of discontinuity. As we saw earlier, Paul pits Habakkuk 2:4 up against Leviticus 18:5 in order to fight off any hint of law-obedience that might try to work its way into Habakkuk. The two concepts—faith and law-works—are incompatible as paths to life, according to Paul. And such opposition is crucial when it comes to justification, which is by faith and *therefore* not by the law (Gal 3:11). It is here that Qumran and Paul part company. For the Habakkuk commentator, law-obedience is not only compatible with faith but is a necessary component of it. Habakkuk's "righteous man" who "will live because of their faith in him" refers to "all doers of the law in the House of Judah, whom God will free from the house of judgment on account of their toil and of their faith in the Teacher of Righteousness" (8:1-3).[47] The phrase "doers of the law," or ʿûśy htôrh,[48] is strikingly similar to Paul's own "works of the law," and it is closely correlated with the very language of Leviticus 18:5. "The one who does *these things*," which refers to "works of the law" or mʿśy htôrh, will not be justified by them. Deliverance comes by faith—and faith

---

[45]See Watson, *Hermeneutics of Faith*, pp. 120-21. This view is also supported by the phrase "their *toil* and *their faith in* the Teacher of Righteousness" (1QpHab 8:2-3). If we take "faith" as "faithfulness" here, this would border on a synonymity, since *faithfulness* and *toil* are similar in meaning.

[46]Watson, *Hermeneutics of Faith*, p. 124.

[47]"Fidelity to the Teacher of Righteousness and accomplishment of the Law are put side by side" (Walter Grundmann, "The Teacher of Righteousness of Qumran and the Question of Justification by Faith in the Theology of the Apostle Paul," in *Paul and Qumran*, ed. J. Murphy-O'Conner [Chicago: The Priory Press, 1968], p. 97).

[48]For the phrase "doers of the law," see also 1QpHab 7:11; 4Q171 2:15, 23.

alone—in the saving work of God, according to Paul. But for the Qumran author, deliverance from the house of judgment comes upon those who observe the law by means of "their toil" (*'mlm*), which refers to the law-obedience of the "righteous one."[49] So faith and works of the law are seen as essential partners in humanity's justification and deliverance.[50] Paul's interpretation of Habakkuk 2:4 would have been quite suspect, if not unacceptable and offensive, to the Qumran pesherist.

Justification and Righteousness in 1QS 10-11. We have argued thus far that Paul's idea of the justification of the ungodly by faith, which stresses God's agency in pronouncing the wicked to be righteous, is not paralleled among the Scrolls. From the passages we have surveyed, it seems that the community at Qumran would not only have disagreed with this idea but abhorred it. God justifies the righteous; otherwise, God himself would not be just.

But one passage seems to sing a different theological tune with regard to justification. The hymn at the end of the *Manual of Discipline* (1QS)[51] in many ways reflects the God-centeredness of the *Hodayot*, as we have seen, and uses the language of righteousness to do so.[52] For the author, God's righteousness and his righteous acts are the agency of salvation.[53] For instance:

> To God belongs my judgment (*mšpṭî*). In his hand is the perfection of my behavior with the uprightness of my heart, and with his righteous acts (*wbṣdqôtû*)[54] he cancels my iniquities. . . . From the source of *his righteousness*

---

[49]Cf. 1QpHab 10:12; Watson, *Hermeneutics of Faith*, p. 122.

[50]Kuhn, "Impact," pp. 171-72; Watson, *Hermeneutics of Faith*, pp. 122-23.

[51]There are multiple authors who contributed to the *Manual of Discipline*, and it is likely that the hymn in 1QS 10-11 was added sometime later in the redactional stage. I will use "author" for simplicity's sake, acknowledging that multiple authors contributed to the document as a whole.

[52]The *Hodayot* also makes the frequent claim that righteousness belongs to God and not humanity (see, e.g., 1QHᵃ 4:32; 6:26; 7:37; 8:27, 29; 9:28; 12:32; 20:22, 34).

[53]1QS 10:11, 23, 25; 11:5, 6, 12, 14, 15; see the discussion in Markus Bockmuehl, "1QS and Salvation at Qumran," in Carson, O'Brien and Seifrid, *Justification and Variegated Nomism*, 1:397-99.

[54]I am following the majority reading of "his righteous acts" rather than Mark Seifrid's proposed reading of "my righteous acts" in his "Righteous Language in the Hebrew Scriptures and Early Judaism," in Carson, O'Brien and Seifrid, *Justification and Variegated Nomism*, 1:435-38. Bockmuehl is correct to point out that "the context repeatedly denies human righteousness, and stresses instead that it is only *God's* righteousness and righteous acts that are *instrumental* to salvation" ("1QS and Salvation," p. 398n60). Though I agree with Bockmuehl about the near context and therefore his reading of 11:3, Seifrid is correct to point out the emphasis on human righteousness in behavioral terms throughout 1QS.

(*ṣdqtû*) is *my judgment* (*mšptî*) and from the wonderful mystery is the delight
in my heart. . . . If I stumble, the mercies of God will be my salvation always;
and if I fall in the sin of the flesh, *by the righteousness of God* (*bṣdqtû*), which
endures eternally, will be *my judgment* (*mšptî*). . . . *He will judge me* (*mšptî*) *by
the righteousness* (*bṣdqt*) of his truth, and in his abundant goodness he will
always atone for all my sins. *And in his righteousness* (*wbṣdqtû*) he will cleanse
me from the uncleanness of the human being. (1QS 11:2-3, 5, 11-12, 14-15)

One would have to search long and hard to find any hint of works-
righteousness or merit theology in this passage. And if Paul were writing
Romans 4:4 polemically, it certainly was not against the view expressed in this
hymn. The author clearly relies on God, not his own merit, for his justification.[55] Several other passages from the *Hodayot* also express similar "justification by grace alone" sentiments. The most explicit is 1QH[a] 5:22-23: "*Only*
(*rq*) by your goodness is man justified (*yṣdq*), [purified] by the abundance of
[your] compa[ssion.]"[56] In fact, the hymnist aligns well with Luther's Paul by
applying the emphatic "only" or "alone" (*rq*) to the justification formula.[57]

How do we reconcile such radical statements about God's grace and
mercy in justification with the passages we looked at above that condemn
the justification of the ungodly? (Assuming, again, that reconciliation is a
worthy path to pursue.) Would the author of 1QS 10–11 have sided with Paul
against the author of CD?

While a good deal of continuity is undeniable, two observations reveal
more *discontinuity* between 1QS 10–11 and Paul than is often recognized.
First, Paul's concept of God justifying the ungodly is reserved for the initial

---

[55]The word *mšpt* can be translated as "judgment," as in, e.g., P. Wernberg-Møller, *The Manual of
Discipline* (Leiden: Brill, 1957), pp. 36-39, or as "justification," as in, e.g., P. Garnet, *Salvation and
Atonement in the Qumran Scrolls*, WUNT 2.3 (Tübingen: Mohr Siebeck, 1977), pp. 76-77. In
some cases it clearly refers to punishment in 1QS (10:11, 20, 25). But in column 11, the writer
expects a favorable verdict on judgment day, and therefore the term should be translated as
"justification" in 11:2, 5, 10, 12 and 14. This translation is further supported if the meaning of
mšpt is derived from *ṣdqh*, which seems likely in 1QS 11:5: "From the spring of his justice (*ṣdqtû*)
is my judgment (*mšptî*)." See the discussion in Garnet, *Salvation and Atonement*, pp. 76-77.
[56]"You, you alone, have [created] the just man, and from the womb you determined him for the
period of approval, to keep your covenant, and to walk on all (your paths)" (1QH[a] 7:17-18); "For
I leaned on your kindnesses and the abundance of your compassion. for you atone iniquity and
cleanse man of his guilt through your justice" (12:36-37); "There is an abundance of forgiveness
and a multitude of [compass]sion when you judge me" (17:34).
[57]See Kuhn, "Impact," pp. 179-80.

acceptance of the sinner, not the final judgment, which is according to works (see the next chapter). 1QS 10–11, however, is oriented toward the final judgment.[58] The significance of this should not be missed. For the Qumran author, justification must take into account righteous obedience, since this was fundamental for membership and continuance in the community.[59] This still does not mean that 1QS 10–11 is governed by merit theology. In fact, as we will see in the next chapter, Paul believes that works are necessary for final justification. But the hymn in 1QS 10–11, which is wholly future orientated, does not match Paul's peculiar assertion that God *initially* justifies the wicked. Moreover, righteous behavior was considered a means of atonement in at least some places in the Scrolls. The men of the council "atone for sin by doing justice" (*bᶜôśy mšpt*; 1QS 8:2) and "make atonement for all who freely volunteer for holiness" (1QS 5:6).[60] In short, God will justify *in the end* those who are part of the righteous remnant, those who have demonstrated *through obedience to sectarian law* that they are not of the Sons of Darkness. Even if such obedience is divinely empowered and ultimately insignificant compared to God's own righteousness—hence the pessimism in the hymn—justification according to 1QS 10–11 is not of the ungodly in the Pauline sense.

Second, as we saw in the previous chapter, this hymn paints humanity in such dark terms largely in light of the God/human contrast. As in the *Hodayot,* when one is compared to God, he cannot be considered righteous, since only God is righteous. But when one is compared to fellow human,

---

[58]This is clear in light of the phrases "the day of vengeance" (1QS 10:19), "until he carries out my judgment" (10:20), and the unqualified "the judgment" (11:10); so most interpreters. Seifrid, "Righteous Language," p. 432; Gathercole, *Boasting,* p. 99: "The hymn at the end of 1QS (esp. 11:13-18) is described in wholly futuristic terms"; contra VanLandingham, pp. 126-31.

[59]1QS 1:3-5, 13, 26; 8:2; see also the phrase "perfection of way" in 1QS 1:8; 2:2; 3:9, 20, 22; 4:22; 8:1, 9, 10, 18, 20, 21; 9:2, 5, 14, 19.

[60]Cf. 1QS 9:3; 4Q400 *frag.* 1 i 14-16; 4Q504 *frags.* 1-2 ii 9-10, iv 5-7; vi 5-6; Seifrid, "Righteous Language," p. 437. Atonement is also seen to be an act of God (1QHᵃ 12:37; 1QS 11:3; CD 2:4; 3:18; 4:6-7; 20:34). 1QS 3:6-8 says atonement is by the "spirit," though this could emphasize divine or human agency (I side with the latter). Given the acknowledgement of both God and humanity's role in atonement, Bockmuehl is correct to conclude: "For the Qumran Community, therefore, atonement for sin remains the prerogative of God himself. Its appropriation, however, is possible only to repentant members of the sect, since its sacrificial locus comes to be situated very specifically in the worship and praxis of the *yahad* " ("1QS and Salvation," p. 402). But this only confirms our conclusion that this is remarkably different from Paul's formulation of justification in terms of God's *initial* declaration that the ungodly are in fact righteous through faith. Such formulation can only be sustained through emphasizing divine agency.

then he can be considered righteous or unrighteous (e.g., 1QH[a] 17:14-17). "At the judgment you pronounce guilty all those who harass me, separating the just from the wicked through me" (1QH[a] 15:12). The same is probably assumed by the hymnist who wrote 1QS 10–11. This would allow him to affirm the rest of 1QS, which assumes that righteousness is possible—indeed necessary—for the covenant members, and at the same time sing about his unrighteousness before God.

Therefore, the authors of 1QS 10–11, the *Hodayot*, the *Habakkuk Pesher* and the *Damascus Document* can all affirm with a good measure of consistency, though not uniformity, that God does not *initially* justify the wicked and that God *will* justify the righteous remnant, who have persevered in sectarian law. What sets Paul apart are his radical statements about God's *initial* acceptance of the wicked, who have demonstrated no measure of righteousness, not even in comparison to other seemingly more wicked people. Indeed, 1QS 10–11 stands closer to Paul than other documents we have examined, but there are still observable points of discontinuity; Paul and Qumran do not have the same understanding of justification.

CONCLUSION

The assertion that "Paul's doctrine has exactly the same *shape* as that of MMT" or other documents from Qumran simply cannot be sustained.[61] When Paul brings the future verdict forward into the present, he erases all preconditions for God's justifying act and therefore radicalizes it. While there are some aspects of continuity in their views of justification, Paul's emphasis on God's initial act of justification of the ungodly through grace is unparalleled—even rebutted—in the Scrolls. And their respective understandings of Abraham, Genesis 15:6 and Habakkuk 2:4 only magnify the disagreement.

---

[61]N. T. Wright, "4QMMT and Paul: Justification, 'Works,' and Eschatology," in *History and Exegesis: New Testament Essays in Honor of Dr. E. Earle Ellis for His 80th Birthday*, ed. Aang-Won (Aaron) Son (New York: T & T Clark, 2006), pp. 104-32 (esp. 120). Wright begins his article by surveying 1QS 10-11 and then seeks to show that MMT assumes the same shape of justification (pp. 104-6). Wright correctly notes the future orientation of justification language in Qumran and also points how that Paul brings this future verdict forward into the present; however, I do not think that Wright recognizes how the difference in timing alters the shape of justification in Paul.

But what do we do with Paul's statements about future judgment according to works? While Paul and Qumran do not share the same perspective on initial justification, do they see eye to eye concerning human deeds and the final day? To these questions we now turn.

7

JUDGMENT
ACCORDING TO WORKS

In the previous chapter, we saw that Paul and Qumran exhibit a good deal of discontinuity in their views on justification. For Paul, the human agent brings nothing to the table in the initial act of justification. He is, in other words, in the state of wickedness when God declares him to be righteous. According to Qumran, justification is God's future verdict pronounced on the members of the community and therefore assumes a measure of obedience—God would never justify the wicked.[1] But how does this relate to the final day? Do Paul and Qumran exhibit continuity in their views on the role of works in future judgment?

Paul clearly views works as a necessary criterion for final judgment. He says, for instance, that "each one's work will become manifest, for the Day will disclose it" and "if the work that anyone has built on the foundation survives, he will receive a reward" (1 Cor 3:13-14). Again, "we must all appear before the judgment seat of Christ, so that each one may receive what is due for what he has done in the body, whether good or evil" (2 Cor 5:10). According to Paul, Christian obedience will matter on judgment day—though the exact way in which it will matter is teased out by scholars in a variety of ways. This is why Paul affirms the principle that Christians reap what they

---

[1]"Wicked" in the sense of outside the covenant community. Of course, 1QS 10–11 and other passages reveal that compared to God, no one—not even covenant members—are righteous, and yet they are still not part of the Sons of Darkness. Though plagued with sin, it is the Sons of Light who will be justified.

sow, and if one sows by the spirit, he "will from the Spirit reap eternal life" (Gal 6:8). This is also why Paul compares the Christian life to a race, where the runner rushes toward the finish line so as to receive a prize (1 Cor 9:24-27), and why Paul commands the Philippian church to "work out your own salvation with fear and trembling" (Phil 2:12). Paul says all of this because works will matter on judgment day for believers.[2]

Similar statements can be found throughout the Dead Sea literature. In the *Manual of Discipline,* we find an extensive reflection on judgment in column 4, where the wicked are punished for their evil deeds (1QS 4:11-14, 18-19) and the righteous are rewarded: "The reward of all those who walk in it will be healing, plentiful peace in a long life, fruitful offspring with all everlasting blessings, eternal enjoyment with endless life, and a crown of glory with majestic raiment in eternal light" (4:6-8). Later in the same document, it is said: "For to God (belongs) the judgment of every living being, and it is he who pays man his wages" (1QS 10:18). This eschatological repayment is affirmed in 11QPs 22:10: "Man is examined according to his path, each one is rewarded according to his deeds" (cf. Ps 62:12), and is implied in other passages, where eternal life is conditioned on perseverance (CD 3:20; 7:5-6; cf. 20:34).[3]

Paul and Qumran are in agreement that judgment is according to works. But the phrase "according to" is ambiguous and says little about the interaction between divine and human agency. This chapter, then, will seek to clarify the matter by asking the question: What is the relationship between divine and human agency in the works that pertain to judgment day?

As expected, there is no scholarly consensus on this question. The disagreement can be exemplified in two important works published around the same time. In 1999, Kent Yinger published his doctoral dissertation, *Paul, Judaism, and Judgment According to Deeds,*[4] which argued that Paul and Judaism resemble each other in framework when it comes to divine and human agency in final judgment. According to Yinger, both Paul and Qumran believe that initial salvation is by grace and election, while final

---

[2] See also Rom 14:10-12; 1 Cor 4:1-5; 2 Cor 9:6; 11:15.
[3] See also 1QH 12:18-22.
[4] Kent Yinger, *Paul, Judaism, and Judgment According to Deeds,* SNTSMS 105 (Cambridge: Cambridge University Press, 1999).

judgment is according to works. Such works, though, are not meritorious but evidence of covenant fidelity. "In both patterns," argues Yinger, "salvation is not earned by human initiative, but is given by God's grace; *and it is contingent upon continuance in the faith and obedience which are required by that relationship.*"[5] In short, human deeds matter on judgment day, since they are "the *necessary manifestation* of that which has already been obtained and assured through faith."[6]

A few years later, Simon Gathercole published his dissertation, *Where Is Boasting?*,[7] which concluded, against Yinger, that there is more discontinuity between Paul and Judaism in their views of the final judgment. Gathercole agrees with Yinger that final judgment is according to deeds for both Paul and Judaism, but argues that "Paul has an understanding of obedience that is radically different from that of his Jewish contemporaries."[8] Divine agency, for Paul, "is both the source and the continuous cause of obedience for the Christian."[9] Therefore, while there is "continuity as to obedience being a criterion for final judgment," there is "discontinuity as to the character of the obedience."[10] Gathercole admits, however, that Qumran exhibits closer parallels to Paul's theology of empowerment than what we find elsewhere in Judaism, since both have comparable pneumatologies. The main difference is that Qumran emphasizes the spirit's role in illuminating the believer, which leads to obedience, while Paul believes that Christian obedience is the byproduct of the spirit's internal work.[11]

In short, both Gathercole and Yinger affirm the presence of a judgment according to works theme in Qumran and in Paul, though they disagree over the relationship between God's verdict and the character of human obedience.[12] In the following, we will look at judgment according to works

---

[5]Ibid., p. 289.

[6]Ibid., p. 290.

[7]Simon J. Gathercole, *Where Is Boasting? Early Jewish Soteriology and Paul's Response in Romans 1–5* (Grand Rapids: Eerdmans, 2002).

[8]Ibid., p. 264.

[9]Ibid.

[10]Ibid., p. 133.

[11]Ibid., pp. 132-35.

[12]Yinger does not believe that works determine one's future salvation at Qumran, while Gathercole does. For Yinger, "judgment according to deeds meant almost exclusively *the punishment of the wicked,*" and not the reward for the righteous for their obedience. Obedience, for Yinger, is a response to God's gracious initiative in salvation. "Only belonging to this

in Paul and Qumran in order to understand how they relate divine and human agency with regard to the final day.

JUDGMENT ACCORDING TO WORKS IN PAUL

I will first demonstrate that Gathercole's conclusion about the divinely empowered character of Christian obedience is not only fundamental to Paul, but is often the driving force behind his confidence concerning the final day. This will be an important point when we consider some judgment passages where divine agency in human works is in the purview. I will then show that select eschatological passages envision unmediated divine action that secures the final verdict for the believer. Works are conspicuously left out of the equation. Last, I will examine Romans 2, which seems to contradict my first two points. In the end, we will see that Paul argues (and sometimes assumes) that Christian obedience is derived from and empowered by Christ and the spirit, and this feeds his confidence toward the final day.

Divinely Empowered Obedience. Paul's letter to the Philippians will be a fitting starting point—it is replete with moral exhortations, yet the possibility of obeying such commands is grounded in divine agency.[13] The key text is Philippians 2:12-13: "Work out your own salvation with fear and trembling, for it is God who works in you, both to will and to work for his good pleasure." Divine agency not only initiates the process of salvation but carries it through and completes it. The very desire to obey is the byproduct of God's influence in the human will. The attitude of "fear and trembling" that accompanies such obedience does not mean that the believer's judgment-day verdict is in question; rather, it describes the posture of one who is encountering the presence of God.[14] Divine initiative is also under-

---

remnant or 'planting' assures salvation from the coming judgment" (Yinger, *Paul, Judaism, and Judgment*, p. 137). So the obedience that matters on judgment day does not determine one's future standing; rather, it gives evidence that they were a genuine, elect member of the community. Gathercole, however, surveys various passages among the Scrolls, where the obedience of the righteous and the disobedience of the wicked are rewarded symmetrically. In other words, the deeds of the righteous are rewarded in the same manner that the deeds of the wicked are punished. We will survey texts below that support Gathercole's view.

[13]For a fuller treatment of the following reading of Philippians, see J. Ross Wagner, "Working Out Salvation: Holiness and Community in Philippians," in *Holiness and Ecclesiology in the New Testament*, ed. Kent E. Brower and Andy Johnson (Grand Rapids: Eerdmans, 2007), pp. 257-74.

[14]This is the typical response when one encounters God in the Old Testament: Ex 15:16; Ps 2:11; Is 19:16; 66:2, 5; Dan 4:37; 10:11. Wagner, "Working Out Salvation," p. 263, following P. T.

scored by the phrase "for good pleasure," which points to God's electing grace as seen throughout the New Testament.[15] J. Ross Wagner rightly sums up the logic of this passage by saying, "God stands right at the center of human volition and action; divine and human agency are inextricably woven together in the lives of those Christians whom God is saving."[16]

The letter as a whole is shaped by the same emphasis on divine agency that we see in Philippians 2:12-13. Paul began the letter with the assurance that "he who began a good work in you will bring it to completion at the day of Jesus Christ" (Phil 1:6). The eschatological direction (i.e., the "day of Christ") implies that divine action is necessary not only for initial justification but also for final judgment. Human obedience, which is altogether necessary for that positive verdict, is elicited by the ongoing work of God in the believer.[17] Later in the chapter, Paul exhorts the church in Philippi to stand firm against persecution (Phil 1:27-28) and grounds his exhortation in the divine authorship of both their faith and their suffering. God is at work behind the scenes to shape their faith through suffering; Paul himself was a beneficiary of this type of divine shaping (Phil 2:17-18). Unlike Romans and Galatians, the work of the spirit is not as thoroughly pronounced in Philippians, and yet his empowering presence is still evident. In Philippians 3:3, Paul says that true worship can only come through the agency of the spirit, in contrast to human achievement (i.e., "confidence in the flesh").[18] This initiates a lengthy discussion where Paul affirms God's past and continuing work in the life of the believer. On the one hand, Paul discusses his own pursuit of Christ and "straining forward to what lies ahead" (Phil 3:13), but on the other hand, such human activity is governed by God's ongoing work. It is "the power of his [Christ's] resurrection" that enables Paul to "attain" his own "resurrection from the dead" (Phil 3:11). Again, after expressing his

---

O'Brien, *The Epistle to the Philippians: A Commentary on the Greek Text*, NIGTC (Grand Rapids: Eerdmans, 1991), pp. 282-84.

[15]Mt 11:26; Luke 10:21; Eph 1:5, 9; cf. 1 Cor 1:21; Gal 1:15; Col 1:19; see further Wagner, "Working Out Salvation," p. 260.

[16]Wagner, "Working Out Salvation," p. 259.

[17]According to Paul, the community is the necessary location where this salvation is worked out. There is no room in Paul's theology for individual sanctification, as Wagner points out ("Working Out Salvation").

[18]The same connection between heart circumcision and the agency of the spirit is made in Rom 2:29.

desire to "press on to make it my own" (Phil 3:12a), he quickly qualifies this with, "because Christ Jesus has made me his own" (Phil 3:12b). Paul is consciously aware, it would seem, that God's power shoulders his own process of obedience—hence his careful phrasing, which prevents an undue emphasis on his own agency. Such obedience is necessary to receive a positive verdict on judgment day, as Paul will say elsewhere. However, Paul envisions the day of Christ as the climax of God's dynamic work in the life of the believer. When Jesus appears on that day, he "will transform our lowly body to be like his glorious body, according to *the working of his power (tēn energeian tou dynasthai)* even to subject all things to himself" (Phil 3:21).[19] On that day, the ongoing work of God (Phil 1:6; 2:13) and power of God (Phil 3:10) will bring to completion what he initiated.

Galatians also bears witness to the same priority of divine agency in human obedience.[20] We can take as a starting point Paul's theologically packed testimony in Galatians 2:20-21: "I have been crucified with Christ. It is no longer I who live but Christ who lives in me. And the life I now live in the flesh I live by faith in the Son of God, who loved me and gave himself up for me. I do not nullify the grace of God, for if righteous were through law, then Christ died fo no purpose" (Gal 2:20-21). Paul's new life is not simply a response to God's grace given at conversion, but has been reconstituted by Christ, who now "lives in me." Christ's self-giving death, summed up as "the grace of God," enables and energizes[21] Paul's vigorous subsequent obedience. "The whole context," says Richard Hays, "portrays Christ as the active agent and Paul as the instrument through which and/or for whom Christ's activity comes to expression." Hays goes on to suggest that "this unrelenting emphasis on the priority of Christ's (or God's) willing and doing over any human will or action is the theo-

---

[19]My translation.

[20]For an in-depth treatment of the following reading of Galatians, see Preston M. Sprinkle, *Law and Life: The Interpretation of Leviticus 18:5 in Early Judaism and in Paul*, WUNT 2.241 (Tübingen: Mohr Siebeck, 2008), pp. 153-56; see also John M. G. Barclay, "Paul's Story: Theology as Testimony," in *Narrative Dynamics in Paul: A Critical Assessment*, ed. Bruce Longenecker (Louisville, KY: Westminster John Knox, 2002), pp. 133-56.

[21]The word "energize" is from John Barclay, who coins the word *energism* (as opposed to *monergism* or *synergism*) to capture the relationship of divine and human agency. John M. G. Barclay, "'By the Grace of God I Am What I Am': Grace and Agency in Philo and Paul," in *Divine and Human Agency in Paul and His Cultural Environment*, ed. John M. G. Barclay and Simon J. Gathercole, LNTS 335 (New York: T & T Clark, 2006), p. 156n39.

logical keynote of the entire letter."[22] A brief tour of Galatians validates Hays's assertion.

Throughout Galatians, Paul describes both his apostleship and the origin of his gospel in terms of God's sovereign action (Gal 1:1, 11-12). In the midst of Paul's human pursuit of religion (Gal 1:13-14), God revealed Jesus to him and reconstructed his life and ministry (Gal 1:15-16). Divine action is central not only in Paul's conversion (Gal 1:15-16) but also in his apostolic work for the gospel, as he testifies in Galatians 2:8-10: "He who worked through Peter for his apostolic ministry . . . worked also through me for mine." Paul will call this ongoing divine work "the grace that was given to me" (Gal 2:9), which is expressed more fully in Galatians 2:20-21 (cited above). We saw earlier that Paul is quick to qualify statements about his desire to pursue Christ with recognition of Christ's own pursuit of him (Phil 3:12). The same qualification is seen in Galatians 4:9, where Paul affirms that the Galatians "have come to know God," but then quickly adjusts his language to prioritize divine action: "or rather to be known by God." God's involvement in the life of the Galatian church is prior to and generative of the Galatians' own pursuit of God—and Paul's self-qualification reveals that this distinction is important. Insofar as the church is obedient to God, Paul considers this to be an outworking of the spirit's activity, the means through which God elicits what he demands (Gal 5:16-26).

Galatians 5:4-6 is of particular importance, since it discusses Christian obedience in light of judgment day: "You are severed from Christ, you who would be justified by the law; you have fallen away from grace. For by the Spirit, by faith, we ourselves eagerly wait for the hope of righteousness. For in Christ Jesus neither circumcision nor uncircumcision counts for anything, but only faith working through love" (Gal 5:4-6). Paul contrasts justification by the law and justification by the spirit ("by the Spirit . . . the hope of righteousness"). On one level, this is a clear contrast between human and divine agency in justification. Paul affirms that the spirit, who operates in the realm of Christian faith (*ek pisteōs*), is the agent (*pneumati*) of future justification ("the hope of righteousness").[23] This correlates with the work

---

[22] Richard Hays, *The Faith of Jesus Christ: The Narrative Substructure of Galatians 3:1–4:11*, 2nd ed. (Grand Rapids: Eerdmans, 2002), p. 155; Barclay, "By the Grace of God," p. 152.
[23] The use of the verb *dikaiousthe* in Gal 5:4 suggests a contrast with the noun *dikaosynēs* in Gal 5:5,

of the spirit in Galatians 5:16-26; 6:8, where Paul says that everlasting life will be attained "from the Spirit." It is nonsensical, therefore, to claim that the "Last Judgment" in Paul "is not a judgment . . . over what the Holy Spirit has done in the believer" but "a judgment over the individual and what he or she has done."[24] Quite the opposite. Obedience will matter on judgment day, but it is impossible—or at least un-Pauline—to separate what the believer has done from what the spirit and Christ have done in the believer.

So the race is not run alone. The Christian does not leave grace behind in order to pursue works under her own power. Rather, the intrusion of grace produces the works that God demands, a thought captured in Paul's concise statement in 1 Corinthians 15:10: "But by the grace of God I am what I am, and his grace toward me was not in vain. On the contrary, I worked harder than any of them, though it was not I, but the grace of God that is with me." Much more is at work here than a nebulous affirmation of salvation by grace. Paul speaks of grace as a perpetual power that propels him toward the finish line—"his grace toward me *was not in vain*"; grace works continually. Paul's response was to work harder than the rest. Grace and (Christian) works are not antithetical in Paul. The former activates the latter. But it is not a zero-sum game, where grace fades out and human agency takes over.[25] For Paul, his own performance is not a product of the unmoved human will (cf. Phil 2:13), but due to "the grace of God that is with me" (1 Cor 15:10). Paul's articulation of the divine/human relation is both explicit and profound. He acknowledges the possibility that grace could be received "in vain," as he says elsewhere (1 Cor 15:2, 14; 2 Cor 6:1), but then stresses that this grace did indeed take effect "not in his passivity but in his (hyper-) activity."[26] In the words of John Barclay, "divine grace calls forth, or takes effect in, human labour," but then Paul qualifies this by "denying" in some

---

and therefore the latter probably has the idea of a future justification. This future verdict should not be separated from initial justification, but is a public declaration of what has been accomplished in the past (cf. Rom 5:19; 1 Cor 4:4). See the excellent discussion in J. Louis Martyn, *Galatians: A New Translation with Introduction and Commentary*, AB (New York: Doubleday, 1997), pp. 472, 478-79; contra Ronald Y. K. Fung, *The Epistle to the Galatians*, NICNT (Grand Rapids: Eerdmans, 1988), pp. 224-28, 232-35.

[24]Chris VanLandingham, *Judgment and Justification in Early Judaism and the Apostle Paul* (Peabody, MA: Hendrickson, 2006), p. 335.

[25]See John M. G. Barclay, "Introduction," in Barclay and Gathercole, *Divine and Human Agency in Paul*, pp. 1-8; see also Barclay, "'By the Grace of God,'" p. 151.

[26]Barclay, "'By the Grace of God,'" p. 151.

sense "the agency of the 'I' in the labour, or at least *strongly qualifying* it by reference to the grace of God which is 'with me.'"[27] This verse then is a crisp summary of the dialectic between God and humanity that we saw throughout Philippians and Galatians, where the human agent has been empowered by the grace of God. And the eschatological orientation of Paul's thought throughout those letters (Phil 1:6, 19; 3:20-21; Gal 1:4; 5:5; 6:8) suggests that divine agency will play a determinative role at the final judgment in that it creates and sustains the obedience that is necessary for a positive verdict.

Romans 8:1-13 also underscores divinely empowered obedience leading to judgment day. We have already seen (Rom 8:1-4) that God's radical intervention through Christ and the spirit satisfies the sum total of the law and transforms believers so that they can walk according to the spirit—something that the law could not do. The ensuing verses (Rom 8:5-13) speak of the ongoing nature of this transformed life, and all credit is given to the spirit. Romans 8:5-9 sums up Paul's argument in Romans 7:6–8:4; namely, that seeking liberation through the law will bring death, but being liberated through Christ and living by the spirit issues in life. Paul then sums up his argument (Rom 8:9-11) by looking forward to resurrection—the reward given to believers on judgment day. But this reward is not simply a response to an obedient life, it is created through the agency of the spirit: "If the Spirit of him who raised Jesus from the dead dwells in you, he who raised Christ Jesus from the dead will also give life to your mortal bodies through his Spirit who dwells in you" (Rom 8:11). This concurs with other "judgment according to works" passages, since the spirit's living presence in the believer will generate the works necessary for a positive verdict (Rom 8:5-8, 12-13). In short, the overwhelming emphasis in the full spectrum of salvation—the initial, ongoing and final work of God—is on divine agency.

Divine agency lingers in the background of three other "judgment according to works" passages. 1 Corinthians 3–4 contains several troubling statements (to Protestant ears) that seem to contradict Paul's belief that justification is by faith.

Each will receive his wages according to his labor. (1 Cor 3:8)

Each one's work will become manifest, for the Day will disclose it, because it

---

[27]Ibid.

will be revealed by fire, and the fire will test what sort of work each one has done. If the work that anyone has built on the foundation survives, he will receive a reward. (1 Cor 3:13-14)

Therefore do not pronounce judgment before the time, before the Lord comes, who will bring to light the things now hidden in darkness and will disclose the purposes of the heart. Then each one will receive his commendation from God. (1 Cor 4:5)

Assuming that Paul refers to believers in general and not just missionaries or apostles, the passage states clearly that works will matter on judgment day.[28] But as with the rest of the passages surveyed above, such works are a result of God's transformative work in and through the believer. Paul began the letter by reminding the Corinthians that "the grace of God . . . was given you" (1 Cor 1:4), and is confident that Christ "*will sustain (bebaiōsei)* you to the end, guiltless in the day of our Lord Jesus Christ" (1 Cor 1:8). The following assertion that "God is faithful" (1 Cor 1:9) refers back to Paul's confidence in the sustaining power of God through Christ that ensures their guiltless position on judgment day (1 Cor 1:4-8).[29] Fee rightly acknowledges that in 1 Corinthians, "Paul is concerned to remind the church that they have not yet arrived," yet here in the opening statements "he holds out before them his great confidence that by God's own action they will indeed make it in the end."[30]

Such confidence in the power of God at work in the Corinthians—despite the way some are living—underlies Paul's argument over the next four chapters (1 Cor 1:10-4:21). Paul maintains a consistent contrast between the power of God and the weakness of humanity in 1 Corinthians 1:18-31, where the power of God at work in the gospel shames the wise by electing the foolish. The purpose is "so that no human being might boast in the presence of God" (1 Cor 1:29). Paul emphatically grounds his eschatological expectation in the work of God: "Because of him you are in Christ Jesus, who

---

[28]Both H. Räisänen, *Paul and the Law* (Philadelphia: Fortress Press, 1986), p. 185n116, and T. R. Schreiner, *Paul, Apostle of God's Glory in Christ: A Pauline Theology* (Downers Grove, IL: InterVarsity Press, 2001), p. 288, limit this passage to apostolic ministers, such as Apollos and Paul.

[29]J. Gundry-Volf, *Paul and Perseverance: Staying In and Falling Away* (Minneapolis: Westminster John Knox, 2991), pp. 76-79; Gordon Fee, *The First Epistle to the Corinthians*, NICNT (Grand Rapids: Eerdmans, 1987), pp. 43-44.

[30]Fee, *1 Corinthians*, p. 44.

became to us wisdom from God, righteousness and sanctification and redemption, so that, as it is written, 'Let the one who boasts, boast in the Lord'"
(1 Cor 1:30-31). Boasting is excluded because the whole saving process is
wrought by the power of God. It was the spirit of God who created faith in
the Corinthian believers (1 Cor 2:5) and the same spirit reveals the wisdom
of God to them (1 Cor 2:6-16). The factions in the Corinthian church expose
a faith in human wisdom and not faith in divine wisdom and power (1 Cor
3:1-4). Paul therefore grounds his argument in God's creating and sustaining
power at work in the church and the missionary efforts of the apostles:
"What then is Apollos? What is Paul? Servants through whom you believed,
as the Lord assigned to each. I planted, Apollos watered, but God gave the
growth. So neither he who plants nor he who waters is anything, but only
God who gives the growth" (1 Cor 3:5-7). The work of Apollos and Paul is
sidelined in order to highlight the fundamental work of God. The growth
that is credited to God's agency is the same "labor" that will be vindicated
on judgment day, as the next verse says: "He who plants [i.e., Paul] and he
who waters [i.e., Apollos] are one, and each will receive his wages according
to his labor" (1 Cor 3:8). Again, Paul has already declared the "labor" that is
to be rewarded to be *nothing apart from the generative work of God who
gives the growth* (1 Cor 3:7). Paul reiterates the point in 1 Corinthians 3:10 by
crediting his apostolic labors to "the grace of God given to me." Paul's work
is an outgrowth of God's work in him.

God's activity in believers weaves its way through Paul's argument in
1 Corinthians 1–3. And this is seen at the end of chapter 3, when Paul returns
to his original boasting motif (cf. 1 Cor 1:30-31): "So let no one boast in men.
For all things are yours, whether Paul or Apollos or Cephas or the world or
life or death or the present or the future—all are yours, and you are Christ's,
and Christ is God's" (1 Cor 3:21-23). Paul previously emphasized that divine
agency is the formal cause of the believer's confidence toward judgment day
(1 Cor 1:4-9), and now asserts that it is fundamental for all of Paul and Apollos's missionary labors (cf. 1 Cor 3:5-23). To think otherwise is tantamount
to boasting in human beings (1 Cor 3:21). In short, the judgment according
to works passages in 1 Corinthians (1 Cor 3:8, 13; 4:5) must be read within
these bookends; God is the author and sustainer of the works that will be
repaid on judgment day.

Other judgment passages exhibit the same assumption regarding human deeds and divine agency. In 2 Corinthians 5:10 Paul says that each believer will "receive what is due for what he has done in the body, whether good or evil." This passage is ultimately rooted in the power of God and the work of the spirit in the new covenant, which Paul described in 2 Corinthians 3:1–4:6, and it is more immediately grounded in the claim that "He who has prepared us for this very thing [i.e., resurrection] is God, who has given us the Spirit as a guarantee" (2 Cor 5:5; cf. 2 Cor 1:21-22). Paul's statement in 2 Corinthians 5:10, therefore, is not a naked assertion that judgment is according to works; rather, it flows from the ongoing empowerment of God through the spirit guaranteeing that a positive verdict awaits the genuine believer in Christ.

The same confidence is true of Romans 14:10-12, where Paul says that the believer "will stand (*parastēsometha*) before the judgment seat of God" and "give an account of himself to God." Not only is this passage connected with the larger argument of Romans 1–11 (especially Rom 5:1; 8:1), but it is also more immediately prefaced by Paul's confidence that "*he will be made to stand* [in judgment] (*stathēsetai*), *for the Lord is able* (*dynatei*) *to make him stand* (*stēsai auton*)" (Rom 14:4).[31] Judgment day will not lay bare the works of an autonomous human agent but will consider whether or not the human agent has been overcome and empowered by God's dynamic grace.

So tethered is God's activity to human obedience that Paul can sum up an entire argument about sanctification (Rom 6:1-22) by saying: "For the wages of sin is death, but the free gift of God is eternal life in Christ Jesus our Lord" (Rom 6:23).[32] Paul has been exhorting the Roman believers to

---

[31]"The emphasis in this passage is on the power of the *kurios*." R. Jewett, *Romans: A Commentary*, Hermeneia (Minneapolis: Fortress, 2007), p. 843; see also D. Moo, *The Epistle to the Romans*, NICNT (Grand Rapids: Eerdmans, 1996), p. 841.

[32]The term "wages" (*opsōnia*) is a commercial term that refers to compensation of services performed. John the Baptist, for instance, told the soldiers to be content with their "wages" (*opsōniois*; Lk 3:14). When Paul here contrasts "wages" with "free gift," the contrast can only be between the services (= sin) performed, which was compensated with death, and no services performed, which was rewarded with the "free gift" of eternal life after judgment day. A similar contrast between "wages" and "grace" was given in Rom 4:4-5 and Rom 5:15-16 to refer to the unilateral act of God in Christ, which secured our *initial justification*. Paul, therefore, goes beyond his Qumran contemporaries—and even beyond his own "judgment according to works" statements—by viewing "eternal life" as an undeserved reward "without regard to whether or not one has fulfilled the requirements of the law" (Jewett, *Romans*, 426).

respond to grace with obedience and even affirmed that such sanctification will lead to eternal life (Rom 6:22), but he sums up his argument by calling eternal life a free gift of God. Paul can say this, since God's grace not only demands but creates the obedience necessary for gaining the reward of life on judgment day.[33]

Gathercole's assertion that "divine action is both the source and continuous cause of obedience for the Christian" is thus far confirmed, and it sharpens Paul's confidence in judgment day, even though it is according to works. But there is more. Paul's understanding of divine agency at the final judgment is even more pronounced in passages where God's act in Christ is determinative not only for initial justification but for the final judgment—even when spirit-empowered obedience is not in view.

Divine Agency at the Final Judgment. Previously, we noted the focus on divine agency for initial justification in Romans 5:6-9, where enemies are justified by the death of Christ. The same emphasis is applied to judgment day, where the risen Christ secures the believer's final salvation. Paul writes: "Since, therefore, we have now been justified by his blood," referring to initial justification, "much more shall we be saved by him from the wrath of God" (Rom 5:9), which says that Christ is the agent of our future salvation from the wrath of God. The term judgment is not in the passage, but the concept is. Paul believes that Christ not only secured our initial acceptance but also our final acceptance before God. The underlying logic is that if he could do the former—the more difficult thing—then surely he could do the latter, which is much easier.[34] He goes on to say: "For if while we were enemies we were reconciled to God by the death of his Son" (initial acceptance) "much more, now that we are reconciled, shall we be saved by his life" (Rom 5:10). The phrase "shall we be saved by his life" refers to our future salvation by means of the risen and living Christ.[35] Divine agency through the death and

---

[33]The phrase "eternal life" refers to the reward given to believers on judgment day. Paul explicitly said this in Rom 2:7, and future life is probably in view in Rom 5:21, though the latter is less clear (cf. Gal 6:8; 1 Tim 1:16; 6:12; Tit 1:2; 3:7). This is probably the sense here in Rom 6:22-23 in light of the word "end" (*telos*). Therefore, it is the "not yet" aspect of eternal life that is being highlighted here; namely, the reward of life given to the believer on judgment day.

[34]"The prepositional phrase *di' autou* ('through him') makes the risen Christ the instrument of eschatological salvation" (Michael F. Bird, *The Saving Righteousness of God: Studies on Paul, Justification, and the New Perspective* [Milton Keynes: Paternoster: 2007], p. 52).

[35]"His life" is a reference to the resurrection of Christ. See Bird, *Saving Righteousness*, pp. 56-57;

resurrection of Christ accomplishes our initial justification and ensures that we will receive a positive verdict on judgment day. Or in the words of Peter Stuhlmacher, "Jesus Christ is the living guarantor of believers' justification from Easter until the end of this world."[36]

The same point is reiterated in Romans 8:31-34, where Paul argues against the possibility of any future condemnation for believers:

> What then shall we say to these things? If God is for us, who can be against us? He who did not spare his own Son but gave him up for us all, how will he not also with him graciously give us all things? Who shall bring any charge against God's elect? It is God who justifies. Who is to condemn? Christ Jesus is the one who died—more than that, who was raised—who is at the right hand of God, who indeed is interceding for us. (Rom 8:31-34)

Here, it is the death, resurrection and continuing intercession of Christ that assures us that we will receive a positive verdict on judgment day.[37] God's gracious intervention is highlighted with the verb *charisetai* ("graciously give"). Paul's use of this term ties the passage in with previous *charis* terminology, which is marked by God's unilateral act in the atoning work of Christ (Rom 3:24; 4:4-5; 5:16-19, et al.). The assurance of final salvation, here described with justification language (*theos ho dikaiōn*), is underwritten by divine agency. A similar idea is stated two times in 1 Thessalonians, where the risen Christ "delivers us from the wrath to come" on his return (1 Thess 1:10); again, "God has not destined us for wrath, but to obtain salvation," referring to final salvation, "through our Lord Jesus Christ, who died for us so that whether we are awake or asleep we might live with him" (1 Thess 5:9-10). As in Romans 5:9-10, Paul grounds our assurance of a positive verdict in the death and continuing agency of Christ.

In summary, Paul believes that divine agency is fundamental for judgment according to works, both in empowering the obedience necessary for a positive verdict and through the unilateral grace of Christ.

Moo, *Romans*, p. 311; Wright, "The Letter to the Romans," in *New Interpreter's Bible Commentary*, vol. 10, ed. Leander Keck (Nashville: Abingdon Press, 2002), p. 520.

[36]Peter Stuhlmacher, *Revisiting Paul's Doctrine of Justification: A Challenge to the New Perspective* (Downers Grove, IL: IVP Academic, 2001), p. 59.

[37]Bird, *Saving Righteousness*, pp. 53, 56-57; Gundry and Volf, *Paul and Perseverance*, pp. 65-69. Jewett argues that this passage does not refer to final judgment (*Romans*, p. 539).

Justification According to Works in Romans 2. The passages we have examined thus far, however, appear to contradict what Paul says in Romans 2:6-15, where God will "render to each one according to his works" (Rom 2:6) and that "the doers of the law . . . will be justified" (Rom 2:13). Uncharacteristically, Paul makes no clear reference to divine agency in Romans 2:1-16.[38] It would appear that Paul is reverting back to a Deuteronomic paradigm of justification and judgment, and in some ways he is (see below). In any case, the passage is among the more difficult in Paul and therefore has incited a whole host of interpretive options.[39] Some claim that Paul is being inconsistent, while others suggest he is speaking hypothetically. Most recent interpreters, however, say that Paul is referring to Gentile Christians in Romans 2:13-16, who have the law written on their hearts (Rom 2:15; cf. Jer 31:33). Paul later says they have established the law through faith (Rom 3:30) and fulfilled the law through love (Rom 13:8-10). Therefore, while initial justification is by faith, future justification will be through the product of that faith, namely, doing the law (Rom 2:13).[40]

Though popular, the latter view does not adequately answer the apparent contradiction between Romans 2:13 and Romans 3:20:

> For it is not the hearers of the law who are righteous before God, but the doers of the law who will be justified. (Rom 2:13)

> For by works of the law no human being will be justified in his sight, since through the law comes knowledge of sin. (Rom 3:20)

One way to relieve the tension is to interpret "works of the law" in Romans 3:20 as something different than "doing the law" in Romans 2:13; the latter referring to general obedience, while the former refers to ethnic boundary markers that exclude Gentiles from the covenant.[41] This view of "works of the law" finds some affirmation in Galatians 2:16 where Paul first uses the phrase, but does not carry much validity in Romans 2–4 for reasons stated

---

[38]Rom 2:15-16 may hint at divine agency. Romans 2:29 highlights it explicitly (although see Moo, *Romans*, pp. 170-71, who does not see a reference to believers in Rom 2:26-29).

[39]In addition to the commentaries, a survey of views can be found in S. J. Gathercole, "A Law unto Themselves: The Gentiles in Romans 2.14-15 Revisited," *JSNT* 85 (2002): 27-49.

[40]For this view, see, among others, Jewett, *Romans*, pp. 211-18; N. T. Wright, "The Law in Romans 2," in *Paul and the Mosaic Law*, ed. J. D. G. Dunn (Grand Rapids: Eerdmans, 1996, 2000), pp. 131-50; Gathercole, "Law unto Themselves."

[41]E.g., James D. G. Dunn, *Romans*, WBC 38A (Dallas: Word, 1988), pp. 153-55.

in the preceding chapter. Moreover, this view still has to account for the rather un-Pauline reference to God justifying the "doers of the law." The text does not merely say that judgment will be according to works (i.e., spirit-led Christian obedience), but that justification will come to those who have obeyed (not "fulfilled") the Mosaic law.[42] The best argument for this position is to see in Romans 2:15 a reference to Jeremiah's prophecy of God "writing the law on their hearts" (Jer 31:33/38:33 LXX) and therefore a redefinition of what "law" means in Romans 2:13. In other words, what Paul has in mind is not raw adherence to the demands given at Sinai, but the reception of God's unilateral work through Christ and the spirit, which together have fulfilled the "righteous requirement of the law . . . in us," as Paul will articulate more clearly in Romans 8:1-4. This view has much to commend it, and it fits in well with everything we have said about Paul's thought thus far. However, it seems to take the steam out of what Paul has been saying in Romans 2:1-12, where he consistently affirms that justification will come to those who have sufficiently done the law—neither Christ nor the spirit play an explicit role here. Moreover, Paul's argument from Romans 1:18–3:26 must be taken as a whole, and we therefore have a tension not only between Romans 2:13 and Romans 3:20, but also between Romans 2:1-13, where the obedient will be rewarded regardless of their ethnicity, and Romans 3:9-20, where no one is obedient regardless of their ethnicity. It is for these reasons and others listed below that I find more merit in the slowly dying hypothetical view: Paul does not envision Romans 2:13 to be a real possibility in our *post Christus* redemptive-historical situation.

That last phrase is important, because it adds a slight modification to the standard hypothetical view.[43] I do not think Paul believes that "*if* someone does the required works, he or she will be righteous before God" but since "no one keeps the law . . . the only pathway to a right relation with God is

---

[42]"When Paul speaks clearly of believers' fulfilling the law . . . they do so by the power of the indwelling Spirit (8:1-11), not 'by nature.'" Frank Thielman, *Paul and the Law: A Contextual Approach* (Downers Grove, IL: IVP Academic, 1994), p. 191; see also Ernst Käsemann, *Commentary on Romans* (Grand Rapids: Eerdmans, 1980), p. 65.

[43]The best articulation of this view is still by Thielman, *Paul and the Law*, pp. 169-76. To my mind, the greatest weakness to this view, as Tom Schreiner pointed out to me (personal conversation), is Rom 2:26-29, which seems to speak of Christian Gentiles keeping the law by the power of the spirit; however, see Thielman, *Paul and the Law*, p. 174; Moo, *Romans*, p. 166-77.

faith in Jesus Christ."[44] This version of the hypothetical view misses the steady undertone of redemptive history in Paul's argument. In other words, the view I am advocating understands Paul to be arguing along the lines of salvation history: Israel was presented with a conditional covenant in which obedience to the law would bring blessing, while disobedience would bring a curse. But Israel failed, and therefore God promised to restore the covenant by his own initiative, through his saving righteousness enacted in Christ. In this reading, Paul is essentially reverting back to the *Deuteronomic* paradigm of the old covenant in Romans 2 in order to condemn the law-possessing Jew on his own terms (i.e., by his own covenant). By possessing the law yet disobeying it, Paul's interlocutor identifies with and mimics the Israel of old and thereby places himself under God's wrath (Rom 1:18; 2:5), the same wrath that God pours out on Gentiles. In turn, everyone is in need of the same solution—the atoning sacrifice of Christ (Rom 3:21-26).

Several observations support this interpretation. First, it is often said that dismissing Romans 2:13 as hypothetical is nonsensical, since Paul says the same thing elsewhere—judgment is according to works (Rom 14:10-12; 1 Cor 3:13-15; 2 Cor 5:10; 9:6; 11:15; Gal 6:7). However, here Paul does not say that judgment is according to (Christian) works, but that "the doers of the law" will receive justification—something that is explicitly denied in many passages elsewhere, not least in Romans 3:20; 4:4-5. When Paul refers to judgment according to deeds, in other words, he never describes the deeds as works of law but as acts of Christian obedience. Paul's statement in Romans 2:13 is never repeated in full color elsewhere in his letters.

Second, and most significantly, Paul alludes to *Deuteronomic* themes throughout Romans 2, suggesting that he is arguing within the retributive structure of the old covenant. For instance, in Romans 2:8 the terms "wrath and fury" (*orgē* and *thymos*) allude back to the phrase "in anger and fury and great wrath" of Deuteronomy 29:28 (29:27 LXX). In Romans 2:9, the phrase "there will be tribulation and distress" (*thlipsis* and *stenoxōria*) is similar to the phrase "in the siege and in the distress" (*en tē stenoxōria sou kai en tē thlipsei sou*) scattered throughout Deuteronomy 28 (see Deut 28:53, 55,

---

[44]Schreiner's articulation of the hypothetical view (*Paul, Apostle of God's Glory*, p. 280).

57). In Romans 2:24, Paul refers to the "word of God being blasphemed," which is a typical *Prophetic* critique lobbed against impenitent Israel (Is 52:5; Ezek 36:20) and is ultimately rooted in Deuteronomy 29:25-29 (29:24-28 MT, LXX).[45] And integrated throughout these allusions is the general theme of *Deuteronomic* eschatology, where obedience to the law is rewarded with blessing while disobedience is recompensed with curse. Paul might as well have been on Mount Gerizim when he rehearsed his blessings and curses in Romans 2:6-11 (cf. Deut 27:11-26).

The most striking piece of *Deuteronomic* theology that sets up Paul's argument comes in Romans 2:4-5: "Or do you presume on the riches of his kindness and forbearance and patience, not knowing that God's kindness is meant to lead you to *repentance* (*metanoian*)? But because of your hard and *impenitent heart* (*ametanoēton kardian*) you are storing up wrath for yourself on the day of wrath when God's righteous judgment will be revealed" (Rom 2:4-5). Paul affirms that the Jew ought to repent (Rom 2:4), but then "diagnoses them with a bad heart that is unable to accomplish such an action" (Rom 2:5).[46] His audience is incapable (*ametanoēton*) of performing the very repentance necessary for eternal life. The solution, therefore, can only be a transformation of the heart as an act of God, as will be revealed in the spirit's circumcision of the heart in Romans 2:29. But to read the spirit's work back into Romans 2:6-13 does not allow Paul's argument to unfold with the *Prophetic* power it is intended to carry. Paul's rhetoric, in other words, follows the script of the Hebrew prophets (see chapter two above), who urged Israel to turn from their sin yet concluded that their hard hearts were not capable of doing so.[47] Not only does Romans 2:4-5 ground Paul's argument in a *Prophetic-Deuteronomic* dialogue, it also sets up the following works-based eternal life passage. That is, when Paul articulates the *Deuteronomic* theology of Romans 2:6-13—blessings to the one who does good; curses to the one who does bad—this must be read in light of what he says in Romans 2:4-5. The sinner needs to repent (Rom 2:4) but is incapable of doing so (Rom 2:5). Rewards come to those who do

---

[45]A. Ito, "Romans 2: A Deuteronomistic Reading," *JSNT* 59 (1995): 21-37 (esp. 27).

[46]David Morlan, "Luke and Paul on Repentance," in *Paul and the Gospels: Christologies, Conflicts and Convergences,* ed. Michael F. Bird and Joel Willitts, LNTS 411 (New York: T & T Clark, 2011), p. 125.

[47]E.g., Jer 13:13; 17:1-9; Ezek 3:1-8.

good (Rom 2:7, 13), and yet "no one does good" (Rom 3:12). Eternal life is awarded to the one who seeks it (Rom 2:7), and yet "no one seeks for God" (Rom 3:11). Paul is not contradicting himself, but is setting up "foils to be negated" in Romans 2–3.[48]

This reading is born out of the *Prophetic* style so typical in Paul and solves many problems inherent in the other views.[49] The one problem that still remains is how to understand Romans 2:15-16, where Paul says: "They show that the work of the law is written on their hearts, while their conscience also bears witness, and their conflicting thoughts accuse or even excuse them on that day when, according to my gospel, God judges the secrets of men by Christ Jesus." The one phrase that is problematic for my view is "work of the law . . . written on their hearts." The language is very close to Jeremiah 31:33 (38:33 LXX). But if Jeremiah is in view, this would almost have to be taken to refer to Gentile Christians rather than a hypothetical law-abider. Syntactically, these are the same people as the "doers of the law" in Romans 2:13, and therefore we would have to understand them as genuine believers who will be justified in the future through law-obedience. But while this may be a reference to Jeremiah, it is not conclusive. Indeed, Jeremiah's prophecy refers to a decisive event where God transforms the sinner and produces wholehearted obedience. In Romans 2:13-16, however, Paul "leaves the issue of final judgment in doubt."[50] That is, the Gentile Christian view does not have a satisfactory explanation for the emphasis in Romans 2:15-16 on the *condemnation,* not salvation, of these same people, whose "conscience also bears witness, and their conflicting thoughts accuse or even excuse them on that day when, according to my gospel, God judges the secrets of men by Christ Jesus" (Rom 2:15-16).[51] The

---

[48]Morlan, "Luke and Paul," p. 27.

[49]See, e.g., Karl O. Sandnes, *Paul—One of the Prophets? A Contribution to the Apostle's Self-Understanding,* WUNT 2.43 (Tübingen: Mohr Siebeck, 1991); Sigurd Grindheim, "Apostate Turned Prophet: Paul's Retrospective Self-Understanding and Prophetic Hermeneutic with Special Reference to Galatians 3:10-12," *NTS* 53 (2007): 545-65; and most recently, Jeffrey W. Aernie, *Is Paul Also Among the Prophets? An Examination of the Relationship Between Paul and the Old Testament Prophetic Tradition in 2 Corinthians,* LNTS 467 (New York: T & T Clark, 2012).

[50]Moo, *Romans,* p. 152.

[51]The syntax here is complicated and can be understood to allow for less of an emphasis on condemnation and more of a neutral view of judgment day, where both salvation and condemnation are in view. For a detailed examination, see Jewett, *Romans,* pp. 214-17.

whole context from Romans 2:12-16 unravels God's impartial judgment and condemnation of all people—which is the driving theme of Romans 1:18–3:20—suggesting that Romans 2:13 should also be read in this light. Paul affirms a *Deuteronomic* soteriology as a foil to be later denied.

Another option is that Paul may be alluding to the Stoic notion of the natural law being implanted on the minds of all people, which serves to condemn them,[52] though this is not altogether clear. Interestingly, the *Testament of Judah* refers to "man's works" which "are written on the heart" (*T. Jud.* 20:4), and yet Jeremiah 31 is not in view. The context, in fact, is clearly on judgment: "the spirit of truth testifies to all things and brings all accusations" and "he who has sinned is consumed in his heart and cannot raise his head to face the judge" (*T. Jud.* 20:5). So even if a Stoic background for Romans 2:12-16 is not in view, Paul may be using language without intentional allusion, much like the *Testament of Judah*.

Though not without its problems, a hypothetical view washed in redemptive history makes good sense of Romans 2. Paul moves from the *Deuteronomic* paradigm of the old covenant in order to condemn both Jew and Gentile. Under the old covenant, repentance was set forth as a means of restoration, but Israel's stubborn heart rendered them incapable of returning to God. Therefore, restoration will come through divine agency, which Paul hints at in Romans 2:29 (circumcision of the heart) and fully articulates in Romans 3:21-26. While Paul believes that works will matter on judgment day, this is not his main concern in Romans 2. And yet at the end of the day, even if the Gentile Christian view is correct, this still necessitates an emphasis on divine agency in future judgment, since the "work of the law . . . written on their hearts" would then allude to Jeremiah 31:33—a clear reference to God transforming the heart (cf. Rom 2:29). This would qualify what Paul meant by "the doers of the law will be justified." They do the law by virtue of God's transformation of their heart.

Summary. Divine agency is seen as fundamental on judgment day, not only in the form of empowering obedience but also in terms of God's un-

---

[52]"Law is the highest reason implanted in Nature, which commands what ought to be done and forbids the contrary. This reason, when firmly fixed and perfected in the human mind, is law." Cicero, *De legibus* 1.6.18, cited in Morlan, "Luke and Paul," p. 34. See J. Martens, "Romans 2:14-16: A Stoic Reading," *NTS* 40 (1994): 55-67.

aided work through Christ—Romans 2 notwithstanding. We turn now to the Dead Sea Scrolls for a final look at how they relate to Paul's soteriology.

JUDGMENT ACCORDING TO WORKS IN QUMRAN

For Paul, divine agency is fundamental for judgment day. Do we see anything paralleled to this in Qumran?

Divinely Empowered Obedience. Several scrolls speak of God enabling obedience, a theme clearly seen throughout the *Hodayot*.[53] The hymnist(s) calls on God to "[Prevent] your servant from sinning against you, from violating all the things of your will." He asks God to "strengthen" him so that "he can walk in all that you love, and abhor all that [you] hate" (1QH[a] 4:23-24). When the hymnist(s) speaks of his obedience, he often adds the qualification that this is only possible through God's empowerment: "I have appeased your face by the spirit which you have placed [in me]." This work of God is followed by three infinitive constructions stating the goal of the divine work: "to lavish your [kind]ness on [your] serv[ant] for[ever,] to purify me with your holy spirit, to bring me near by your will according to the extent of your kindnesses" (1QH 8:18-20 *DSSSE*).[54]

Some passages speak of God enabling obedience with a view toward eschatological acceptance and reward. For instance, the hymnist believes that God has created "the just man, and from the womb you determined him for the period of approval." God's election is the ultimate determining factor in one's righteousness and acquittal. He goes on to add several comments about the goal of election: "*to keep* your covenant, and *to walk* on all (your paths), and to [. . .] on him with the abundance of your compassion, *to open* all the narrowness of his soul to eternal salvation and endless peace, without want" (1QH 7:17-19). The phrase "eternal salvation and endless peace" shows that the author is looking forward to judgment day, when these rewards will be given to those who have obeyed torah. But here, as elsewhere, such obedience is made possible through God's electing grace.[55]

---

[53]For the emphasis on divine agency in the *Hodayot*, see Jason Maston, *Divine and Human Agency in Second Temple Judaism and in Paul*, WUNT 2.297 (Tübingen: Mohr Siebeck, 2010), pp. 95-123.

[54]For an in-depth discussion of this hymn, see ibid., pp. 95-97.

[55]Maston interacts extensively with the role of election and obedience in the *Hodayot* (ibid., pp. 97-113).

Again, in 1QH 15, the author says that God "establish[ed] my heart [with] your [tea]chings and with your truth, to straighten my steps on the paths of justice, to walk in your presence on the frontier of [lif]e along tracks of glory [and life] and peace without e[nd which will ne]ver stop" (1QH 15:13-15). God is the source of obedience, and the result is eternal life and peace.[56]

Other hymns underscore judgment according to works without clear emphasis on divine agency:

> At the ju[dgm]ent you will destroy all deceitful men, seers of delusion will no longer be found. For these is no folly in any of your deeds, and there is no deceit [in] the intentions of your heart. Those who are aligned with you will stand in your presence always. Those who walk on the path of your heart, will be established forever. (1QH[a] 12:20-22)

This passage leads Chris VanLandingham to conclude that "salvation and eternal life result from human effort,"[57] citing several other hymns in support.[58] Such a description may reflect this passage in itself, but it does not take into account the *Hodayot*'s emphasis on predestination.[59] The presence of predestination in these hymns is undisputed, but its relationship to human obedience is debated among scholars. Eugene Merrill, for instance, understands predestination in terms of foreknowledge, which amounts to God knowing ahead of time who will be righteous and who will be wicked.[60] In this view, human action still forms the basis of divine action. Similarly, Chris VanLandingham understands predestination as a natural reflex of the genre. However, the hymnists believe in free will, since they frequently make vows (1QH 6:17-18), give exhortations (1QH 9:24-26), and encourage repentance (1QH 10:8-9)—all of which demand a robust belief in the human capacity to obey.[61] Jason Maston, however, is probably closer to the mark by understanding the hymnists' belief in predestination and human action as noncompetitive. For the *Hodayot*, "underlying every action taken by a

---

[56]In this passage, eternal life and peace seem to be a future reality that is partially experienced in the present.

[57]VanLandingham, *Judgment & Justification*, p. 125.

[58]1QH[a] 4:10-15; 6:23-24; 7:12-19; 8:12-13; ibid., VanLandingham, *Judgment & Justification*, p. 125n216. None of these hymns support his point, however.

[59]1QH 7:15-22; 9:7-15, 19-20; 11:16-17; 18:1-2, 5-7.

[60]Eugene Merrill, *Qumran and Predestination: A Theological Study of the Thanksgiving Hymns*, STDJ (Leiden: Brill, 1975), p. 50.

[61]VanLandingham, *Justification & Judgment*, pp. 113-14.

human is a corresponding action made by God."[62] God's predestination of the community is the prior and formal cause of all subsequent human action. So when a member obeys, his "actions reveal the category to which one belongs, and one's actions are the outworking of a decision made by God" who is "the ultimate cause."[63]

Maston's view is the most sensitive to the complex thought bundled up in these hymns. And though a thorough look at predestination in the Scrolls is beyond the scope of this book, Maston's study serves only to support our point above; namely, that obedience is ultimately the result of divine action (see esp. 1QH^a 7:25). I would hesitate, however, in understanding obedience as the inevitable outcome of being a covenant member, given the *Hodayot's* anthropological pessimism toward its community (see chapter five above). But when a member obeys, God has enabled it. And therefore, even if divine agency is not explicitly mentioned in some judgment passages such as 1QH^a 12:20-22, there is an underlying assumption about God's action, which enables human obedience. It may not take the same form as in Paul, but it is present nonetheless.[64]

Other hymns at Qumran also speak of divinely enabled obedience. The *Barki Nafshi* hymns (4Q434-438) affirm this with the same clarity as the *Hodayot*. Here, obedience from the heart is made possible by the power of God. The term "heart" is a key word in these hymns, occurring no less then

---

[62]Maston, *Divine and Human Agency*, p. 112.

[63]Ibid. As a slight modification of Maston's view, we may view the predestinarian thinking of the *Hodayot* (and perhaps at Qumran as a whole) as asymmetrical, where the wicked are condemned based on God's foreknowledge of their behavior, while the righteous are saved based on God's electing grace. For instance, the hymnist says, "the wicked you have created for [the time] of your wrath, from the womb you have predestined them for the day of slaughter. For (*kî*) they walk on a path that is not good, they reject your covenant" (1QH 7:20-21). The wicked here are predestined to wrath *because* they rejected God; human action is the basis for divine action (see Merrill, *Qumran and Predestination*, p. 50). In the same hymn, however, "the just man" is "determined" not because he kept the covenant but in order "to keep your covenant" (7:18). See further Kyle Wells, "Grace, Obedience, and the Hermeneutics of Agency: Paul and his Jewish Contemporaries on the Transformation of the Heart" (Ph.D. diss., Durham University, 2010), pp. 72-75.

[64]At least two aspects of divine agency are different in Paul and Qumran. First, the spirit as the formal cause of human obedience is more pronounced in Paul than in the *Hodayot*. Paul seems to argue that the spirit not only enables human obedience but inevitably causes it. Second, Paul's statements that focus on Christ's death, resurrection and advocacy for the believer on judgment day (e.g., Rom 8:31-34) push the envelope of divine agency and are unparalleled in Qumran.

fifteen times, and in several places God is the agent who changes the heart
to produce obedience: "he circumcised the foreskin of their heart" (4Q434 1
i 4); "he gave them another heart" (4Q434 1 i 10); "my heart you have commanded it and my inmost parts you have taught well, lest your statutes be
forgot" (4Q436 1 i 5); "and you have placed a pure heart in its place" (4Q436
1 i 10).[65] The hymnist alludes to several biblical passages (Deut 29:4; 30:6; Jer
32:39; Ezek 36:26-27)[66] to announce a thoroughly *Prophetic* picture of God's
restorative act in enabling heartfelt obedience from the community. The
references to God circumcising their hearts and giving them "another heart"
are particularly noteworthy. These metaphors come from Deuteronomy
30:6 and Jeremiah 32:39, two passages that are shaped by God's unilateral
intervention to restore Israel.[67] Through and through, these hymns underscore the belief that "the spiritual attributes of the individual or the community" are "conferred by divine intervention."[68]

However, while obedience is clearly enabled by God in *Barki Nafshi,* such
obedience is not oriented toward judgment day.[69] The focus seems to be
more on God's initial act of salvation in enabling obedience through en-
lightening his people (4Q434 1 i 3-4) and giving them a new heart. We can
assume that if the author believes that future judgment is according to
works, then such works are only possible in light of divine action, though
this is never explicitly stated.

The same initial endowment of power seems to drive several statements in the *Words of the Luminaries* (4Q504). The hymnist calls on God

---

[65]Translations are from D. R. Seely, "The 'Circumcised Heart' in 4Q434 Barki Napshi," *RevQ* 17
(1996): 527-35 (esp. 529-30).

[66]For these allusions, see ibid., pp. 530-35.

[67]See chapter two above.

[68]D. R. Seely, "Implanting Pious Qualities as a Theme in the *Barki Nafshi* Hymns," in *The Dead Sea
Scrolls: Fifty Years After Their Discovery: Proceedings of the Jerusalem Congress, July 20-25, 1997,*
ed. L. H. Schiffman, et al. (Jerusalem: Israel Exploration Society, 2000), pp. 322-31 (esp. 324). The
only possible exception comes in 4Q434 1 i 11, where the text could read: "He has brought them
on the path of his heart, *because* (*kî*) . . . they pledged their spirit." Wells points out that this
reading suggests that "God is ultimately responding to an eagerness on the part of the people as
in CD 1:10" (Wells, "Grace," p. 63). However, the text is fragmentary and open to other
reconstructions and translations. For instance, F. García-Martínez and E. J. C. Tigchelaar, *The
Dead Sea Scrolls Study Edition,* 2 vols (Leiden: Brill, 1997) translate the last line as "for . . . their
spirit at ease." Therefore, we need to be cautious in using this passage to supplant the divine
priority reading offered above.

[69]Several lines speak of judgment, but these refer to present acts of God, not judgment day (see,
e.g., 4Q434 1 i 5-8).

to "circumcise the foreskin of [our heart]" (*frag.* 4 11), to "implant your law in our heart, [so that we do not stray from it]" (*frags.* 1-2 ii 13-14), and acknowledges to God, "[you have] poured your holy spirit upon us, [to be]stow your blessings to us" (*frags.* 1-2 v 15-16) and have "strengthened our heart so that we can recount your mighty works" (*frags.* 1-2 vi 9).[70] All of these statements affirm God's initiative in restoring the covenant to Israel. As with the *Barki Nafshi* hymns, however, the explicit connection between divinely empowered works and final judgment is not clear.

A final text that is relevant for the question of agency in judgment according to works is one that is now familiar to us: the hymn at the end of the *Community Rule* (1QS 10–11). We have already looked at this passage in the previous chapter, where we saw that final justification is ultimately based on God's goodness and mercy. Judgment will bring a reward for righteousness and punishment for wickedness,[71] but the hymnist (compared to God) does not possess the righteousness needed for a positive verdict on judgment day.[72] It is only by the hand of God that he can do anything good.[73] But even this righteousness, constituted by divinely empowered works, is nothing compared to God's own righteousness, and therefore the hymnist anticipates—and acknowledges that he desperately needs—God's mercy in order to receive a positive verdict on that day.[74] While there is discontinuity between the final justification of 1QS 10–11 and Paul's understanding of initial justification of the ungodly, there is continuity between the Qumran hymn and Paul regarding the final day. Divinely empowered works are a condition of final salvation.

Thus far, Paul and Qumran are singing a similar tune. Both agree that judgment is according to works and that such works are only possible by the power of God, though the explicit connection between the final day and di-

---

[70]Cf. *frags.* 1-2 v 11-13: "You did favors to your people Israel among all [the] countries amongst whom you had exiled them, *to place upon their heart to turn to you and to listen to your voice.*" Wells points out that this comes from Deut 30:1 but the writer actually changes the text to heighten the sense of divine agency that is not apparent in the Deuteronomy verse (Wells, "Grace," p. 63).

[71]1QS 10:18, 21-26.

[72]1QS 11:9-10.

[73]1QS 11:2-3, 10-11.

[74]1QS 11:11-15.

vinely empowered works is not as pronounced in Qumran (save the *Hodayot* and 1QS 10–11) as it is in Paul. And the pessimistic anthropology in Qumran, as we saw in chapter five, applies not only to the reprobate but also to the covenant member who looks ahead to judgment day. Paul, however, draws a closer connection between divinely empowered obedience and judgment day, and his pessimistic anthropology does not apply to the covenant member, who has been transformed by Christ and the spirit. Sins still plague the believer, but the power of sin has been broken. But these points of discontinuity do not outweigh the significant measure of continuity observed thus far. Both Paul and the hymnists of Qumran believe that all goodness that flows from covenant members is ultimately due to God's mercy.

Such continuity, however, is limited to the hymns. We discussed the issue of genre in chapter five, so we do not need to review it here. For the purpose of this chapter, it is important to note that Qumran's nonhymnic texts that speak of judgment according to works or the reward of eternal life for obedience are not so quick to qualify human deeds as being divinely empowered. In other words, there is, once again, a good deal of discontinuity between the didactic literature at Qumran and the didactic letters of Paul, while there is more continuity between Paul and the Qumran hymnists.

For instance, at the end of the *Damascus Document,* the writer concludes with a reflection about torah obedience and judgment day: "But all those who remain steadfast in these regulations . . . will exult and rejoice and their heart will be strong, and they shall prevail over all the sons of the world. And God will atone for them, and they will see his salvation, because they have taken refuge in his holy name" (CD-B 20:27-34).[75] The final line here envisions eschatological salvation being given to the obedient, and there is nothing in the context that qualifies obedience as the result of God's internal work. This may be an assumption, but it is not explicitly stated.

The theme of final judgment occurs throughout the wisdom text known as 4Q*Instruction,*[76] which usually highlights the final annihilation of the

---

[75]The intervening section that I left out lists examples of obedience demonstrated by the righteous—e.g., they "listen[ed] to the Teacher's voice" (20:28) and "they do not raise their hand against his holy regulations and his just judgment[s]" (20:30-31).

[76]At least six surviving manuscripts constitute this work: 1Q26, 4Q415-18, 423. The work "combines traditional wisdom with an apocalyptic worldview" and contains themes related to eschatological judgment and eternal life throughout. Matthew J. Goff, *Discerning Wisdom: The*

wicked.[77] Several sections, however, seek to foster wisdom and obedience so that one can anticipate an eschatological reward on the final day.

> in upright understanding are disclos[ed the sec]rets of his thoughts, while one walks [per]fect[ly in all] one's [w]orks. Be constantly intent on these things, and understand [al]l their effects. And then you will know et[ernal] glory [wi]th his wonderful mysteries and his mighty works. And you, understanding one, inherit your reward in the remembrance of the [. . . f]or it comes. (4Q417 2 i 11-14)

The passage has several lacunae, but the idea of judgment according to works is apparent.[78] The author exhorts his subjects to understand ("constantly intent on these things") the ways of God that will be disclosed on judgment day.[79] By meditating on "his wonderful mysteries" and by walking "[per]fect[ly in all] one's [w]orks," the addressee will "inherit your reward,"[80] which implies that works will play a role on judgment day. Elsewhere the author discusses the "soteriological rewards of the humble,"[81] whose elect status is connected to his poverty: "Be like a poor man when you strive for his judgment . . . then God will see, and his anger will turn away, and he will forgive your sins" (4Q417 2 ii 14-16).[82] Little can be said either way about the nature of God's involvement in the obedience of the righteous in 4QInstruction. The author's intention is certainly not to parse out the relationship

Sapiential Literature of the Dead Sea Scrolls, VTSup 116 (Leiden: Brill, 2007), p. 13 (for an introduction to 4QInstruction, see pp. 9-13; on the theme of eschatological judgment and salvation, see pp. 44-47); T. Elgvin, "Early Essene Eschatology: Judgment and Salvation According to Sapiential Work A," in *Current Research and Technological Development on the Dead Sea Scrolls: Conference on the Texts from the Judean Desert, Jerusalem, 20 April 1995,* ed. D. W. Parry and S. D. Ricks, STDJ 20 (Leiden: Brill, 1996), pp. 126-65.

[77] 4Q418 *frags.* 212, 213; frag. 122 ii 6-13.

[78] See Gathercole, *Where Is Boasting?,* pp. 105-7.

[79] That judgment day is in view can be seen in a previous line, where the author refers to "their visitations for all eternal periods, and eternal visitation" (4Q417 2 i 7). The word "visitation" (*pqd*) refers to God's future judgment throughout the Scrolls and this is probably what is in view here.

[80] "Inherit" (*nḥl*) is an eschatological term connoting the reward given on judgment day.

[81] Goff, *Discerning Wisdom,* p. 59.

[82] I have translated *'nî* as "poor" instead of "humble" in light of the context, following Goff, *Discerning Wisdom,* p. 59. The next line (4Q417 2 ii 16-17) reads: "And who will be considered just in his judgment, and without forgiveness [h]ow . . . a poor man." This further confirms that judgment day is in view. Since the author has already shown confidence that economic integrity will secure forgiveness of sins, and the same idea is carried over here. Timothy Lim, however, finds evidence in lines 16-17 for Paul's understanding of unattainable righteousness. "The Qumran Scrolls and Paul in Historical Context," *The Dead Sea Scrolls as Background to Postbiblical Judaism and Early Christianity,* ed. J. R. Davila (Leiden: Brill, 2002), p. 154.

between divine and human agency, and the lacunae in the text only adds to the ambiguity. In any case, it is safe to say that throughout 4Q*Instruction*, judgment day will weigh the works of the righteous, and yet there is little (if any) emphasis on such obedience being divinely empowered.[83] The author speaks freely of human deeds in the context of final salvation without feeling the need to qualify it.[84]

Judgment according to works is particularly acute in the Qumran *Pesherim*.[85] These commentaries are laden with an "eschatological urgency,"[86] as they look forward to the new age when God will punish the wicked and reward the righteous. Humanity is divided in terms of the covenant members and non–covenant members, depicted by various identity markers such as "the elect,"[87] "the community of the poor ones"[88] and "doers of the law"[89] for the former; and "wicked,"[90] "traitors"[91] and "violators of the covenant"[92] for the latter. Obedience to the law helps secure one's standing among the righteous community and is vital for one's survival on the "day of judgment."[93] For instance, 1Q*Pesher Micah* says that "a[l]l those volun-

---

[83]See, e.g., 4Q417 *frag.* 1 ii + 23 13; *frag.* 2 i 19; 4Q418 *frag.* 81 6-8. Some passages may hint at divine empowerment, but the text is too fragmentary (e.g., "[. . .] all the sons of Eve, and through the strength of God and his abundant glory with his goodness [. . .]" 4Q418 *frags.* 122 ii + 126 ii 12).

[84]Jason Maston (in personal conversation) suggested that this may be due to the wisdom genre of the document. Just as the hymns lend themselves to emphasize divine agency, so wisdom texts more readily emphasize human responsibility.

[85]The *Pesherim* include seventeen manuscripts that cover seven biblical books: Isaiah (3Q4, 4Q161-65), Hosea (4Q 166-67), Micah (1Q14, 4Q168), Nahum (4Q169), Habakkuk (1QpHab), Zephaniah (1Q15, 4Q170) and the Psalms (1Q16, 4Q171, 4Q173). For an overview of the *Pesherim* at Qumran, see T. Lim, *Pesherim*, CQS 3 (London: Sheffield Academic Press, 2002). For a recent study on the soteriology of the *Pesherim*, see Alex P. Jassen, "Survival at the End of Days: Aspects of Soteriology in the Dead Sea Scrolls *Pesherim*," in *This World and the World to Come: Soteriology in Early Judaism*, ed. Daniel M. Gurtner, LSTS 74 (New York: T & T Clark, 2011), pp. 193-210; cf. Gathercole, *Where Is Boasting?*, pp. 102-5.

[86]Jassen, "Survival," p. 199.

[87]1QpHab 5:4; 9:12; 10:13 ("elect of Israel"); 4Q164 (*Pesher Isaiah D*) 1 3; 4Q169 (*Pesher Nahum*) 1-2 ii 8.

[88]4QpHab 12:3, 6, 10; 4Q171 ii 9-12; iii 10.

[89]4Q171 2:15, 23; 1QpHab 7:11; 8:1.

[90]1QpHab 5:5; 4Q171 ii 18-20; 4Q171 iii 12.

[91]1QpHab 2:3; 5:8.

[92]1QpHab 2:6; 4Q167 7-8 1-2. The descriptions of "traitors" and "violators of the covenant" imply that these people were once part of the covenant. This means that there are two different types of "wicked," those who were never part of the covenant and those who fell away. For all these terms, see Jassen, "Survival," pp. 198-204.

[93]For "day of judgment," see 1QpHab 12:14; 13:2-3; 3Q4 6; 4Q275 2; 4Q418 212 2.

teering to join the chosen of [God, observing the law] in the council of the Community" are "those who will be saved from the day of [judgment]" (1Q14 8-10 7-9). Or more explicitly, as noted in the previous chapter, the Habakkuk commentator understands Habakkuk 2:4 to predict that "God will free from the house of judgment" all the "doers of the law . . . on account of their toil and of their faith in the Teacher of Righteousness" (1QpHab 8:1-3). But as for the wicked, "their sins will be doubled against them [and they will] n[ot] find favor when they come to judgment" (1QpHab 7:14-16).[94] We should not take these and other passages to promote a sort of works-righteousness devoid of grace, since both covenant membership and obedience to the law work together in securing one's verdict on the final day.[95] Nevertheless, there is no explicit divine empowerment that governs human obedience. There is the general sense that the "doers of the law" are at the same time "elect" and therefore part of the covenant; however, such election, while allowing for obedience, does not necessitate it. Unlike the hymns of Qumran, it is the human agent, not God, who circumcises the heart to compel one to obey.[96]

To bring us back full circle, it may be helpful to take into account the texts considered in previous chapters that deal with some form of eschatological salvation. In chapter three, we saw that God responds to Israel's (or the community's) obedience by lifting the curse and granting them blessing (e.g., 11QT^a 59; 4QMMT C), and in chapter four, God rewards the righteous for their faithfulness and toil (4QPseudo-Ezekiel). These texts can also be read within the purview of eschatological salvation and therefore contribute to our understanding of Qumran's view of judgment according to works, even if the judgment day theme is less explicit. And with Qumran's *Deuteronomic* return to the law, such repentance is rarely seen explicitly as divinely empowered.[97] Again, divine agency may be assumed, but there is no clear indication that the authors of these texts were as eager to qualify obedience as divinely wrought as we saw in Paul.

---

[94]The translation is from Jassen, "Survival," p. 208.

[95]"Thus, it is not the law that saves, but one's status as a member of the community that secures survival at the end of days" (Jassen, "Survival," p. 206).

[96]Explicitly in 1QpHab: "the Priest whose disgrace exceeded his glory because he did not circumcise the foreskin of his heart and has walked on paths of excessiveness" (1QpHab 11:11-14).

[97]With the exception of 4Q504, noted in chapter three.

In summary, Qumran clearly affirms that judgment is according to works, yet there is much diversity on how divine and human agency interact in those works. On the one hand, the *Hodayot* and *Barki Nafshi* hymns affirm that all obedience is enabled by the power of God. On the other hand, the didactic literature is much more *Deuteronomic,* viewing obedience to the law as necessary for judgment day without explicitly crediting human action to God's empowerment.

PAUL, QUMRAN AND JUDGMENT ACCORDING TO (DIVINELY EMPOWERED) WORKS

Both Paul and Qumran believed that future judgment will be according to works, and yet this formulation begs for further inquiry. In particular, what is God's involvement in the works that will be judged? Having surveyed several passages from Paul and Qumran, we can now consider elements of continuity and discontinuity between the two. In terms of continuity, Paul's emphasis on divine empowerment in obedience is paralleled in several hymns from Qumran; namely, 1QH^a, 1QS 10–11, 4Q434 and 4Q504. For Paul and these writers, God is the ultimate source and enabler of human obedience. However, this emphasis at Qumran is largely limited to hymnic material. While not all the hymns emphasize divine agency in obedience, virtually all of the clear statements about divine agency are limited to the hymns. Didactic material is quite comfortable speaking about God responding to human obedience and repentance, rather than causing it. But Paul reveals a consistent urgency *in his didactic letters* to locate the source and ultimate cause of all human obedience in God. The genre distinction, therefore, creates a slight wedge of discontinuity between Paul and Qumran, especially when we compare didactic texts from Qumran with didactic texts from Paul. When we get the two on the same playing field, there is more discontinuity than is often noticed.

With the hymns in general, and the *Hodayot* in particular, can we conclude that there is pure continuity with Paul in terms of judgment according to works, and specifically with God's involvement in those works?

To answer this, we should first review our previous chapters, where we have identified elements of discontinuity between Paul and the *Hodayot.* For instance, the role of Ezekiel's spirit as the divine agent that effects obedience (Ezek 36–37) is present in the hymns but not as prominent as it is in Paul (chapter four). The anthropological pessimism in these hymns is unmistakable and overlaps a good deal with the apostle. However, there are still traces of discontinuity, since for the hymnist such pessimism is usually articulated in the context of humanity in comparison to God, while Paul's pessimism pervades all levels of discourse (chapter five). As far as justification is concerned, Paul's understanding of God's initial justification of the ungodly is not clear in the *Hodayot* or 1QS, which focuses on the community's orientation toward judgment day. And yet, in one of the only hymns that reflects on one's entrance into the community—which would roughly parallel Paul's understanding of initial justification—it is human, not divine, agency that is emphasized (chapter six).[98] Despite such discontinuity, this chapter on judgment according to works has shown that the *Hodayot* and Paul have much in common. While the difference in genre prevents an exact parallel, both Paul and the hymnist(s) agree that the obedience of the covenant member, which is necessary for judgment day, is enabled by the grace of God.

But there may be yet another facet of discontinuity between Paul and the *Hodayot* in terms of the strength of divine agency in obedience. Throughout 1QH^a, for instance, all human obedience is ultimately credited to divine empowerment, whether explicitly or through the underlying assumption of predestination. God, in the *Hodayot*, certainly makes obedience *possible* (1QH 12:30-37). However, Paul's discourse reveals a stronger sense of agency. The human agent is bound up "in Christ" and infused with the divine spirit, who acts not only as an *enabler* of obedience but also as a *compeller* (Rom 8:1-11; Gal 2:20-21; 5:16-25). Obedience for Paul is not just made possible but

---

[98]"I know, thanks to the abundance of your goodness, and I have enjoined my soul with an oath not to sin against you [and n]ot to do anything which is evil in your eyes. In this way I was brought near in the community of all the men of my counsel. According to his [int]elligence I bring him near, I love him in proportion to the abundance of his inheritance" (1QH^a 6:17-19). The agent of "bring him near" ('*gyšnû*) in the final line is the writer of the hymn, probably the Teacher of Righteousness, who sees a measure of intelligence in the aspiring member before he enters the community. Although the writer acknowledges God's goodness in his own entrance into the community, it is his commitment "not to sin" and "not to do anything which is evil" that enables him to enter the community. Even if there is an underlying theme of predestination (as Maston wants to affirm; *Divine and Human Agency*, p. 114), the passage in itself would rule out a Pauline view of initial justification of the ungodly by grace.

inevitable through Christ and the spirit.[99] This is why Paul's anthropological pessimism becomes tempered after the convert has been baptized into the death and resurrection of Christ (Rom 6:1-11). Paul's view is tamed, of course, by the real presence of sin in the believer's life (Rom 6:12-23), and yet his anthropological outlook is one of optimism rather than pessimism. Hence, he looks toward judgment day with confidence (Rom 8:31-39). For the hymnists at Qumran, obedience is made possible through divine empowerment, but the dark picture of humanity is still dark, and therefore the writers express a measure of reluctance toward the final day (1QH^a 17:14-17; 20:24-32). None of this is conclusive, but it is at least suggestive that Paul's pneumatology and anthropology indicate a wedge of discontinuity between him and the Qumran hymnists in how they anticipate judgment day.

Aside from divinely empowered obedience, the most significant point of discontinuity is the role of the Christ event for final justification. For Paul, the death, resurrection and intercession of Christ is a (if not *the*) definitive cause for the acquittal the believer will receive on judgment day (Rom 4:25; 5:8-11; 8:31-34). So it is more than just divinely energized obedience that will push the believer through the pearly gates, but the unilateral act of God on Calvary and in the vacant tomb that secures both the initial and final verdict for those in Christ. I have not seen anything in Qumran—not even in the *Hodayot*—which parallels Paul's thinking on this.[100]

---

[99]See D. B. Smith: "Just because a Jew may be under the influence of a principle of obedience does not mean that obedience to the Law necessarily follows." *What Must I Do to Be Saved? Paul Parts Company with His Jewish Heritage* (Sheffield: Sheffield Phoenix Press, 2007), p. 237.

[100]Maston, *Divine and Human Agency*, p. 158. Sometimes the hymnists hope to find mercy on judgment day, since it will lay bare all their failings: "only by your goodness is man acquitted" (1QH^a 5:22-23). But Paul's radical view of *charis* as divine action, which refashions the sinner into legal saint and conquers the power of the flesh, is not paralleled.

Excursus

Justification by Grace and
Future Judgment Not by Grace?

We have argued that initial justification is by grace and final justification is conditioned (in part) on spirit-empowered works. Both assertions are clear in Paul, but the logical question is: if grace excludes works as a precondition (Rom 4:4-5), then is final justification, which includes works, *not* by grace? The very question seems absurd. Could Paul consider any aspect of our salvation—including our final salvation—not a product of grace? One could say that since the works are spirit-compelled, and since the agency of Christ is determinative for the positive verdict (Rom 8:31-34), then final justification can be viewed as a gracious event. But again, Paul has defined grace as a gift given without any preconditions, so even spirit-empowered works would preclude grace as Paul defines it from the final verdict. If initial justification is by grace, then it would seem that final justification cannot be by grace.

The dilemma is well known and has inspired several attempts at reconciling the incongruence.[101] Nigel Watson, for instance, argues that the judgment passages are rhetorical—they do not speak of a real situation—and need to be understood in light of the occasional nature of Paul's letters.[102] This is seen by the fact that most of the judgment passages are given in Corinthians, where Paul is battling licentiousness.[103] The other passages in Romans (Rom 2:1-17; 14:7-12) are directed at Christians "who are guilty either of censoriousness or contempt towards their brethren and thus, in different ways, of presumption."[104] The passages in Galatians (Gal 5:19-25; 6:7-10) are directed against those who wrongly use freedom as an excuse for indulging in the flesh. In short, "Paul's warnings of future judgment are di-

---

[101]For a survey of views, see Yinger, *Paul, Judaism, and Judgment*, pp. 6-15; D. Ortlund, "Justified by Faith, Judged According to Works: Another Look at a Pauline Paradox," *JETS* 52 (2009): 323-39.
[102]N. Watson, "Justified by Faith, Judged by Works: An Antinomy?" *NTS* 29 (1983): 209-21.
[103]Ibid., p. 214.
[104]Ibid., p. 215.

rected at those who are 'puffed up', guilty of presumption, living in a state of illusion."[105] The warning of judgment is not an assertion of what is to come but is meant to hover over these people "as long as they remain in a state of illusion."[106] Paul's messages of judgment, therefore, "are addressed to Christians whose faith has degenerated to a false security" and are meant to shake the believer from their apathetic state.[107]

Karl Donfried views the judgment motif as more real.[108] Put simply, initial justification is by faith, but final justification is by works. Donfried points out that Paul's language of justification has a past referent while language of salvation has a future reference (see for instance, Rom 5:9-10; 13:11; 1 Thess 5:8; 1 Cor 1:18 ["being saved"]). Second Thessalonians 2:13 is representative: "God chose you . . . to be saved, through sanctification by the Spirit."[109] So "even though Paul stresses that justification is purely an act of God's mercy and that sanctification is entirely the gift of God's spirit, he is quick to warn his audience that these involve their active participation and obedience to God's continued goodness."[110] And this is the basis of Paul's many (real) warnings for Christians to remain holy and blameless until the end (1 Cor 1:8; Col 1:22; 1 Thess 3:13; 5:23; Phil 2:15). Therefore, judgment will fall on Christians who are disobedient, as is clear from 1 Corinthians 10:6-13; 11:27, and Galatians 5:21 (cf. Gal 6:7-8), since they are in paranaetic sections.[111] A Christian can, quite explicitly, lose their justified status through failing to persevere in works.

Both of these approaches contain an element of truth. Watson has highlighted the rhetorical force of Paul's statements and reminded us that the goal of the doctrine is to squelch apathy and spur on obedience. Donfried has shown that works play a real role in final salvation. But neither captures the full contours of the interplay between initial and final justification and how these relate to his understanding of grace.

Recently, John Barclay has, to my mind, solved the apparent contradic-

---

[105]Ibid., p. 216.
[106]Ibid.
[107]Ibid., p. 220.
[108]K. Donfried, "Justification and Last Judgment in Paul," *ZNW* 67 (1976): 90-110.
[109]Ibid., pp. 101-2.
[110]Ibid., p. 104.
[111]Ibid., p. 107.

tion.[112] Barclay argues that Paul's understanding of initial and final salvation does not betray two different soteriological principles—the former is by grace, while the latter is by works—but reveals a proper understanding of grace. The gift of grace, Barclay argues, was understood in the Mediterranean world as an undeserved gift given without preconditions. And yet, the benefactor would normally consider the worthiness of the recipient of such gifts, since wasting grace on an unworthy recipient would be foolish.[113] Paul goes beyond the typical Greco-Roman conception of grace by highlighting the *un*worthiness of the recipient. However, both Paul and his culture agreed on one important aspect of grace, one which helps solve the tension between justification by grace and judgment according to works: the unconditioned gift of grace, while undeserved, carried with it obligations.[114] These obligations are not the condition of grace, but the expected response to grace and its intended goal. Barclay says: "The notion that gifts are in principle 'purer' by expecting nothing in return is a peculiarly modern conception that has almost no counterpart in antiquity."[115] This is why Paul "can call eternal life both the *telos* of holiness (6.22) and the *charisma* of God (6.23), without a hint of tension or contradiction, because he expects that the abnormal, unfitting gift will be completed"[116] by the divinely empowered response of the human agent. Again,

> Paul can describe the fulfilment of the gift in conditional clauses (e.g. Rom 8.13; 11.22-23), but this is not such that an unconditioned gift (the Christ-event) is then followed by a separate and conditioned gift (eternal life, if you do this or that), but rather that the one unconditioned gift can only be fulfilled on the condition that it is neither repudiated nor refused.[117]

---

[112]John Barclay, "Believers and the 'Last Judgment' in Paul: Rethinking Grace and Recompense," in *Eschatologie—Eschatology*, ed. H.-J Eckstein, C. Landmesser and H. Lichtenberger (Tübingen: Mohr Siebeck, 2011), pp. 195-208. I was unable to find this essay, but I thank professor Barclay for sending me a prepublished copy of it. I will be working from his original document.

[113]See, e.g., Philo, *Leg. All.* 3.164; *Somn.* 2.176; *Abr.* 200-204; Seneca, *De Beneficiis* 1.1.2; 1.2.1; John M. G. Barclay, "Paul, the Gift and the Battle over Gentile Circumcision: Revisiting the Logic of Galatians," *ABR* 58 (2010): 36-56 (esp. 48-49).

[114]Barclay prefers the term "unconditioned" over "unconditional," since the latter suggests that there are no conditions *nor subsequent obligations* to the gift, while the former only indicates that there are no preconditions (p. 50n45).

[115]Barclay, "Believers and the 'Last Judgment,'" p. 10.

[116]Ibid., p. 12.

[117]Ibid., p. 15.

In short, the very idea of initial justification as a gift of grace *necessitates* that its completion—judgment day—will integrate a response by the one receiving the gift. There is no contradiction between initial and final justification in Paul, only a responsible understanding of the meaning of *charis*.

8

DIVINE AND HUMAN AGENCY
IN EARLY JUDAISM

A Survey

Thus far, we have compared Paul with the Dead Sea Scrolls in their understanding of divine and human agency in salvation. As stated in the introduction, comparing Paul with the Scrolls makes good sense, since both share similar eschatological paradigms (i.e., inaugurated eschatology) and theological motifs. In order to situate our study in the wider context of early Judaism, however, this chapter will survey other Second Temple documents, which will provide a more historically rooted depiction of both Paul and Qumran. We can more accurately understand Paul and Qumran if we have a broader understanding of the theological world in which they lived. The nature of such a survey is laden with problems, however. The historical context, rhetorical purpose, social location and textual tradition of the writings under scrutiny must be ignored if we are to achieve such a survey.[1] Our conclusions, therefore, must be tentative and cautious, yet the short-

---

[1] I echo the words of Stephen Westerholm, who prior to his brief journey through vast tracks of Jewish literature admitted: "The deficiencies inherent in rapid overviews will be on bold display here: the social context, rhetorical purpose, and literary and textual history of the sources we look at will all be ignored; nor is there place here for subtlety or novelty in interpretation" ("Paul's Anthropological 'Pessimism' in Its Jewish Context," in *Divine and Human Agency in Paul and His Cultural Environment*, ed. J. M. G. Barclay and S. Gathercole [New York: T & T Clark, 2006], p. 74).

comings of this approach are offset by the cumulative benefit of looking at a broad range of sources.

In the following, we will survey seven early Jewish documents, which I have chosen in light of their affinities to the thought world of either Paul or Qumran (or in some cases, both). Many of the following works exhibit soteriological concerns that correlate with the questions we have posed throughout this study. I have chosen *Jubilees* since it contains restoration motifs and was widely read by the Qumran community. Sirach could not be overlooked, since it directly wrestles with our question of divine and human agency. The collection of hymns known as the *Psalms of Solomon* displays many commonalities with both Paul and Qumran, and may have been written by a member, or members, of the Pharisaic community. As is well known to Pauline scholars, the so-called Wisdom of Solomon may have been one of Paul's implicit dialogue partners when he wrote his epistle to the Romans. The apocalypse of *4 Ezra* wrestles with questions that fall outside the scope of our study (e.g., theodicy, the afterlife, the messianic kingdom), and yet salvation, covenant and law are central throughout. Lastly, two first-century Palestinian works, Pseudo-Philo's *Biblical Antiquities* and the so-called *Testament of Moses,* will be examined for the simple reason that despite their geographical and theological relevance, they have been somewhat neglected in discussions surrounding Pauline and early Jewish soteriology. As we will see, they both have much to say.[2]

Before we begin our survey, we need to widen the parameters of our prior definition of soteriology, which was tailored to the specificities of Paul

---

[2]For the sake of space, I had to leave out several documents relevant for our study. The composite book *1 Enoch* would have been next on my list, especially the Book of the Watchers (*1 Enoch* 1–36), the Parables of Enoch (37–71) and the Epistle of Enoch (91–105). I examined this literature in previous drafts of this book but later found that pressing them to answer questions related to *Deuteronomic* and *Prophetic* restoration only yielded artificial conclusions. The apocalypse known as *2 Baruch* is also relevant, and yet its affinities to *4 Ezra* led me to choose one or the other for convenience. The so-called *Life of Adam and Eve* (Greek *Apocalypse of Moses*) contains some relevant motifs, as does *2 Enoch,* and yet the dating of these books is widely disputed—some say they were written well after the first century. Several other books could have been studied (Judith, Tobit, the *Testaments of the Twelve Patriarchs*, etc.), but were excluded for the simple reason that they display less relevance for our topic than the seven that were chosen. The soteriology of these books and many others are treated in D. A. Carson, P. T. O'Brien and M. A. Seifrid, eds., *Justification and Variegated Nomism*, Vol. 1: *The Complexities of Second Temple Judaism*, (Grand Rapids: Baker Academic, 2001); and Daniel M. Gurtner, ed., *This World and the World to Come: Soteriology in Early Judaism* (New York: T & T Clark, 2011).

and Qumran. Previously, we broke down the meaning of "salvation" into various motifs that are evident in both Pauline and Dead Sea literature: the curse of the law, the eschatological spirit and others.[3] However, not all books in the following survey appear to be concerned about these themes, so we will consider the "soteriology" of the seven books along the lines of the broad contours of *Deuteronomic* and *Prophetic* paradigms of restoration. All of the following works show some interest in divine deliverance, where God's people—the righteous—need to be rescued from something (sin, wrath, idolatry, ignorance, their pagan environment, etc.). Some focus more explicitly on the restoration of God's covenant with Israel,[4] while others are more centered on God's eschatological deliverance of the righteous on judgment day.[5] Aside from specific soteriological motifs evinced in Paul and Qumran, therefore, we will consider how divine and human agencies relate in the paradigms of salvation evident in each work.

DIVINE AND HUMAN AGENCY: PARADIGMS OF PROPHETIC AND DEUTERONOMIC RESTORATION

Jubilees. The book of *Jubilees* makes an apt inroad into the broader stream of early Jewish thought, since it was cherished as a significant—if not inspired—work among the Qumran community.[6] *Jubilees* exhibits many commonalties with the Scrolls in matters of calendar, interpretive practices and general theological outlook. Concerning its soteriology, scholars have long recognized a strong *Deuteronomic* tone, where Israel's restoration is conditioned on its repentance, which is seen in the prologue of *Jubilees* 1. In the context of national restoration, the author writes:

> And they will forget all of my laws and all of my commandments and all of my judgments. . . . And afterward they will turn to me from among the nations with all their heart and with all their soul and with all their might. And

---

[3]See chapter one above.

[4]*Jubilees, Biblical Antiquities* and the *Testament of Moses.*

[5]The Wisdom of Solomon, Sirach, the *Psalms of Solomon* and *4 Ezra* (the latter two include notions of covenant restoration).

[6]*Jubilees,* composed between 170 and 150 B.C., is a retelling of Gen 1–Ex 24 through the lens of Moses' revelation on Sinai. The work exhibited an extensive influence on the Dead Sea community and probably had scriptural status (see CD 16:1-6); see most recently, Ian Werrett, "Salvation Through Emulation: Facets of Jubilean Soteriology at Qumran," in Gurtner, *This World,* pp. 211-28.

I shall gather them from the midst of all the nations. And they will seek me so that I might be found by them. (*Jub.* 1:14-15)[7]

Israel initiates restoration by its repentant turning to God, in the same vein that we saw in 4QMMT and 11QT[a]. The structure of salvation, therefore, appears to be *Deuteronomic*. D. Lambert, however, argues otherwise, suggesting that while *Jubilees* "inherits a paradigm of sin-exile-repentance-restoration," the author "chooses to modify that paradigm" by "introducing the divine circumcision of the heart language of" Deuteronomy 30:6.[8] This divine initiative reading is supported by the latter part of *Jubilees* 1, where the author depicts a revised plan of restoration in light of Moses' plea:[9]

> And the LORD said to Moses, "I know their contrariness and their thoughts and their stubbornness. And they will not obey until they acknowledge their sin and the sins of their fathers. But after this they will return to me in all uprightness and with all of (their) heart and soul. And I shall cut off the foreskin of their heart and the foreskin of the heart of their descendants. And I shall create for them a holy spirit, and I shall purify them so that they will not turn away from following me from that day and forever." (*Jub.* 1:22-23)

Divine agency is certainly highlighted more than in the previous restoration passage (*Jub.* 1:14-15); however, it is not at all clear that *Jubilees* "anticipates a dramatic, *divinely* initiated transformation of human nature,"[10]

---

[7]Unless otherwise stated, all translations of the Pseudepigraphic books are from James H. Charlesworth, ed., *The Old Testament Pseudepigrapha*, 2 vols. (Garden City, NY: Doubleday, 1983, 1985), and translations of the Apocrypha are from the NRSV.

[8]D. Lambert, "Did Israel Believe that Redemption Awaited Its Repentance? The Case of *Jubilees* 1," *CBQ* 68 (2006): 640.

[9]Lambert argues that there are two versions of restoration articulated in *Jubilees* 1. The first version (*Jub.* 1:15-18) follows the *Deuteornomic* pattern of Deut 4:29-31, where human initiative precedes divine action, but the second pattern (*Jub.* 1:22-25) flows from Deuteronomy 30:1-10, where God's circumcision of the heart (Deut 30:6) precedes Israel's response ("Did Israel Believe?," pp. 638-40).

[10]Ibid., p. 633. A divine initiative reading is also taken by A. Andrew Das, "Paul and Works of Obedience in Second Temple Judaism: Romans 4:4-5 as a 'New Perspective' Case Study," *CBQ* 71 (2009): 795-812 (esp. 798-99). Passages that may support this interpretation include *Jub.* 5:12; 10:1-14; 50:5. For instance, the latter passage anticipates Israel's future "purification from all the sin of fornication, and defilement, and uncleanness, and sin and error" (50:5). However, the relationship between divine and human agency in how the purification takes place is not explicitly stated; therefore, this passage in itself cannot support either view of restoration. E. P. Sanders points to the emphasis on covenant and election throughout the book (*Jub.* 1:17, 25, 28; 16:18, 26; 19:18; 21:24; 22:11, 27; 24:29; 25:3; 33:20; 36:6) to garner support for his view that the soteriology of *Jubilees* is one of covenantal nomism. See *Paul and Palestinian Judaism: A*

as Lambert asserts. Here in 1:22-23, God's transformative act of heart circumcision is prefaced by Israel's initiative; it comes after they "obey," "acknowledge their sin and the sins of their fathers," and "return to me in all
uprightness and with all of (their) heart and soul" (*Jub.* 1:22-23). Human
turning still precedes divine transformation.[11]

A number of other passages in *Jubilees* follow the same program. In another restoration narrative (*Jub.* 23:8-31), the author depicts the post-flood
fall of humanity, which unfolds much like CD 2:14–3:20 (cf. Rom 1:18–3:20).
The "evil generation" (*Jub.* 23:14, 15, 16) goes from bad to worse as they pollute
the land with fornication (23:15) and disobedience to parents (23:16), and
they ultimately "forsake the covenant which the LORD made" with Israel
(23:16). God responds by raining down punishment in the form of covenant
curses: the LORD "will give them to the sword and to judgment and to cap-
tivity and pillage and destruction" (23:22). And much like Deuteronomy
(e.g., Deut 4:29-31), restoration hinges on the nation's repentance: "In those
days, they will cry out and call and pray to be saved from the hand of the
sinners. . . . And in those days, children will begin to search the law, and to
search the commandments and to return to the way of righteousness" (*Jub.*
23:24-26). God responds to their repentance by extending their life (23:27-
29), granting the covenant blessing of peace (23:30), and executing judgment
on their enemies (23:30-31).[12] Like *Jubilees* 1, this narrative follows a *Deuteronomic* pattern of restoration.[13]

In another passage, the author of *Jubilees* discusses the flood and affirms
a conditional restoration in patent *Deuteronomic* terminology: "If they

---

Comparison of Patterns of Religion (Philadelphia: Fortress, 1977), pp. 362-85. However, while
election terminology may contribute to the author's understanding of the gracious *establishment*
of the covenant, it does not determine the relationship between divine and human agency in
restoring the covenant.

[11]J. C. Vanderkam critiques Lambert on the same point, showing that "the 'returning' of the
people in exile *precedes* the divine transformation of their nature." See "Recent Scholarship on
the Book of Jubilees," *CBR* 6 (2008): 425, emphasis his; see too Kyle Wells, "Grace, Obedience,
and the Hermeneutics of Agency: Paul and His Jewish Contemporaries on the Transformation
of the Heart" (Ph.D. diss., Durham University, 2009), pp. 112-14.

[12]Resurrection may be included in these blessings: "They will *rise up* and see great peace. . . . And
their bones will rest in the earth, *and their spirits will increase joy*" (*Jub.* 23:30-31); see, e.g., N. T.
Wright, *The Resurrection of the Son of God* (Minneapolis: Fortress, 2003), pp. 143-44. The
language, however, is inconclusive.

[13]Divine action is actually not stated until 23:30: "And then the LORD will heal his servants" (see
Wells, "Grace," pp. 116-17).

return to him in righteousness, he will forgive all of their sins and he will pardon all of their transgressions. . . . He will have mercy on all who return from all their error, once each year" (*Jub.* 5:17-18). Here, as in *Jubilees* 1 and 23, the author "seems to foreground human agency as the mechanism which brings about restoration."[14] Such *Deuteronomic* soteriology may be supported by the author's depiction of Abraham (*Jub.* 11:1–23:10). Unlike the biblical portrait of a thoroughly human patriarch (and everything that implies), *Jubilees* depicts Abraham as "a paragon of faith and obedience who heeds the commandments of God and, as a result, becomes a 'friend' of the Lord" (*Jub.* 17:15, 18; 23:10; cf. CD 3:2).[15] According to *Jubilees*, "Abraham was perfect in all of his actions with the LORD and was pleasing through righteousness all of the days of his life" (23:10). The glowing portrait of the patriarch, however, does not in itself confirm a *Deuteronomic* soteriology. One's obedience could be understood as a human response to divine grace—though this would not fit the pattern we have seen thus (1:22-23; 5:17-18; 23:16-32). What makes *Jubilees'* reading of Abraham more *Deuteronomic* is the way his obedience exhibits a "paranaetic function" where the author "wishes to make clear that only strict obedience to covenant stipulations secures deliverance from earthly and heavenly threats against the covenant people."[16] In the retelling of the Aqedah (17:15–18:9), Abraham's unswerving faithfulness wards off the evil attacks of the evil Prince Mastema (17:16; 18:9, 12). Abraham's demonic foe is not relegated to the biblical past but is very much preventing second-century Jews from rendering God wholehearted obedience. Mastema, in other words, stands in the way of God's covenant blessings being poured out on the nation, and it is up to Israel to follow Abraham's example of obedience and withstand the demonically charged power of sin.[17] So for *Jubilees*, Abraham "is intended to function as a model of obedience and covenantal faithfulness that must be emulated in order for subsequent generations to secure their own protection from Mastema's deceptions and to ensure the

---

[14]Ibid., p. 115.

[15]Werrett, "Salvation Through Emulation," p. 227.

[16]Leroy A. Huizenga, "The Battle for Isaac: Exploring the Composition and Function of the *Aqedah* in the Book of Jubilees," *JSP* 13 (2002): 36, cited in and followed by Werrett, "Salvation Through Emulation," p. 226.

[17]See, e.g., *Jub.* 10:10-14; 48:2-3, 9-19.

promise of countless offspring, unending peace, and God's eternal blessings,"[18] which come to the fore in the restoration narratives of *Jubilees* 1 and 23.

The reworking of the Abraham narrative (11:1–23:10), together with Israel's initiative in restoration (1:14-15, 22-23; 23:8-31) and use of retributive terminology drawn from Deuteronomy (*Jub.* 5:17-18), suggest that the author anticipated that Israel's restoration will come through *Deuteronomic* means. This is not to say that the author believes in salvation attained purely by human merit any more than the author of Chronicles does. But neither does it mean that "salvation depends on the grace of God,"[19] unless we define grace to include notions of humanly initiated repentance that preface divine restoration.

Sirach. The Wisdom of Jesus Son of Sirach (hereafter, Sirach) is pertinent for our topic, not because it contains restoration narratives like *Jubilees*, but because the author addresses the relationship between human and divine agency directly.[20] The author not only emphasizes human agency more explicitly than most Jewish authors, he argues against a type of determinism that must have been in the air at his time.[21] And Sirach sets forth his case within the framework of the Sinaitic covenant: "Obedience brings covenantal blessing, while disobedience results in death."[22] Such *Deuteronomic* theology is explicitly articulated in Sirach 15:

---

[18]Werrett, "Salvation Through Emulation," p. 226.

[19]Sanders, *Paul and Palestinian Judaism*, p. 383, followed with some modification by Peter Enns, "Expansions of Scripture," in Carson, O'Brien and Seifrid, *Justification and Variegated Nomism*, 1:92-97.

[20]Originally written in Hebrew, Sirach was composed around 180 B.C., just prior to the persecution of Antiochus IV. The book was then translated into Greek by Ben Sirach's grandson sometime after 117 B.C. in Egypt. For these and other introductory issues, see Patrick W. Skehan and Alexander A. Di Lella, *The Wisdom of Ben Sira: A New Translation with Introduction and Commentary*, AB 39 (New York: Doubleday, 1987), pp. 3-92.

[21]Ben Sirach uses a debate formula ("do not say . . .") throughout his work, which exposes views about God that he is seeking to confront (see, e.g., 5:1-6; 15:11-12; 16:17). One of the theological views that Sirach is correcting is a form of determinism that has "eliminated the human agent," forging many passages into a discussion about "the problem of divine and human agency." Jason Maston, *Divine and Human Agency in Second Temple Judaism and in Paul*, WUNT 2.297 (Tübingen: Mohr Siebeck, 2010), p. 26. Maston is interacting with, and slightly modifying, the view of James Crenshaw, who says that the underlying problem in Sirach is theodicy, God's apparent failure to judge bad behavior. See James L. Crenshaw, "The Problem of Theodicy in Sirach: On Human Bondage," *JBL* 94 (1975): 47-64.

[22]Maston, *Divine and Human Agency*, p. 27.

> It was he who created humankind in the beginning,
>> and he left them in the power of their own free choice.
> If you choose, you can keep the commandments
>> and to act faithfully is a matter of your own choice. . . .
> Before each person are life and death,
>> and whichever one chooses will be given. (Sir 15:14-15, 17)

The author argues against a determinism that limits human free will and confirms his view by citing Deuteronomy 30:15, 19.[23] Central to his concern is anthropological optimism; namely, that humans possess the moral capacity to obey the torah.

The emphasis on torah obedience as a pathway to blessing is seen again in the author's hymn of creation (16:24–17:24). The author moves from the beginning of creation (esp. 17:1-4) to the theophany at Sinai, where God revealed the law to Israel:

> He bestowed knowledge upon them
>> and allotted to them the law of life.
> He established with them an eternal covenant,
>> and revealed to them his decrees. (17:11-12)

The passage is significant since the author has skipped from creation to the establishment of the Sinaitic covenant with Israel. The coupling of "eternal covenant" (cf. Gen 9:16; 17:1-8) and the Sinaitic "law of life"[24] shows that for Sirach, it is not God's unconditional covenant with Abraham, but "the giving and observing of commandments" that "is fundamental to God's relationship to Israel."[25] When God's covenant with Abraham is mentioned in 45:20, the emphasis is on God's response to Abraham's deeds:

> He kept the law of the Most High,
>> and entered into a covenant with him;
> he certified the covenant in his flesh,
>> and when he was tested he proved faithful.

---

[23]Deut 30:15: "See, I have set before you today life and good, death and evil"; Deut 30:19: "I call heaven and earth to witness against you today, that I have set before you life and death, blessing and curse. Therefore choose life, that you and your offspring may live."

[24]The phrase "law of life" is used again in 45:5 in the context of God's revelation to Moses on Sinai.

[25]Francis Watson, *Paul and the Hermeneutics of Faith* (New York: T & T Clark, 2004), pp. 9-10.

Therefore the Lord assured him with an oath

  that the nations would be blessed through his offspring. (45:20-21)

Abraham's obedience on the mountain of Moriah (Gen 22) is smuggled back into the initial covenant ceremony of Genesis 15, making the divine oath at least partially based on Abraham's deeds. This *Deuteronomic* paradigm is confirmed throughout Sirach 17, where those who have disobeyed are encouraged to repent. God "will rise up and repay" sinners for their evil deeds (cf. 17:20), but "to those who repent he grants a return" (17:23-24). The author exhorts his audience to "turn back to the Lord and forsake your sins. . . . Return to the Most High and turn away from iniquity" (17:25-26). Given his optimistic view of humanity's capacity to obey (cf. 15:14-15), we can assume that unlike Jeremiah and Ezekiel, Sirach believes his audience has the ability to heed the call.

Sanders wants to assume that God's gracious covenant underlies all exhortations to obey the law, but this does not seem to be the author's main concern. For Sirach, the focus is not on God's past acts of grace but on the present offer of life to all who obey the law.[26] Even Sanders, who wants to maintain an element of covenantal nomism in Sirach, believes that an individual's salvation is ultimately determined by their obedience to torah.[27] Such emphasis on obedience as the pathway to covenantal blessing is seen throughout the so-called Hymn to the Fathers (Sir 44:1–50:29), where the author sweeps through Israel's history and highlights the obedience of the righteous. Those who live uprightly have "left behind a name" (Sir 45:8) and their "righteous deeds have not been forgotten" (Sir 45:10), while those who were disobedient "have perished as though they had never existed" (Sir 45:9).[28] Like the biblical Chronicler, Sirach highlights the righteousness

---

[26]See Maston: "Deuteronomy 30.15-20, for Ben Sira, functions as the hermeneutical guide for how the rest of the Torah should be read" (*Divine and Human Agency*, p. 42).

[27]Sanders, *Paul and Palestinian Judaism*, p. 333: "What Ben Sirach has to say about the fate of the individual, whether happy or dolorous, does not depend on whether or not the individual is elect . . . but on whether or not he is counted among the wicked or the righteous; that is, on whether or not he more or less satisfactorily keeps the commandments of the covenant" (see also p. 346).

[28]Teresa Brown points out that "the distinguishing factor between the 'good guys and bad guys' is idol worship." See "God and Men in Israel's History: God and Idol Worship in Praise of the Fathers (Sir 44–50)," in *Ben Sira's God: Proceedings of the International Ben Sira Conference: Durham—Ushaw College 2001*, ed. Renate Egger-Wenzel, BZAW 321 (Berlin: Walter de Gruyter, 2002), p. 220.

of Old Testament heroes and is constrained to whitewash a few of them in the process.[29]

Judgment according to works is consistently affirmed throughout Sirach, and the nature of reward stems from a *Deuteronomic* view of retribution. For Sirach, "on the day of death . . . one's deeds are revealed," and the Lord will "reward individuals according to their conduct" (Sir 11:26-27). God "judges a person according to one's deeds" and "everyone receives in accordance with one's deeds" (Sir 16:11, 14). On judgment day, God "does justice for the righteous and executes judgment" when "he repays mortals according to their deeds, and the works of all according to their thoughts" (Sir 35:22, 24). The theme of judgment according to works is pervasive and clear, such that the author concludes his work with yet another reminder: "Do your work in good time, and in his own time God will give you your reward" (Sir 51:30). Such strict judgment is not devoid of mercy, however; for mercy will rain down "as clouds of rain in time of drought" (Sir 35:26), and the righteous will "rejoice in his mercy" (Sir 35:25) on judgment day. But divine mercy is viewed as a response to repentance and obedience: "How great is the mercy of the Lord, and his forgiveness for those who return to him" (Sir 17:29).[30]

Despite many differences in genre, occasion for writing and theological concerns, the author's explicit emphasis on human agency in obedience as a means of covenantal blessing correlates with a *Deuteronomic* paradigm of restoration. Such a view is not unbiblical; as we saw in chapter two, it forms the heartbeat of one theological strand in the Old Testament. But it is different from the *Prophetic* emphasis on unilateral redemption, which governed Paul's soteriological framework.

Psalms of Solomon. The collection of hymns known as the *Psalms of Solomon* exhibit many parallels with Paul's letters and may give us a first-

---

[29]As we saw above, Abraham is presented in glowing light (Sir 45:19-22). Also, Moses is viewed as a "a godly man" from the beginning (Sir 44:23–45:5, esp. 44:23): "For his faithfulness and meekness he consecrated him, choosing him out of all humankind" (Sir 45:4). Aaron's lengthy presentation ignores his sin with the golden calf (Sir 45:6-22; cf. Ex 32). The judges are vaguely yet curiously praised for not falling into idolatry or turning from the Lord (Sir 46:11). And David's debacle with Bathsheba is not explicitly mentioned (Sir 47:2-11, though cf. Sir 47:11), while he is highlighted (along with Hezekiah and Josiah) as an exception to the "great sinners" who "abandoned the law of the Most High" (Sir 49:4).

[30]"Divine mercy is the reward given to the obedient" (Maston, *Divine and Human Agency*, p. 69).

hand account of Pharisaic thought.[31] As far as soteriology is concerned, the psalms exhibit a good deal of retribution theology, where the righteous are rewarded and the wicked are punished. The author writes:

> Our works (are) in the choosing and power of our souls,
>> to do right and wrong in the works of our hands,
>> and in your righteousness you oversee human beings.
> The one who does what is right saves up life for himself with the Lord,
>> and the one who does what is wrong causes his own life to be destroyed.
> (*Pss. Sol.* 9:4-5)

This passage is similar to Sirach 15:14-15 above in that it affirms the moral capacity to do good or evil. The reference to saving up "life for himself with the Lord" refers to the afterlife reward of resurrection,[32] which is contingent on doing what is right (*ho poiōn dikaiosynēn*). Again, in *Psalms of Solomon* 14, the author writes:

> The Lord is faithful to those who truly love him,
>> to those who endure his discipline,
> To those who walk in the righteousness of his commandments, in the Law,
>> which he has commanded for our life.
> The Lord's devout shall live by it forever. (*Pss. Sol.* 14:1-3)

As in the previous hymn, the author affirms that obedience to the law is a precondition for eternal life.[33] And such retribution theology is evident

---

[31]Pharisaic authorship is debated. Advocates include: S. Holm-Nielsen, *Psalmen Salomons,* JSHRZ 4/2 (Gütersloh: Gütersloher Verlagshaus, 1977), pp. 58-59, and M. Winninge, *Sinners and the Righteous: A Comparative Study of the Psalms of Solomon and Paul's Letters* (Stockholm: Almqvist & Wiksell, 1995), pp. 141-80. For a recent review of the literature devoted to authorship, see K. Atkinson, *An Intertextual Study of The Psalms of Solomon,* SBEC 49 (Lewiston, UK: Edwin Mellen Press, 2000), pp. 420-24. I am inclined to N. T. Wright's view, who says that the *Psalms of Solomon* shows "strong traces of a revolutionary Pharisaism" (*Resurrection,* p. 162). For studies that compare these *Psalms* with Paul, see Mark A. Seifrid, *Justification by Faith: The Origin and Development of a Central Pauline Theme,* NovTSup 68 (Leiden: E. J. Brill, 1992), pp. 109-32; and Preston Sprinkle, *Law and Life: The Interpretation of Leviticus 18:5 in Early Judaism and in Paul,* WUNT 2.241 (Tübingen: Mohr Siebeck, 2008), pp. 87-100.

[32]See too *Pss. Sol.* 2:31; 3:11-12; 13:11-12; 14:1-5; 15:10-13; Sprinkle, *Law and Life,* pp. 89-90.

[33]That eternal life is in view here is confirmed later in the hymn: "Their [the wicked] inheritance is Hades and darkness and destruction, and they will not be found in the day of mercy of the righteous; but the pious of the Lord will inherit life in happiness" (*Pss. Sol.* 14:9-10). This means that the phrase "live *by it* forever" in 14:3 should be taken as instrumental—the life in question is the reward of eschatological life, and the law is the means by which the pious gain it. In contrast to Paul, the author alludes to Lev 18:5 ("the one who does these things will live by

throughout the collection: "The Lord's mercy is upon those who fear him with judgment, to separate between the righteous and the sinner to repay sinners forever according to their actions and to have mercy on the righteous" (2:33-35); God "atones for (sins of) ignorance *by fasting and humbling* his soul" (3:8); "(Because of) our sins, sinners rose up against us. . . . You rewarded them, O God, according to their sins" (17:5, 8). Throughout the work, the sinners will be punished and the righteous will be rewarded.

It is not altogether clear, however, on what basis the righteous will be rewarded. Some say that God's mercy is given to the righteous *because of* their righteous deeds,[34] while others say "the salvation of the righteous is due . . . purely to the mercy of God."[35] But neither of these views does justice to the complex thought in the collection—these psalms defy tidy systemization. On the one hand, retribution theology is evident throughout, as seen above. But on the other hand, God's mercy is sometimes viewed as the basis for the righteousness of the pious. This is explicit in *Psalms of Solomon* 16, where the author credits God's sovereign grace with keeping him from falling away: "My soul was drawn away from the Lord God of Israel, unless the Lord had come to my aid with his everlasting mercy. He jabbed me as a horse is goaded to keep it awake; my savior and protector at all times saved me" (16:3-5). Later the author calls on God to "direct the works of my hands before you, and protect my steps in your remembrance" (16:9); and "if I sin, discipline (me) that (I may) return" (16:11). Again, God's sovereign control is at work in the fate of every individual: "an individual and his fate (are) on the scales before you; he cannot add any increase contrary to your judgment, O God" (5:4); "His ways are directed by the Lord, and the works of his hands are protected by the Lord his God" (6:2).

It is therefore complicated to unravel the relationship between divine and human agency in passages such as 6:6, where the author says that the Lord "show[s] mercy to those who truly love him."[36] In itself, this could mean that the author affirms that God's mercy is a response to human

---

them") in 14:2-3 to show that obedience to the law is the pathway to eschatological life. Paul uses the same text to argue the opposite (Rom 10:5; Gal 3:12). For the soteriology of this hymn, see further Sprinkle, *Law and Life*, pp. 90-93, 97-100.

[34]Seifrid, *Justification by Faith*, pp. 109-32.

[35]Sanders, *Paul and Palestinian Judaism*, p. 393, cf. 391.

[36]Cf. 10:3; 14:1.

action—those who "truly love him." And yet even human action cannot be divorced from God's prior mercy, as we saw above (5:4; 6:2; 16:3-5, 9, 11).

The theology of the *Psalms of Solomon* is not uniformly *Deuteronomic*. Divine and human agency work together in keeping the pious in the covenant and ultimately securing mercy before God on judgment day. However, the *Psalms* do not exhibit a wholly *Prophetic* theology either, where God justifies the wicked and infuses dry bones with resurrection life. Divine agency is present, but the *priority* of divine agency in the face of a pessimistic anthropology (e.g., Rom 1:18–3:26) is not apparent. It seems best to view these *Psalms*—much like the biblical Psalms—as standing somewhere in the middle of the *Deuteronomic* and *Prophetic* paradigms.

The Wisdom of Solomon. The Wisdom of Solomon is important for our survey, since it is likely that Paul was aware of it—and may have been critiquing it—when he penned his letter to the Romans.[37] The book exhibits a complex blend of philosophical reasoning and Jewish wisdom theology derived from rigorous exegesis in the Greek translation of the Jewish Scriptures. The author writes the book in order to remind his Diaspora audience "about the superiority of the Jewish way of life" and exhort them "to remain faithful to their tradition."[38] Throughout his exhortation, the author explores the contours of God's justice in the world and "argues from and for a consistent theological vision shaped by the rational exercise of divine justice and the predictable patterns of moral order."[39] And soteriology—broadly defined—is a major theme throughout.[40]

---

[37]See W. Sanday and A. C. Headlam, *A Critical and Exegetical Commentary on the Epistle to the Romans*, ICC (Edinburgh: T & T Clark, 1900), pp. 51-52; and recently Joseph Dodson, *The "Powers" of Personification: Rhetorical Purpose in the Book of Wisdom and the Letter to the Romans*, BZNW 161 (Berlin/New York: W. de Gruyter, 2008), pp. 2-13. The book was originally written in Greek by a Jew (probably) living in Alexandria. The date of composition falls somewhere between 50 B.C. and A.D. 50, though some cast the net even wider. David Winston says that it was written during the reign of Caligula (A.D. 37-41). See *The Wisdom of Solomon: A New Translation with Introduction and Commentary*, AB 43 (Garden City, NY: Doubleday, 1979), p. 23.

[38]Daniel J. Harrington, "'Saved by Wisdom' (Wis. 9.18): Soteriology in the Wisdom of Solomon," in Gurtner, *This World*, p. 182.

[39]Jonathan Linebaugh, "God, Grace, and Righteousness: *Wisdom of Solomon* and Paul's Letter to the Romans in Conversation" (Ph.D. diss., Durham University, 2011), p. 26.

[40]Harrington defines "soteriology" in its most basic sense as "the process of healing or making whole and well those who need to move from one state or status to another," and notes that "the meaning of what the audience is being saved from" in Wisdom "ranges from 'ungodly' or unrighteous behavior, to ignorance, and to idolatry" ("Saved by Wisdom," p. 181).

Like the *Psalms of Solomon*, the author of Wisdom contrasts the wicked and the righteous through the lens of retribution theology (esp. Wis 1:1–6:11). The wicked will be punished for their sins,[41] and the righteous will be rewarded with immortality for their faithfulness.[42] On a basic level, therefore, Wisdom maintains a *Deuteronomic* theology of blessings and curses; the righteous will be blessed while the wicked are cursed.[43] However, the *Deuteornomic* rewards are transferred to the afterlife, since in this life the righteous are persecuted and the wicked prosper, which is seen clearly in Wisdom 3. Here, the author argues that "the barren woman who is undefiled" and therefore has the *appearance* of transgression (Deut 28:4, 11, 18) is actually "blessed" since "she will have fruit when God examines souls" on judgment day (Wis 3:13). In contrast, "children of adulterers will not come to maturity, and the offspring of an unlawful union will perish" *even though* they may "live long" (Wis 3:16-17). They will have "no consolation on the day of judgment, for the end of an unrighteous generation is grievous" (Wis 3:18-19). By delaying the rewards of the retributive system, "the symmetrical justice of deuteronomic theology is preserved by being postponed."[44]

But such retribution theology is augmented by divine agency in the form of Lady Wisdom—who creates and governs the material and moral fabric of the universe.[45] Without her, righteousness and salvation would be impossible. Lady Wisdom is "the breath of the power of God, and a pure emanation of the glory of the Almighty" (Wis 7:25). "She is a reflection of eternal light, a spotless mirror of the working of God, and an image of his goodness"

---

[41]Wis 3:10-13; 4:18-19; 8:13; 11:12, 16; 16:18; 18:18-19.

[42]Wis 2:22; 3:1, 13-15; 5:1-2, 15. Although the righteous suffer in this life, it is not conceived as punishment but as discipline to refine them for eternal life (Wis 3:5-7; 11:23; 12:1-2, 10, 20).

[43]Wisdom, while endorsing *Deuteronomic* themes, also redefines them. Moses promises life to those who keep the law (Deut 30:11-19; cf. Lev 18:5), which Wisdom redefines as a "blameless life" (Wis 4:9). Deuteronomy connects fertility with God's favor (Deut 28:4, 11) and infertility with curse (Deut 28:18), while Wisdom connects infertility with virtue (Wis 4:1). Deuteronomy critiques the status of the eunuch (Deut 23:1), while Wisdom offers blessing on him if he keeps the law (Wis 3:14; cf. Is 56:4-5). See further Linebaugh, "God, Grace, and Righteousness," p. 32.

[44]Ibid., p. 34. Linebaugh's statement refers to the *Epistle of Enoch* (*1 En.* 92:1-5; 93:11–105:2), which he says exhibits conceptual parallels with Wisdom.

[45]The identity of Lady Wisdom in the book is notoriously debated, ranging from "an attribute of God; an autonomous power, or something in between" (Dodson, *"Powers" of Personification*, p. 15; see his discussion and survey on pp. 15-18, 101-14). Whichever view one takes, Lady Wisdom is portrayed (at the very least) as an extension of God's agency in the world (cf. esp. Wis 7).

(Wis 7:26). The author also calls her "the active cause of all things" and the "fashioner of what exists" (Wis 8:5-6); "because of her," says the author, "I shall have immortality" (Wis 8:13). Indeed, Lady Wisdom is the gift of grace, who performed acts of salvation throughout Israel's history, saving the earth by "steering" Noah in the ark (Wis 10:4), ensuring the blamelessness of Abraham by keeping "him strong in the face of his compassion for" Isaac (Wis 10:5), rescuing Lot from destruction (Wis 10:6) and Jacob "from his brother's wrath" (Wis 10:10). Lady Wisdom "delivered" Joseph "from sin" and "brought him the scepter of a kingdom" (Wis 10:13-14). She delivered Israel from Egypt, parted the sea before them (Wis 10:15-21), and brought water out of the "flinty rock" (Wis 11:4). In sum, "the paths of those on earth were set right, and people were taught what pleases you, and *were saved by wisdom*" (*tē Sophia esōthēsan*, 9:18).

Such emphasis on God's action in the world through Lady Wisdom may suggest a soteriology that parallels Paul's, and some have taken this view.[46] The priority of divine agency is not altogether clear, however, when one considers the *worthiness of the agents whom Wisdom saves*. John Barclay points out that "wisdom's benevolence is not without rationale," and that "all five individuals saved by wisdom [Noah, Abraham, Lot, Jacob and Joseph] are accorded moral, and not just social, worth."[47] For example, all five characters are already considered "righteous" when Wisdom delivers them,[48] a telling feature captured in Wisdom 10:9: "Wisdom rescued from troubles *those who served her*."[49] For the author of Wisdom, "there is always a reason why some perish and some are rescued from destruction, and discerning that moral or social principle makes history both comprehensible and

---

[46]Das, "Rom 4," pp. 799-800, who agues for divinely initiated obedience in Wisdom.

[47]John M. G. Barclay, "Unnerving Grace: Approaching Romans 9–11 from The Wisdom of Solomon," in *Between Gospel and Election*, ed. Florian Wilk and J. Ross Wagner, WUNT 257 (Tübingen: Mohr Siebeck, 2011), pp. 96-97.

[48]Wis 10:4, 5, 6-8, 10-12, 13-14.

[49]To be precise, the "righteousness" of the patriarchs is not the formal cause of their salvation, for Wisdom is clear that God is the causal agent of salvation. Righteousness may be viewed as a condition of salvation, but such righteousness cannot be autonomously produced or sustained by the human agent. Linebaugh rightly points out that the righteous behavior of Jacob and Joseph is "attributed to the guiding and delivering activity of" Wisdom and therefore "cannot be separated from its divine cause" (Linebaugh, "God, Grace, and Righteousness," p. 55). Salvation, therefore, is not unilateral, but neither is it synergistic.

hopeful."[50] This theological axiom underlies Wisdom 11:15–12:27, an excursus on the justice of God's power and mercy.[51] Here, the author smoothes out any potential claim of arbitrariness that may be lobbed at God's dealings in the world. The reason why the Egyptians and Canaanites were punished was that they deserved it, for God would not "condemn anyone who does not deserve to be punished" (Wis 12:15). On the flip side, God's salvation and preservation of his people through the agency of Lady Wisdom is not wrought through the absolute freedom of God—which would be arbitrary and chaotic—but within the confines of a *Deuteronomic* system of retribution and reward. God is responsible and just, and therefore he evaluates the worthiness of the beneficiary of his gifts, which is why "immortality" is considered both a gift (*charis*, Wis 3:5-9; 4:10-15) and a reward (*misthos*, Wis 2:22; 3:13-15).[52]

The soteriological incongruence of Wisdom and Romans is witnessed especially in their respective interpretations of the biblical narrative. According to Wisdom, for instance, God's dealings with the Egyptians follow the *Deuteronomic* structure of reward and punishment, though the author must rework the biblical narrative to maintain his agenda.[53] For Wisdom, God's righteousness and power prevent him from condemning "anyone who does not deserve to be punished" (Wis 12:15), and this is the reason he destroyed the Egyptians. They refused to heed God's warnings through the plagues and therefore "will experience the deserved judgment of God" (Wis 12:26). This stable rationale for punishment provides a convincing answer for the one "who will say, 'What have you done?' Or will resist your judgment?" (Wis 12:12). For Wisdom, no one can "confront you about those whom you have punished" (Wis 12:14), since the "punishments did not come upon the sinners without prior signs in the violence of thunder, for they justly suffered because of their wicked acts" (Wis 19:13).[54] Likewise, as we

---

[50]Barclay, "Unnerving Grace," p. 97.

[51]Ibid. On this passage, see too Monya McGlynn, *Divine Judgment and Divine Benevolence in the Book of Wisdom*, WUNT 2.139 (Tübingen: Mohr Siebeck, 2001), pp. 25-53.

[52]Linebaugh, "God, Grace, and Righteousness," pp. 35, 150; Barclay, "Unnerving Grace," p. 94; see also Simon Gathercole, *Where Is Boasting? Early Jewish Soteriology and Paul's Response in Romans 1-5* (Grand Rapids: Eerdmans, 2002), p. 71.

[53]Watson, *Hermeneutics of Faith*, p. 399.

[54]Regarding the Canaanites, Wisdom writes: "But judging them little by little you gave them an opportunity to repent, though you were not unaware that their origin was evil and their

saw above, Wisdom provides theological rationale for saving the heroes of old. Noah, Abraham, Lot, Jacob, Joseph and Moses are all worthy of Lady Wisdom's saving graces: "She gave to holy people the reward of their labors; she guided them along that marvelous way" (Wis 10:17). Salvation, therefore, is an act of God mediated through Lady Wisdom, but it is not arbitrary or irresponsible. It considers the worthiness of the agent being saved (cf. Wis 2:22; 3:13-15).

Paul's understanding of the biblical story is not only different from than Wisdom's but seems to be in critical dialogue with it. God's election of Abraham, Isaac and Jacob is based on God's free selectivity; it is explicitly not based on anything they have done (Rom 9:10-12). Paul anticipates the same objection that Wisdom raised concerning God's justice (Rom 9:14: "Is there injustice on God's part?"; Wis 12:12: "Who will say, 'What have you done?'"), yet gives an entirely different answer. "Paul's answer to the question about divine injustice is the sheer 'thatness' of God's selectivity: God has mercy; God hardens."[55] Paul's rationale for divine justice is rooted in the absolute freedom of God, which governs both salvation and judgment. God's mercy and wrath are determined by the will of God and cannot be manipulated by human action. Pharaoh (the embodiment of Egypt) is not judged through a system of retribution but was raised up as a conduit for God's power (Rom 9:14-18; contrast Wis 12:23-27; 19:1-5). "Considered from this vantage point, Romans 9.6-18 reads like an intentional and flagrant un-raveling of the fabric of *Wisdom's* stable and just moral universe."[56]

In short, while Wisdom modifies the strict *Deuteronomic* paradigm to include notions of the afterlife and introduces a new emphasis on divine agency through Lady Wisdom, the soteriological structure of retribution is maintained. Elements of continuity notwithstanding, there are recognizable discontinuities between Wisdom's more *Deuteronomic* and Paul's *Prophetic* understandings of divine and human agency.

4 Ezra. In many ways, Moses' *Deuteronomic* theology confronts Paul's

---

wickedness inborn, and that their way of thinking would never change" (Wis 12:10).

[55]Linebaugh, "God, Grace, and Righteousness," p. 175; see too John M. G. Barclay, "'I Will Have Mercy on Whom I Have Mercy': The Golden Calf and Divine Mercy in Romans 9–11 and Second Temple Judaism," *EC* 1 (2010): 82-106.

[56]Linebaugh, "God, Grace, and Righteousness," p. 176.

anthropological pessimism in the apocalypse known as *4 Ezra*.[57] This late first-century work has been studied quite frequently with an eye to its soteriology since Sanders labeled it the exception that proves the rule of covenantal nomism back in 1977.[58] That is, of all the Jewish texts examined by Sanders, only *4 Ezra* confirms the legalistic theology that most scholars had assumed was characteristic of all early Jewish thought in the first century, and therefore it stands out—according to Sanders—as an anomaly. But scholars have recently shown that *4 Ezra* is more in line with Sanders's own view of Judaism. According to Richard Bauckham, in *4 Ezra* "the terms of the covenant . . . make salvation for the righteous both a matter of reward, within the terms God has given, but also a matter of God's grace, in that he freely chose to make such a covenant with Israel."[59] Rather than an exception to the norm, this apocalypse, according to Bauckham, fits the general paradigm of covenantal nomism that Sanders so eloquently revealed in Second Temple Judaism.[60]

But does *4 Ezra* mirror Paul's view of divine and human agency in salvation? In some ways, it does. First, Ezra[61] believes that humankind is

---

[57] *4 Ezra* was probably composed originally in Hebrew in Palestine during the reign of Domitian (A.D. 81–96). It was written in response to the destruction of the temple in A.D. 70. Much like the first temple's destruction in 586 B.C., which is the fictive setting of the book, *4 Ezra* wrestles with God's apparent merciless judgment poured out on Israel through the destruction of the second temple. Ezra addresses "the wise among your people" (12:38), which probably refers to the religious leaders of Israel. Richard Bauckham suggests that these may be the rabbis who gathered at Yavneh between the two Jewish revolts ("Apocalypses," in Carson, O'Brien and Seifrid, *Justification and Variegated Nomism*, 1:135-87 [esp. 162-63]). The book unfolds in seven episodes, which consist of dialogues between Ezra and the angel Uriel: (1) 3:1–5:20, (2) 5:21–6:34, (3) 6:35–9:26, (4) 9:27–10:59, (5) 11:1–12:51, (6) 13:1-58, (7) 14:1-48; *4 Ezra* 1–2 and 15–16 are not part of the original work (Bauckham, "Apocalypses," p. 161). Through the dialogues, Ezra becomes more convinced of Uriel's worldview, so that by the fourth episode (9:27–10:59), he has fully accepted Uriel's view. Bauckham, "Apocalypses," p. 162, following Michael E. Stone, *Fourth Ezra: A Commentary on the Book of Fourth Ezra*, Hermenia (Minneapolis: Fortress Press, 1990), pp. 24-28.

[58] Sanders, *Paul and Palestinian Judaism*, pp. 409-18; Bruce Longenecker, *Eschatology and the Covenant: A Comparison of 4 Ezra and Romans 1-11*, JSNTSup 57 (Sheffield: JSOT Press, 1991); Bauckham, "Apocaplyses"; Jonathan Moo, "The Few Who Obtain Mercy: Soteriology in *4 Ezra*," in Gurtner, *This World*, pp. 98-113.

[59] Bauckham, "Apocalypses," p. 173; followed by Moo, "Few Who Obtain Mercy."

[60] Bauckham, however, qualifies this reading of the book in his closing remarks: "*4 Ezra* . . . importantly illustrates how the basic and very flexible pattern of covenantal nomism could take forms in which the emphasis is overwhelmingly on meriting salvation by works of obedience to the Law" ("Apocalypses," p. 174).

[61] I will refer to the author as Ezra with the understanding, of course, that the historic Ezra did not pen the book.

hopelessly sinful, and his predicament is due to Adam's transgression in the garden: "Adam, what have you done? For though it was you who sinned, the fall[62] was not yours alone, but ours also who are your descendants" (7:118).[63] Adam's sin has infected the entire cosmos (9:20; cf. 7:12) and everyone (3:22), including Israel (7:116-26; cf. 8:35) is guilty. Second, in light of his anthropological pessimism, Ezra has doubts that Israel will actually keep the law (3:20-22, 25-26). The righteous are promised an everlasting reward (4:34-37; 5:44, 48-49; 6:33-34; 7:16, 19; 8:51-55; 9:13),[64] but because of sin, there seem to be very few who actually are righteous, who will keep the law and obtain salvation (7:47, 60-61). Such pessimism about the condition of humankind reveals a good deal of theological congruence between Ezra and Paul.

But Ezra does not wholly abandon the *Deuteornomic* worldview. Although tempered by a *Prophetic* anthropology, Ezra still maintains that the few who find mercy are the ones who "keep the commandments" of God (4 *Ezra* 7:45, 88, 94), "have a treasure of works stored up with the Most High" (7:77), "laboriously served the Most High . . . so that they might keep the law of the Lawgiver perfectly" (7:89),[65] and therefore "will be saved and will be able to escape on account of their works, or on account of the faith by which they have believed" (9:7; cf. 13:23).[66] In contrast to Deuteronomy 30:11-14, keeping the law is exceedingly difficult, yet it is still a necessary condition of future life (4 *Ezra* 7:129).[67] This does not mean that grace is absent from Ezra's apocalypse. But Ezra's understanding of grace is not the same as Paul's. For Ezra, God "is gracious to those who turn in repentance to his law; and patient, because he shows patience toward those who have sinned, since they are his own works" (7:133-34). Grace here is defined as God forgiving

---

[62]The Latin *casus* here translated as "fall" is better translated as "misfortune" (Stone, *Fourth Ezra*, p. 253) or "evil" (Moo, "Few Who Obtain Mercy," p. 103).

[63]Cf. 3:22; 7:48, 68.

[64]See Moo, "Few Who Obtain Mercy," p. 101.

[65]Moo rightly notes that "keeping the law *perfectly*" does not refer to sinless perfection but to the Old Testament notion of "sincerity and blamelessness" (Gen 6:9; 17:1; Ps 15:2; 37:18; 84:12); Moo, "The Few Who Obtain Mercy," p. 110; see too Bauckham, "Apocalypses," p. 172; contra Sanders, *Paul and Palestinian Judaism*, p. 422.

[66]Moo, "The Few Who Obtain Mercy," p. 109. Bauckham points out the statements about rigorous law-obedience initially stated by Ezra (3:35-36; 7:45; 8:27, 32-33, 36; 9:32) are repeated by Uriel (7:35, 77, 79, 88, 94; 14:35); "Apocalypses," p. 171.

[67]Given 4 *Ezra's* clear belief in resurrection, it would appear that the passages that speak of life contingent on obedience to the law refer to resurrection life.

those who repent, whereas Paul defines grace as God's justification of the wicked—a theme that we do not see in Ezra's book.

Four Ezra, therefore, maintains a *Deuteronomic* theology of restoration, where covenant blessing is conditioned on obedience, as seen in Uriel's only explicit quotation of Scripture: "Moses, while he was alive, spoke to the people, saying, 'Choose for yourself life, that you may live!'" (*4 Ezra* 7:129, citing Deut 30:19). The covenantal blessing of life through obeying the law is affirmed throughout. "God strictly commanded those who came into the world, when they came, what they should do to live, and what they should observe to avoid punishment" (7:21). Those who died having despised the law are pitied, "because they cannot now make a good repentance that they may live" (7:82). The "law of life" revealed on Sinai was transgressed by the nation and resulted in exile (14:30-32). At the end of the apocalypse, Ezra petitions God for the holy spirit to enable him to write "the things which were written in your law that men may be able to find the path, and that those who wish to live in the last days may live" (14:22).[68] Therefore, Ezra's pessimism has shaken the *Deuteronomic* paradigm but not destroyed it. While sin has prevented most people from keeping the law, it has not totally suffocated humanity's moral capacity to obey the torah. The eschatological blessing of life is still conditioned on obeying the law, and the few who keep it will find mercy on judgment day.

What is the role of divine agency in this *Deuteronomic* eschatology? Two features are worthy of note. First, Ezra's emphasis on rigorous law-obedience is not, in the author's conception, divorced from God's mercy and grace. At the judgment, God "will deliver in mercy the remnant of my people" (12:34; cf. 10:24; 14:34). Mercy here probably refers to God overlooking the minor imperfection of the lawkeepers since sinless perfection is most likely not required.[69] Law-works, therefore, are conceived as a condition of future reward, although "human achievement takes center-stage" in *4 Ezra* "and God's grace, while presupposed, is effectively marginalized."[70]

---

[68]For the law and life theme in *4 Ezra*, see Shannon Burke, "'Life' Redefined: Wisdom and Law in Fourth Ezra and Second Baruch," *CBQ* 63 (2001): 55-71.

[69]Richard Bauckham, however, understands mercy as referring to "God's favor to the covenant people"—his "free grace that he chose Israel and made his covenant with this people" (Bauckham, "Apocalypses," p. 173).

[70]Ibid., p. 174.

Another feature of divine agency that is evident, though rarely stated, is God's empowerment of those who keep the law.[71] On a couple of occasions, divine agency in obedience is mentioned—God's "plant" is "saved, because with much labor" he has "perfected them" (9:22), and God "will guide" the righteous in his mercy (8:11)—but such allusions find only a trace in 4 Ezra's theology. This Jewish apocalypse does not mirror Paul's thoroughgoing emphasis on divine agency in obedience leading to eschatological salvation.

In short, 4 Ezra may fit the general contours of covenantal nomism—with a clear and consistent emphasis on nomism. Yet in terms of its view of divine and human agency, it remains within a *Deuteronomic* paradigm of restoration, since final salvation is ultimately contingent on law-obedience.[72] The author on a couple occasions does hint that divine agency is necessary for obedience, but this is certainly not a main emphasis in the book. For Ezra, salvation is conceived as an eschatological reward for the few righteous, who through rigorous law-obedience will find mercy from God and attain resurrection life.

Pseudo-Philo's Biblical Antiquities. The first-century Palestinian work

---

[71]Both Moo ("Few Who Obtain Mercy," p. 112) and Bauckham ("Apocalypses," p. 173) see divine agency in obedience as a marginal feature in 4 Ezra.

[72]One possible exception to my reading, as pointed out by Jonathan Moo (personal conversation), is 4 Ezra 6:18-28, which is the "first prophecy of redemption in the predictions of 4 Ezra" (Stone, *Fourth Ezra,* p. 171). Here, God intervenes to judge the wicked and save his people. God judges the wicked based on their evil deeds ("I require from the doers of iniquity the penalty of their iniquity," 6:19), but the basis of the salvation of "Zion" (cf. 6:19) is not clearly articulated: "It shall be that whoever remains after all that I have foretold to you shall be saved and shall see my salvation and the end of my world . . . and the heart of the earth's inhabitants shall be changed and converted to a different spirit" (6:25-26). There is no explicit mention of Israel's prior return to the law that prefaces God's cosmic intervention, and the fact that those who are saved "shall be changed and converted to a different spirit" (6:26) may suggest that salvation was more unilateral. However, the relationship between divine and human agency is not specified in this early vision; God simply says that he will intervene to judge and save. Later in the book (especially the lengthy third vision of 6:35–9:25), Uriel and God argue unambiguously that the few righteous who will be saved are those who have kept the law. The cosmic intervention of God in 6:18-28, therefore, seems to describe future salvation in more general terms, while divine and human agencies are specified in more detail throughout the rest of the book. This is further supported by 9:1-13, a passage that is parallel to 6:18-28. It begins with the same cosmic signs preceding God's intervention, and then states: "And it shall be that everyone who will be saved and will be able to escape *on account of his works,* or *on account of the faith by which he has believed,* will survive the dangers that have been predicted, and will see my salvation in my land and within my borders" (9:7: "works" and "faith" are used synonymously). So when the author discusses the role of works in salvation, he clearly says that they are a necessary precondition.

known as Pseudo-Philo's *Biblical Antiquities* has been somewhat neglected in recent discussion on divine and human agency in early Judaism, though I have attempted to fill this void in several recent publications.[73] The following survey will summarize my previous conclusions.[74]

The clearest and most ubiquitous theme in *Biblical Antiquities* (hereafter *L.A.B.*)[75] relevant to its soteriology is the irrevocable nature of God's covenant with Israel.[76] No matter what Israel does, no matter how much they sin, God will remain faithful to the covenant and restore the nation. In commenting on Israel's future apostasy in Deuteronomy 31, Pseudo-Philo writes: "I know that you will rise up and forsake the words established for you through me, and God will be angry with you and abandon you and depart from your land. And he will bring upon you those who hate you, and they will rule over you, *but not forever, because he will remember the covenant that he established with your fathers*" (*L.A.B.* 19:2). The dark future revealed through Moses at Moab is supplanted with an affirmation that God will restore the covenant. The author, therefore, prioritizes divine commitment over human action. Such prioritization is seen quite clearly in *L.A.B.* 13, where the author highlights the unconditionality of the covenant and even twists the words of Moses to foster his agenda:

If you walk in my statutes and observe my commandments and do them, *then I will give you your rains in their season, and the land shall yield its increase,* and the trees of the field *shall yield their fruit.* (Lev 26:3-4)

If they walk in my ways, I will not abandon them but will have mercy on them always and bless their seed; *and the earth will quickly yield its fruit, and there*

---

[73]See Sprinkle, *Law and Life*, pp. 115-30; idem, "Covenant Nomism Revisited: The Soteriological Framework of *Pseudo-Philo*," in *Christian Origins and Hellenistic Judaism: Literary and Social Contexts for the New Testament*, ed. Stanley E. Porter and Andrew W. Pitts (Leiden: Brill, forthcoming); idem, "The Hermeneutic of Grace: The Soteriology of Pseudo-Philo's *Biblical Antiquities*," in Gurtner, *This World*, pp. 50-67. Peter Enns's study of Pseudo-Philo's soteriology was limited to four pages ("Expansions of Scripture," pp. 88-92).

[74]*Biblical Antiquities* was written from Palestine in Hebrew probably in the latter half of the first century A.D. The book is a running commentary on the biblical narrative from Genesis to 2 Samuel, though many of the individual stories are reworked (sometimes significantly) in order to capture the author's own theological agenda. The most thorough study of the book is still Howard Jacobson's magisterial commentary, *A Commentary on Pseudo-Philo's Liber Antiquitatum Biblicarum with Latin Text and English Translation*, 2 vols., AGAJU 31 (Leiden: E. J. Brill, 1996).

[75]*L.A.B.* is the abbreviation for the Latin title *Liber Antiquitatum Biblicarum*.

[76]*L.A.B.* does not show signs of being a sectarian work, so all references to Israel must be taken to refer to the nation as a whole.

will be rains for their advantage, and it will not be barren. But I know for sure that they will make their ways corrupt and I will abandon them, and they will forget the covenants that I have established with their fathers; *but nevertheless I will not forget them forever.* (*L.A.B.* 13:10)

A close reading of *L.A.B.*'s commentary against its biblical counterpart reveals a subtle yet striking maneuver: the author erases the "if . . . then" conditionality of Leviticus by inserting the confident notion that God "will not forget them forever." The idea of ultimate restoration is not foreign to Leviticus 26 (see Lev 26:40-45), but in the biblical text restoration is conditioned on the nation's repentance.[77] Pseudo-Philo, however, rewrites Leviticus 26 to correct Moses' conditional theology and therefore underscores God's unconditional covenant.

The climax of God's commitment to Israel is resurrection, and herein lies the heart of Pseudo-Philo's soteriology.[78] While the book is filled with accounts of God's earthly deliverances from evil, the author is quick to incorporate notions of the afterlife, even where there are none in the biblical text. And while human agency plays a role in "Israel's deliverance (salvation!) from her gentile oppressors,"[79] it is God who will resurrect the nation, even if law-obedience is lacking. In his final speech to the nation, Joshua addresses the entire nation and says:

But also at the end of the lot of each one of you [i.e. the nation] will be life eternal, for you and your seed, and I will take your souls and store them in peace until the time allotted the world be complete. And I will restore you to your fathers and your fathers to you, and they will know through you that I have not chosen you in vain. (*L.A.B.* 23:13)

Earlier in his speech, Joshua indicates that he is speaking to the entire

---

[77]Repentance does not play a major role in Pseudo-Philo's soteriology. The author mentions it in on occasion (*L.A.B.* 21:6; 33:2, 5), but it does not play an important role in the book—in some cases, in fact, it is downplayed (e.g., 19:2-5; cf. 25:7).

[78]For resurrection, see *L.A.B.* 3:10; 19:12-13; 23:13; 26:13; 51:5; 64:7. For damnation in hell, see *L.A.B.* 16:3; 31:7; 51:5; 63:6.

[79]George W. E. Nickelsburg, "Salvation Among the Jews: Some Comments and Observations," in Gurtner, *This World*, p. 301. Nickelsburg, commenting on my essay in the same volume, rightly points out that salvation is a "multifaceted event" in *L.A.B.*, referring to "deliverance from Israel's enemies in this world, and the future resurrection from the dead" (301-2). I still think, however, that Pseudo-Philo had a special interest in resurrection as the pinnacle of God's saving acts.

nation and not just those who keep the law. He addresses "all the people . . . woman and children" (23:1, 2, cf. 4), "each one of you" (23:13), "you and your seed" (23:13). The statement in 23:13, that "the end of the lot of each one of you," suggests that God will resurrect the entire nation.[80]

Chris VanLandingham is incorrect, therefore, to argue that "Pseudo-Philo affirms again and again a strict application of the Deuteronomic formula for reward and punishment"[81] and that "God's salvation . . . depends on the nation's repentance."[82] Israel will be rewarded with salvation, but not through a formula of retribution. Howard Jacobson represents the majority of scholars when he states: "If there is a single predominant theme in L.A.B., it is the following: No matter how much the Jewish people suffer, no matter how bleak the outlook appears, God will never completely abandon His people and in the end salvation and triumph will be the lot of the Jews."[83]

As Jacobson points out, salvation depends on God's unconditional faithfulness to the nation regardless of how sinful they are. This is not to say that Pseudo-Philo is indifferent to sin. The book encourages obedience and re-

---

[80]See further Sprinkle, "Hermeneutic," p. 58. Pseudo-Philo refers to judgment according to works in two other places (*L.A.B.* 3:10; 64:7). In *L.A.B.* 3:10, however, the "works" in question are most likely the evil deeds of those being damned, and not the good deeds of those being saved. *L.A.B.* 64:7 mentions the resurrected Samuel being "render[ed] the rewards of" his deeds, and this may be the one instance in *L.A.B.* where works play a role in future salvation. Another possible reference to future life being contingent on law-works is *L.A.B.* 23:10: "I gave them my Law and enlightened them in order that by doing these things they would live and have many years and not die." Pseudo-Philo cites Lev 18:5 here, which suggests a *Deuteronomic* outlook on Israel's future (resurrection) life. But this is only stated as the law's intention and does not say that this is how God will end up giving life to the nation. Moreover, in 23:13, as we have seen, the entire nation is promised resurrection, which qualifies the Leviticus allusion in 23:10. See further Sprinkle, *Law and Life*, pp. 115-30.

[81]Chris VanLandingham, *Judgment & Justification in Early Judaism and in the Apostle Paul* (Peabody, MA: Hendrickson, 2006), p. 32.

[82]Ibid., p. 31.

[83]Jacobson, *Commentary*, pp. 241-42. Cf. *L.A.B.* 18:10: "It is easier to take away the foundations of the topmost part of the earth and to extinguish the light of the sun and to darken the light of the moon than for anyone to uproot the planting of the Most Powerful or to destroy his vine." See also *L.A.B.* 4:11; 7:4; 9:4, 7; 10:2; 13:10; 19:2; 30:7; 35:3 and 49:3; see especially John Levinson, "Torah and Covenant in Pseudo Philo's *Liber Antiquitatum Biblicarum*," in *Bund und Torah: Zur theologischen Begriffsgeschichte in alttestamentlicher, frühjüdischer und urchristlicher Tradition*, ed. Friedrich Avemarie and Hermann Lichtenberger (Tübingen: J. C. B. Mohr, 1996), pp. 111-27; F. J. Murphy, "The Eternal Covenant in Pseudo-Philo," *JSP* 3 (1988): 43-57; Bruce Fisk, *Do You Not Remember? Scripture, Story and Exegesis in the Rewritten Bible of Pseudo-Philo*, JSPSup 37 (Sheffield: Sheffield Academic Press, 2001), pp. 45-50; Peter Enns, "Expansions," pp. 88-92.

pentance throughout. The author, in other words, does not preclude all forms of *Deuteronomic* theology; rather, he only "limits the Deuteronomic motif to this world and temporary punishment."[84] But when it comes to God's commitment and ultimate salvation of the nation, nothing will prevent God from saving his people.

In terms of divine and human agency in salvation, Pseudo-Philo emphasizes the former—perhaps more than the other books examined in this chapter. Covenantal nomism is not a fitting description of his soteriology, since God will restore the covenant apart from any nomism on Israel's part. This book, then, evinces a first-century Palestinian soteriology akin to the apostle Paul, even though the correlation is not exact. For instance, Paul's pneumatology, doctrine of justification, and belief in the empowering presence of the risen Christ for obedience and final justification are unparalleled in *L.A.B.* But Paul and Pseudo-Philo are in agreement that the salvation of the Israel of God is created, sustained and will ultimately be consummated by the unconditional grace of God, enacted in Abraham and reaching its dramatic conclusion on the final day.

Testament of Moses. The final book I will examine is the early first-century work titled the *Testament of Moses*.[85] Contextually situated at the eve of Moses' death, this book narrates the future of Israel from a covenantal perspective. The author believes that Israel has broken the covenant, and he is concerned with how God will restore it, which makes this book wholly relevant for our study. Unfortunately, scholars have come to different conclusions over whether the paradigm of restoration is *Deuteronomic* or *Prophetic* (though they do not use those terms).[86] In this brief review, I will first summarize the story line and then discuss which paradigm of restoration best reflects the author's perspective.

The book begins with Moses' deathbed exhortation to Joshua, who will assume leadership over Israel (*T. Mos.* 1:1-18). Much like Deuteronomy 31-32, Moses prophetically reviews Israel's future to Joshua. Joshua is told that he

---

[84]Sprinkle, "Hermeneutic," p. 66.

[85]The book was probably written in the early first century A.D. in Hebrew from Palestine. For a discussion of the issues surrounding date, authorship and occasions, see Johannes Tromp, *The Assumption of Moses: A Critical Edition with Commentary* (Leiden: Brill, 1993), pp. 115-18.

[86]See the discussion in Robert A. Kugler, "Testaments," in *Justification and Variegated Nomism*, 1:189-213 (esp. 193).

will lead the nation into the land, distribute the allotted portions, and then the nation will end up establishing a kingdom (2:1-9). Ultimately, however, they will rebel against the covenant (2:7), resulting in their exile in Babylon (3:1-3). From exile, they will call on God to rescue them and restore his covenant made with Abraham (3:8-14), when God "swore to them by yourself, that their seed would never fail from the land which you have given them" (3:9). After "crying out to heaven" (3:8), the people "will remember me" (3:10) and confess that their exile is the result of their transgression of God's commandments (3:11-13).[87] Then enters Daniel,[88] who echoes his biblical petition (cf. Dan 9) and calls on God to remember his promises made to the fathers (4:1-5), which sets the stage for God's restorative action. This brings us to a crucial transition in the narrative; what happens next will most likely reveal the author's assumptions about divine and human initiative in restoring the covenant. The author writes: "Then God will remember them because of the covenant which he made with their fathers and he will openly show his compassion. And in those times he will inspire a king to have pity on them and send them home to their own land" (4:5-6). The initiative to restore the covenant is taken by God, and there is no clear indication that he responded to repentance.[89] Israel previously cried out and remembered God while in exile (3:8-10), but this does not in itself mean that they repented. It could very well indicate that they acknowledged their weakness and pled for divine intervention.

In any case, restoration is not yet complete. After God restores two tribes back to the land (*T. Mos.* 4:8-9; cf. Ezra 1:1-4), the other ten tribes "will grow and spread out among the nations" (4:9) and remain in exile. They will "pollute the house of their worship with the customs of the nations" and "play the harlot after foreign gods" (5:3)—which probably refers to the sins of Israel during the Hasmonean period.[90] Wickedness continues to mount,

---

[87]At this point, it is not clear that their "crying out" is itself an act of repentance (human initiative) or an acknowledgment of human weakness and a plea for unilateral intervention.

[88]Daniel is not named, but he is almost certainly in view.

[89]While Tromp believes that "the people's restoration . . . is not presented as some kind of reward for their repentance" and "is based solely on the covenant with the fathers," he still thinks that *T. Mos.* 4:5-6 indicates that the people do repent and that such penitence is a condition for God's promised restoration (*Assumption,* p. 178).

[90]J. Priest, "Testament of Moses," in Charlesworth, *Old Testament Pseudepigrapha,* p. 919-34 (esp. 929).

leading to the rise of Herod the Great (6:1-4). God responds with judgments reminiscent of the plagues of Egypt (6:5-6), yet sin continues to pollute the nation during the Hasmonean and Herodian era (7:1–8:5), evoking God's "wrath such as has never happened to them from the creation" (8:1). The punishments rained down on Israel at this time are seen as the "second punishment" (9:2)—the first being the punishment on Israel by the hands of Babylon in 586 B.C. The point, therefore, is that the initial return during the days of Ezra, though divinely initiated, is not the full restoration of the covenant. Israel, in the time of the author (early first century) is still in spiritual exile.

Chapter 9 introduces the mystifying and highly disputed character of Taxo (*T. Mos.* 9:1-2), who exhorts his seven sons not to reject the commandments: "Let us die rather than transgress the commandments of the Lord ... for if we do this, and do die, our blood will be avenged before the Lord" (9:6-7).[91] Taxo's exhortation is followed by an apocalyptic vision of the kingdom of God (10:1), who will execute vengeance on his enemies (10:1-7) and bring salvation (resurrection?) to Israel (10:8-10).[92] After the vision, the scene reverts back to Moses' deathbed, where we find him exhorting Joshua to take up the mantle of leadership (10:11-15). Joshua mourns the future rebellion of Israel and the death of his "master" (11:1-8), especially since Moses seems to possess unparalleled intercessory powers (11:9-19, esp. 11:17). Nevertheless, in a fragmentary final scene,[93] Moses grabs hold of Joshua (literally, 12:2) and reminds him of God's foreknowledge of "the end of the age" (12:4, 13) and power to restore his covenant (12:13). Thus ends the narrative, according to our manuscripts, though the original composition may well have continued on.

Deciphering which paradigm of restoration governs the author's conception of acquiring divine favor is difficult, which is probably why there is

---

[91]For a discussion of the identity and rhetorical function of Taxo, see Tromp, *Assumption,* pp. 124-28.

[92]N. T. Wright argues that 10:9 ("And God will raise you to the heights. Yea, he will fix you firmly in the heaven of the stars, in the place of their habitations") alludes to resurrection (*Resurrection,* p. 157). While the imagery parallels Dan 12:3 and other Second Temple passages where resurrection is probably in view (cf. *1 En.* 104:2-7; *2 Bar.* 51:5-12), the book as a whole does not reflect concerns for the afterlife, and therefore 10:9 does not seem to be a clear affirmation of resurrection.

[93]Several lacunae occur in *T. Mos.* 12:4-6, 13.

such stark disagreement among scholars. Space prevents us from a thorough examination, but we can make three observations that are fairly clear from our summary of the *Testament*.

First, while the Sinaitic covenant is mentioned throughout, it is understood through the lens of God's unconditional covenant with Abraham.[94] References to "covenant" and "oath" occur together throughout the book (*T. Mos.* 1:8; 2:7; 3:9; 11:17; 12:13), which allude to God's words to both Moses (Deut 29:9-14) and Abraham (Gen 22:16-18). But when the content of the "covenant and oath" is given, it is the unilateral promise to Abraham that is in view: "Remember your covenant which you made with them, and the oath which you swore to them by yourself, that their seed would never fail from the land which you have given them" (*T. Mos.* 3:9, cf. Gen 22:16-18; Ex 32:13). When God is called on to restore this covenant at the end of the book (according to our manuscript), it is most likely his commitment to Abraham and his seed that is in view.[95]

Second, God's initial restoration of Israel from Babylon was governed by divine intervention (*T. Mos.* 4:5-9), and it seems that his future restoration of the kingdom (10:1-10) contains the same emphasis, though it is not as clear. Some say that the martyrdom of Taxo and his sons "compel God to exercise His vengeance,"[96] but this is far from explicit. Taxo says that if they are martyred, their "blood will be avenged before the Lord" (9:7), but this merely indicates that the righteous will experience persecution and will be vindicated. J. Priest is more cautious in saying that Taxo "is better seen as a singular example of the extreme woes that will beset God's people in the last days than as one who plays a significant part in precipitating the advent of these days."[97] Moreover, the book as a whole displays a deterministic outlook, highlighting not only God's foreknowledge of future events but also his power to intervene and carry out his will on earth. This does not necessarily rule out the possibility that human action may trigger divine

---

[94]The same collocation of covenants occurs in Pseudo-Philo; see, e.g., Levinson, "Torah and Covenant," pp. 111-27.

[95]Both *T. Mos.* 3:9 and 12:13 occur in the context of Israel remaining in the land ("their seed would never fail from the land" 3:9; "it is not possible for the nations to drive them out or extinguish them completely" 12:12).

[96]See J. Licht, "Taxo, or the Apocalyptic Doctrine of Vengeance," *JJS* 12 (1961): 95-103, quoted in Priest, "Testament of Moses," p. 923.

[97]Priest, "Testament of Moses," p. 923.

intervention, but lack of explicit statements along these lines makes such a view suspect.

Third, while the book displays some *Deuteronomic* elements, they seem to be limited to God's blessing and curse in daily affairs and not the ultimate salvation of Israel. For instance, Joshua is encouraged to "do everything which has been commanded" (*T. Mos.* 1:10), Israel in exile remembers that "we should not transgress God's commandments" (3:12, cf. 9:4), and Taxo exhorts his sons to "die rather than transgress the commandments of the Lord" (9:6). But none of these statements in themselves necessitate a *Deuteronomic* restoration, nor do they preclude a *Prophetic* one. The one passage that may be an exception is 12:10-11: "Therefore, those who truly fulfill the commandments of God will flourish and will finish the good way, but those who sin by disregarding the commandments will deprive themselves of the good things which were declared before." This is the most *Deuteronomic* statement in the book, but it is not clear that Moses is talking about restoration here. The surrounding context refers to Joshua's conquest, which God previously said will come about *not* "on account of the piety of this people" (12:8) but by the power of God who creates and sustains all creation (12:9).[98] After 12:10-11, the author returns again to speak of God's power in the conquest: "God, who has foreseen all things in the world, will go forth, and his covenant which was established . . . " (12:13). The statement that God "will go forth" (*exivit*) probably refers to his eschatological intervention, as it does in 10:3.[99] It would seem, therefore, that 12:10-11 reflects the theology of Joshua 1, where obedience will bring a measure of success in the land, but ultimate victory over the Canaanites is fundamentally accomplished by the sovereign hand of God.

The *Testament of Moses* on the whole does not reveal a clear emphasis on either a *Deuteronomic* or a *Prophetic* paradigm of restoration, although it leans closer to the latter. The book warns against transgressing the commandments and committing apostasy, but it does not clearly preface God's

---

[98]The contrast between the people's lack of piety and God's power is seen throughout 12:1-9, where God's "predetermined course of history and the people's own responsibility are artfully combined" (Tromp, *Assumption*, p. 260).

[99]"For the Heavenly One will arise from his kingly throne. Yea, *he will go forth* (*exiet*) from his holy habitation with indignation and wrath on behalf of his sons." See the discussion in ibid., pp. 232-33, 269.

restoration with Israel's return to the law. However, the emphasis on God's unconditional commitment to Abraham, along with the expectation of God's apocalyptic intervention in ushering in the kingdom, suggest that the author assumed a more *Prophetic* paradigm of how God would restore the covenant. But as with *L.A.B.*, we do not find explicit *Prophetic* motifs, such as the resuscitating power of the eschatological spirit or God's justification of the wicked. Perhaps the author would agree with Pseudo-Philo that if God is going to restore the covenant, he cannot wait for Israel to repent—for such repentance is not likely to happen.

SUMMARY

Our survey has revealed a good deal of diversity in how the authors understand the mechanics of divine and human agency in salvation. On one end of the spectrum stands Sirach, who is unyielding in his belief that Israel possesses the moral capacity to obey torah. On the other end stands Pseudo-Philo and (to some extent) the author of the *Testament of Moses,* both of whom believe that salvation will come without prior human action. In between stand *Jubilees,* the *Psalms of Solomon,* Wisdom and *4 Ezra,* which contain elements reminiscent of the *Prophetic* paradigm of restoration (e.g., *4 Ezra*'s pessimistic anthropology and Wisdom's emphasis on the agency of Lady Wisdom), though they still expect salvation to come through *Deuteronomic* means.

In light of our study, we can make the following observations. First, the categories of *Deuteronomic* and *Prophetic* restoration (as defined in chapter one and examined in chapter two above) form a fitting lens to understand paradigms of restoration in the previously examined early Jewish books. Some works express more blatant concerns for how God will restore Israel (e.g., *Jubilees* and *L.A.B.*), while others consider the interaction between divine and human agency in ways that are relevant for soteriology (e.g., Sirach). Our survey, therefore, helps to provide historical validity to our overarching categories of divine and human agency in *Deuteronomic* and *Prophetic* restoration, through which we have examined Pauline literature and the Dead Sea Scrolls. Second, our survey helps to situate Paul and the Scrolls within the Judaisms of their day. The soteriological concerns that we have examined in Paul and Qumran were shared—to some extent—by other Jewish writers. For instance, Paul, Qumran, and *Jubilees* argue for a specific way in which God has rescued Israel from the curse of the covenant. Paul, Qumran, *4 Ezra* and the *Psalms of Solomon* all discuss the life-giving benefit of law observance (Paul, of course, argues that there is no such benefit). The moral capacity or incapacity of humankind to obey the law is explicitly discussed by Paul and Sirach. Our study as a whole, therefore, has not ventured into hopeless anachronism, but has sought to understand ancient writers through their own soteriological lenses. And, third, despite some commonalities between Paul and other soteriological structures in *4 Ezra*, the *Testament of Moses*, and to a greater extent *L.A.B.*, Paul still exhibits significant points of discontinuity (esp. with *4 Ezra*) and displays more intricately developed soteriological motifs. Based on our admittedly brief assessment, Paul's interaction between pneumatology and anthropology, his *Prophetic* view of God's justification of the ungodly and his nuanced understanding of judgment according to works construct a rather complex paradigm of restoration, where divine agency is not only present but explicitly emphasized at nearly every turn. Paul, therefore, exhibits some congruence with Pseudo-Philo's view of divine agency, and is especially close to some of the hymnists at Qumran, but he still seems to push the envelope of God's role in salvation with a complexity and precision that is unparalleled in the literature of early Judaism.

9

PAUL AND JUDAISM

Soteriology Revisited

Throughout this book, we have compared the soteriological structures of Paul with Qumran, noting points of continuity and discontinuity. In the previous chapter, we surveyed seven books in early Judaism with an eye to similar questions in order to situate our discussion in the wider stream of Jewish thought. The depiction of salvation we have unearthed has not been one of clear and comprehensive continuity, nor have we seen wholesale discontinuity. Sensitivity to the complex and diverse theological thought evident in the examined portions of Judaism (especially the Scrolls) and in Paul has prevented us from embracing either extreme. At the very least, therefore, this study should deter careless assertions made by scholars and students on both sides of the debate. Paul does not exhibit total continuity with Qumran (nor Judaism) regarding divine and human agency, but neither is there complete discontinuity. Extreme new (continuity) or old (discontinuity) perspectives on Paul are not, to my mind, historically viable. In this final chapter, therefore, we will summarize our findings in order to contribute to our understanding of—and the debate surrounding—Paul and Jewish soteriology.

    Continuity and Discontinuity in Paul, Qumran and Early Judaism. As far as the curse of the law is concerned, Paul believes, in contrast to his pre–Damascus road beliefs, that the curse of the law cannot be relieved by a return to the law, since it has already been removed unilaterally by God through Christ and the spirit (Gal 3:10-14). The prayers collected in the *Words of the Luminaries* (4Q504) share a similar perspective. Even though these hymns anticipate Israel's return to the law, they believe that God must take the initiative to empower Israel to do so.[1] Obedience to the law and restoration from the curse will materialize only after God has circumcised the heart of Israel, poured out his spirit on them and put it into the core of their being to obey. The *Deuteronomic* worldview is not abandoned, but it is reread through a *Prophetic* lens. Divine agency is prior to and the cause of human agency in Israel's return to the law. Pseudo-Philo's *Biblical Antiquities* reveals some resonance with this *Prophetic* paradigm, where the resurrection of Israel is anticipated without reference to a prior return to the law.[2] God's conditional covenant through Moses is swallowed up by his unconditional commitment to Abraham, and a similar (albeit less clear) view is witnessed by the *Testament of Moses*. Despite Israel's unswerving wickedness, God's irrevocable covenant stands firm, forming the bedrock for God's restoration of the nation. Aside from the *Words of the Luminaries*, all other Scrolls that bear witness to the curse of the law motif betray an unmistakable *Deuteronomic* means of restoration from the curse of the law.[3] The same pattern is seen throughout *Jubilees*[4] and to some extent in Sirach and *4 Ezra*, though the motif is not as explicit in these latter two books. With the curse of the law, therefore, we have discovered a mosaic of beliefs, ranging from an uncompromising *Deuteronomic* paradigm to an unswerving *Prophetic* emphasis on divine agency, with Paul unequivocally embracing the latter.

The agency of the eschatological spirit in bringing about restoration is unyielding in Paul, 4Q504 and other hymns from Qumran. We have shown a direct connection between Ezekiel's prophecy of the unilateral agency of the spirit (Ezek 36–37) and Paul's understanding of the transformation of the human heart.[5] A similar picture is seen in at least four texts from

---

[1] 4Q504 *frag.* 4 11; *frags.* 1-2 ii 13-14; v 12-13; vi 8-9.
[2] E.g., *L.A.B.* 23:13.
[3] 11QT^a 59:4-13; CD 1:13-17; 3:10-16; 1QS 2:11-18; 4QMMT C 12-32.
[4] *Jub.* 1:22-23; 5:17-18; 23:16-32.
[5] 2 Cor 3:3-6; Rom 8:1-13.

Qumran.[6] Aside from these four, we did not find the same Ezekielian emphasis on the spirit's unilateral agency at Qumran—its own commentary (4QPseudo-Ezekiel) went so far as to flip Ezekiel's logic on its head. Rather than granting life to dead bones, the Qumran pesherist believes that God will reward the bones for their obedience. The seven Jewish books surveyed in the previous chapter do not reveal much continuity with either Paul or Ezekiel. Perhaps the closest parallel would be the agency of Lady Wisdom, who fulfills in many ways a function analogous to Ezekiel's spirit in enabling Israel to obey. But as we saw, the gift of Wisdom is not given indiscriminately but considers the worthiness of the one receiving the gift. Paul's continuity with Ezekiel 36–37, therefore, does not find many parallels in the Jewish literature we examined, aside from a few instances in Qumran.[7] So while there are discernible points of continuity between Paul and Judaism regarding the empowering work of the spirit, we have found that the overall picture is primarily one of discontinuity. That is, Paul locates the transformation of the human heart in the eschatological work of the spirit; all obedience flows from God's prior work and is underwritten by the spirit's agency. While a few Qumran texts mirror this pattern, the very fewness of these texts paints a portrait of discontinuity.

Anthropological pessimism runs rampant in the *Hodayot* and the hymn at the end of 1QS (10–11).[8] It is also assumed in the *Barki Nafshi* hymns and the *Words of the Luminaries*. In all of these scrolls, we find much continuity with Paul's pessimistic view of the human condition, where the human agent is unable to turn to God under their own power. And yet there still seem to be aspects of discontinuity because the pessimism in Qumran is largely limited to hymns. Even within the hymns, the view of the human condition is more complex than is sometimes recognized. Qumran's pessimism is largely limited to places where humanity is compared to God, but Paul's pessimism is more comprehensive, even when humanity is not being compared to God. The human condition is not portrayed as pessimistically in the didactic texts of Qumran as it is in Paul's didactic letters—and the

---

[6] 4Q504 *frags*. 1-2 v 11b-16 and 1QH[a] 8:19-20. 1QH[a] 15:6-7 speaks of God's spirit as an empowering agent, though without reference to Ezekiel 36–37. 1QS 4:20-22 alludes to the Ezekielian promise, though the depiction is reserved for a time yet future for the Qumranites.

[7] But see *Jos. As.* 8:10-11; 16:14; 19:11; *T. Reub.* 2:4; *T. Abr.* 18:11.

[8] See 1QH[a] 5:21-22; 9:22; 11:9-10, 23-24; 17:13, among others.

similarities in genre only augment the discontinuity. Our comparison between CD 2:14–3:20 and Romans 1:18–3:26 reveals this quite clearly. The
author of CD argues that God has established the new covenant with
the remnant of Israel, who has demonstrated a measure of obedience to the
revealed law. Human action prefaces God's eschatological restorative act, a
concept that signals a bundle of theological assumptions, including a
measure of anthropological optimism. The theology of CD is mirrored in
Jubilees, Sirach, Wisdom of Solomon and even *4 Ezra*, despite the latter's
pessimistic anthropology: obedience to the law, though extremely difficult,
is still possible. In all these Jewish texts, there is some obedience or worthiness within Israel that precedes God's restorative action—a tenet directly
countered by Paul in Romans. Other books such as *L.A.B.* and the *Testament of Moses* do not parse out the details of the human condition to the
same extent as Paul, *4 Ezra* and the *Hodayot*, but they do seem to retain
doubts about the nation's ability to render sufficient obedience to God so as
to remove the curse (*Testament*) or attain resurrection (*L.A.B.*). But neither
L.A.B. nor the *Testament* make explicit assertions about humanity's inability
to obey; they simply refer to restoration without reference to Israel's prior
turning. Aside from some hymns at Qumran, therefore, the early Jewish
literature that speaks to the issue of the moral capacity of humankind exhibits a measure of anthropological optimism, echoing Moses' assertion
that obeying the law is not all that difficult (Deut 30:11-14): if humans will it,
they can choose life and shun evil.[9]

Justification language is evident in both Paul and Qumran,[10] though it is
not a major category in the other books we examined.[11] As far as final justification is concerned, Paul finds some agreement with Qumran: on the
final day, justification will be according to works. However, aside from 1QS
11 and some hymns in the *Hodayot*, the Scrolls do not reveal the clear and
persistent emphasis on God's empowerment (in some cases, causation) of
the works necessary for final justification that we see in Paul.[12] Moreover,

---

[9]E.g., Sir 15:14-15, 17; *Pss. Sol.* 9:4-5; 14:1-3; *4 Ezra* 7:129.

[10]Rom 3:21-26; 4:4-5; 5:1; Gal 2:16, 19-20; 3:11; 1QS 11:2-15; CD 1:19; 4:7.

[11]Although see Wis 15:3: "For to know you is complete righteousness, and to recognize your
power is the root of immortality." Cf. Sir 42:2.

[12]Other hymns at Qumran speak of empowerment but do not connect this clearly to future
justification or judgment.

the presence of the risen Christ as an advocate for the redeemed on the final day—an unparalleled emphasis on divine agency in final justification—finds no correspondence in the Scrolls.[13] Within a large swath of continuity, therefore, there is a measure of discontinuity. But aside from their perspectives on the final day, it is Paul's unique emphasis on justification as an initial event, where God pronounces the wicked to be righteous apart from any prior obedience, which distances him from even the most radical statements in the hymns at Qumran, though both hold an already-not-yet soteriology. And clear statements to the contrary in Qumran, that God explicitly does *not* justify the ungodly,[14] only reinforces the disparity—a Son of Darkness would not receive a divine pronouncement declaring that he is righteous apart from any prior demonstration of law-works. Paul's understanding of God, therefore, as the one "who justifies the ungodly" locates his view of divine agency on the extreme end of the spectrum of early Jewish soteriological paradigms.

However extreme, Paul's soteriology remains within the Jewish spectrum of beliefs. His soteriology is born out of the Old Testament *Prophetic* restoration texts, which prioritize the agency of God in the face of a radical pessimism toward the human condition. In Judaism, we see some books (mainly hymns from Qumran) that reveal a similar emphasis on divine agency, others that may allow for it, and many that embrace a much more *Deuteronomic* view, where salvation—broadly defined—hinges on prior human action. Within this diversity, we have seen more points of soteriological discontinuity than continuity.

But how did Paul arrive at his view? He certainly was not born with it; the soteriological thought pursued in his letters is the product of a long hermeneutical journey, refracted no doubt through his encounter with Christ. By cautiously yet imaginatively tracing Paul's path of discovery, beginning in his Pharisaic past, we will find one plausible explanation for the emergence of his soteriological beliefs. This exercise will help us to both compare and contrast Paul's writings with his Jewish upbringing, which will provide a fitting close to our study.

History, Conversion and the Soteriological Renovation of Saul the

---

[13]Rom 8:31-34; cf. 5:6-11.
[14]E.g., CD 4:7.

Pharisee: A Reading. Saul of Tarsus was a Jew. He was not just any Jew, however, but a religious revolutionary, steeped in the tradition of Phineas, Elijah and more recently Mattathias, who violently sought to preserve the Jewish faith.[15] The Hasmonean revolt of the second century fostered an aggressive optimism toward the establishment of the kingdom of God, and the sons of Mattathias enjoyed a (somewhat complicated) foretaste of it for several decades.[16] Sometime in the wake of the revolt, a Jewish school of thought[17] that became known as Pharisaism. These Jews, like others of their ilk,[18] were animated by the early Hasmonean desire for independence; if the time was ripe, they would don the Hasmonean sword to purify Israel and, if possible, establish the kingdom of God by force.[19] For the most part, however, the fear of Rome and the heavy hand of Herod kept the seething unrest of the Pharisees at bay.

The establishment of the Hasmonean state spawned many different reactions. While the Pharisees remained sympathetic, the Essenes reacted

---

[15]Num 25:1-13; Ps 106:30-31; 1 Kings 18:36-40; 1 Macc 2:15-28. For the portrait of Saul as a religious revolutionary, see N. T. Wright, *The New Testament and the People of God* (Minneapolis: Fortress, 1992), pp. 181-203; N. T. Wright, *What Saint Paul Really Said: Was Paul of Tarsus the Real Founder of Christianity?* (Grand Rapids: Eerdmans, 1997), pp. 25-37.

[16]The Jews established a relatively independent state from 142–63 B.C., largely due to the crumbling Seleucid rule, and there is no doubt that this independence fostered a sense of messianism. Note the description of Simon's reign in messianic terms in 1 Macc 14: "He established peace in the land, and Israel rejoiced with great joy. All the people sat under their own vines and fig trees, and there was none to make them afraid. . . . He made the sanctuary glorious, and added to the vessels of the sanctuary" (1 Macc 14:11-12, 15).

[17]The term "sect" is often applied to the Pharisees, but it is problematic. See Anthony J. Saldarini, *Pharisees, Scribes and Sadducees in Palestinian Society: A Sociological Approach* (Livonia, MI: Dove, 1988; Grand Rapids: Eerdmans, 2001), pp. 70-75. I am using the term "school of thought" in its place (following Saldarini, pp. 75, 123-27).

[18]Josephus's "fourth philosophy," known as the Zealots, were recognized as violently militant, and yet this sect was like-minded with the Pharisees.

[19]For example, during the rule of John Hyrcanus (134–104 B.C.), a Pharisee named Eleazar confronted John on his illegitimate birth (he basically called John's mother a whore; *Ant.* 13.292), which created a civil uprising (*Ant.* 13.299). Around 20 B.C., despite Herod's support for the Pharisees, two of their leaders, Pollion and Samaias, refused to swear an oath to Herod, demonstrating political resistance (*Ant.* 15.368-372). Sometime near the end of Herod's life (7–4 B.C.), six thousand Pharisees refused to swear an oath to Caesar, which promoted civil disorder (*Ant.* 17.71-75). In 4 B.C., the description of Judas and Matthias, who daringly tore down the golden eagle from the Temple, suggests that they were Pharisees (*Ant.* 17.149-167; *War* 1.648-155). The revolt of A.D. 6 led by Judas the Zealot seems to have been started in collaboration with some Pharisees (*Ant.* 18.4-10, 23). One of the leaders of the Jewish war, Simon ben Gamaliel, was a Pharisee and close companion of John of Gischala, a violent leader of the Zealots (*War* 4.159). See further, Wright, *New Testament*, pp. 190-94; Saldarini, *Pharisees*, pp. 85-105.

more critically, especially toward the "Wicked (High) Priest" Jonathan, who lacked the genealogical credentials to occupy the office.[20] In the early years of Hasmonean rule, the Pharisees and Essenes probably collaborated in their pursuit of torah and separation from the influx of Hellenization. At some point, however, an Essene leader known as the "Teacher of Righteousness" confronted Jonathan and a leader of the Pharisees regarding some of their aberrant interpretations and practices of torah.[21] Jonathan and the Pharisees responded with violence, trying to kill the Teacher of Righteousness. The assassination failed, however, and the Teacher escaped into exile.[22] Sometime later, his followers established a monastic community at Khirbet Qumran near the Dead Sea.[23] There in the desert, this new covenant community studied the law, maintained strict purity, enjoyed a glimpse of God's inaugurated kingdom, and remained stubbornly opposed to the corrupted temple cult and religiously lenient Pharisees—the so-called "seekers of smooth things."[24] But the kingdom, they believed, would not come through revolt, but by main-

---

[20]That is, he was not a Zadokite. Several Hasmonean leaders have been suggested as candidates for the "Wicked Priest," most notably Jonathan, Simon and Alexander Jannaeus. Jonathan, however, still seems to be the best candidate, especially since he was first to occupy the high priesthood (152 B.C.) after the seven-year hiatus (159-152 B.C.). The death of the "Wicked Priest" mentioned in the Scrolls also fits the his identification with Jonathan. See 1QpHab 8:13–9:2; 9:8-12; 11:9-12:3; 4QpPs^a 4:7-10; Hanan Eshel, *The Dead Sea Scrolls and the Hasmonean State* (Grand Rapids: Eerdmans, 2008), pp. 43-46. For the fanciful suggestion that the Wicked Priest was Jesus of Nazareth, see Barbara Thiering, *Redating the Teacher of Righteousness* (Sydney: Theological Explorations, 1979).

[21]The one identified as the "Man of Lies," who rejected the teaching of the Teacher of Righteousness, was probably a leader of the Pharisees (1QpHab 5:8-12; 10:6-13; CD 8:12-13). The religious debate between the Teacher of Righteousness and the Pharisees may also form the backdrop of the writing of 4QMMT, which confronts some halachic practices that we know to be Pharisaic: the pouring of liquid from a pure vessel into an impure one, and the level of purity required by the priest who burns the red heifer (4QMMT B 14-16, 56-57; see *m. Yadayim* 4:7; *m. Parah* 3:7; and the discussion in Eshel, *Dead Sea Scrolls*, p. 51).

[22]See 1QpHab 11:2-8 and 4QpPs^a 4:7-9 for the Wicked Priest's attempted murder of the Teacher of Righteousness. 4QpPs^a 2:16-20 suggests that the Pharisees were involved, since "the wicked ones of Ephraim" (2:18) most probably refers to Pharisees in light of 4QpNah *frag.* 3+4 i 2-8, which identifies the Pharisees ("those looking for easy interpretations") as "the simple folk of Ephraim" (cf. CD 7:10-13; Eshel, *Dead Sea Scrolls*, pp. 29-46).

[23]Apparently, the Sadducees also tried to kill the Teacher of Righteousness and his followers (4QpPs^a 2:16-20). It is unknown where the Teacher of Righteousness fled to immediately after the skirmish between Jonathan and the Pharisees. The first attempt on his life was probably sometime around 152 B.C., when Jonathan began occupying the high priesthood, and the first signs of Qumran occupation can be dated to around 100 B.C.

[24]CD 1:14-2:1; 1QH 10:31-32; 12:11; 4Q163 *frag.* 23 ii 10-13; 4QpNah *frags.* 3-4 i 2-4.

taining torah allegiance and waiting on God to apocalyptically intervene.

Sometime in the first century, Saul joined the Pharisees and glowed with the same zeal for the law that fueled Phineas and Mattathias to pick up arms.[25] Saul sought to inaugurate the kingdom by first purifying his own religion, which had seen quite a number of apostates lured into the grip of Hellenization. A recent sect known as "the Way" had broken out in Jerusalem and spread to the surrounding regions,[26] and although it retained an apparent allegiance to the Scriptures and claimed to worship Yahweh, it was blinded by a Hellenistic spirit and even taught against certain laws of torah. The spread of this heretical sect would only ensure that God's covenant curse remain over the nation; crushing the sect was necessary if God's kingdom were to be established. As Saul was en route to Damascus to continue his religious crusade, he had a traumatic vision that would forever change his life and reconfigure his beliefs.[27] Jesus, the martyred leader of the Way, appeared to Saul and revealed to him that this sect was actually the embodiment of the remnant of Israel, and that the curse of the covenant had been exhausted in his sacrificial death. Saul's religious zeal was genuine, but misguided, and through God's grace and forgiveness, Saul would be used to "carry my name before the Gentiles and kings and the children of Israel" (Acts 9:15). The kingdom that Saul was seeking to establish had already been inaugurated through God's intervention in Jesus.

Saul's encounter with the risen Messiah did not just provide him with new identity markers for his faith, but also reconfigured the structure of his soteriology.[28] In other words, salvation from Rome, the purification of

---

[25]Although Paul indicates that he sat at the feet of the Hillelite Gamaliel (Acts 22:3), his violent actions as a zealous persecutor of "the Way" (Acts 22:3-4; Phil 3:6) suggest that at one point he switched over to the more militant Shammaite wing of Pharisaism; see Seyoon Kim, *The Origin of Paul's Gospel*, WUNT 2.4 (Tübingen: Mohr Siebeck, 1981; Grand Rapids: Eerdmans, 1982), pp. 41-50; Wright, *What Saint Paul Really Said*, pp. 26-29.

[26]Acts 8:1-3; 9:1-2.

[27]Acts 9:1-9; recounted in 22:3-11; 26:12-18.

[28]Kim, *Origin*, pp. 269-329. I am not suggesting that Paul received a neat and tidy soteriology from Jesus immediately after his Damascus encounter. Rather, as Seyoon Kim more recently suggests, "the main features of Paul's gospel took firm shape within the first few years, although they continued to be refined through his biblical reflection, his controversies with his opponents, and his other experiences in the mission fields, eventually reaching the state in which they are now found in his epistles" (Seyoon Kim, *Paul and the New Perspective: Second Thoughts on the Origin of Paul's Gospel* [Grand Rapids: Eerdmans, 2002], p. 4).

Israel, and the establishment of God's kingdom—all of which Saul was seeking to accelerate through his violent actions—had been accomplished through the death and resurrection of Jesus of Nazareth. The impact that Saul's Damascus road vision had on his beliefs is retold in Galatians 1:13-16:

> For you have heard of my former life in Judaism, how I persecuted the church of God violently and tried to destroy it. And I was advancing in Judaism beyond many of my own age among my people, so extremely zealous was I for the traditions of my fathers. But when he who had set me apart before I was born, and who called me by his grace, was pleased to reveal his Son to me, in order that I might preach him among the Gentiles, I did not immediately consult with anyone.

The violent nationalism that led Saul to rid Judaism of dissenters in order to help bring about the kingdom of God came to a halt with God's revelation of Jesus, who had already inaugurated the kingdom unilaterally. Or in the words of N. T. Wright, "The one true God had done for Jesus of Nazareth in the middle of time, what Saul had thought he was going to do for Israel at the end of time."[29] No longer would Saul need to be a *Deuteronomic* catalyst in prompting salvation for Israel; Paul would now be a herald of God's *Prophetic* intervention in Jesus, who has rescued us "from the present evil age" (Gal 1:4). While it is true that Saul the Pharisee was certainly not trying to pull himself up by his moral bootstraps and earn his way to heaven,[30] his life was devoted to triggering God's end-time salvation through torah devotion and the violent purification of Israel. More than just a call to a new vocation, Paul's Damascus road encounter would entail a rereading of salvation history—a transposition of the divine and human dynamics in bringing eschatological salvation into the present through the death and resurrection of the Messiah.[31]

---

[29]Wright, *What Saint Paul Really Said*, p. 36, emphasis original.

[30]E.g., ibid., p. 32.

[31]Here, I am following B. R. Gaventa, "Galatians 1 and 2: Autobiography as Paradigm," *NovT* 28 (1986): 309-26, who argues that Paul's autobiographical account of his conversion, along with his apostolic origin, is not apologetic but paradigmatic. Paul, here, is not primarily defending his apostleship but giving a paradigm of how the gospel has laid claim to Paul's own life. See also John M. G. Barclay, "Paul's Story: Theology as Testimony," in *Narrative Dynamics in Paul: A Critical Assessment*, ed. Bruce Longenecker (Louisville, KY: Westminster John Knox, 2002), pp. 133-56 (esp. 141-42); J. L. Martyn, *Galatians: A New Translation with Introduction and Commentary*, AB 33A (New York: Doubleday, 1997), pp. 152-53, 159-61.

Moreover, the Damascus encounter became a paradigm for the shape of the gospel that Paul would preach. Bernard Lategan righty states: "The nature of the gospel as contrary to human expectations, not based on human effort, is first and foremost illustrated by Paul's conversion from persecutor to preacher and his calling as apostle."[32] Paul implicitly reveals this throughout Galatians 1–2, where human and divine agencies are contrasted.[33] Paul opens the letter by asserting that his apostolic commission was "not from a human source nor through a human agent but through Jesus Christ and God the Father who raised him from the dead" (Gal 1:1 my translation). He later identifies God in contrast to man as the source of his gospel; he "neither received it (the gospel) from a human nor was I taught it, but (I received it) through a revelation of Christ" (Gal 1:11-12 my translation). He describes his experience in Galatians 1:14-16 along the same contrasting lines of human and divine agencies. His former wrongheaded pursuit of God was countered by God's invasive pursuit of Paul, whose former zeal for God through the law brought death (Gal 2:19), whereas Christ's unilateral deliverance of Paul brought life (Gal 2:20). Paul's encounter with Jesus, in other words, embodies the gospel that he is commissioned to preach—the reprioritization of God as the prior and primary agent of salvation is cemented in his message.[34]

More than just a call to a new vocation, therefore, Paul considers his encounter with Jesus an embodiment and showcase of the divine and human dynamics that would shape the gospel he was commissioned to herald. In 1 Corinthians, Paul describes his encounter with Christ as a revelation of grace, where God transformed him from persecutor to preacher (1 Cor 15:9-10). Again in 2 Corinthians, he alludes to his experience on the road to Damascus as a work of re-creation, where God generated faith through the gospel in the same way that he had called light out of darkness (2 Cor 4:4-6). In his letter to the Philippians, Paul recounts his former life in Judaism in a similar way to how he did in Galatians. Paul again contrasts his violent zeal

---

[32]Bernard Lategan, "Is Paul Defending His Apostleship in Galatians?" *NTS* 34 (1988): 426.

[33]For the following reading of Gal 1–2, see Preston Sprinkle, *Law and Life: The Interpretation of Leviticus 18:5 in Early Judaism and in Paul*, WUNT 2.241 (Tübingen: Mohr Siebeck, 2008), pp. 153-56.

[34]Cf. 1 Cor 3:18-23. This is probably why Paul often refers to his apostolic office as an act of "grace given to me" (Rom 12:3; 15:15; 1 Cor 3:10; Gal 2:9; Eph 3:2, 7, 8); cf. Kim, *Origin*, pp. 288-98.

as a persecutor of the church with Christ's pursuit of him, saying that Christ "made me his own" (Phil 3:12).[35]

As Paul relates this account of coming into contact with Christ, he explains that his own human initiative in purifying Israel in order to hasten God's kingdom was superseded by God's own agency in transforming him. And the unilateral revelation of Jesus left its stamp on the theological contours of Paul's newly forged *Prophetic* gospel. The same divine and human dynamics that collided on the Damascus road took up residence in the message itself. Paul's Pharisaic view of God as the one who will justify the righteous on the final day was not simply adjusted—it was substantially transformed. The Jewish God is now understood as the one who justifies the ungodly.

So Paul remained a Jew. His theology, however, reconstituted through his encounter with the risen Messiah, shifted from the *Deuteronomic* conventions of Moses to the *Prophetic* framework of Isaiah, Jeremiah, Ezekiel and others, and therefore embraced a heightened awareness of divine agency and anthropological pessimism. Such emphasis is not only born out of the Hebrew Scriptures themselves but finds resonance in the perspectives of some of his own countrymen. Pseudo-Philo, the author of the *Testament of Moses,* and some of the hymnists at Qumran all heralded a similar (though still somewhat distinct) message that eschatological salvation will not come through Israel's initiative but God's decisive intervention. Paul's emphasis on divine agency is not unparalleled, even if it is more intricately developed and filled out than others. But the most unique element in Paul's soteriology, one which used to offend his Pharisaic sensibilities and no doubt continued to sound outlandish, is the sacrificial death, bodily resurrection, subsequent enthronement, and personal indwelling, intercession and love that the risen Messiah accomplishes in and for wicked people— Jesus' enemies, whom God stubbornly sought to justify.

---

[35]Paul's encounter with Christ, however, does not nullify human agency, but empowers him to live and pursue true righteousness all the more (Phil 3:8-11; cf. Gal 2:19-20; 1 Cor 15:10).

Author Index

Barclay, John M. G., 14, 26-28, 87-88, 128, 130, 132, 152, 177-79, 205-6, 208, 222-24, 247

Bauckham, Richard J., 30, 225-28

Brueggemann, Walter, 38, 57

Byrne, Brenden, 107

Cranfield, C. E. B., 154

Cranford, Michael, 152-53

Davies, Philip R., 161

Donfried, Karl, 205

Dunn, J. D. G., 12, 23-25, 81, 83, 147-48, 150, 152

Fee, Gordon, 102-3

Foreman, Benjamin, 14, 53

Gathercole, Simon J., 12, 14, 26-29, 33, 128, 132, 134, 151-52, 158, 169, 174-75, 177, 179, 184, 186, 198-99, 208, 223

Hafemann, Scott, 96-101

Hays, Richard B., 12, 82, 84, 86-89, 97, 122-24, 177-78

Jacobson, Howard, 231

Käsemann, Ernst, 24

Kvalvaag, R. W., 117-18

Laato, Timo, 27, 126-27, 132

Lim, Timothy, 32, 36

Longenecker, Bruce W., 26, 29, 177, 225, 247

Longenecker, Richard, 87, 93

Martyn, J. Louis, 88

Maston, Jason, 28, 138-39, 143, 193-94

Merrill, Eugene, 193

Moo, Douglas J., 103-7, 183, 185-87, 190

Moo, Jonathan, 14, 225-28

Noth, Martin, 84

O'Brien, P. T., 126-27, 132

Potter, Harry D., 54-55, 57, 59-60

Sanders, E. P., 12, 22-25, 28-29, 126, 134, 139, 146-47, 149, 216, 225

Schreiner, Thomas, 11, 14, 103, 106, 132, 181, 187-88

Scott, James M., 84

Seifrid, Mark A., 22, 30, 146, 148-49

Stendahl, Krister, 12, 24

Stuhlmacher, Peter, 185

VanLandingham, Chris, 138-39, 193, 231

Wagner, J. Ross, 159, 175-76

Watson, Francis, 12, 21, 26-28, 47, 84-85, 88, 91, 100, 151, 158, 165-67, 215, 223,

Watson, Nigel, 204-5

Wells, Kyle, 14, 28, 75, 111, 113, 131-32, 136, 141

Westerholm, Stephen H., 9-10, 22, 26-27, 91, 127-28, 132, 208

Wright, N. T., 11-12, 24-25, 76-78, 81-82, 84, 89, 110, 146-47, 170, 185-86, 212, 218, 234, 244, 246-47

Yinger, Kent, 25-27, 29, 155, 173-75, 204

Subject Index

blessing
    of covenant. *See* covenant
    of Christ/Spirit, 87-88
Christ
    cross/crucifixion of , 88, 177
    faith of, 24, 133, 150
circumcision
    of the flesh, 23, 87-88, 101, 148, 154, 178
    of the heart, 46, 75, 102, 137, 189, 191, 211-12
covenant
    blessing of, 39-40, 43-47, 61-62, 65, 68-70,
        72, 73-81, 83, 89, 91-94, 101, 119-20, 164,
        173, 188-89, 196, 200, 212-17, 221, 227, 236
    conditional, 38-67, 91, 108, 188, 206, 212,
        230, 240
    new, 31-32, 34, 56-57, 71-72, 96-97, 99-102,
        108-9, 122-24, 132-33, 183, 244-45
covenantal nomism, 22, 126, 216, 225, 228, 232
creation, 50, 215, 234, 236,
curse
    of the law, 68-94, 118, 125, 136, 210, 239, 240
    of covenant, 34-36, 39-44, 46, 68-94, 120,
        163, 188-89, 200, 212, 221, 236, 238, 242,
        246
divine and human agency, 13, 25, 27-28, 36-37,
    51, 95, 145-48, 153, 162, 173, 175-176, 199, 201,
    208-38
death
    of Christ, 33, 150-51, 159, 160, 177, 184-85,
        203, 246-49
    of people (punishment), 63, 65, 92,
        98-100, 103-5, 108, 122-24, 129-30, 132-33,
        141, 180, 182-83, 214-15, 217
election, 152-53, 173, 192, 200, 224
ethnocentrism, 23, 148
Essenes, 244-45
faith
    in Christ, 23, 32, 91, 177-78, 182, 188, 246
    of people (general), 25, 36, 89, 91, 174, 176,
        200, 205, 213, 226
    content of, 26
    report/message of, 87-88

    justification by. *See* justification
flesh, 64, 87-88, 97-99, 101, 104-5, 114, 130-31,
    137, 140-42, 156, 176, 204, 215
glory
    of God, 50
    of believers (glorification), 117, 141
    of the covenant(s), 122-24
gospel, 25-26, 150, 178, 181, 190, 248-49
grace, 22-28, 32, 47-48, 50-52, 61-62, 134, 136,
    143, 147-48, 150, 152-56, 161, 163, 168, 170,
    173-74, 176-85, 192, 200, 202, 204-7, 213-14,
    216, 219, 222, 224-27, 232, 246-48
judgment, 40, 42, 47, 50, 53, 55, 60-62, 85, 91,
    128, 133, 136, 140, 149, 158, 166-71, 172-207,
    210, 212, 217, 219-21, 223-24, 227, 234, 238
justification, 180, 186, 205
law
    works of, 23, 35, 75-89, 94, 129, 148, 150,
        152-54, 163, 166-67, 186, 188
    of life, 215, 227
legalism, 23, 100, 148
life, covenant blessing of, 65, 92-94, 101, 227
New Perspective, 22-25, 126, 146-50
Pharisee, 244-247
perfection, 161, 167, 169, 227
restoration, 33-34, 37, 38-94, 110, 114-15, 119-20,
    125, 157-60, 191, 209-15, 217, 227-28, 230,
    232-38, 240, 242-43
resurrection
    of believers, 107, 110, 176, 180, 183, 218, 220,
        228, 230, 234, 240, 242
    of Christ, 33, 150, 159, 176, 185, 203, 247, 249
soteriology
    definition of, 33-34
    of Paul and Judaism, 21, 25-27, 29, 33-34,
        146, 239-49
    of early Judaism, 210-38
Spirit, 26, 32, 50, 64-66, 68, 74, 80, 87-89, 93,
    95-124, 130, 142, 173-76, 178-80, 182-83, 187,
    189, 191-92, 196-97, 203, 204-5, 227, 237,
    240-41
Truth, absolute, 250

Scripture Index

OLD TESTAMENT

Genesis
1, 88, 210
1:2, 115, 116
6:9, 226
6:17, 108
7:15, 108
9:16, 215
15, 163, 164, 216
15:6, 29, 77, 78, 81, 146, 149, 151, 156, 159, 161, 163, 164, 170
17:1, 226
17:1-8, 215
17:11, 88
17:13, 88
17:14, 88
17:23-25, 88
22, 156, 164, 216
22:16-18, 235
26:5, 152
45:26, 90

Exodus
15:16, 175
15:26, 127
23, 158, 165
23:7, 158, 161
24, 210
25–31, 69
32, 217
32–34, 100
32:13, 235
34, 124
34:29-35, 96

Leviticus
5:1-6, 162
18, 63, 91, 92
18:5, 12, 13, 29, 63, 72, 79, 82, 83, 84, 89, 90, 91, 92, 93, 94, 108, 134, 153, 157, 166, 177, 218, 221, 231, 248

26, 41, 69, 79, 92, 230
26:3-4, 229
26:15, 69
26:16, 41
26:17, 41
26:19, 41
26:25, 41
26:25-26, 41
26:31-32, 69
26:32, 69
26:40-45, 230
26:41, 102

Numbers
12:1, 54

Deuteronomy
4, 40
4:1, 39
4:10, 58
4:13, 97
4:20, 86
4:26-28, 40
4:29, 59
4:29-30, 40
4:29-31, 211, 212
4:31, 40
5:22, 97
5:29, 58
6:1-2, 39
6:2, 58
6:5, 40, 42, 59
6:6-7, 57
6:9, 57
6:17-19, 39
6:24-25, 39
6:25, 164
7:8, 86
7:12-13, 39
8:1, 39
8:18, 86
9:9-10, 97
10, 75
10:12, 59
10:16, 46, 75, 102
11:26, 127
12–23, 69
12–26, 47
12:25, 39

12:28, 39
19:13, 39
22:7, 39
23:1, 221
26:8-9, 86
27, 73, 85, 86
27–29, 74
27–30, 81, 89
27–32, 84, 85
27:11-26, 189
27:15-25, 86
27:15-26, 86
27:26, 82, 83, 84, 85, 86, 94
28, 39, 41, 188
28–29, 72
28–30, 84
28–31, 69
28–32, 84, 86
28:1-14, 39
28:4, 221
28:5, 188
28:11, 221
28:15-44, 39
28:18, 221
28:21, 80
28:21-23, 41
28:25, 41
28:28, 80
28:36-37, 69
28:38-42, 41
28:44, 188
28:48, 41, 69, 80
28:55, 188
28:59, 80
28:63, 58
28:64, 69
29–30, 47
29–32, 47, 85
29:1, 47
29:4, 47, 195
29:9, 47
29:9-14, 235
29:12, 73
29:17-27, 60
29:19, 72, 73, 74
29:19-21, 70
29:20, 38, 73
29:22-29, 85
29:25, 72

29:25-29, 189
29:28, 58, 72, 92, 188
29:29, 134
30, 73, 216
30:1, 85, 196
30:1-2, 76
30:1-4, 78
30:1-10, 60, 85, 119, 211
30:2, 42, 77
30:3, 70
30:6, 46, 75, 102, 195, 211
30:9, 58
30:10, 42
30:11-14, 226, 242
30:11-19, 221
30:11-20, 47
30:15, 215
30:19, 215, 227
31, 229
31–32, 232
31:12-13, 47
31:13, 58
31:14-22, 85
31:16-29, 47
31:17-18, 69
31:20, 86
31:27-29, 85
31:29, 76, 85
32, 47
32:1-43, 85
32:36, 47
32:39, 47
33:1, 47
34, 83

Joshua
1, 236
8, 73

Ruth
2:12, 110

1 Samuel
24:19, 110

2 Samuel
18:21-32, 54

1 Kings
2:1-4, 40
2:4, 48, 59
8, 38, 40, 41
8:25, 40, 48
8:33, 41
8:33-34, 40
8:34, 41
8:35, 41
8:35-36, 41
8:36, 41
8:37, 41
8:46-53, 60
8:47, 41
8:47-50, 41
8:48, 41
8:50, 41
9:4-5, 40, 48
11:9-13, 40
11:34, 48
11:38, 40
12:1-24, 45
14:1-18, 40
14:21, 45
14:21-31, 45
14:22-24, 45
14:25-28, 45
15:4, 48
18:36-40, 244

2 Kings
8:19, 48
9:26, 110
16:1-4, 48
21:1-15, 48
22:19, 41
23:3, 59
23:31–25:26, 48
24:4, 38
25:27-30, 48

1 Chronicles
4:10, 44
5:20, 44
10:13-14, 44
21:26, 44
22:19, 44
28:9, 44

2 Chronicles
6:21, *45*
6:25, *45*
6:27, *45*
6:30, *45*
6:39, *45*
7:13-14, *38*
7:13-15, *44, 45*
7:15, *45*
10-12, *45*
10-36, *44*
11:5-12, *45*
11:13-17, *45*
11:16, *44*
11:18-22, *45*
12:1-2, *45*
12:6, *44*
12:7, *44, 45*
12:12, *44, 45*
12:14, *44*
13:12-15, *44*
14-16, *44*
14:4, *44*
14:7, *44*
14:11, *44*
15:2, *44*
15:4, *44*
15:12, *44*
15:13, *44*
15:15, *44*
16:12, *44*
17:4, *44*
18:4, *44*
18:31, *44*
19:3, *44*
20:4, *44*
20:9, *44*
22:9, *44*
25:20, *44*
26:5, *44*
28:19, *44*
30:6, *44*
30:9, *44*
30:11, *44*
30:18, *44, 45*
30:19, *44*
30:20, *45*
30:27, *44*
31:21, *44*
32:20, *44*
32:24, *44*
33:12, *44*
33:13, *44, 45*
33:18-19, *44*
33:19, *44, 45*

33:23, *44*
34:3, *44*
34:27, *44*
36:12, *44*
36:13, *44*
36:16, *45*

Ezra
1:1-4, *233*
8:21, *43*
8:21-22, *43*
8:21-23, *43*
8:22, *43*
8:23, *43*
9:1-4, *42*
9:6, *42*
9:15, *42*
10:2-3, *43*
10:18-44, *42*

Nehemiah
8, *43*
8-10, *43*
9, *43*
9:8, *43*
9:38, *43*
9:38-10:32, *43*
10:29, *43*
13:23-29, *43*
13:23-31, *42*

Job
28:19, *54*
33:28, *160*
33:30, *160*
34:6, *55*

Psalms
1, *160*
2:11, *175*
15:2, *226*
37:18, *226*
38:8, *90*
49:19, *160*
51, *102*
51:11, *116*
62:12, *173*
77:2, *90*
84:12, *226*
103, *137*
104, *137*
106, *163*
106:30-31, *244*
106:31, *77, 78, 81, 163*

Proverbs
17:15, *158*
20:22, *110*
24:24, *158*

Ecclesiastes
12:7, *112*

Song of Solomon
4:8, *54*

Isaiah
1-39, *49*
5:23, *158, 161*
6:7, *49*
11:6, *54*
12:1-6, *64*
17:11, *55*
19:16, *175*
30:18-21, *49*
40-54, *52*
40-55, *49, 50, 51, 52, 53, 66, 159, 160*
40-66, *51, 52, 53*
40:12-17, *50*
40:21-31, *50*
41:17-20, *50*
41:28, *52*
42:1, *112*
42:8-12, *50*
42:10-13, *159*
42:13-44:23, *50*
42:14-25, *50*
42:14-43:7, *50*
42:15-16, *50*
42:22, *52*
43:1-7, *50*
43:7, *50*
43:9, *159*
43:13, *52*
43:16-19, *50*
43:16-21, *64*
43:19-21, *50*
43:20-21, *50*
43:22-24, *49*
43:25, *50*
43:26, *159*
44:3, *50, 119, 120*
44:19, *52*
44:22, *50, 52*
44:24-28, *50*
44:25, *52*
45, *159*

45:6, *50*
45:9-10, *159*
45:18, *50*
45:20-23, *159*
45:22-23, *159*
45:23, *52*
45:24-25, *159*
45:25, *159*
46:8, *52*
46:12-13, *49*
47:10, *52*
48:11, *50*
48:20-21, *50*
49:5, *52*
49:6, *52*
49:13, *159*
50:8, *159*
50:8-9, *159*
51:4-11, *159*
51:9-11, *50*
51:11, *52*
52:5, *189*
52:8, *52*
52:10-12, *64*
52:11-12, *50*
53, *160*
53:10-11, *160*
53:11, *159, 160*
55, *52*
55:1-5, *52*
55:1-9, *53*
55:3, *62*
55:6-7, *52*
55:6-9, *53*
55:7, *52*
55:10, *52*
55:11, *52*
56, *52*
56-64, *51*
56-66, *49, 51, 52, 53*
56:1, *51*
56:1-59:15, *51*
56:4-5, *221*
57:14-21, *49*
57:17-19, *51*
58:1-14, *51*
59:1-15, *51*
59:14-21, *51*
59:15-21, *49*
59:16-17, *51*
59:18-20, *51*
59:20, *51*
60-62, *52*
60:1-62:12, *49*

61:8, *62*
63:7-66:17, *51*
63:10-12, *116*
65-66, *51*
65:6, *110*
66:2, *175*
66:5, *175*

Jeremiah
1, *86*
1-25, *86*
2, *58*
2:23-24, *55*
3, *56*
3:17, *57*
4:4, *102*
4:22, *54*
5:6, *54*
7:24, *57*
8:20, *58*
9:14, *57*
9:25, *102*
11, *86*
11:3, *85*
11:3-5, *86*
11:5, *86*
11:8, *86*
11:10, *86*
13:10, *57*
13:13, *189*
13:23, *53, 56*
15:18, *55*
16:12, *57*
17:1, *54, 55, 57*
17:1-9, *189*
17:1-13, *54*
17:9, *55, 57*
17:16, *55*
18:12, *57*
21:5, *58*
23:17, *57*
24:4-7, *59*
24:7, *57, 59*
26:3, *53, 59*
29:10-11, *59*
29:13-14, *59*
29:14, *59*
30:12, *55*
30:12-13, *55*
30:15, *55*
31, *56, 59, 97, 99, 101, 191*
31:31, *55, 97, 99*
31:31-34, *38, 59, 60, 62, 119*

31:32, 57
31:33, 97, 186, 187,
   190, 191
32, 57
32:31, 58
32:37, 58
32:37-41, 38, 58,
   59, 60, 62
32:39, 195
32:39-41, 57
32:40, 62
33:5, 58
36:3, 53, 59
36:7, 58
38:7, 54
39:16, 54
42:18, 58
50:4-5, 59
50:5, 62
50:17, 55
50:19, 56
50:19-20, 56

Lamentations
3:42, 38

Ezekiel
1–19, 62
1–20, 62, 66
1–24, 62
1:20, 108
1:21, 108
2:3, 60
2:4, 60
2:5, 60
2:6, 60
2:7, 60
2:8, 60
2:10, 60
3, 109
3:1-8, 189
3:6-7, 60
3:7, 60
3:24-25, 61
3:26, 61
10:17, 108
16, 61, 63
16:3-6, 61
16:8, 61
16:15-19, 61
16:15-52, 61
16:20-22, 61
16:23-43, 61
16:44-50, 61
16:61, 62

16:63, 61
18, 66
18:2, 66
18:5-23, 66
18:23, 65, 66
18:25, 66
18:29, 66
18:31, 66
18:32, 65, 66
20, 61, 62, 64, 97
20:4, 61
20:5-26, 62
20:5-32, 63
20:7-8, 62
20:11, 63, 65, 92,
   99, 108
20:13, 63, 65, 92,
   99, 108
20:21, 63, 65, 92,
   99, 108
20:25, 63, 65
20:25-26, 99, 108
20:33, 64
20:33-38, 63, 64
20:34, 64
22:2, 61
29:21, 61
33:10, 65, 92, 99
33:10-11, 108
33:11-16, 65
33:21-22, 61
36, 66, 97, 108,
   114, 115
36–37, 61, 62, 64,
   65, 95, 96, 101,
   102, 103, 107,
   108, 113, 115,
   116, 119, 120,
   202, 240, 241
36:20, 189
36:22-37:14, 38
36:25-26, 115
36:25-27, 114
36:26, 97
36:26-27, 64, 92,
   107, 108, 143,
   195
36:27, 65, 97, 107,
   108, 120
37, 64, 65, 99, 102,
   107, 109, 110,
   113, 114, 115,
   120, 121
37:1-14, 64, 92,
   99, 100, 108

37:2, 65
37:5, 108
37:6, 99, 112, 114
37:10, 108
37:11, 108
37:12-14, 101
37:14, 65, 99, 112,
   114
37:26, 62
44:6-9, 102

Daniel
4:37, 175
9, 233
10:11, 175
12:3, 234

Hosea
4:16, 70
13:7, 54

Micah
1:9, 55

Habakkuk
1, 17
1:4, 90, 91
1:5-11, 91
2:2-3, 90
2:2-4, 90, 91
2:2-5, 90, 91
2:3, 165
2:4, 29, 82, 89, 90,
   91, 94, 146, 149,
   157, 159, 161,
   165, 166, 167,
   170, 200
2:4-5, 91
2:6-20, 91
3, 91

Zechariah
1:3, 53

Malachi
3:7, 53

APOCRYPHA

Tobit
13:5-18, 83
14:4-7, 83

Judith
10:13, 108

**Wisdom of
Solomon**
1:1–6:11, 221
2:22, 223, 224
3:5-7, 221
3:5-9, 223
3:13, 221
3:13-15, 223, 224
3:14, 221
3:16-17, 221
3:18-19, 221
4:1, 221
4:9, 221
4:10-15, 223
7, 221
7:25, 221
7:26, 222
8:5-6, 222
8:13, 222
10:4, 222
10:5, 222
10:6, 222
10:10, 222
10:13-14, 222
10:15-21, 222
10:17, 224
11:4, 222
11:23, 221
12:1-2, 221
12:10, 221, 224
12:12, 223, 224
12:14, 223
12:15, 223
12:20, 221
12:23-27, 224
12:26, 223
15:3, 242
19:1-5, 224
19:13, 223

Sirach
11:26-27, 217
15, 214
15:7, 131
15:11-20, 127
15:14-15, 215, 218,
   242
15:17, 215, 242
16:11, 217
16:14, 217
17, 216
17:29, 217
35:22, 217
35:24, 217
35:25, 217

35:26, 217
36:1-17, 83
42:2, 158, 161, 242
44–50, 216
44:1–50:29, 216
44:20, 156
44:20-21, 156
44:21, 156
44:23–45:5, 217
45:4, 217
45:6-22, 217
45:8, 216
45:9, 216
45:10, 216
45:19-22, 217
46:11, 217
47:2-11, 217
47:11, 217
49:4, 217
51:30, 217

Baruch
1:15–3:8, 83
4:5–5:9, 31

1 Maccabees
1, 17
2:15-28, 244
2:51-52, 156, 163
2:52, 163
14, 244
14:11-12, 244
14:15, 244

2 Maccabees
1, 83
4, 17
7, 83

**NEW
TESTAMENT**

Luke
3:14, 183
10:21, 176
15:24, 104

Acts
9:15, 246
22:3, 246
22:3-4, 246

Romans
1–2, 155
1–3, 128, 132, 134,

135, 141, 150,
151, 153, 154
1–4, 155, 157
1–5, 26, 174, 223
1–8, 23
1–11, 29, 183, 225
1:16-17, 157
1:17, 157
1:18, 188
1:18-23, 128, 133
1:18-32, 131, 133,
135
1:18–3:20, 132,
150, 191, 212
1:18–3:26, 132, 152,
187, 220, 242
1:18–4:25, 157
1:21, 131, 141
1:21-23, 141
1:24-32, 128
1:28, 131, 141
1:32, 106, 133, 154
2, 24, 102, 154,
175, 186, 188,
189, 191, 192
2–3, 190
2–4, 186
2:1-5, 133
2:1-12, 187
2:1-13, 187
2:1-16, 150, 186
2:1-17, 204
2:1-29, 128, 133,
135
2:4, 189
2:4-5, 189
2:5, 188, 189
2:5-11, 133
2:6, 155, 186
2:6-11, 189
2:6-13, 189
2:6-15, 186
2:7, 184, 190
2:7-13, 133
2:8, 188
2:9, 188
2:12-16, 191
2:12-24, 154
2:13, 154, 186, 187,
188, 190, 191
2:13-16, 186, 190
2:14-16, 191
2:15, 154, 186, 187
2:15-16, 190
2:16, 102

2:17-24, 133
2:17-29, 150
2:17–3:9, 133
2:24, 189
2:25, 154
2:25-29, 154
2:26, 154
2:26-29, 186, 187
2:27, 154
2:28-29, 100, 101,
102
2:29, 101, 102, 141,
176, 186, 189,
191
3–5, 150
3:4-5, 102
3:5, 133
3:9, 129
3:9-10, 150
3:9-20, 187
3:10-11, 129
3:10-20, 133
3:11, 190
3:12, 102, 129, 190
3:12-18, 133
3:19-20, 129, 133,
157
3:19-26, 155
3:20, 148, 154,
186, 187, 188
3:21-22, 157
3:21-26, 129, 132,
133, 135, 150, 151,
157, 159, 162,
188, 191
3:21–4:5, 151
3:22, 24, 134
3:22-26, 150
3:23-24, 150
3:24, 185
3:26, 24, 134, 150,
151
3:28, 23, 148, 153
3:29, 154
3:30, 186
4, 29, 148, 150,
151, 152, 154,
155, 156, 163,
222
4–5, 158
4:1-5, 156
4:1-6, 102
4:1-8, 152
4:1-25, 134
4:2-5, 151, 164

4:2-6, 151, 152, 155
4:4, 153, 154, 155,
168
4:4-5, 135, 152, 155,
183, 185, 188,
204, 211
4:5, 151, 162
4:9-16, 155
4:9-25, 152
4:15, 129
4:17, 151
4:18-22, 91
4:24, 151
4:25, 159, 160,
203
5, 151
5–8, 129
5:1, 183
5:5, 131
5:6-8, 151
5:6-9, 151, 184
5:6-11, 129, 135
5:8-11, 203
5:9, 151, 184
5:9-10, 185, 205
5:10, 162, 184
5:12-21, 129
5:15-16, 183
5:16, 106
5:16-19, 185
5:18, 106
5:18-19, 107, 160
5:19, 160, 179
5:21, 129, 184
6:1-11, 203
6:1-22, 183
6:2, 104
6:6, 104, 129
6:11, 104
6:12-13, 104
6:12-23, 203
6:17, 131
6:17-23, 129
6:18-22, 104
6:22, 184
6:22-23, 184
6:23, 183
7, 103, 104, 105,
137
7–8, 108
7:1-4, 103
7:5, 103, 104, 130
7:5-6, 100, 103
7:6–8:4, 180
7:6–8:11, 141

7:6–8:13, 96, 102,
103
7:7, 103
7:7-12, 104
7:7-25, 103, 104,
105, 108
7:7–8:11, 103
7:7–8:13, 103
7:8, 129
7:8-9, 103
7:10, 104, 105
7:11, 129
7:12-14, 123
7:13, 129
7:13-25, 104
7:14, 104, 137
7:14-25, 103, 104,
142
7:17, 129
7:18, 104, 130, 137
7:23, 104
7:25, 104
8, 102, 103, 107,
108, 206
8:1, 183
8:1-4, 102, 104,
105, 106, 107,
108, 131, 180,
187
8:1-11, 103, 108,
202
8:1-13, 103, 118,
125, 180, 240
8:2, 102, 103, 104,
105, 108
8:2-4, 107
8:3, 105, 106, 130
8:4, 106
8:4-13, 107
8:5-8, 106, 130, 180
8:5-9, 180
8:5-13, 107, 180
8:6-8, 129
8:7-8, 129, 130
8:8, 131, 142
8:9-11, 102, 107,
180
8:9-16, 23
8:11, 103, 180
8:12-13, 180
8:13, 103, 107
8:18-23, 141
8:31-34, 185, 194,
203, 204
8:31-39, 203

8:33-34, 159
9, 224
9–11, 27, 222, 224
9:2, 131
9:10-11, 152, 153
9:10-12, 155, 224
9:10-16, 153, 155
9:11, 153
9:14, 224
9:14-18, 224
9:20-21, 159
9:30-32, 153
9:31-32, 153
9:32, 153
10:1, 131
10:5, 12, 219
10:5-11, 153
10:9-10, 131
10:16-17, 87
10:19-20, 131
11, 153
11:1, 21
11:6, 153, 155
12:1-2, 131, 141
12:3, 248
13, 106
13:8-10, 106, 186
13:10, 106
13:11, 205
13:14, 130
14:4, 183
14:5, 131
14:7-12, 204
14:10-12, 173, 183,
188
14:11-12, 159
15:15, 248
16, 130

1 Corinthians
1–3, 182
1:4, 181
1:4-8, 181
1:4-9, 182
1:8, 181, 205
1:9, 181
1:10–4:21, 181
1:18, 205
1:18-31, 141, 181
1:21, 176
1:29, 181
1:30-31, 182
2:4-5, 91
2:5, 182
2:6-16, 182

2:10, 91
2:14-16, 141
3–4, 180
3:1-3, 88
3:1-4, 182
3:5-7, 182
3:5-23, 182
3:7, 182
3:8, 155, 180, 182
3:10, 182, 248
3:13, 182
3:13-14, 172, 181
3:13-15, 188
3:14, 155
3:16, 123
3:18-23, 248
3:21, 182
3:21-23, 182
4:1-5, 173
4:4, 179
4:5, 131, 181, 182
6:9-11, 141
6:19-20, 123
7:32-34, 131
9:24-27, 173
10:6-13, 205
11:27, 205
15:2, 179
15:9-10, 248
15:10, 179, 249
15:14, 179
15:42-49, 96
15:56, 129

2 Corinthians
1:21-22, 183
2:4, 131
2:14–4:6, 96
3, 96, 102, 103, 108, 118
3:1, 96, 98
3:1-3, 98
3:1-7, 96, 102, 122, 124
3:1-18, 96
3:1–4:6, 141, 183
3:3, 96, 97, 98, 100, 101, 123
3:4-18, 96

3:6, 96, 97, 99, 100, 101, 102, 104, 122, 123
3:7, 100, 122, 123, 124
3:7-11, 122
3:7-18, 96, 122
3:8-18, 122, 123, 124
3:9, 122
3:10, 100
3:11, 122
3:13, 122, 123
3:14, 122
3:14-15, 131
3:15, 123
3:16, 124
3:16-18, 123
3:17-18, 96
3:18, 123, 124
4:1-6, 123
4:4, 124, 129
4:4-6, 248
4:6, 91, 124
5:5, 183
5:10, 155, 172, 183, 188
6:1, 179
6:16-17, 123
9:6, 173, 188
10:3, 130
10:6, 106
10:10, 96
10:12, 96
11:4, 96
11:4-5, 123
11:6, 96
11:12, 96
11:15, 173, 188
11:18, 96
11:21-22, 96
11:22-23, 96
12:12, 96

Galatians
1, 242, 247
1–2, 248
1:1, 178, 248
1:4, 141, 180, 247

1:11-12, 178, 248
1:13-14, 178
1:13-16, 247
1:14-16, 248
1:15, 176
1:15-16, 178
2–3, 84
2:8-10, 178
2:9, 178, 248
2:12, 81
2:16, 23, 24, 83, 86, 87, 88, 148, 186, 242
2:19, 248
2:19-20, 242, 249
2:20, 130, 248
2:20-21, 89, 177, 178, 202
3, 81, 84, 89, 91, 94, 122
3:1-5, 87
3:1–4:11, 87, 178
3:2, 83, 86, 148
3:2-5, 83, 87
3:3, 88
3:5, 83, 86, 88, 148
3:6, 81
3:8-9, 87
3:8-14, 81, 83, 89
3:10, 81, 82, 83, 84, 86, 88, 89, 94, 148
3:10-12, 190
3:10-13, 94
3:10-14, 81, 82, 84, 240
3:11, 90, 91, 157, 166, 242
3:11-12, 82, 89, 94, 157
3:12, 12, 84, 91, 94, 219
3:13, 93, 94
3:14, 87
3:15-25, 141
3:16-19, 84
3:21, 83, 89
3:22, 129

4:1-7, 141
4:2, 178
4:3, 129
4:9, 178
4:21-31, 102
4:23, 88
4:29, 88
5:4, 178
5:4-6, 178
5:5, 178, 180
5:14, 106
5:16-24, 130
5:16-25, 96, 202
5:16-26, 141, 178, 179
5:17, 88, 104
5:19-25, 204
5:21, 205
5:24, 88
6:7, 188
6:7-8, 205
6:7-10, 204
6:8, 173, 179, 180, 184
6:12-13, 88
6:16, 21, 32, 81

Ephesians
1:5, 176
1:9, 176
2:1-3, 129
2:1-10, 141
2:2, 129
3:2, 248
3:7, 248
3:8, 248
4:17-24, 141
4:23, 131
5:6-14, 141
5:18, 106

Philippians
1:6, 176, 177, 180
1:6-7, 131
1:11, 106
1:19, 180
1:22, 130
1:27-28, 176
2:10-11, 159

2:12, 173
2:12-13, 175, 176
2:13, 177, 179
2:15, 205
2:17-18, 176
3:3, 88, 176
3:6, 246
3:8-11, 249
3:10, 177
3:11, 176
3:12, 177, 178, 249
3:13, 176
3:20-21, 180
3:21, 177

Colossians
1:9, 106
1:19, 176
1:22, 205
2:11, 102

1 Thessalonians
1:10, 185
2:13, 87, 91
2:14-16, 21
3:13, 205
4:1, 131
4:8, 96
5:8, 205
5:9-10, 185
5:23, 205

1 Timothy
1:16, 184
6:12, 184

Titus
1:2, 184
3:7, 184

Hebrews
7:16-19, 88

James
2:14-26, 156
2:21, 164

Revelation
11:11, 108